COMMUNITY ECONOMIC DEVELOPMENT

Problems and Potentials for Minority Groups

John C. Weistart
Editor

OCEANA PUBLICATIONS, INC.

Dobbs Ferry, New York

1972

HD
82
.C5732
1972

Library of Congress Cataloging in Publication Data
Main entry under title:

Community economic development.

(Library of law and contemporary problems, no. 16)
Reprint of the 1971 ed., which was issued as v. 36, no. 1-2 of Law and contemporary problems.
  1. Economic policy. 2. Community development.
I. Weistart, John C., ed. II. Series: Law and contemporary problems, v. 36, no. 1-2.
HD82.C5732 1972   330.9   72-5855
ISBN 0-379-11516-6

© Copyright 1971, 1972 by Duke University

Manufactured in the United States of America

BLACKWELL LIBRARY
SALISBURY STATE COLLEGE
SALISBURY, MARYLAND

WITHDRAWN

Titles Published in

The Library of Law and Contemporary Problems

POPULATION CONTROL, The Imminent World Crisis
Melvin G. Shimm, *Editor*

EUROPEAN REGIONAL COMMUNITIES
A New Era on the Old Continent
Melvin G. Shimm, *Editor*

AFRICAN LAW, New Law for New Nations
Hans W. Baade, *Editor*

ACADEMIC FREEDOM, The Scholar's Place
in Modern Society
Hans W. Baade, *Editor*

THE SOVIET IMPACT ON INTERNATIONAL LAW
Hans W. Baade, *Editor*

URBAN PROBLEMS AND PROSPECTS
Robinson O. Everett and Richard H. Leach, *Editors*

ANTIPOVERTY PROGRAMS
Robinson O. Everett, *Editor*

INTERNATIONAL CONTROL OF PROPAGANDA
Clark C. Havighurst, *Editor*

HOUSING
Robinson O. Everett and John D. Johnston, Jr., *Editors*

MEDICAL PROGRESS AND THE LAW
Clark C. Havighurst, *Editor*

THE MIDDLE EAST CRISIS: TEST OF INTERNATIONAL LAW
John W. Halderman, *Editor*

AIR POLLUTION CONTROL
Clark C. Havighurst, *Editor*

CONSUMER CREDIT REFORM
Clark C. Havighurst, *Editor*

THE INSTITUTIONALIZED PRESIDENCY
Norman C. Thomas and Hans W. Baade, *Special Editors*
John C. Weistart, *Series Editor*

HEALTH CARE
Clark C. Havighurst, *Special Editor*
John C. Weistart, *Series Editor*

COMMUNITY ECONOMIC DEVELOPMENT
John C. Weistart, *Editor*

CONTENTS

Part I

FOREWORD 1
John C. Weistart

THE POLITICS OF COMMUNITY ECONOMIC
    DEVELOPMENT 3
Milton Kotler

COMMUNITY PARTICIPATION: A CRITICAL VIEW 13
J. A. C. Hetherington

COMMUNITY DEVELOPMENT CORPORATIONS: THE
    PROBLEM OF MIXED OBJECTIVES 35
Frederick D. Sturdivant

NEW DIRECTIONS FOR MINORITY ENTERPRISE 51
Samuel I. Doctors and Sharon Lockwood

GAMES THE GOVERNMENT PLAYS: FEDERAL FUNDING
    OF MINORITY ECONOMIC DEVELOPMENT 68
Otto J. Hetzel

A TAXPAYER'S CHOICE INCENTIVE SYSTEM: AN
    EXPERIMENTAL APPROACH TO COMMUNITY
    ECONOMIC DEVELOPMENT TAX INCENTIVES 99
Robert S. Robin

MINORITY ECONOMIC DEVELOPMENT: THE PROBLEM
    OF BUSINESS FAILURES 119
William A. Strang

PROFIT MOTIVATION AND MANAGEMENT ASSISTANCE
    IN COMMUNITY ECONOMIC DEVELOPMENT 136
John E. Oxendine and Alvin N. Puryear

Part II

FOREWORD 145
   John C. Weistart

MANAGERIAL ASSISTANCE: PROMISES AND PITFALLS . 147
   Thomas P. Ference

MARKETING TECHNIQUES FOR THE COMMUNITY-BASED ENTERPRISE 173
   Carl E. Block

COMMUNITY ECONOMIC DEVELOPMENT AND LOW-INCOME HOUSING DEVELOPMENT 191
   Paul G. Garrity

ECONOMIC DEVELOPMENT IN THE MODEL CITIES PROGRAM 205
   Charles E. Olken

OPPORTUNITY FUNDING CORPORATION: AN ANALYSIS 227
   Samuel I. Doctors and Sharon Lockwood

THE EFFECT OF THE PRIVATE FOUNDATION PROVISIONS OF THE TAX REFORM ACT OF 1969 ON COMMUNITY DEVELOPMENT CORPORATIONS 238
   Jordan D. Luttrell

POLITICS AND BUREAUCRACY IN COMMUNITY-CONTROLLED ECONOMIC DEVELOPMENT 277
   Geoffrey Faux

NATIONAL POLICY AND THE COMMUNITY DEVELOPMENT CORPORATION 297
   Stewart E. Perry

COMMUNITY ECONOMIC DEVELOPMENT

Part I

COMMUNITY PARTICIPATION: A CRITICAL VIEW

J. A. C. HETHERINGTON*

INTRODUCTION

Since the problem of urban poverty was discovered and began to receive significant public attention in the early 1960's, much has been written about the various strategies and tactics by which the conditions of life of the urban poor might be improved. In this substantial body of literature there are wide areas of agreement. Perhaps the principal area of consensus is the view that an essential first step in any successful ghetto improvement program is the creation of jobs for ghetto residents and the development in the ghetto of business enterprises which are locally owned and operated.[1] These two allied objectives are in several significant respects quite distinct. The creation in the short run of large numbers of jobs for ghetto residents is a task which could probably be best accomplished by having existing manufacturing enterprises establish facilities in ghetto areas. Accordingly, the goal of immediate jobs in the ghetto[2] suggests programs, such as tax incentive arrangements, that would induce established businesses to operate in the ghetto. The focus of these programs would be on protecting employers against the special risks and higher costs attendant on ghetto operations;[3] the tactic would be to make ghetto operation profitable for them.

Proposals for the development of black-owned and operated businesses in ghetto areas reflect a different order of priorities. Here the aim, expressed variously by different writers, is to redress the inequality of the economic opportunity structure and to build a black middle class. It is obvious that this effort would be successful— if at all—only over a longer period of time, while the number of ghetto residents directly benefited, at least initially and probably even in the long run, would be considerably smaller. The two approaches are mutually complementary, and both can be pursued simultaneously. Mutual interference occurs only to the extent that resources devoted to one are necessarily denied to the other. Since the resources that we are prepared to devote to alleviating poverty are limited (and may be in-

---

* Professor of Law, University of Wisconsin. The writer is pleased to acknowledge the assistance of Miriam Witlin, a third year law student at the University of Wisconsin Law School, in the preparation of this paper.

[1] Among the many works dealing with various aspects of the subject, notable recent contributions include NEGROES AND JOBS (L. Ferman, J. Kornbluh & J. Miller eds. 1968); T. CROSS, BLACK CAPITALISM (1969); R. KRAMER, PARTICIPATION OF THE POOR (1969); BLACK ECONOMIC DEVELOPMENT (W. Haddad & G. Pugh eds. 1969); L. SULLIVAN, BUILD, BROTHER, BUILD (1969).

[2] For an eloquently stated analysis which places the primary emphasis on employment, see Kennedy, *The Urban Ghetto and Negro Job Problems: A Diagnosis and a Proposed Plan of Action*, in NEGROES AND JOBS, *supra* note 1, at 256, 262, 264.

[3] There are numerous discussions in the literature on this point. *See, e.g.*, CROSS, *supra* note 1, at 73-110; Garrity, *Red Ink for Ghetto Industries?*, HARV. BUS. REV., May-June 1968, at 4; Skala, *Inner-City Enterprises: Current Experience*, in BLACK ECONOMIC DEVELOPMENT, *supra* note 1, at 151.

adequate even if wisely expended), it becomes important to compare and appraise as carefully as possible the relative cost effectiveness of the two strategies. The remainder of this paper deals with only one part of this comparison: its purpose is to consider and evaluate the suggestion that business organizations operating in ghetto areas be owned and controlled by local residents. The discussion is divided into five parts: (1) the social significance of control; (2) the traditional function of business; (3) the concept of control of business enterprises; (4) community control of ghetto business enterprises; and, finally and somewhat anticlimactically, (5) some suggestions for future action in view of the conclusions reached in the preceding sections.

I

THE SOCIAL SIGNIFICANCE OF CONTROL

In the growing literature dealing with urban poverty such phrases as black capitalism, compensatory capitalism, black ownership and control, economic separatism, and local ownership and control, have become familiar terms. While these various phrases express related, and to some extent common, meanings there are at least two distinct ideas which need to be clearly identified: one is black ownership and control, and the other is community or local ownership and control. These ideas share some common ground because the populations of our urban ghettos are predominantly black, and therefore community ownership and control means black ownership and control. But black ownership and control need not be in any sense community ownership and control, although it could mean ownership and control by members of the local black community.

A. Black Capitalism

The argument for black capitalism is basically unrelated to community control; it simply asserts that there ought to be more businesses owned and operated by blacks than there are.[4] Everyone concerned with the urban poverty problem agrees on this and the only questions concern how to stimulate black entrepreneurship and what priority to accord it in the overall antipoverty effort.

Further, there is a solid consensus among writers on the subject that black entrepreneurship is of great importance in the effort to bring economic vitality to the urban ghetto. This means ownership at different levels, ranging from the traditional sole proprietorship, which typically in the ghetto has meant a corner store, to larger and more ambitious enterprises. To a people who have been denied access to economic opportunity, ownership of a business is a symbol of personal

---

[4] *See generally* Goodpaster, *An Introduction to the Community Development Corporation*, 46 J. URBAN L. 603, 638-45 (1968). "Of the nearly five million private businesses in the United States fewer than one percent are non-white owned." Statement of Robert A. Levine, in *Financial Institutions and the Urban Crisis, Hearings Before the Subcomm. on Financial Institutions of the Senate Comm. on Banking and Currency*, 90th Cong., 2d Sess. 101, 106 (1968). *See also* SULLIVAN, *supra* note 1, at 165; Samuels, *Compensatory Capitalism*, in BLACK ECONOMIC DEVELOPMENT, *supra* note 1, at 60, 61-66; Johnson & Smith, *Black Managers*, in BLACK ECONOMIC DEVELOPMENT, *supra* note 1, at 112, 115.

emancipation.[5] The person who owns a business is entitled to manage it, within the limits of the law, for his own benefit and without regard to other interests. Hence, the owner-controller has a degree of autonomy and independence not generally enjoyed by those who earn their livelihoods by selling their services in the labor market. Some aspects of this freedom-of-enterprise doctrine have been challenged in the case of large publicly-held enterprises[6] in which ownership and control are separated. But for small businesses, even of the marginal type known in the ghetto of past and present, the dogma continues to be unquestioned. The entrepreneur symbolizes both independence and a degree of security which members of a minority group need. Black ownership and control therefore appears to be an appropriate form of redress for the fact that in this, as in other industrial countries, it has been the historical fate of the black to earn his livelihood as an employee of the white. To make a meaningful and symbolic social and economic contribution to the solution of urban poverty, black capitalism must be developed far beyond the meager experience of "mom and pop" establishments known in the ghetto. Any program for economic development of the ghetto must include measures aimed at promoting entrepreneurship among ghetto residents to the greatest possible degree.

B. Community Control

Community ownership and control is a very different matter. The central idea here is that business enterprises established in the ghetto should be owned and controlled by the ghetto community as a community. This is a remarkable and an important idea, because it is a major departure from the pattern of ownership and control in American industry and is without important modern precedent in our economy. There are, of course, some community-owned enterprises, such as municipal utilities. In addition, there are large and important producers' cooperatives in various agricultural commodities, and there are many, usually local, consumer cooperatives. These enterprises, which are owned by the producers or consumers whom they serve, perform functions which are quite different in relation to their owners from those of a profit-making business enterprise. Of course, the stockholders of companies whose shares are not regularly traded or are locally traded are often residents of the locality in which the businesses operate. In any case, they would be a small fraction of the local population; in no sense would such enterprises be considered by the owners or other local residents as community-owned or controlled.

Hence, the idea of community ownership is certainly not an obvious step to take toward the economic development of ghetto areas. Nevertheless, it has already

---
[5] *See, e.g.*, McKersie, *Vitalize Black Enterprise*, HARV. BUS. REV., Sept.-Oct. 1968, at 88. "The importance of business ownership and management in helping a minority group to achieve pride and influence cannot be overstated." *Id.* at 88-89. Johnson & Smith, *supra* note 4, at 117-18.

[6] The corporate social responsibility doctrine and the concept of the corporate good citizen are a challenge to the conventional view of the role of business at least in the case of large industrial firms. *See* notes 11, 16, and 17 *infra*.

had considerable impact on current thinking about solutions to urban poverty.[7] It may reflect tendencies to think about poverty in community rather than individual terms and, based on past experience, to think of privately-owned business, at least in relation to blacks and the ghetto, as exploitative and antisocial. In any event, the idea of collective community ownership is the basic principle underlying the Community Self-Determination Act of 1969 and the prior version of substantially the same proposal which was sponsored by twenty-six senators.[8]

The bill reflects the strongly-held opinion of an important segment of the black leadership.[9] The desire of the black community to control its own social and economic affairs after decades of discrimination and neglect is certainly understandable. This does not mean, however, that collective community ownership would be a desirable or effective organizing principle for building economic enterprise in the ghetto. As has been pointed out, community ownership of economic enterprises has not been an important aspect of the economic development in this country, and there is no convincing reason to think that ghetto residents in their attitudes and aspirations on this matter are significantly different from other segments of the population. Presumably the successful operation of communal enterprise requires a strong, cohesive social organization among the members of the

---

[7] A good statement of the community ownership position appears in Innis, *Separatist Economics: A New Social Contract*, in BLACK ECONOMIC DEVELOPMENT, *supra* note 1, at 50.

[8] S. 33, 91st Cong., 1st Sess. (1969); S. 3875, 90th Cong., 2d Sess. (1968). An informative account of the draftsmen's views of the problem and of the thinking underlying the proposed solution, appears in McClaughry, *Black Ownership and National Politics*, in BLACK ECONOMIC DEVELOPMENT, *supra* note 1, at 38.

The organization of a community development corporation under S. 33 is prescribed in great detail in the bill and is a model of complexity without equal under general corporation law. The process is initiated by a letter of intent from residents which, among other things, must prescribe the precise boundaries of the area in which the corporation would function; articles of incorporation are then prepared and filed, providing for the issuance of $5 par value shares; an organizational certificate is then issued, and pledges for the purchase of shares must be obtained from at least 5% of the area residents. S. 33, 91st Cong., 1st Sess., in 115 CONG. REC. 834 (1969). The National Community Corporation Certification Board, which would be established under the bill to administer the statute, must then open an office in the area to disseminate information concerning the proposal (unless the Board finds the proposal to have been filed "for a patently frivolous purpose or with respect to a patently frivolous area"); thereafter additional stock subscriptions must be obtained to increase the total number of subscribers to 10% of the residents of the area over 16 years of age. *Id.* at 835. Finally a referendum must be held in the area on the question whether the corporation should function in the area; and if more than one corporation has been proposed, successive referenda must be held until all but one is eliminated or until "it becomes clear that community sentiment opposes the establishment of a CDC in any of the proposed communities." The theme of democratic control is maintained in the internal arrangements: shareholders have only one vote regardless of the number of shares owned (*id.* at 834), and proxy voting is allowed only if the proxy specifies the "particular matter" to be voted on. However, the quorum may be reduced to one-twentieth of the shareholders. Management is divided between a board of directors and a business management board (which manages the "business and assets" of the corporation) elected by the directors. *Id.*

The bill has been severely criticized. *See, e.g.*, CROSS, *supra* note 1, at 196 ("quasi-socialist enclave"); Sturdivant, *The Limits of Black Capitalism*, HARV. BUS. REV., Jan.-Feb. 1969, at 122.

A new bill, the Community Development Act of 1970, significantly changes some of the provisions of S. 33.

[9] S. 33 was largely prepared by the staff of the Congress on Racial Equality. *See* McClaughry, *supra* note 8.

group. A disciplined social structure of this sort is inconsistent with the emphasis on individualism and independence which is the dominant theme of the social philosophy of this country. Nor is there reason to think that such a structure exists in the ghetto. The fact that ghetto residents have been excluded from the benefits of this loose system does not mean that they are or have been immune from its influence. On the contrary, the emphasis of the movement for equal opportunity for the blacks has been on access to the benefits of an open society and economy.

The idea of a cohesive communal black society working together for common betterment has strong appeal to those who feel the urgency of the need for change, who want the black American to be free to control his on future, and who would be the leaders of such a community if it existed. The idea reflects the sense of frustration and isolation of black leadership. The fact is that in many of their attitudes, values, and aspirations, blacks are like other citizens of this country. Consequently, the vision of an harmonious black community working together to develop its own economy for the good of all is only a vision. It is based on a misconception of the values and goals which the black community shares with American society at large. On the basis of precedent and experience in this country, community ownership and control seems to be of questionable value in the effort to eliminate black poverty. The point of this discussion, then, is simply that in view of the nature of the black community, communal ownership and control is not a workable mechanism for economic development. We will consider subsequently whether, from the economic standpoint of business enterprise itself, community control (if it were feasible) could provide effective business management.

This criticism of the community control concept does not in any way apply to black capitalism. In one sense, the community control concept is merely one tactic for achieving black capitalism. The discovery of the most effective means of developing black ownership and control of business enterprise must be a matter of high priority in the search for ways to end urban poverty. However, as the foregoing discussion indicates, in the context of urban poverty, ownership and control of business enterprise has dimensions which are very different from those fundamental to economics and business law. Economic and legal ideas about ownership and control have become tools for basic social reform which Roy Innis has called "a *new social contract.*"[10] In attempting to evaluate this development, it may be useful to reconsider briefly some conventional learning about business enterprise.

II

The Traditional Function of Business

In a time when the need for reform and social change seems paramount, tradition becomes a dirty word. Nevertheless, the effort to utilize business enterprise

---

[10] Innis, *supra* note 7, at 51.

as a vehicle for achieving social reform must take account not only of its own goals and objectives, but of the nature and strucure of the institutions through which it seeks to accomplish its purposes. And the values and structure of the business community in this country are in a proper sense traditional. The rhetoric of the poverty literature, which advocates the use of business enterprise as a vehicle for promoting the welfare of the poor, is preoccupied with the needs of the poor and is relatively unconcerned or perhaps unaware of the nature and function of business enterprise. The fact is, however, that business enterprises as institutions have certain unique characteristics. The principal one is that business enterprises are unilinear institutions: they exist and operate to serve a single specific purpose—profit-making—and all corporate activities must be evaluated in the light of that end. It is this characteristic which more than anything else is responsible for the remarkable achievements of the business system. The fact that successful operation of the enterprise directly inures to the material and personal benefit of both owners and operators is the heart of the system. Discussions of social responsibility and corporate good works tend to obscure this basic yet essential fact about business enterprise. This oversight leads to misconstruction of such activities as corporate charity and to failure to apprehend the limitations on the capacity of business to contribute to the solution of social crises. In a business enterprise, nothing can take precedence over successful economic operation, including the public-spirited desire of its managers to train and hire the unemployed, to contribute to social causes, and to uplift the ghetto. The rhetoric and the record of corporate good citizenship amount to nothing more than the fact that a financially healthy enterprise can and may direct some of its profits to good works. It does not alter the case a fraction to say that enlightened corporate leadership has a moral obligation to devote some of the enterprise's assets to cleaning up the environmental mess that business has created, or to say that alleviating poverty is a part of the cost of doing business, because if poverty is not alleviated there will be a revolution. The critical fact for present purposes is that business must make a profit first, so that when costs rise, avoidable and deferrable commitments and expenditures will be avoided and deferred—*Business and Society*[11] and the

---

[11] *Business and Society* is a biweekly newsletter which reports current developments in the area of social and environmental responsibilities of business. It has responded vigorously to assertions of the priority of the profit motive. For example, when an article by Professor Milton Friedman espousing the traditional role of business recently appeared (Friedman, *The Social Responsibility of Business Is to Increase Its Profits*, N.Y. Times, Sept. 13, 1970 (Magazine), at 32), *Business and Society* responded with a piece of its own. *See Friedman's Folly*, Business and Society, Sept. 22, 1970, at 1. More recently, the paper attacked statements along this line by the president of Ford Motor Company in a piece entitled "The Iacocca Doctrine." The article attributed to Mr. Iacocca the view that profit comes first, and that this is true even of "equal opportunity jobs."

A trivial but eloquent illustration of the basic misunderstanding that occurs on this point concerns a businessman who stated, concerning the problem of environmental pollution, that he saw no alternative to government regulation. Business and Society, Mar. 3, 1970, at 1. The column writer suggests that this view represents failure of the "entrepreneurial spirit." The assumption must be that management has the right and the duty voluntarily to allocate a portion of a corporation's available funds to public service. The argument for such executive authority is liberal in the same sense that embezzlement is liberal; it is an appropriation of property by a fiduciary for purposes not consented to by the owner-beneficiaries. The

Harvard Business Review[12] notwithstanding. All the corporate charity that has occurred, and all that can reasonably be hoped for as a contribution to the solution of social problems, is an insignificant but well-intentioned gesture which can be justified or rationalized in traditional terms as tax deductible institutional advertising.[13]

The idea that the antipoverty effort must begin with an understanding of private enterprise would seem obvious, were it not for the fact that in several significant aspects a major proposal for developing business in the ghetto advocated arrangements that are basically inconsistent with the fundamental facts of business life. In trying to bring the ghetto into the normal economy, we must utilize the basic strengths of the business system. The task is to create conditions under which business enterprises outside the ghetto will have an economic incentive to operate within ghetto areas, and under which locally-owned and operated businesses may be organized and developed. Within this larger framework, the particular assignment of this paper is to discuss the function and role of local control in the light of the objectives described and the nature of business enterprise.

III

The Concept of Control of Business Enterprises

Some of the special problems which arise in connection with an effort to develop extensive community participation in business enterprises in ghetto areas can perhaps be seen most clearly through a brief discussion of the role of ownership and the relationship between ownership and control in business corporations generally.

---

argument is not saved by the suggestion that not all the earnings of the enterprise should be so allocated —that is like advocating "only a little embezzlement." Of course, the legal power to make charitable donations has long since been settled, and moderate charitable donations are a generally accepted usage that is unlikely to be successfully challenged. However, shareholder proposals to limit corporate giving regularly appear (along with resolutions to place a ceiling on management compensation) in the proxy statements of publicly-held corporations. *See also* note 17 *infra*.

[12] The *Harvard Business Review* has apparently taken a strong stand in favor of corporate social responsibility. Articles appearing in recent issues include Carr, *Can an Executive Afford a Conscience?*, July-Aug. 1970, at 58; Brower & Little, *White Help for Black Business*, May-June 1970, at 4; Cohn, *Is Business Meeting the Challenge of Urban Affairs?*, Mar.-Apr. 1970, at 68; Nadler, *Helping the Hard-Core Adjust to the World of Work*, *id.* at 117.

[13] It is totally unrealistic to expect that business is capable of making the sustained effort needed to bring economic life to the ghetto on a non- or low-profit basis. Gestures, even very significant gestures, are one thing; large scale performance is another. In 1967 the business community expended about 1% of its pre-tax revenues on charity. Albrook, *Business Wrestles with Its Social Conscience*, Fortune, Aug. 28, 1968, at 88. In 1967, one of the more impressive business antipoverty efforts was announced: the life insurance industry pledged $1 billion for slum mortgages. The money was to be "diverted from the normal channels of life insurance investments in a special effort to help alleviate the problems of the central cities. This sum was to be invested in core city areas to improve housing and to finance job-creating enterprises—projects which would not have ordinarily been financed under usual business practices because of their type, location or risk." Life Insurance Fact Book 5 (1968). By September 1968, $658 million had been lent, creating 46,800 housing units and 16,060 new jobs. Cross, *supra* note 1, at 244. The total assets of the U.S. life insurance industry in 1967 were $177.4 billion (including an increase during the year of $10.3 billion). Life Insurance Fact Book 8 (1968). The industry had therefore agreed to commit .56% of its assets to this antipoverty effort.

A. Small Businesses—Sole Proprietorships, Closely-Held Corporations

Special considerations apply to small, closely-held businesses, those in which the owners, often all of them, characteristically are directly involved in operations. Here there is, of course, no separation of ownership and control. Businesses of this kind are extremely common and exist in the ghetto as well as elsewhere. The development of this type of business in the ghetto is highly desirable because it contributes to community stability and creates a class of independent businessmen within the community of the poor. Encouragement of such small enterprises primarily involves making credit and insurance available on reasonable terms and improving the stability and physical safety of the ghetto community. An important part of the effort to promote such enterprises is the preservation of the independence and sense of independence of the operators. If the cost of these essential services is prohibitive, not only will fewer ghetto residents attempt to develop their own enterprises, but those who do will be demoralized by their inability to generate a profit sufficient to afford them a livelihood and to accumulate savings for expansion.

B. Medium and Large Size Enterprises

Discussions of community control and participation largely focus on businesses which are substantially larger than the corner store. These are enterprises which in the normal economy may be publicly or closely held. Enterprises in this range are of major importance to the antipoverty effort because of their capacity to make substantial short-run contributions toward the eradication of unemployment and underemployment, problems which are generally considered to be the point at which the principal attack on poverty should be directed.

In the normal economy, control and ownership are typically separated in publicly-owned companies. Over the years this separation has received much attention and has been the subject of extended scholarly discussion, as it is inconsistent with the basic dogma that owners should control because the productivity of private enterprise is derived from the avarice and energy of owners. This conventional, simplistic free enterprise psychology does not account for the competitive ardor of concerns not run by owners or by managers directly under the watchful eye of owners. It has been suggested that the explanation for this theoretical anomaly is to be found in the nature and aspirations of American business managers[14] who are intensely competitive[15]

---

[14] A powerful and widely-discussed analysis of the commitment of corporate management to growth and earnings (but not necessarily to the payment of dividends) appears in J. GALBRAITH, THE NEW INDUSTRIAL STATE (1967). The argument is that the managerial hierarchy seeks to preserve itself and to protect itself from outside interference, and that these objectives are promoted by financially successful operations. The security of the management is promoted by growth, profitable operation, and above all by the absence of losses, which may lead to borrowing and consequent loss of independence to outsiders. Avoidance of risk of loss is not the equivalent of profit maximization; loss avoidance as a goal leads to conservative management practices and does not aim at increased profit where there is an attendant increased risk of loss. *See generally id.* at 166-78.

[15] In psychological terms, corporate executives are "high need achievers." *See* D. McCLELLAND, THE ACHIEVING SOCIETY 226-35 *et seq.* (1961).

and measure their own performance by growth, and in the fact that the owners collect their dividends, watch the price-earnings ratio, and sell their stock if they dislike what they see.[16] In the recent discussions about the irresponsibility of corporate power, shareholders have been rarely heard from;[17] and when they have, their complaint has usually been that management has not been sufficiently aggressive or effective in its pursuit of profit. The conclusion to be drawn from this seems to be that if managers and owners share a common goal, and if the owners can withdraw their investment from the business if they become dissatisfied, it is not necessary for the protection of the interests of the latter that management be directly under their control.

The other aspect of the control dilemma is concerned not with the responsibility of management to the owners, but with its responsibility to society at large. The suggestion is not that corporate managers should become socially responsible, but that responsibility to a range of public interests and values should be imposed upon business organizations through regulation in the public interest. There is nothing novel about this suggestion, since many aspects of business conduct have been regulated for years; certain values about competition have long been protected by the antitrust laws and recently the public interest in motor vehicle safety and in environmental deterioration has produced both state and federal regulatory legislation. The initial inquiry when restriction or regulation of corporate conduct is proposed concerns what interests are sought to be advanced. Discussion in general terms of the control of business enterprises in the public interest is quite useless; one must know the specific purpose for which control is sought. After this is determined, it becomes possible to talk about means. In the case of large publicly-held companies, most of the groups whose interests and welfare are immediately affected by the operation of the business have available devices or remedies of greater or lesser effectiveness by which they can protect themselves against corporate conduct which is detrimental to their interests.[18] In any given case there may be no remedy

---

[16] The author has developed this theme at length elsewhere. See Hetherington, *Fact and Legal Theory: Shareholders, Managers, and Corporate Social Responsibility*, 21 STAN. L. REV. 248 (1969).

[17] The annual reports of the brothers Gilbert are a diary of the stockholder movement in publicly-held companies. The most recent report discusses 1969 annual meetings and reports of various companies. It emphasizes adequacy of disclosure and shareholder concern over executive compensation and pensions, cumulative voting, and related matters. See L. & J. GILBERT, THIRTIETH ANNUAL REPORT OF STOCKHOLDERS ACTIVITIES AT CORPORATION MEETINGS 129, 142, 154, 173 (1970). Notably absent are materials dealing with corporate responsibility. The efforts of Mr. Ralph Nader and his associates to procure representation on corporate boards of other groups whose interests are affected by corporate operations continue. One such proposal was to have some members of the board of directors of General Motors "named by GM employees, purchasers of new GM vehicles and GM auto dealers." Wall Street Journal, Nov. 20, 1970, at 1, col. 2. It is unlikely that the constituency represented by the Gilberts will look with favor on such innovations.

[18] Among these groups are shareholders (the stock market, managerial duties of competence and loyalty, derivative suits, proxy fights); employees (unions, employment contracts); customers (rights and remedies under the law of sales, power to bargain in certain cases, antitrust law, freedom to deal elsewhere, appeals for government aid, the mass media); dealers and suppliers (trade associations, state laws in certain cases); and competitors (price changes or other alterations in their own competitive conduct, antitrust litigation). The list is incomplete and is intended to be only suggestive.

or none that is effective, and there may be important questions of costs to be considered, but at least mechanisms are available to limit the ability of business enterprise to impose upon the interests of various groups affected by its operations. Those in control of an enterprise do not have anything approaching complete and unrestricted freedom in decision making on behalf of the company. In general, management has the broadest discretion in connection with proposed *new* undertakings—where to locate a new facility or whether to develop a new product. In decisions concerning existing operations it may be forced to take account of the views of various groups having established interests and relationships with the company.

In summary, control of a business enterprise means power, but not unrestricted power, and it is therefore necessary to think in terms of power to perform a specific act or to make and implement a specific policy under particular circumstances. In speaking of ghetto enterprises, it is similarly necessary to know as exactly as possible what is meant by community participation and control and what are the reasons and the purposes for which community control is advocated.

IV

COMMUNITY CONTROL OF GHETTO BUSINESS ENTERPRISES

This section is concerned with whether widespread community participation and control can be achieved in ghetto economic enterprises and, if it can, what is likely to be the effect of such control on the operation of the businesses involved. In order to reach these questions it is necessary to comment briefly on the legal forms of organization that are being used in community development efforts.

A. Membership Corporations

There are presently two types of corporate vehicles being used in efforts to develop business activity in ghetto areas: profitmaking (stock) and nonprofit (nonstock) corporations.[19] Nonprofit corporations, which apparently are more prevalent, are exempt from income tax and are eligible to participate in certain government programs. The nonstock form of organization also simplifies the mechanical aspects of arranging for community participation;[20] membership may be open to any interested person or to any resident of a particular area. Stock corporations, on the other hand, may engage directly in profitmaking activities, must pay taxes, and must limit membership to stockholders, although nonstockholder participation in particular corporate decisions may easily be arranged.[21]

---

[19] For example, Zion Investment Associates, Inc. (Philadelphia), began as a stock corporation, while Action Industries, Inc. (Venice, California), and East Central Citizens Organization, Inc. (Columbus, Ohio), were initially financed through grants. Hough Area Development Corporation (Cleveland) is a nonprofit corporation initially financed by a group of trustees. *See* Note, *Community Development Corporations: Operations and Financing*, 83 HARV. L. REV. 1558, 1562-77 (1970).

[20] *Id.* at 1585.

[21] There is no principle or rule of corporation law which would prohibit the creation of an advisory board selected for any purpose from any interested group or constituency so long as ultimate decision-making authority is retained by directors elected by shareholders.

In view of the consensus on the desirability of community control, the question of how to bring about this result arises in both types of organization. Experience thus far with community development corporations organized under state corporation laws has produced no example in which broadly-based community participation and control has been achieved. A distinction must be observed between participation and control. In at least one case, a degree of community participation was achieved through a representative structure, but the amount of direct control by residents appears to have been limited as a consequence.[22] In other nonprofit community development corporations the number of community members involved in the organization has been relatively small.[23] This experience suggests that development of large-scale community participation may take considerable time and effort to achieve, and even if it is attained it may be of dubious benefit to the organization.

Clearly the question of community participation in a nonprofit organization is very different from ownership in a conventional profitmaking enterprise. Since the corporation issues no stock and cannot make a distributable profit, the motive for individual participation is community benefit, and personal benefit is only derivative. The member of such an organization lacks the characteristic interest of an investor in a business enterprise. Similarly, the position of the management of a nonprofit organization is significantly different from its counterpart in a for-profit corporation in that it lacks the personal incentive for material success on which a normal business venture depends. It is clear therefore that the selection of the nonprofit corporation as the primary structure for developing business activity in a ghetto deprives the organization, for better or worse, of the incentives and pressures which move participants in normal business corporations. The selfless devotion and determination of the community members in the cause of community betterment are substitutes for the usual incentives, but this makes the organization entirely dependent upon the energy and skill of the leadership in motivating and directing the efforts of the members. It seems questionable whether an organization which depends so heavily on the personal commitment of its leaders and members to the public good can sustain its vigor and effectiveness through the long pull. One wonders whether there may not be an inescapable tendency for this form of organization to develop a bureaucracy with a depressing resemblance to a government administrative agency or department. However excellent bureaucracies may be for regulatory and

---

[22] The organization is East Central Citizens Organization, Inc. (ECCO), of Columbus, Ohio. All neighborhood residents over the age of 16 years (as well as nonresidents regularly employed in the neighborhood) are eligible for membership. Articles of Incorporation of East Central Citizens Organization art. 7, § 1. The members comprise the Neighborhood Assembly, which elects the Executive Council. *Id.* art. 9, § 1. The Council has "the power to represent the Corporation in all matters." *Id.* § 4. The Council has apparently taken an active interest in management: its activities are said to have "impinged . . . on operations . . . . Council activity has been characterized by devotion of much time to minor operating matters and by lack of ability to move swiftly and secretly on business matters." 83 HARV. L. REV. at 1575.

[23] Hough Area Development Corporation is an example of limited participation. 83 HARV. L. REV. at 1572.

supervisory functions, we have little experience to indicate that either governmental or eleemosynary cadres can provide the sustained, imaginative, and creative leadership required to build and maintain soundly-managed economic enterprise.

B. Stock Corporations

Stock corporations organized for community development face similar problems. In order to obtain any degree of community ownership, stock must be sold to a substantial number of residents who are inevitably not in a position to contribute substantial amounts of money.[24] Consequently, the stock must be offered at a low price.[25] Even so, it is unlikely that front-end money adequate to launch a significant effort can be raised from the local community, and outside financing will be necessary. This presents difficulty with the control problem; if outsiders buy shares of the class offered to residents, local control will be lost. Consequently, either debt or a non-voting or limited-voting stock must be used, but in any event local control may still be impaired. Further, if voting shares are issued to local residents, restrictions on transfer must be imposed to prevent stock from passing into the hands of outsiders.[26] Thus the price for the preservation of control is the destruction of any possible market for the shares.[27]

Offering shares of such an organization to local residents differs in significant

---

[24] An impressive apparent exception on this point is Zion Investment Associates, Inc., where 600 members of the congregation of Zion Baptist Church had by 1968 bought shares of stock. *Id*. at 1564. Under the original subscription arrangement, congregation members were asked to invest $10 per month for 36 months. SULLIVAN, *supra* note 1, at 168. Subsequently, 7000 people purchased or were purchasing shares on the installment plan. 83 HARV. L. REV. at 1564. The venture was launched as "a new kind of experiment in racial economic emancipation." SULLIVAN, *supra* note 1, at 166. However, the appeal was to the economic self-interest of the purchasers: "Put your ten-dollar bills down and keep them there . . . and within the years to come they will multiply themselves a hundred times." *Id*. at 168.

The special circumstances under which this success was attained are important. First, the appeal was launched to members of a well-organized, highly successful local church. Second, the appeal was to personal economic advantage. Third, the persons appealed to clearly were not the destitute poor of the community, and the amounts invested were not nominal. Fourth, there was not broad community participation.

[25] It is for this reason that corporations organized under S. 33, discussed at note 8 *supra*, were limited to a single class of stock, which was required to be offered to community residents at its par value of $5 per share.

[26] For example, under S. 33 the shares of a community development corporation are nontransferable, and are redeemable by the corporation at par if the owner leaves the community. S. 33, 91st Cong., 1st Sess. § 118 (1969). Under these circumstances, share ownership is a contribution to the community and offers no personal economic incentive to the resident.

[27] The S. 33 proposal is destructive of proprietary incentive in other ways. For example, local businesses may be entitled to borrow from a community development bank on advantageous terms. However, eligibility for borrowing from the bank is limited to businesses "at least 75-percent owned by resident CDC stockholders." 115 CONG. REC. 835 (1969). If there is lesser degree of ownership the owners must agree they will not sell the business without first offering it to the local community development corporation under terms prescribed by the Comptroller of the Currency. Loans will also be made if the borrowing business is at least 51% owned by the community development corporation, or if it is an outside corporation operating under a turn-key arrangement with the CDC. *Id*. These restrictions appear to impose substantial disincentives to participation in the program by businessmen whose objective is profit.

ways from the sale of shares in a normal corporation. There is, first, the great difficulty of finding a large enough number of local residents with money and the disposition to invest. While the investment being offered should have substantial appeal to community pride, such a venture is undeniably risky. One could well ask whether it is a service or a disservice to local residents to ask them to put what little money they can spare into such an enterprise. Perhaps one answer to this criticism is that the money would not otherwise be put to better use, and that, to gain local support, local people must have a financial stake in the enterprise. But in fact they already have a stake in the community by living there, and the desirability as well as the need for imposing a price on their participation in a community development program seems questionable. Further, the stock purchase requirement discriminates against the residents who cannot afford to make the investment, and this discrimination cannot be justified on the usual ground that the proprietor of a business ought to be required to put in the first, or front, money. The local residents are not proprietors whose active personal interest and participation can be engaged by requiring them to put their own money down; the possibility of personal gain is remote and speculative, and the gain—if any—would be small because the amounts invested would be small. Under these circumstances an investment intended as earnest money and required as a symbol of support seems hardly essential and may not even be desirable. In addition, neither wide distribution of stock nor issuance of a large number of memberships will assure a substantial degree of actual community participation. In publicly-held stock corporations, as is well known, the vast majority of shares are usually represented by proxies gathered by management through strenuous and often repeated solicitation. In cooperative organizations, where proxies are sometimes not allowed, quorum requirements are reduced to less than ten per cent of the members so that meetings can be held.[28] The emphasis on community control of community development corporations is a hollow gesture if the sole intention is to create the possibility of local control without concern for its exercise.

The question therefore arises, what is the purpose for which control of business activity in ghetto areas is considered to be critical? What particular decisions made in the course of operating a business enterprise ought to be subject to control by local residents? We have already noted that shareholders in publicly-held companies neither have nor need control of the enterprise to protect their interests under most circumstances. The law merely requires that they elect managers and approve, after full disclosure, certain basic changes in the enterprises. As for day-to-day operation, shareholders are content (perhaps fortunately for us all) to leave things to management.

In the daily operation of the business, ghetto residents are in the same position

---

[28] *See, e.g.,* WIS. STAT. ANN. § 185 *et seq.* (1957). Proxies are not permitted—except that representation of members may be "by delegates apportioned territorially." *Id.* § 185.12(3). The quorum requirement is "10 per cent of the first 100 members plus 5 per cent of additional members," but not more than 50 members unless the bylaws provide otherwise. *Id.* § 185.14.

as shareholders. As shareholders of a community development corporation they are neither qualified nor probably disposed to participate in the operation of a going concern; the same is true of the affairs of a nonprofit corporation trying to promote and finance other concerns. However, as shareholders, or members, or neither, local residents have a substantial interest in being kept advised of the activities of the corporation and in being given ample advance opportunity for communication on corporate activities which affect community interests. A substantial degree of community acceptance and support is not only highly desirable, but it may be essential to successful operation of an industrial facility in the ghetto. Here the position of the shareholder in a publicly-held company ceases to be remotely analogous to that of the shareholder or member of a community development corporation. The importance of the corporation to the residents of a ghetto exists regardless of investment or membership in the enterprise; the typical shareholder's interest in a typical publicly-held corporation, on the other hand, begins and ends with his investment. He may discontinue his connection and concern with the corporation by a telephone call to his broker; the prospects and the life of a ghetto resident may continue to be affected by the activity of a community corporation regardless of his personal involvement with it. It is this continuing nonproprietary interest that gives him a stake in the corporation and requires that his voice and interests be interpreted to the corporation and that its activities and programs be communicated to and, in some measure, understood by him. A ghetto resident may or may not be a stockholder or a member of a community development corporation; he may or may not be a customer, employee, or trainee either of the corporation itself or of a corporation which it is promoting; he is in any event a neighbor and an intended beneficiary of the social and economic consequences of its operation in the ghetto. The aggregate of all these relationships, of which stock ownership or membership is the least significant, are the substance of his relationship with and stake in a community development organization.

What is needed is an arrangement that accommodates the unique relationship between the ghetto community and business enterprises established as part of the antipoverty effort. Neither the business corporation nor the nonstock membership corporation is an adequate model for this purpose. Reported experience thus far casts serious doubt on the possibility that an organizational form can be devised that will produce a broad, effective, and continuing community participation and control in a community development organization. The difficulty of this approach is illustrated in the recently proposed federal legislation which would provide for inflexible structure with forced community participation.[29] The elaborate structure thus created would exercise control over various privately-owned community enterprises within a specifically defined area.[30]

---

[29] *See* note 8 *supra.*
[30] *See* note 27 *supra.*

There have been other proposals for the creation of new institutional forms to manage the ghetto economy. One scheme would create both local and regional development corporations.[31] The local organization would be project-oriented and would work with and through "interested groups in the community."[32] The organization would be divided into two parts, one a functional staff concerned with specific developmental problems (housing, business development, manpower, and financing), and the other an area staff concerned with "internal relationships with community organizations."[33] It is suggested that "sustained interaction between directors and members of the community would insure sensitivity to changing community attitudes and needs."[34] The author advances a very plausible argument that the structure advocated would be both effective and beneficial.

There does not appear to be any provision in the proposal, however, for solving the problem encountered by existing community development corporations—lack of broad participation by residents. Nor does there appear to be any way to solve this problem by manipulating the organizational structure.[35] The federal proposal would solve it by requiring community approval by referendum and by requiring community purchase of shares. Again, the overwhelming difficulty is that there is no evidence that broad, ongoing, active participation can be achieved in this way.

The proposed federal legislation and the proposal for regional and local development corporations are both based on the view that in order to bring economic vitality and growth to the ghetto a new institutional form is required. The proposals share the further assumption that the new form must be based on broad participation and actual control of the organization by the community. The organizations proposed are designed to achieve this requirement of local control, and also are designed to have special and unique powers and goals (such as community improvement) that distinguish them from conventional business enterprises.

The critical factor concerning both designs is that profit, the normal entrepreneurial incentive, has been removed from the organization. This is true under the federal proposal despite the fact that it involves stock corporations, and despite the fact that in certain events the boards of directors may authorize a distribution of earnings to shareholders.[36] The possibility of a distribution is so remote, and the individual investments of ghetto residents certain to be so small, that there is no serious possibility that personal gain would play any role at all in the shareholders'

---

[31] Rosenbloom, *Corporations for Urban Development*, in SOCIAL INNOVATION IN THE CITY 161 (R. Rosenbloom & R. Marris eds. 1969).
[32] *Id.* at 164.
[33] *Id.* at 165.
[34] *Id.* at 164.
[35] The author states, "The initiative must come from within the community, provided by an individual or small leadership group." *Id.* at 167. In other words, structure is secondary. If the local leadership or group exists, no new structures are needed; and there seems to be no reason to think that new structures will serve better than those available under present law to facilitate the mobilization and development of local leadership.
[36] *See* note 8 *supra*.

relationship to the corporation or in management's view of its responsibilities to them. The abandonment of the profit motive is made more explicit in the proposal for local and regional corporations, which offers as a "working definition of entrepreneurship" that its function is to "seek to attract talent and capital from new sources and to coordinate their application in the task of development."[37] The distinction is between entrepreneurs who are "profit-seeking" and those who are not.

The effective destruction of any meaningful profit motive is probably the unavoidable consequence of any arrangement for widespread community control. The amounts of capital available from large numbers of residents are necessarily so small, and the programs sought to be promoted so uncertain of financial success at least within any reasonable time, that no shareholder could regard his prospects for personal return as significant. This raises a very serious question about the desirability and the feasibility of the community ownership and control idea. Once the traditional motivating force of business enterprise is removed, the community ownership and control principle appears in a very different light, as an attempt to build a functioning economy in the ghetto on a basis wholly different from that on which the economy of the rest of the country was built and operates. It is ironic, to say the least, to offer to ghetto residents as a device for improving their economic situation a type of organization which denies its participants access to the benefits which owners of businesses normally expect. It is true, of course, that both existing CDC's and the forms proposed are in large part envisioned as organizations which assist others, rather than operating businesses directly. However, in the case of the federal bill at least, provision is made for preserving a right in the CDC under certain circumstances to acquire privately-owned businesses which it assists.[38] Since one of the avenues of business profit is sale of the enterprise, this provision would destroy one of the incentives of the operators of the businesses assisted.

To recapitulate, it seems that an organizational form which seeks broad participation in the community is extremely ill-suited to develop the ghetto economy, because the dispersion of ownership in the effort to build ghetto industry destroys the entrepreneurial element. The assumption behind this criticism is that permanent and dynamic business enterprises must be built on, and for, profit. Specifically, the effort to build ghetto business enterprise ought to focus on profit such that those involved, like businessmen anywhere, can see an apparently realistic probability of future profit from the beginning. The proposals to create special organizations to develop and control ghetto business would be subject to another less critical but nevertheless important objection, namely, that the proposed community control arrangements would tend to segregate ghetto business enterprises from the normal economy. Such

---

[37] Rosenbloom, *supra* note 31, at 161.

[38] Nonresident owners of ghetto businesses would be required as a condition for obtaining a loan from a National Community Development Bank to agree to give the local CDC a right of first refusal if they should decide to sell. S. 33, 91st Cong., 1st Sess. § 1942(c)(2) (1969).

a private ghetto business system has been advocated by responsible commentators.[39] It is clear that even if an economic segregation program were in any degree feasible, it could not under any reasonably foreseeable circumstances provide employment in the near future for large numbers of ghetto residents. The economy of the area would of necessity retain substantial connections and dependence on the outside economy. Artificial barriers restricting access of outsiders who would establish businesses in the ghetto inure to the detriment of ghetto residents, tend to retard economic development of the area, and operate to encourage second-rate noncompetitive black businesses whose future would be confined to the area of special privileges. Isolation of the ghetto economy on any terms is bad policy from the standpoint of those on both sides of the barriers.

The justification for efforts to design special organizational structures to build up the economy of the ghetto lies in the implicit assumption that since normal economic forces permitted ghettos to develop, they cannot be the basis for reviving the ghetto economically.[40] Hence the need for special arrangements. It seems to me that this conclusion is very dubious. The alternative is to attack directly the conditions in slum areas which perpetuate their economic underdevelopment. Instead of building new organizations, this approach suggests a program which would attempt to remove the economic barriers preventing growth in the ghetto economy.

V

TOWARD A LOW-PROFILE APPROACH TO COMMUNITY PARTICIPATION

The following suggestions about programs for building up the economy of our urban ghettos are based on three assumptions. First, from the beginning and over the long run, the objective of the effort to reduce and eliminate the poverty of the ghetto should be to integrate the ghetto into the national economy. Second, this objective should be achieved by creating conditions in which business can be organized and allowed to grow in the ghetto on the same basis and principles on which it functions elsewhere in the economy. Third, neither the experience of community development corporations in recent years, nor the arguments advanced in favor of community ownership and control, make a persuasive case that community ownership and control has been or can be an effective technique for developing successful business enterprise in the urban ghetto.

Credit and business insurance (fire and theft) must be made available to ghetto businessmen to develop and assist the entrepreneurial talent which presently exists but is prevented from attaining fruition by the nonavailability of the essential business services without which no enterprise can grow, or even survive.[41] Credit should be available through normal channels and in large amounts. This would require gov-

---

[39] *See* Innis, *supra* note 7.
[40] *See, e.g.*, Goodpaster, *supra* note 4.
[41] Hellman, *Your Policy Is Hereby Cancelled*, N.Y. Times, Nov. 8, 1970 (Magazine), at 32.

ernment subsidies to lenders to absorb the extra costs of slum lending.[42] Further, it would undoubtedly be desirable to have black financial institutions play a leading role in this effort.[43] The small independent retailer (mom-and-popism) is a symbol not only of the ghetto's backwardness and of the failure of national firms to service the ghetto market, but also of the ghetto residents' belief that business ownership is the way to economic security.[44] The local small business operator is an important figure in the neighborhood economy. Because he is self-employed he has a degree of independence which other residents lack. At the same time his dependence on the local market, his personal relationships with his customers, and his involvement and commitment to the area make him a stabilizing factor in the community. In this regard he is quite unlike the semi-itinerant professional executive who manages the local plant of a national firm.

In addition to services essential to business, job skill training needs to be made available on a large scale to ghetto residents. Probably the most encouraging development in this field has been the OIC program which began in Philadelphia.[45] The success of this program has been attributed in large part, by its founder, to the feeling of the participants that it was their own program[46] and to the fact that the students knew the program would lead to personal economic advantage.[47] The same initiative is and must be kept as the basis of the growth of black capitalism. Community job training programs not only develop job capability, they also stimulate interest in business and proprietorship.

On the basis of events to date, there is no way to estimate the capacity of ghetto communities to generate profitable economic activity in the conventional forms of business enterprise once credit, insurance, and training have been made available.

---

[42] For a full discussion of this subject, see CROSS, *supra* note 1, at 156-82. For an account of one bank officer's experiences in lending to ghetto businessmen, see Allen, *Making Capitalism Work in the Ghettos*, HARV. BUS. REV., May-June 1969, at 83.

[43] Racial problems may result when white-controlled banks seek to collect loans in urban ghettos. CROSS, *supra* note 1, at 168. There are a number of banks controlled by blacks in ghetto areas. *See* Business and Society, Sept. 22, 1970, at 2. Aggregate assets of the 24 largest black-owned banks are $3.7 million, while the 50th largest bank in the United States has assets of $1.3 billion. *Id.*

[44] Johnson & Smith, *supra* note 4, at 112, 118-19. It has been persuasively argued that the provision of adequate financing for ghetto businesses would in itself be a grossly inadequate antipoverty strategy because of the inherent weaknesses and disadvantages of the ghetto businessman. McLaurin & Tyson, *The GHEDIPLAN for Economic Development*, in BLACK ECONOMIC DEVELOPMENT, *supra* note 1, at 126, 130. Clearly, provision of adequate financing will not solve the problems of the ghetto businessman, but it would undoubtedly strengthen his position. Hence this device can properly be a part of the overall attack on urban poverty. Building on and from local institutions has been recognized as necessary for the success of the campaign against poverty, and ghetto business is such an institution. Those who have survived in the hostile business environment of the ghetto have demonstrated a strength that should be encouraged.

[45] A personal and informative account of this venture appears in Reverend Leon Sullivan's book, BUILD, BROTHER, BUILD, *supra* note 1, at 85-142.

[46] "They [the students] saw it as their program, they believed in what it was doing, and it made each of them feel like somebody. In OIC the student feels that the teacher is there because of him. He is the most important individual." *Id.* at 108.

[47] *Id.* at 85-86.

There are indications, such as the Philadelphia program, that the potential may be very great. The most direct way of trying to develop ghetto enterprise is to offer the ghetto businessman financing at reasonable cost and insurance against business risks.

Major industrial firms must be given a business incentive to establish facilities in ghetto areas. The encouragement of local enterprise as proposed above would inure, at the beginning, to the benefit of consumer sales and service businesses. The inability of developing local enterprise to create a significant amount of employment and to bring new money into the ghetto, at least initially, is apparent.[48] For this purpose established businesses and large-scale industrial enterprises are needed. The costs of establishing industrial facilities in ghetto areas are high.[49] These operations must be profitable[50] to induce outside companies to establish substantial operations in ghetto areas, perhaps necessitating an incentive or subsidy arrangement to absorb the high costs. Strong opposition to this strategy has been expressed by some black leaders, who see in this proposal a perpetuation of "colonialism."[51] In economic terms, this contention is difficult to understand. Under modern conditions, the relationship between a large industrial firm and its employees or the plant community in which it operates is not in any sense "colonial." There obviously are areas of both mutual and adverse interest between employers and employees. But the relationship between them is also obviously mutually advantageous: the company is interested in profitable operation, and the employees are interested in steady work and good wages. The degree of employer dominance of the local community implied by the term "colonialism" is highly unlikely in large urban centers. If the term is applied to the overall relationship between the ghetto and society or the economy at large, the meaning is still obscure. The relationship of the ghetto community with the "outside" social forces is complex; ghetto residents are sellers of labor, consumers of goods, borrowers of credit, and, to some extent, suppliers of goods and services. It should hardly be necessary to say that mutually advantageous economic relationships are not exploitative, and the history of exploitation and discrimination against blacks cannot be made a justification for attacking any employment relationship between whites and blacks. It is difficult to see how ghetto employment created by such a plan differs from the relationship between large business firms and their employees in other communities.

When a national firm establishes a ghetto facility, its interest would plainly dictate that it adopt and implement a program to develop local executive talent as

---

[48] This fact has been the principal basis of the criticism of the proposal discussed at pp. 15-19 *supra*.
[49] *See, e.g.*, Garrity, *supra* note 3; Skala, *supra* note 3, at 151, 154.
[50] *See* Cross, *supra* note 1, at 137-41. The author's point is that economic incentive must be offered to the organization which is in the position to decide, on a normal profitmaking basis, whether to establish a ghetto business operation.
[51] Innis, *supra* note 7. This article is a concise presentation of a separatist position. It argues in part from an analogy between colonies and parent country, on the one hand, and the situation of the urban ghetto in American cities, on the other. *Id.* at 53-54. The author approves the 1968 Community Development proposal (S. 3875) as providing "incentive for broad-based community ownership." *Id.* at 57.

rapidly as possible. Employment of blacks as managers,[52] whether local residents or not, directly benefits relations between the company and the community. Corporations have in recent years made susbtantial efforts to hire and promote black executives, and as immediate, tangible evidence of changed attitudes toward blacks by industry, the presence of black executives in ghetto plants is plainly important to ghetto residents. In a recent project in which a local community organization developed a shopping center, the national firms renting space in the project were required to employ black managers.[53]

The contribution other than in symbolic terms to the ghetto community is probably not great. Black executives, and for that matter, black owners of substantial profitable businesses, will not continue as residents there any more than the executives of industrial firms generally reside in working class neighborhoods. Possession of marketable management skills is a ticket out of the ghetto, and few who acquire it will not use it. The development of black executive talent is a useful and important part of the effort to gain for black citizens their rightful place in the society and economy. It is not of major significance, other than as a symbol, in the achievement of the immediate objectives of the attack on ghetto poverty.[54]

If immediate ghetto employment on a substantial scale is the primary goal of the attack on poverty, direct community ownership and control of economic development must be substantially limited. A program which attempts to deliver training and jobs to ghetto residents as quickly as possible must work primarily through existing business enterprise. This does not mean that ghetto residents would be or could be excluded from consultation or involvement in the affairs of businesses operating in the ghetto. On the contrary, the legacy of bitterness and resentment engendered by decades of discrimination is a fact which must be taken into account in any effort to establish a ghetto business operation. The feasibility and success of any training and employment plan is dependent upon an effective community relations program. The ghetto poor have suffered so long from active discrimination and indifference that the task of convincing them (and ourselves) that a change has really come is very great. They must be informed through every means possible, beginning with communication with community leaders and social workers, and including meetings at which questions are encouraged and dealt with by people who

---

[52] Johnson & Smith, *supra* note 4, at 112, 118. "It has been estimated that 100 jobs exist at the management level for every five trained black managers in existence." *Id*. at 124. Apart from employment contracts, which are probably not common, there are no legal devices which protect the interest or expectancy of managers in fair or equal treatment by their employers. Traditionally there has been no tenure in business hierarchy. *See, e.g.*, R. EELLS, THE GOVERNMENT OF CORPORATIONS 211 (1962): "Least protected, at the administrative core of corporate governments, are the rights of persons in middle management." The author proposes an intracorporate structure to protect the constitutional rights of this group, who may lose their positions or be denied advancement on grounds unrelated to merit or performance.

[53] This is Progress Plaza in Philadelphia. SULLIVAN, *supra* note 1, at 170.

[54] Ghetto employment and executive training for blacks are aimed at different objectives; one seeks to improve the economics of ghetto residents, and the other to provide an exit from the ghetto. *See* note 50 *supra*.

know the facts. This means that small neighborhood meetings are required. Further, the enterprise must be responsive to their requests and suggestions. It is reported time and again that what the poor need is to be informed about issues and developments in programs which affect them. The information and community involvement programs must be on a sufficiently large scale to convince community residents that something is really happening and that they are a part of it. Management of such a program requires a high degree of skill and insight as well as persistence. (A member of an academic faculty must have at least some passing qualms before suggesting that the poor be subjected to the joys of the committee system.) However, involvement is impossible if it does not begin with communication, and communication must be as immediate and personal as possible. The most effective vehicles for initiating communication in many instances are existing community organizations. The primary need in this type of project is information—where, when, how many jobs, what about the training programs, and the like.

This level of communication and participation falls far short of control by ghetto residents. The degree of influence by residents on a business enterprise operating in the community should be determined by their respective needs and interests. There is no evidence to show that ghetto residents as employees of large companies do or would feel differently than other employees of large companies do about their prerogatives and interests as employees.[55] Where the purpose of the enterprise is to establish a business involving ghetto residents, the scope of the interaction which is feasible and needed is guided by that fact. Where the objective of the organization is otherwise, such as planning community services and housing, the role for local participation is determined by the fact that community residents are the consumers of these services.

Conclusion

In conclusion, it is difficult to explain our apparent reluctance to make a major effort to develop the ghetto economy in "normal" ways. The explanation may in part lie in the fact that for decades the normal economy permitted the ghetto to grow and to become what it is. There is an understandable reluctance among black leaders and others who are committed to the fight against ghetto poverty to look to the institutions of the economy which created a national disgrace to correct it. The sense of urgency about poverty is the product of the 1960's, and the undoing of the damage of decades in a few years seems to require special measures. Hence, the call for community ownership and control. The difficulty is that there is nothing in this idea, in the structures designed to implement it, or in recent experience

---

[55] The bitterness and antagonism of many ghetto residents toward "the establishment" is undoubtedly reflected in their attitudes toward "outside" society and institutions. These attitudes are destructive of the work relationship, and must be dealt with as part of the communication between the employer and the community and as part of the training of "hard core unemployables." It does not follow, however, that ghetto residents think that as employees they should have different rights vis-à-vis their employer than other employees do.

to support confidence that this is the way to promote economic growth. In failing to make full use of the resources, techniques, and incentives of normal economic growth we may be overlooking the best—and the least costly—remedy.

The critical aspect of the war on poverty is money. We have been unwilling in the past to give the antipoverty effort a high fiscal priority. It seems likely that for one reason or another efforts of the federal government in this field will continue to receive inadequate funding. Changes in the military budget and in economic conditions constantly threaten even modest poverty appropriations. Further, if there is not a recurrence of violence in the ghettos, the country and the ghetto communities themselves may well settle for a modest continuing effort in the poverty field. If this evaluation of fiscal prospects and hazards is correct, there would appear to be special advantage in an antipoverty program designed to promote permanent employment by integrating the ghetto into the national economy through normal economic institutions. In this process, community acceptance, participation, and support are essential, but community-owned and controlled business enterprise is not. Experimental business institutions do not appear to be a strategy which is well-suited to bring prosperous, stable economic activity to the ghetto. The message from our black urban ghettos is that the residents want to participate on an equal basis with others in the economic life of this country. The policy which is most responsive to that just and overdue demand is one which moves directly to bring ghetto residents into the normal economy.

COMMUNITY DEVELOPMENT CORPORATIONS: THE PROBLEM OF MIXED OBJECTIVES

FREDERICK D. STURDIVANT*

In commenting on the urban riots of the 1960's, W. H. Ferry has noted that the most important force to emerge "was the explosive renascence of the idea of black manhood, of black dignity and worth, of the black's desire to run his own affairs." Ferry added that he regarded "this welling-up within the black psyche as a permanent force in our national life and a matter for great rejoicing."[1] Indeed, this rebirth of racial pride is the foundation for much of the discussion and activity centering around the concept of community development corporations (CDC).

In any discussion of community development corporations it is important to distinguish between those already established corporate entities (of which there are some one hundred in the United States) and the provisions contained in the Community Self-Determination Bill[2] which was introduced during the Ninetieth Congress. This paper will focus primarily on the organizational effectiveness of the existing community or local development corporations rather than on the provisions of proposed legislation designed to accelerate the expansion of such corporations. It should also be noted that while a number of these established CDC's are operated by low-income American Indian and Mexican-American communities in rural as well as urban areas, this paper will primarily treat the role of the CDC's in black urban ghettos.

In general, these corporations are "community-based organizations that conduct revenue-generating business with the primary purpose of economic and social development of their community."[3] In most cases these CDC's either involve or ultimately call for widespread ownership of shares in the corporation by members of the local community. Furthermore, most of the earnings of the business usually are committed to community well-being rather than to the economic enhancement of individual shareholders. While the specific organizational forms among the various community development corporations vary widely, it should be possible to treat the question of whether such a type of corporate ownership provides an effective base upon which to construct viable economic-social institutions. In approaching the problem, it will be necessary to analyze the types of challenges facing those who would create and direct such corporations in their communities, and to evaluate the capability of these organizations to surmount those challenges.

---

* Associate Professor, Harvard University School of Business Administration.
  I am indebted to my research assistant, Steven L. Diamond, and to Miss Elizabeth Burnham, Associate in Research, for their assistance and comments on this paper.
  [1] Ferry, *The Case for a New Federalism*, SATURDAY REVIEW, June 15, 1968, at 14.
  [2] S. 3876, 90th Cong., 2d Sess. (1968).
  [3] Note, *Community Development Corporations: Operations and Financing*, 83 HARV. L. REV. 1559, 1560 (1970).

Fields of study ranging from architecture to biology to organization theory suggest that organisms must be adaptive to their *environment* if they are to be effective—indeed, if they are to survive. A closely related matter is the issue of *resources*. An organizational form must be evaluated not only in terms of the availability of resources such as capital and expertise, but also with respect to the capacity of the organization to marshall these resources through effective management. Finally, the *objectives* of the enterprise must be evaluated in light of the environment and the resources of the organization.

I
THE BUSINESS ENVIRONMENT OF THE NEIGHBORHOOD

The rediscovery of poverty by the dominant society in the United States during the 1960's produced a seemingly unending series of portraits of the physical and emotional decay that characterizes the urban slum. Most of the books, articles, television documentaries, and speeches treating poverty in the United States focused on the most visible and seemingly fundamental aspects of the problem: education, medical care, housing, and unemployment. The issue of business development within the ghetto, however, was largely ignored. Even the discussions of unemploymnet generally concentrated on training and employment opportunities in businesses outside the ghetto. Gradually, however, it came to be recognized by people both inside and outside these depressed areas that economic development was central to dealing effectively with the nation's urban crisis.

An important segment of any economy is the retail sector. The state of its health is often a vital sign of the overall well-being of the community. This is indeed the case in black ghettos. As psychologist Kenneth Clark has noted, "The dark ghetto is not a viable community. It cannot support its people; most have to leave it for their daily jobs. Its businesses are geared toward the satisfaction of personal needs and are marginal to the economy of the city as a whole." He further explains that "It has few large businesses. Most of its businesses are small, with what that implies in terms of degree of stability. . . ."[4] The structure of the retailing communities in black ghettos can be best described as atomistic. That is, the predominant form of retail establishment is the small, owner-operated "mom-and-pop" store.

Mass merchandising firms are seriously underepresented in such areas. Clark notes, for example, that in 1965 there was only one large department store in Harlem. In most cases where units of large chain organizations are found in ghetto locations, such stores were established in a period when the area was neither economically depressed nor black. There are generally a few "middle-sized" retail firms often dealing in appliances or groceries, and there are the ubiquitous door-to-door peddlers. It is often in these two categories, as opposed to the the mom-and-pop operations or large retailers, that parasitic practices are found. The inflated prices, bait-and-switch sales techniques, misrepresentation of goods, and illegal rates of interest that have

---
[4] K. CLARK, DARK GHETTO 27-28 (1965).

been documented by David Caplovitz and others too often characterize the buyer-seller relationship in the ghetto.[5]

Inefficiency, however, is an even more significant feature of the ghetto marketplace than exploitation. Inefficiency not only characterizes the generally undercapitalized and poorly managed mom-and-pop stores, but also the consumers who patronize the retail establishments. It is, for example, inefficient to shop frequently and purchase in small lots. This kind of buying behavior maximizes wear-and-tear both on the shopper and on the facilities of the retailer. It eliminates the opportunity for savings through quantity purchases and increases the cost per transaction. Heavy reliance on credit is also inefficient in that the interest charges consume many dollars that could otherwise be used to purchase needed goods and services.

These inefficiencies on the part of the consumer are largely explained by low-income. How can large quantities be purchased when the income is meager? How can large quantities of food, for example, be purchased when not only the income is limited but also the consumer's storage facilities? These limitations coupled with relative immobility of the customer group also discourage comparative shopping and bargain hunting beyond the bounds of the ghetto.

The shopping behavior of the area residents represents only one set of problems faced by the ghetto retailer. While he is often pictured as a nefarious exploiter who every evening tosses a money-stuffed bag in the trunk of his Cadillac and drives off to the suburbs, the description is grossly misleading. A study by the Federal Trade Commission in the Washington, D.C. area of ten low-income market retailers and ten general market retailers of furniture and appliances revealed the following:

Revenue Component	10 low-income market retailers	10 general market retailers
1966 net sales	$5,146,395.	$5,405,221.
	%	
Operating ratios as percent of sales	100.0	100.0
Cost of goods sold	37.8	64.5
Gross profit margin	62.2	35.5
Salary and commission expense[1]	28.2	17.8
Advertising expense	2.1	3.9
Bad-debt losses[2]	6.7	.3
Other expenses[3]	21.3	11.2
Total expenses	58.3	33.2
Net profit return on sales	3.9	2.3

[1] Includes officer's salaries.
[2] Includes amounts held back by finance companies to cover bad-debt losses.
[3] Other expenses, including taxes, after deduction of other income.
Source: FEDERAL TRADE COMMISSION, ECONOMIC REPORT ON INSTALLMENT CREDIT AND RETAIL SALES PRACTICES OF DISTRICT OF COLUMBIA RETAILERS.

[5] D. CAPLOVITZ, THE POOR PAY MORE (1963); THE GHETTO MARKETPLACE (F. Sturdivant ed. 1969).

It can be seen that the substantially higher gross margins are largely consumed by personnel expenses, bad-debt losses, and other expenses which are higher in ghetto locations. Problems of insurance rates, vandalism, and theft are reported to be major problems for ghetto retailers. Indeed, the same FTC report found that while net profit as a percent of sales was higher in the ghetto stores studied, the return on investment was substantially lower than in comparable general market stores. (These data include other stores in the FTC sample in addition to the 20 low-income and general market retailers noted above.)

Type of retailers	Net profit after taxes as a percent of sales	Percent rate of return after taxes on on stockholders' equity
Low-income market retailers	4.7	10.1
General market retailers:		
Appliance, radio, and television stores	2.1	20.3
Furniture and home-furnishing stores	3.9	17.6
Department stores	4.6	13.0

Source: FEDERAL TRADE COMMISSION, ECONOMIC REPORT ON INSTALLMENT CREDIT AND RETAIL SALES PRACTICES OF DISTRICT OF COLUMBIA RETAILERS.

In addition to having limited income opportunities, ghetto merchants are also faced with community hostility. The fact that most retail establishments are white-owned and controlled by outsiders is the cause of much of the bitterness. As Clark notes, "Property—apartment houses, stores, businesses, bars, concessions, and theaters —are for the most part owned by persons who live outside the community and take their profits home."[6] While black-owned businesses have not escaped looting and destruction during riots, much of the dialogue and action associated with efforts by black people to gain local control of economic institutions is based on the bitterness toward white-owned businesses.

Although the role of the manufacturing sector of the ghetto economy is less well documented than that of retailing, it is clear that the industry suffers many of the same environmental problems. James L. Sundquist has summarized the basic elements of the problem as follows:

> The realities of land and production economics suggest that the possibilities of ghetto industry, without substantial subsidies—and possibly even with them—are severely limited. Vacant land is often scarce and costly. Existing commerical buildings are cramped and outmoded. The ghetto labor force lacks skill and experience. Insurance rates are high. So are the city tax rates. Transportation for materials and products is expensive. For all these reasons, ghetto industries are usually at a marked competitive disadvantage.[7]

---
[6] K. CLARK, *supra* note 4, at 28.
[7] Sundquist, *Jobs, Training, and Welfare for the Underclass*, in AGENDA FOR THE NATION 57 (1968).

These barriers to success in part explain why less than one percent of the manufacturing enterprises in the United States are black-owned.[8]

Thus, if one combines the economic forces which have a direct impact on ghetto retailing and manufacturing establishments with the dismal conditions that often prevail in the schools, the problem of narcotics and crime, and the pervasiveness of the dehumanizing and inadequate welfare programs, it can be seen that the total environment for business is not attractive. These factors pose a major challenge to the operation of any successful business whether it be a community corporation or some other form of enterprise.

Does an organization owned by local citizens and committed to the social as well as economic well-being of the community have any unique advantages in dealing with the environmental forces which have been noted? Clearly if the local development corporation is successful in getting wide-spread community involvement and creates an *esprit de corps* among the shareholders, employees, and managers, it may be able to deal effectively with the problem of hostility toward business. It is important to note that if success is achieved in this area, the corporation's chances of survival will have been increased.

Assuming that the CDC spirit does spread through the community, the organization still faces a number of very difficult problems. The CDC certainly does not offer any unique advantages in dealing with the atomistic structure of the ghetto retailing community. Indeed, a number of these corporations have achieved little more than transferring the ownership of inefficient mom-and-pop stores from white to black hands. The most notable attack by a community corporation on the problem of the scale of ghetto enterprises has been made by Zion Investment Associates, Inc., the Reverend Leon Sullivan's well-known Philadelphia-based company.[9] Unfortunately, the fact the Sullivan's enterprises stand out is a reflection of their atypical scale of operation.

Perhaps the most crucial of the challenges are those related to efficiency. The issues of costs, profitability, and customer satisfaction are, of course, interrelated. In order to attain maximum levels of profitability a business must control costs. For the new enterprise, it is especially difficult to arrive at the proper level of expenditures for payroll, supplies, rent, and the like. For example, the general manager of Shindana, the Operation Bootstrap manufacturer of black dolls, has reported: "That first year was a messed-up year. We didn't know anything about business. We had more so-called white-collar workers than factory workers. Then last year, we had about 75 workers. This year we have 65."[10] It should be noted that these reductions were made during a period when output of the manufacturer increased sharply.

---

[8] THE THIRTY-FIFTH AMERICAN ASSEMBLY, BLACK ECONOMIC DEVELOPMENT 5 (1969).

[9] For description of Zion Investment Associates, Inc., see J. HUND, BLACK ENTREPRENEURSHIP 59-61 (1970); Community Development Corporations: Operations and Financing, *supra* note 3, at 1562-67.

[10] *Shindana Discovers the "Together" Dolls*, BLACK ENTERPRISE, Dec. 1970, at 24, 25.

Many of the costs of doing business in the ghetto, as noted above, are external to the firm. These costs are especially burdensome for the ghetto enterprise that must retain the patronage of its local customers and be competitive in the outside market. According to James M. Hund, "In order to compete, both in the ghetto setting and in the wider market, black enterprises beyond the scope of the 'mom and pop' grocery must be able to offer the same quality of services as white counterparts competitively located."[11] One of the unfortunate myths contained in much of the rhetoric surrounding the CDC concept is that "buy black" campaigns will assure black enterprises a guaranteed market. However, as ghetto residents become more affluent and mobile and as racial barriers diminish, the retailers in those areas face increasing competitive pressures. Theodore Cross has suggested that "The Negro entrepreneur is being buffeted by pressures from . . . the growing affluence of his once-captive customers. The mortician, the beautician, the barber is finding much of his clientele deserting him for stronger and 'more prestigious' white competitors."[12] Even the few black-owned firms which have operated in the national market, such as the Supreme Life Insurance Company, have faced intensified efforts of "white" companies to penetrate their traditional markets.

In sum, if the community development corporation's businesses are to be viable, they must have effective control over their internal costs and work to offset those external cost differentials which place them at a competitive disadvantage with firms operating in the general economy. While ethnocentrism is increasingly a fact of life in black communities, it would be dangerous to assume that even local customers will remain loyal if more attractive competitive alternatives are available to them.

II

Neighborhood Resources

A major determinant of whether or not any enterprise can meet such a challenge will be the resources it has at its command. The essential ingredients in creating a successful business can perhaps be summarized as follows: entrepreneurship, managerial skill, and financial strength.[13]

"Entrepreneur" is a much abused word. Often used to describe the MBA who becomes a junior executive in a giant corporation, it also frequently is applied to the owner of the corner gasoline station. Instead, it should be thought of in the Schumperterian sense of the word—innovative, driving men who are agents for change because they conceive of new relationships between products, services, and markets and possess the courage to assume the high risks associated with launching enterprises committed to exploiting those opportunities. They are the type described by Lenin's teacher, G. V. Plekhanov:

---

[11] J. Hund, *supra* note 9, at 25-26.
[12] T. Cross, Black Capitalism 62 (1969).
[13] The most obvious omission from this list is labor. However, there are no labor problems that are essentially unique to CDC's, and thus the topic is not discussed here.

The more or less slow changes in "economic conditions" periodically confront society with the necessity of more or less rapidly changing its institutions. This change never takes place "by itself"; it always needs the intervention of *men*, who are thus confronted with great social problems. And it is those men who do more than others to facilitate the solution of these problems who are called great men.[14]

Does the black community have such men among its numbers? One need only observe the charismatic leadership of articulate and dynamic men within the community to be convinced that the potential seems to exist. Because of racism in the dominant society and the absence of a business heritage among blacks, these talents have often gone untapped or else they have been unleased in other directions; but the potential exists. This view was expressed excellently by Elmer Young, as associate of Leon Sullivan, during a conference on community-based economic development at the Cambridge Institute.

> All of us are starting out as infants in a man's world. If you told me back in 1962 that Elmer Young was going to develop a shopping center I'd have said, "You're crazy." Same thing with Lou Smith who I knew back in Philadelphia. If I'd said, "Lou, you'll be president of a company making black dolls," he'd have told *me* I was crazy. But we had the guts to try it. And I think that's what any black group has to have. You have to stand up and there and say, "White folks can do this, and we can too." This doesn't mean you're not going to stumble. We still have to stumble.[15]

Will community-based forms of organization provide the appropriate mechanism for attracting the talents of local entrepreneurs? Certainly in a limited number of cases they have. Leon Sullivan is probably one of the outstanding entrepreneurs produced by this country in recent years. In too many cases, however, the CDC's have done little more than encourage the development of a class of marginal shop-keepers. Perhaps the essential point to be made is that a black entrepreneur may well view the CDC as one of a number of attractive avenues to be considered along with traditional corporate organizations, partnerships, sole proprietorships, and the like. He must have the freedom to select from among these alternatives the organizational form that is best suited to the opportunities which he has identified. One of the more unfortunate features of the Community Self-Determination Bill was that because of certain tax provisions and lending arrangements, it would have discriminated against existing and would-be entrepreneurs who elected not to participate in the CDC.[16] Any legislation designed to stimulate economic development in the inner-city should not unnecessarily restrict the freedom of action for these agents of change by granting discriminatory advantages to one particular organizational form.

The qualities of innovativeness, drive, and a high propensity for risk taking

---
[14] J. Hughes, The Vital Few 14 (1966).
[15] The Cambridge Institute, Community Based Economic Development, June, 1970, at 18.
[16] Sturdivant, *The Limits of Black Capitalism*, Harv. Bus. Rev., Jan.-Feb., 1969, at 122, 124-25.

that distinguish the entrepreneur do not necessarily make him a good manager of a firm's day-to-day operations. An additional resource that is vital to community economic development, therefore, is managerial talent. Such skills are acquired through formal education or practical experience or some combination thereof. Because of barriers to full participation by blacks in business in the past, the pool of experienced managers in the community is quite shallow.

One of the challenges facing the community corporation, therefore, is to compete effectively for experienced black managers. The black community orientation of the business will in itself represent a strong appeal to many who feel that they have not received equal opportunities in white businesses. Two examples can be cited from Shindana, the black doll company. Phil Gilyard who is 38 and general manager of the company explains that he "was an administrative supervisor at Hughes Tool Company and I couldn't go any farther. I took this job not for the money, but to develop my management potential." Thirty-five year old foreman Ralph Reggin left Eldon Industries, another toy company, where he was a supervisor and came to Shindana at a lower salary. "I felt that I would only go so far because of its being a white company. Here, I can go any place and I'm doing something for the black."[17]

In spite of the strong appeal of "doing something for the black," it is unlikely that experienced managers can be attracted and retained unless they feel the enterprise has sufficient potential to offer them a challenge and an opportunity to develop their "management potential." Thus CDC's must undertake ventures which have excellent growth potential. At the same time they must recognize that their internal organizational structure must allow for maximum managerial freedom in conducting the affairs of the business. The community ownership and social development objectives of many of the local development organizations pose a number of difficulties which will be discussed more fully below. In terms of its implications for management, perhaps a brief analogy with cooperatives will be sufficient.

In its purest form the managerial atmosphere of a community development corporation closely resembles that of a cooperative. As the Cambridge Institute bulletin puts it, "A CDC is simply a corporation based in one geographic area and controlled democratically by the residents."[18] This is not to suggest that all CDC shareholders vote on every management decision. In addition to the traditional board of directors, however, there generally exists a business management board or some such body composed of local residents who are responsible for the management of the enterprise. Democratic management, whether it be in a cooperative or a CDC, according to James Hund "can be stultifying to the conduct of the business."[19] It is not difficult to imagine the frustrations that would be encountered by an experienced manager in such situations. Indeed, it is probably safe to say that the greater the

---

[17] *Shindana Discovers the "Together" Dolls, supra* note 10, at 26-27.
[18] The Cambridge Institute, *supra* note 15, at 1.
[19] J. Hand, *supra* note 9, at 65.

degree of democracy in the enterprise, the less effective its management will be. This weakness is clearly a major flaw in the concept of community-based development corporations.

The third critical resource which needs to be considered is financing. Community development corporations have drawn on a wide range of sources for funds. The Hough Area Development Corporation in Cleveland received its initial capital in the form of a $1.6 million Special Impact grant from the Office of Economic Opportunity. Subsequently, to found a rubber company, Hough raised an additional $350,000 through a Small Business Administration loan guarantee. The Operation Bootstrap company, Shindana, received its initial $200,000 gratis from Mattel, Inc. Another corporation, El Mercado de Los Angeles, raised $1,040,000 for a shopping facility housing forty small businesses in the Mexican-American barrio, the money being obtained through loan under the provision of the Small Business Investment Act of 1958. In addition, some $260,000 was raised in the community through the sale of stock. Zion Investment Associates, Inc., in Philadelphia raised its initial capital through the monthly investments of some 200 members of Sullivan's Zion Baptist Church. The 10-36 plan ($10 per month for 36 months) began in 1962. The corporation now has some 1,000 shareholders and an additional 6,000 persons are making installment payments for shares. Additional funds have been raised through loans from banks.

The *Harvard Law Review* has reported that managements of ten of thirty community development corporations interviewed had "acquired sufficient funding for substantial business activity and [had] begun operating such businesses."[20] In each case, however, even these organizations "were struggling to secure additional venture capital to allow continuation and growth of their businesses."[21] Another third of the organizations interviewed were operating on a very small scale, generally fewer than ten employees, and had received little outside financial or technical assistance. The remaining third had not yet launched their business operations, but several had received funding commitments for operations which were in an advanced stage of planning.

The key to raising funds, either equity, debt, or gifts is, the viability of the enterprise. Investors, loan officers, and benefactors must have confidence in the leadership of the company. This confidence is enhanced by the existence of a well-planned and well-managed venture that holds good promise of achieving its objectives. For the investor and the lending institution the ultimate objective must be the generation of sufficient profits to protect the investment or to repay the debt. Even the funds received by outright grant must be received on the assumption that the funds will assist in the creation of a viable business that will produce long-range benefits for the participants and the community. Thus the definition of the community corporation's goals is closely related to its capability to raise capital.

---

[20] *Community Development Corporations: Operations and Financing, supra* note 3, at 1576.
[21] *Id.*

III

THE OBJECTIVES OF THE CDC

The major problem facing community-based development corporations is the formulation, adoption, and achievement of goals and objectives. The people who come together to create or to participate in virtually any kind of organization generally share in a complex set of goals. Even the traditional business corporation is clearly more than an economic institution. However, its fundamental objective—to make a profit—is well-defined and provides the basis which makes the achievement of all of its other goals possible.

The goals of most CDC's are highly complex and in many cases they make the attainment of this fundamental objective of long-range economic viability difficult if not impossible. While community-based development corporations are not legally bound to the goals called for in the Community Self-Determination Bill, most are committed to similar objectives. Therefore, it is useful to consider what the *Harvard Law Review* described as the three primary goals of the CDC:

> First, as a political institution, it provides a mechanism through which the poor can achieve meaningful participation in the control of significant aspects of their community life. Second, the CDC as a service organization provides needed services to the community while avoiding the handout syndrome surrounding public welfare. Third, as an economic institution, the CDC promotes the economic development of the community through investment in community businesses.[22]

The article notes that the draftsmen of the bill viewed economic development as the most important function. However, Gar Alperovitz, a coauthor of the original bill has emphasized that all three goals are essential elements of the legislation:

> The critical word in the legislation is community development. I want to distinguish that from economic development, because the whole assumption of community development is that jobs or the ownership of stock—either one alone—is insufficient to deal with some of the critical problems of the ghetto. The view here, which relates to community participation and the poverty program, is that some way must be found to bring together some form of cohesive unit in the ghetto, and that is the critical first assumption you must begin with. Thereafter, the questions of economic development, transfer of resources, jobs and capital come up.[23]

Thus Alperovitz views the creation of a sense of community of the forming of a cohesive unit in the ghetto as a necessary precondition to economic development. Alperovitz also explains the linkage between social services and the community's business operations.

---

[22] Note, *Community Development Corporations: A New Approach to the Poverty Program*, 82 HARV. L. REV. 644, 645 (1969).

[23] *A Dialogue on Community Self-Destruction: Problems and Potential*, NEW GENERATION, Fall, 1968, at 22.

What we are trying to do here is to get away from bureaucratic administration of various social service programs. We are attempting to transfer to the people in the community control over decisions that affect their lives. In one sense this approach has grown out of the experience of projects like Crawfordville, a Georgia textile operation which is essentially a non-profit, one-man, one-vote community corporation, like a co-op, only it doesn't give dividends at this stage.

What this new legislation proposes is to link the social services controlled by a community with an economic profit-making enterprise.[24]

The soundness of this organizational form as a vehicle for a dramatic transformation of the nation's ghettos rests with the compatibility of its political and social goals with its economic goals.

A. Compatibility of Political and Economic Goals

The political goals center around community control of economic resources and social services and widespread community participation in the decision making process. Implicit in much of the discussion of political goals, however, is the development of a power base within the community which can be used to deal with outside agencies such as the city or the federal government.

The demand for local control over economic institutions is an interesting anachronism in an era of conglomerates, chain stores, and franchising. While there has been some resistance to these forces throughout the society, the resistance generally has been based on the increasing dissatisfaction with the depersonalization and sameness of the strings of hamburger stands, fried chicken establishments, muffler and automatic transmission repair shops, and discount houses that have spread from coast to coast to deface the landscape. In the ghetto, however, hostility has grown out of years of bitterness associated with the inefficiency, corruption, and insensitivity of the businesses and governmental agencies with whom the residents of the ghetto have normally interacted. Therefore, the desire for local control is understandable. But is it feasible?

If the community corporation had the resources needed to gain control of extant businesses, create new growth firms within the ghetto, and manage these enterprises without outside assistance, then such an objective as local control might well be within its reach. However, when the community corporation turns to outside sources for the capital that is needed, it necessarily incurs restrictions on its freedom of action. Private sources of funds are reluctant at best either to invest equity dollars in or make loans to ghetto enterprises because the risks of failure are greater than in non-ghetto businesses. Therefore, it is not at all uncommon for restrictions to be placed on the use of the funds, the qualifications for members of the management group and the types of businesses to be established or acquired. And certainly restrictions of this kind are imposed when federal funds are obtained be they from the Small Business Administration, the Office of Economic Opportunity, or other agencies.

---

[24] *Id.*

In the same manner, local groups may find encumbrances resulting from the use of outside experts. As Bernard Gifford of FIGHT in Rochester has indicated, the outside consultant may speak a very different language and his role may ultimately be determined by the funding source:

> The white individual who comes in to offer his expertise has to think differently. Basically you have to decide which side of the fence you're talking about: profits or people. If your motivation is detemined by material gain instead of by human beings, then you're going to find yourself hung up in the same kind of situation that created these problems in the first place. People who don't share this kind of philosophy—that people are more important than profit—work against you . . . . Do-gooders who want to come down and give some input may have a lot of expertise in some areas, but they have to be willing to listen to people here with good ideas about what their community needs, what's best for their community, and then try to work out the solutions to do that, which is contrary to the present system. Under this system, your funding source dictates how things are to get done.[25]

The dilemma of outside resources suggests that the more self-sufficient the local corporation the greater the degree of local control possible. If substantial seed money can be raised within the community, as in the case of Zion in Philadelphia, then the corporation is in a stronger position to minimize restrictions tied to outside funds. As Elmer Young explains, "We . . . had to establish credibility. But I'll tell you one thing, a few hundred thousand dollars in a banker's face did an awful lot to help us."[26] Credibility is more readily established, as well, when the management of the community corporation has established programs which are consistent with traditional management practices. Indeed, if the economic structure of the ghetto is to undergo dramatic transformation, it may be necessary that even the strongest community corporations compromise their desire for complete control by inviting outside firms to participate in community-inspired plans for business development. Such, for example, was the case in the Progress Plaza shopping center in Philadelphia. Six of the sixteen units in the center are "white" businesses which not only helped secure financing but also reflected the results of a consumer study conducted in the area to determine the desired make up of the center.[27] In sum, it is essential that realistic priorities be established and that it be recognized that "social" goals may have to be deferred for some time.

A closely related political goal of the community corporation which poses challenges is the desire for community participation. The objective of creating a "cohesive unit in the ghetto" through involving a maximum number of people in the decision making process of the community corporation is one which has proved to be largely impractical. In its survey of CDC's, the *Harvard Law Review* found

---

[25] THE CAMBRIDGE INSTITUTE, *supra* note 15, at 8.
[26] *Id.* at 17.
[27] Sturdivant, *supra* note 16, at 126.

that "In practice there has been little community-wide participation in all but a very few community corporations."[28] Generally, the control of the corporations rests in the hands of the leaders who established them. "This concentration of control appears to be due in large part to the need to devote almost all energies to establishing a viable business organization, rather than expending efforts to inform, motivate, and organize large numbers of community persons."[29]

Again, this political objective appears to be in fundamental conflict with the economic objective of creating a viable enterprise. Frances Fox Piven has suggested that "The corporation is not an organism which lends itself to democratic control by shareholders, as any scrutiny of private corporations in America will confirm . . . [because of] . . . the tendency of a corporation management to acquire control by the mere fact of constant involvement in intricate corporation affairs."[30] To a great extent the lack of democracy is related to shareholder apathy. Shareholders with relatively small investment in a corporation have little incentive to participate in forums designed for shareholder involvement. This problem is even more complicated in a ghetto setting because of the disillusionment experienced in the past. Getting local residents to invest in a community corporation and participate actively in its public meetings would be a formidable task. One critique of the Community Self-Determination Bill stressed this point by noting that:

> if shareholders are to retain their shares in the corporation and are to participate actively in its functions, and if new shareholdres are to be encouraged to invest after formation, then concrete benefits must derive from stock ownership. However, unlike investors in business corporations, shareholders in the CDC cannot realize capital gains because of the restriction on transferability and the continuing offer of shares by the CDC at the five dollar par value. Moreover, distribution of CDC profits to shareholders ordinarily may be made only in the form of community services. Intangible considerations, such as community pride or pride in being a shareholder-owner of visible and tangible assets, may serve to secure participation at the outset, but these are thin reeds on which to rest a continuing financial commitment by the poor.[31]

Even if community development corporations were allowed to pay cash dividends to their shareholders, it is clear that their ghetto enterprises generally will be starved for capital and any profits generated for the forseeable future should be retained in the businesses.

B. Compatibility of Social Service and Economic Goals

The lack of compatibility between political and economic goals is closely related to the conflict between social and economic objectives. If social services are to be

---

[28] *Community Development Corporations: Operations and Financing, supra* note 3, at 1582.
[29] *Id.* at 1582.
[30] Piven, *Community Control: Beyond the Rhetoric*, NEW GENERATION, Fall, 1968, at 7, 8.
[31] *Community Development Corporations: A New Approach to the Poverty Program, supra* note 22, at 649-50.

provided to the community by the corporation then profits must be generated by the corporation's enterprises. Since it is highly unlikely that the enterprises can be effectively managed by means of a democratic decision-making process, the most visible benefits to be derived by the local residents will be the social services. Again, the community corporation faces a difficult problem, as suggested by Louis Smith of Operation Bootstrap in Los Angeles: "If people think you're going to start a business and that business is going to generate any real capital to put back into your community, you're really thinking in terms of years."[32]

While community corporations have been largely unable to contribute to the improvement of health, recreation, housing, and medical services in their communities, they offer other social benefits that are of major importance. By creating businesses of any reasonable scale in the ghetto the corporations are providing training to the unskilled, employment to the unemployed, management development opportunities to blacks who might otherwise face racial barriers on the outside, and a model of business adventure for the younger members of the community. Simply by accepting the challenge of locating in the ghetto and hiring and training local people the corporations have incurred a "social service overhead" which makes their long-range viability that much more difficult. Perhaps one of the major weaknesses of this form of organization is that these basic, enterprise-building activities may not be viewed as being sufficiently dramatic to enlist the support of the community and therefore the organizations may undertake other social services before being in a sufficiently sound economic position to support them.

Frances Fox Piven suggested that "On its own, the ghetto seems better described as an economic backwater than an economic colony, the sluggish backwater of a swift and dynamic economy."[33] Even a brief review of the economic environment in the ghetto suggests that it is far from being a fertile field for business growth. The costs of conducting business there, the limited resources, and the general hostility toward business help explain why the black ghetto has been left to stagnate while the economy of the dominant society has moved ahead at a rapid rate. After first being victimized by racism its residents have become the victims of opportunity costs. In general, there have simply been too many profitable alternatives to investing in or conducting business in the ghetto.

It is of paramount importance, therefore, that it be clearly understood that the establishment of viable enterprises in the ghetto is extremely difficult. It requires imaginative leadership, resourceful management, and substantial funds to create the kinds of enterprises that will transform the economic status of the ghetto. These enterprises must overcome the environmental problems, such as higher costs, and be capable of competing with companies from the general market. It must also be recognized that economic development is a long and difficult process whether it be

---

[32] THE CAMBRIDGE INSTITUTE, *supra* note 15, at 6.
[33] Piven, *supra* note 30, at 8.

Nineteenth Century America or the five year plans in the Soviet Union or China and it is unrealistic to assume that the process can be speeded without the infusion of outside capital and technical assistance. As Bayard Rustin has stated, "we have to get rid of this idea that people can lift themselves by their bootstraps. No social class has ever got out of being in the lumpen proletariat except by social engineering."[34]

This process of social engineering requires the involvement of local groups such as community development corporations, government, and the business system in general. Conceding the fact that local involvement poses certain managerial problems, the notion of local participation is still one of the essential strengths of the CDC concept. If it can be accomplished, at least to the extent of communicating to the community that local people are controlling the direction the economic development is taking, then the general atmopshere for the conduct of business can be improved sharply. On the other hand, the most serious weakness of the concept is the danger of confused objectives. The primary objective must be the establishment of self-sufficient, viable enterprises which are capable of attracting the necessary financial, technical, and managerial resources. In short, many of the broader social service benefits must be viewed as long-range. Shareholders and managers alike must recognize that if resources are to be attracted and utilized effectively the objectives of local control and democratic rule by the area residents must be subordinated.

In communities which enjoy imaginative and strong leaders with a commitment to sound management practices and the capacity to raise the capital for seed money, these compromises should be minimal and relatively painless. Unfortunately, such conditions are found in a minority of locations where community corporations are presently in operation. Thus, while in some cases the community-based development corporation represents a promising and exciting approach to economic development, in a majority of situations the mixed objectives and managerial problems associated with the community decision-making process will probably condemn the local corporation to failure.

These strengths and weaknesses of the community corporation approach to economic development reinforce the view that a variety of approaches must be attempted in dealing with the plight of the ghetto. Among the unfortunate features of the debate which centered around the Community Self-Determination Bill were the claims made for the CDC approach by its more enthusiastic supporters. In discussing the bill, Oscar A. Ornati observed that "there is clearly nothing wrong with the Act as one more tool in the kit of national anti-poverty policies. What is wrong and fundamentally dangerous are the claims made for it. . . . [T]he well-being of slum inhabitants can come only through many and massive national programs geared to maximum employment, effective markets, the ending of discrimination, and more health, housing, and education."[35]

---
[34] J. HUND, *supra* note 9, at 6.
[35] Ornati, *A Noble Cop-Out*, NEW GENERATION, Fall, 1968, at 10.

It was because of the recognition of a need for diversity in the approaches to dealing with black economic development that the American Assembly on that topic listed a series of approaches ranging from CDC's to the location of branch operations of big companies in the ghetto. In support of these efforts, it was recommended that a Marshall Plan commitment of resources be made by the federal government to be coordinated by a "National Development Corporation." This program was to be supported by the creation of a network of regional discount banks to stimulate the infusion of capital and other programs including tax incentives to offset the higher costs of doing business in the ghetto.[36] The attack must be made on a wide front utilizing a variety of vehicles for economic development. The community-based corporation is one such vehicle, but alone it offers relatively little promise because of its organizational weaknesses.

---

[36] T. CROSS, *supra* note 12, at 5-9. For the background papers used by the Assembly, see BLACK ECONOMIC DEVELOPMENT (W. Haddad & G. Pugh eds. 1969).

NEW DIRECTIONS FOR MINORITY ENTERPRISE

SAMUEL I. DOCTORS* AND SHARON LOCKWOOD†

I

THE NEED FOR NEW DIRECTIONS

Minority enterprise has historically been limited to primarily small retail establishments, personal service businesses, and small construction contractors. Despite the fact that minority groups constitute about seventeen per cent of our population,[1] they own less than three per cent of the nation's businesses.[2] Perhaps even more significant is the fact that these businesses control less than one-half per cent of the nation's business assets.[3]

Present programs for minority business development have emphasized loans, grants, and subsidies to small businesses primarily in retail services and construction areas. These businesses are often in crowded business sectors, small margin, low-growth potential areas such as gasoline service stations, barber shops, or small retail food markets and often serve an impoverished clientele. The historic failure rate for these types of businesses is quite high.[4] Although data is scarce in this area, it appears that less than twenty per cent of all new small businesses survive their first five years.[5] New minority businesses are even more vulnerable due to a lack of access to financial and technical resources.[6] However, even those which do achieve

---

* Associate Professor of Management, Northwestern University Graduate School of Management, and Consultant to the National Advisory Council on Minority Business Enterprise (NACMBE) and Acting Associate Director, National Strategies and Goals Task Force; Editor of NACMBE Final Report.
† Economic Advisor to the National Advisory Council on Minority Business Enterprise.
The authors owe a debt of gratitude for assistance in the preparation of this paper to the following persons: Mr. George Aragon, Doctoral candidate, Harvard Business School, and Consultant to the NACMBE; Professor Frank Cassell, Professor of Industrial Relations, Northwestern University Graduate School of Management, and Consultant to the NACMBE; Miss Anita Henry, Candidate for the J.D. degree, Yale Law School, and Research Assistant to the NACMBE.

[1] "Minority group" is defined for this paper to include only blacks, persons of Spanish-speaking ancestry, and American Indians.
[2] Office of Planning, Research, and Analysis of the Small Business Administration, Distribution of Minority-Owned Businesses, June, 1969, at 1 (unpublished report). Theodore Cross has estimated that there are only a dozen black businesses in Manhattan which employ ten or more people. T. CROSS, BLACK CAPITALISM 60 (1969).
[3] Distribution of Minority-Owned Businesses, supra note 2.
[4] See generally THE PRESIDENT'S TASK FORCE REPORT ON IMPROVING THE PROSPECTS OF SMALL BUSINESS 21-27 (1970).
[5] Id. See also Roberts, Entrepreneurship and Technology, in FACTORS IN THE TRANSFER OF TECHNOLOGY 219, 224-25 (D. Marquis & W. Gruber Eds. 1969); A. PARRIS, THE SMALL BUSINESS ADMINISTRATION 51-55 (1968). Of course most business discontinuances are not outright bankruptcies; still for every five new businesses started, another 3.5 go out of business each year.
[6] One estimate of minority business failure or discontinuances may be obtained by examining the relative default rates on SBA loans between non-minority and minority borrowers. Parris estimates that minority defaults were running ten to twenty times the rate of non-minority defaults (three per cent). A. PARRIS, supra note 5, at 116. However, this estimate is based solely on the Economic Opportunity

some modest degree of success are unlikely to achieve growth rates that would create high leverage business opportunities for very many members of the minority community. Moreover, these businesses often lock their owners into a life of long hours, and hard, non-stimulating work with little or no opportunity to branch out of the pattern of marginal growth opportunity.

Surveys of existing minority businesses indicate that there are very few with gross sales as large as one million dollars a year and none which approaches the size of the 500 largest white owned and controlled corporations.[7] Nor do we find minority group members in positions of control or decision making in the large American corporations where they could gain the managerial experience to start companies which might grow to a place among the largest American businesses.

Other data indicate that minority business development, although receiving some stimulus from present public and private efforts, still shows no signs of the exponential growth rate needed to catch up with white business development and may in fact be falling relatively farther behind. We have raised the expectations of our minority groups for examples of such exponential growth but have neither formed nor created models capable of achieving these catchup growth rates.

As may be seen from the sample of minority businesses presented in Tables I and II, the minority entrepreneur tends to enter the more marginal types of businesses. Table I indicates that a disproportionate number of minority entrepreneurs are in the personal service area. While some facets of the service industries are higher growth areas, the more disaggregated data in Table II reveals that the minority entrepreneurs are not in these higher growth areas.

Little effort has been made to guide the minority entrepreneur to more lucrative business opportunities. Most government and non-government programs are grounded in the concept that simply establishing a minority member in a business is sufficient. This reasoning requires serious reconsideration. If minority businessmen are not guided to the higher growth areas, their businesses will not help the minority economy approach the national economy.

To lift minority enterprise from the ghetto and the barrio to which it has been consigned, a strategic thrust must now aim at providing opportunities for higher growth potential models of minority enterprise. These model businesses should be

---

Loan (EOL) program through 1968 and a more recent analysis of the SBA minority loan program indicates that overall default rates are likely to be lower than was previously true for the EOL program. *See* Small Business Administration, Evaluation of the Minority Enterprise Program, Jan., 1971 (unpublished report). For a discussion of the difficulties in running a ghetto-based small business, see T. Cross, *supra* note 2, at 21-30.

[7] *See* Distribution of Minority Enterprise, *supra* note 2. A recent Office of Economic Opportunity (OEO) survey of larger minority businesses attempted to identify minority businesses with annual sales in excess of $500,000, and which showed a profit for the last two years. The largest business so identified was Johnson Publications, Inc., with annual sales in 1969 of about $33 million, and this was three times the size of the next largest minority business, Johnson Products, Inc. About 100 companies were included in this study; of these, 24 met the sales and profitability criteria. OEO memo from Paul London and Susan Davis to Theodore Cross, Minority Business Successes, May 19, 1970. The smallest company listed among the *Fortune* 500 had sales of $162 million in 1969. THE FORTUNE DIRECTORY, May, 1970, at 23.

TABLE I
Distribution of Minority and Non-Minority Business Enterprises

	Minority Owned	Non-Minority Owned
Personal Service	26.9	7.3
Other Service	15.1	20.3
Construction	10.8	9.0
Manufacturing	2.2	7.9
Retail Trade	34.0	34.9
Other Industries	11.0	21.6
All Other Industries	100.0	100.0

Source: Office of Planning, Research, and Analysis of the Small Business Administration, Distribution of Minority-Owned Business, June, 1969, at 7 (unpublished report).

TABLE II
Categories and Types of Black Business Enterprises

Category	Number	Percentage
Food and Beverages	173	30.7
Public Services	101	17.9
Merchandise Sales	37	6.5
Professional Services	35	6.2
Contracting Services	31	5.5
General Sales and Service	169	30.0
Other	18	3.2
TOTAL	564	100.0

Source: F. Coles, Jr., An Analysis of Black Entrepreneurship in Seven Urban Areas, app. I, at i-ii (1969).

capable of growing at the rate of ten to twenty per cent or more per year over the next five to ten year period.[8] Such new enterprises will help meet rapidly rising expectations, provide for true upward mobility, stimulate capital formation, and provide attractive alternative routes for minority employment and provide success models for future programs.[9]

---

[8] The 216 Boston "route 128" spinoff companies studied by Edward Roberts and his colleagues had an annual five year growth rate of over 20 per cent per year. Roberts, *supra* note 5, at 225-27. The same type of growth rate was exhibited by a sample of 13 companies used in a technology transfer study by the author. S. Doctors, The NASA Transfer Program: An Analysis (to be published about November 1971 by Praeger). Much of the growth achieved by these companies has been made possible through the creation of a protected market by the federal government. Clearly this same federal government power could be used in the development of minority enterprise as it has been used to develop an aerospace industry.

[9] It is assumed, contrary to Andrew Brimmer, that the promotion of minority enterprise does not have the sole objective of providing employment for larger numbers of blacks. It is assumed that the creation of numbers of viable minority-owned enterprises may serve a number of other socio-economic objectives. It is also assumed that minority economic development requires a holistic approach to such development, including the parallel provision of improved employment, business, educational, and health care opportunities. Just as in the non-minority community, it is the synergistic interaction of a variety of factors which will result in significant development. *See* A. Brimmer & H. Terrell, The Economic Potential of Black Capitalism, Dec. 29, 1969 (paper presented before the 82nd Annual Meeting of the American Economic Association).

Many new opportunities for minority entrepreneurs to obtain financial assistance have become available, not only in the Small Business Administration, but also in the Department of Commerce, the Office of Economic Opportunity, and in the private sector. New and expanded business opportunities capable of leveraging these expanding sources of capital funds must be provided to stimulate the creation of enterprises which can multiply their initial investments many times over.

Much of this development should occur in higher growth industries, although medium- and low-profit, low-growth potential industries should not be completely excluded. They may provide needed goods and services for the community, and serve to keep a larger amount of capital within the ghettos and barrios. Medium or lower growth potential businesses may also provide some training opportunities for a number of potential minority entrepreneurs and managers. Thus, this latter type of business may also play some role in long term economic development of minority communities.

Today's minority entrepreneur is finally ready to gain a more advantageous position in the economy. Higher minority educational levels, increased minority incomes, a wider range of business opportunities, the changing attitude of public and private institutions toward minority entrepreneurs, and an attitudinal change in the minority community towards business as a career, have combined to bring about an environment which can fit the minority entrepreneur for entering higher growth industries. The educational level of minorities appears to be improving more rapidly than that of the population as a whole. As entrepreneurs are usually drawn not from the most disadvantaged groups, but from the middle classes,[10] this increase in educational level will undoubtedly be reflected in a growing pool of potential and actual entrepreneurs (Table III). The rapidly increasing family income of minority groups (Table IV) is reflected in the growing purchasing power in the minority community. This increased purchasing power can support a larger number of minority businesses and a wider range of products and services. Thus, an increased range of business opportunities should be available within the minority community. The increased educational level and the extensive needs of the general public in the areas of goods and services should increase the range of business opportunities for the minority entrepreneur.

There has been an increasing concentration of the minority community in the urban area during the decade of the fifties and the sixties (Table V). This increasing concentration in the urban areas may, on the one hand, help consolidate purchasing power to the advantage of the minority entrepreneur. On the other hand, with the move to the suburbs by the non-minority middle class, much of the capital and markets needed for economic development is no longer available in the central city.

---

[10] This idea is suggested by the work of Frazier, McClelland, and Roberts. E. Frazier, Black Bourgeoisie (1968); D. McClelland & D. Winter, Motivating Economic Achievement (1969); Roberts, *supra* note 5.

TABLE III
Per Cent Distribution by Years of School Completed for Persons 20 Years Old and Over, by Age, 1969

	Less than 4 years High School	High school 4 years	College 1 year or more	Median Years of school completed
NEGRO				
20 and 21 years old	42.1	36.6	21.2	12.2
22 to 24 years old	43.9	37.1	19.1	12.2
25 to 29 years old	44.3	40.1	15.7	12.1
30 to 34 years old	49.8	36.7	13.5	12.0
35 to 44 years old	62.8	26.8	10.5	10.6
45 to 54 years old	70.8	18.9	10.3	9.1
55 to 64 years old	85.2	8.7	6.2	7.6
65 to 74 years old	89.7	5.5	4.9	6.1
75 years old and over	92.4	4.1	3.5	5.2
WHITE				
20 and 21 years old	18.1	41.6	40.1	12.8
22 to 24 years old	19.6	44.8	35.7	12.7
25 to 29 years old	23.0	44.8	32.1	12.6
30 to 34 years old	27.3	44.9	27.6	12.5
35 to 44 years old	33.9	41.0	25.1	12.4
45 to 54 years old	40.7	39.3	20.0	12.2
55 to 64 years old	55.2	27.5	17.3	10.9
65 to 74 years old	67.6	18.9	13.4	8.9
75 years old and over	75.1	13.8	11.1	8.5

Source: Bureau of the Census, in U.S. Bureau of Labor Statistics, Dep't of Labor, The Social and Economic Status of Negroes in the United States 50 (1970).

TABLE IV
Median Family Income in 1968, and Negro Family Income, 1965-1968, as a Per Cent of White, by Region

	Median family income, 1968		Negro income as a per cent of white			
	Negro	White	1965	1966	1967	1968
United States	$5,359	$8,936	54	58	59	60
Northeast	6,460	9,318	64	68	66	69
North Central	6,910	9,259	74	74	78	75
South	4,278	7,963	49	50	54	54
West	7,506	9,462	69	72	74	80

Source: Bureau of the Census, in U.S. Bureau of Labor Statistics, Dep't of Labor, The Social and Economic Status of Negroes in the United States 15 (1970).

One of the most interesting elements in today's minority enterprise climate is the changing attitude in the minority community toward the status of the entrepreneur. Heretofore, the ambitious black perceived the obstacles to a business career and often chose a career in the professions. He had access to professional education in black educational institutions and he had a captive clientele since white doctors, dentists, or lawyers frequently did not or would not provide these services to the

TABLE V

NEGROES AS A PER CENT OF TOTAL POPULATION BY LOCATION, INSIDE AND OUTSIDE METROPOLITAN AREAS, AND BY SIZE OF METROPOLITAN AREA, 1950, 1960; and 1969

	Per cent Negro		
	1950	1960	1969
United States	10	11	11
Metropolitan areas*	9	11	12
Central cities	12	17	21
Central cities in metropolitan areas of—			
1,000,000 or more	13	19	26
250,000 to 1,000,000	12	15	18
Under 250,000	12	12	12
Suburbs	5	5	5
Outside metropolitan areas	11	10	9

*Population of the 212 SMSA's as defined in 1960.
Source: BUREAU OF THE CENSUS, in U.S. BUREAU OF LABOR STATISTICS, DEP'T OF LABOR, THE SOCIAL AND ECONOMIC STATUS OF NEGROES IN THE UNITED STATES 15 (1970).

black population.[11] Highly motivated blacks, unlike the highly motivated in other racial groups, were discouraged from entering business and were diverted to the professions. The black population valued the contribution of the black professional man, but tended to diminish the contribution of the black businessman. In fact, until recently it was considered prestigious in the black community to purchase name brands from non-minority enterprises. The goods of the black merchant were thought to be inferior, apparently for no reason other than that the proprietor was black.[12]

II

GROWTH POTENTIAL INDUSTRIES

Minority enterprise opportunities should be developed which:

1) contribute to the capacity of the various minorities to take advantage of business opportunities beyond particular ethnic or racial markets;
2) have a capacity for growth and capital creation;
3) capitalize upon the skills and knowledge of all elements of the population;
4) promote areas of comparative advantage such as health care, job training, day care and communications in the minority community;
5) promote short and long-run community development objectives;
6) make effective use of government-created and protected markets, particularly in new, higher growth areas.[13]

---

[11] A recent survey of the graduates (346—1946 to 1969) of Atlanta University's (AU) School of Business Administration, indicated that most of their graduates, prior to 1968, had entered non-business occupations. AU has produced over half of all the black M.B.A.'s in the period 1908 to 1969.

[12] This is especially true for the black middle class. See E. FRAZIER, supra note 10.

[13] The core recommendations of the National Advisory Council on Minority Business Enterprise

Economic indicators show where the potential for minority business lies. Real economic growth of the United States is expected to average 4.4 per cent per year, so that the Gross National Product (GNP) will increase from the third quarter 1970 level of 985.2 billion to almost 1.4 trillion dollars by 1980.[14] With this increase, the consumption rate of nondurable goods is expected to decline from 62 per cent to 60 per cent during the period from 1967 to 1980.[15] At the same time, increases in family formation, rising incomes, and replacement of old and substandard housing will push demand for new housing to 2.4 million units per year in the late 1970's. This factor will account for the rise in private domestic investment growth from the 1967 level of 15 per cent to over 16 per cent of the 1980 GNP.[16]

Expenditures on consumer durable goods will show the highest rate of growth, largely because of rising affluence. Between 1967 and 1980, real disposable income per capita is projected to increase at an annual average of 3.1 per cent, doubling the proportion of families with real incomes of $10,000 or more from around 25 per cent of all consumer units to around 50 per cent. Higher incomes, along with increased leisure time, will influence demands for recreation equipment, such as boats, motors, automobiles, televisions, pleasure aircraft, and sporting goods. There will also be large demands for household furnishings because of the large increase in the 25-34 age group.[17]

Consumer spending for nondurable goods will continue to grow at a slower rate than total spending. By 1980, Americans are expected to spend only 38 per cent of total expenditures on consumer nondurables, compared to 44 per cent in 1967 and 55 per cent in 1968. A large share of the consumer nondurables will be for clothes, household supplies, gasoline and oil, drugs, personal grooming aids, and reading materials. Spending for food and beverages will decrease as a proportion of total nondurable expenditures.[18]

Statistical data from the Department of Commerce indicates that consumers will, for the first time in American history, spend more money on services—air travel, car rentals, beauty parlors, advertising and management consulting, life insurance, and so on—than for nondurable goods. Even though the prices for services have risen at a faster than average rate, services have proliferated and their coming preeminence will present a whole new set of opportunities and challenges. Major components within the services field will be housing, business expenditures, medical services, and education and research.[19] These then are prime areas for minority enterprise to enter.

(NACMBE) placed stress on the need for greatly expanded training and educational opportunities and recommended the allocation of $160 million over the next three years to assist materially in this area.

[14] Labor Department Forecast, November, 1970.
[15] PREDICASTS, April 20, 1970, at 3.
[16] Id.
[17] Id.
[18] NATIONAL CONSUMER FINANCE ASSOCIATION, FINANCE FACTS YEARBOOK (1970).
[19] Sales Management—1970 Survey of Buying Power, June 10, 1970, at A-21.

Using projections from the Bureau of Labor Statistics, an examination of output demand can be used to show a national trend in higher growth businesses. The data reveals obvious business opportunities in those industries with projected substantial increases in growth rate. These include the following industries: optical, ophthalmic, and photographic equipment; electric, gas, and sanitary services; business services; and office supplies.[20]

Industries for which the projected demand for ouput is expected to grow at medium high and increasing rates include the following:

nonferrous metal ores	medical, educational services and non-profit organizations
new construction	
household furniture manufacture	primary nonferrous metals manufacture
manufacture of other furniture and fixtures	manufacture of electrical industrial equipment and apparatus
manufacture of paper and allied products, except containers	manufacture of miscellaneous electrical machinery, equipment and supplies
printing and publishing	scientific and controlling instruments
manufacture of stone and clay products	miscellaneous manufacturing
the wholesale and retail trade industry	hotels, personal and repair services, except automobile repair services

Some discretion must be used in evaluating those industries which will show high rates of growth during the 1965-1980 period, but for which the growth rate has decreased since the 1957-65 period. Whether or not opportunities exist for minority entrepreneurs depends on such factors as: (1) the production capacity of existing firms; (2) the number of new firms to be developed during the coming decade; (3) new product development; (4) the ability of minority firms to reduce costs; (5) the relative sales promotion success of minority versus that of rival firms; (6) the availability of capital; and (7) the availability of trained minority managers and technicians.

A. Technology-Intensive Industries

A large number of higher growth opportunities exist in technology intensive industries.[21] In the past, entry into these industries has been eased in many cases by government contract support, both in terms of direct support for research and

---

[20] It should be noted that the SIC code groupings may, in general, bring together different kinds of growth areas within one industrial code. Thus, further breakdowns of a given area may be necessary to find particularly desirable opportunities.

[21] Technology intensive industries may be defined as those industries which have such characteristics as a much larger than average amount of their funds being spent on research and development, a significantly higher than average percentage of technologists in their employ, and a reliance on the production of new technology based products for their retention and expansion markets. Such industries would include: aircraft, scientific instruments, chemicals and electronics. *See* NATIONAL SCIENCE FOUNDATION, RESEARCH AND DEVELOPMENT IN INDUSTRY, 1968 (1970).

development expenses and through creation of a market for at least a limited number of the new products. The importance of government market creation has been dramatically demonstrated by the hundreds of new firms initiated in the Boston, Palo Alto, and Los Angeles areas since World War II. Research and development is a potentially profitable area, but it presents many problems, such as the need for substantial investments. In addition, these areas require technological expertise, managerial and entrepreneurial expertise, and sale promotion expertise.

Given these requirements, how can a minority enterprise launch itself into a high-growth potential industry? The answer may lie in non-minority corporate support of minority spin-off firms, perhaps in conjunction with direct government grants or tax incentives. For example, a large manufacturing firm could set up a minority-run supplier to manufacture components for the manufacturer, or to provide a specialized service. One example of such a high technology spin-off is that established by the Bendix Corporation's Communications Division—Baltimore Electronic Associates, Inc.[22]

In a study of more than 200 new technology-based firms founded by former employees of the Massachusetts Institute of Technology research and development laboratories, the total proportion of failures found during the first five years of these spin-off firms was only 20 per cent, as compared with 80 per cent failure during the same period for all firms.[23] In addition, the spin-off firms showed an exponential growth in sales during this same five-year period. During their preliminary stages, these firms were mainly preoccupied with government research and development, but tended to diversify rapidly into consumer markets.[24]

Potential minority businessmen seeking out areas of high growth might also look to the industries in which significant technological advances are expected, as there appears to be a correlation between research and development or technological research expenditures and long-run profits.[25] Not only must minority businessmen enter fields in which subsidized research and development will occur, they must also enter fields which are already technology-intensive and in which expenditures on innovation will translate themselves into substantial profits during the coming decade.[26]

One cannot predict with certainty which industries will experience significant

---

[22] Bendix helped several of its minority employees establish a business to manufacture electrical components needed by Bendix. Originally the components were manufactured by the company, but it was thought that they could be produced less expensively by an outside source. Bendix has supplied management and technical assistance as well as help in purchasing for the new corporation, Baltimore Electronics Associates.

[23] Roberts, *supra* note 5, at 224-29.

[24] *Id.* at 228.

[25] *See, e.g.*, U.S. DEP'T OF COMMERCE, TECHNOLOGICAL INNOVATION: ITS ENVIRONMENT AND MANAGEMENT (1967); E. MANSFIELD, THE ECONOMICS OF TECHNOLOGICAL CHANGE 43-98 (1968); Freeman, *Research and Development in Electronic Capital Goods*, NAT'L INSTITUTE REV., Nov., 1965, at 40-91.

[26] S. Doctors, Federal R&D Funding and Its Effects on Industrial Productivity, Jan., 1968 (unpublished paper prepared for the New England Research Application Center, University of Connecticut).

technological changes, nor can one readily predit with absolute certainty where an innovative thought will occur. But the growth of investments in, and profits from, research and development expenditures appear to be closely correlated with government expenditures in any given area.[27] While government expenditures for the 1960's were concentrated in the areas of aerospace, electronics, and atomic energy, increased emphasis will be placed on research and development in such areas as medical research, education, sanitation, housing, and safety.[28] If minorities are seeking high return investments, they must look toward these new areas of large government investment.

America has typically accepted technological advances with insufficient consideration for problems of physical health, sanity, and aesthetics such as the noisiness of airplanes and air pollution from automobiles. Thus, one higher growth business opportunity (in terms of government expenditures) will be the technology-intensive research and development industry which will deal with the problems created as a by-product of advanced technology.

B. Discretionary Purchase Industries

Another source of high growth opportunities is the discretionary purchase industry. Business opportunities may be said to lie in the areas of fad industries and intermediaries for labor-intensive production. The fad industry is one area of business opportunity which can show high growth but which does not necessarily involve a high level of technology. Increasing income and increasing leisure time will stimulate a tremendous increase in goods and services which will soon outgrow their stylishness. Despite the fact that employment for minorities may be cyclical or unpredictable and sporadic in these industries, the fad industires give unusual returns on capital. The toy industry is one example of business opportunity requiring relatively little capital outlay, but much innovation, extremely good sales promotion, and market appraisal.

An additional source of business opportunity is the area of businesses which provide special services as well as social services. The following areas of comparative strength may contribute to rewarding business opportunities by drawing on the strengths and knowledge of an ethnic or racial group: developing minority resources; capitalizing on ethnic or racial identities, experiences, and attitudes; providing (and researching) social services to minorities.

In the first area—resource development, minorities could act as developers and agents for talented minorities. For example, black recording stars, actresses, athletes, artists, and writers might also have black agents—provided adequate training, financing, and necessary contacts were available. The entrepreneurial aspect requires

---

[27] NATIONAL PLANNING ASSOCIATION, LOOKING AHEAD, May, 1969, at 11.

[28] See the discussion of new career opportunities in A. PEARL & F. RIESSMAN, NEW CAREERS FOR THE POOR chs. 3, 4, 5, 7 (1965).

an aggressive sales promoter. Not only might this minority talent-public intermediary operate a highly successful business, but also this business venture would be one means of stopping the flow of minority talent to non-minority capitalists. For Indians and Mexican-Americans (many of whom are engaged in the making of handicraft, pottery, dolls, and carved items), an intermediary might exploit the rising market for custom goods by acting as a go-between for labor-intensive producers and retailers. Where possible, both types of intermediaries might also function in the final stages of trade or production.

Minorities operating in minority-identity fields might have a better understanding of minority needs than would other business firms. A chain of soul kitchens might be highly successful, especially if it combined good food with pleasant surroundings and served both minorities and non-minorities. Cosmetic, clothes, and hair products catering to minorities have, on the whole, met with widespread acceptance, although they are often so expensive that they are beyond the means of many potential customers. In an allied area, Latin minorities could investigate the development of import-export linkages with the increasingly important Latin American market; blacks could likewise involve themselves in African trade exchange.

An important minority comparative advantage includes the administration of social services in minority communities, since a minority individual, capitalizing on shared experiences, can better communicate with others of the same minority group.[29] In the areas of mental health programs, drug and crime rehabilitation, and social welfare, a minority enterprise to administer social services, staffed by professionals in their respective social fields and with para-professional minority community residents, might have considerably more success and prove to be much less expensive than a similar governmental agency.[30] Formal education and professional experience cannot overcome a lack of communications, distrust, and lack of common experience. Among groups with language problems, language training by bilingual minority members may capitalize upon a strategic weakness. In addition, a minority firm could do urban research into the quality of public services, and might well have an advantage over a similar non-minority firm.

III

GOVERNMENT CREATION AND ENCOURAGEMENT OF MARKET DEVELOPMENT

Since World War II, the federal government has become an important force in the creation of new markets in both the public and private sectors of the economy.[31]

---

[29] *Id.*

[30] BUSINESS AND DEFENSE SERVICES ADMINISTRATION, DEP'T OF COMMERCE, SELECTED INDUSTRY PROFILES: DETAILED ANALYSIS OF MINORITY BUSINESS OPPORTUNITIES pt. 1-V (1969).

[31] State and local governments also purchase large quantities of goods and services, and create markets in many other ways, but this article will concentrate on the role of the federal government, leaving for

A familiar example is the visible market created by the federal government in the aerospace area, which has amounted to several hundred billion dollars over the last ten years.[32] But the government also creates market demand in many other ways, such as licensing, grants of insurance, and protection of monopoly status. Perhaps most important for minority enterprise development, the government can use its market creation power to provide numerous protected market areas so necessary for the development of most new enterprise, and the government can assume the role of the primary risk taker.

Of course, there are numerous other ways in which the government may create a protected market, as by the granting of a radio, television, or interstate commission carrier license. As previously noted, the government may also create substantial incentives for non-minority business to assist minority business with financial guarantees, subsidies, and grants. There is a variety of ways in which the federal government may use its powers to promote the development of minority enterprise. The following list is a brief survey of federal government market creation and development powers:

1. *Risk Taker.* The government has become the primary risk taker in many new technical areas such as radar, computer development, micro-electronics, and more recently, supersonic air transportation and artificial organs.

2. *Direct Purchaser of Goods and Services.* Many hundreds of new companies have been initiated and sustained through government contracts, including almost the entire aerospace industry.

3. *Tax Incentives.*[33] The use of tax incentives has stimulated many different types of industrial development. The most widely publicized have been the various mineral depletion allowances and the investment tax credit. However, a large variety of taxes is commonly used by government at all levels for selective stimulation of business development.

4. *Allocation of Scarce Resources.* The issuance of licenses in regulated industries, such as air transport, communications, and interstate transport, have all provided substantial opportunities for business development. The grant of grazing, mineral, or timber rights on federal lands has also been quite important.

5. *Insurance.* The guarantee of investments by agencies, such as the Agency for International Development (AID), or the guarantee of loans by SBA or EDA, have been important in business development. New areas of proposed government

---

future works the exposition of the importance of the non-federal public sector for minority enterprise development. The ratio is about two to one in terms of present tax collection expenditures in favor of the federal government. 1970 DEP'T OF COMMERCE SURVEY OF CURRENT BUSINESS.

[32] Aerospace research and development expenditures alone have totaled over $100 billion during the last decade. *See* NATIONAL SCIENCE FOUNDATION, FEDERAL FUNDS FOR RESEARCH, DEVELOPMENT, AND OTHER SCIENTIFIC ACTIVITIES: FISCAL YEARS 1968, 1969, and 1970 (1969).

[33] NACMBE has recommended the use of tax incentives for both direct non-minority business assistance to minority businesses and for training minority managers.

TABLE VI
Government Spending by Function 1967 Actual and 1980 Projected

Program	Total Government Millions of Current $		Average Annual Growth %
	1967	1980	
Total expenditures	241,253	587,164	7.08
Defense	74,555	116,179	3.47
Nondefense	166,698	470,985	8.32
Education	39,677	123,324	9.12
Health and Hospitals	8,547	35,087	11.48
Sanitation	22,006	7,672	10.87
Social Security and Welfare	40,994	103,683	7.40
Civilian Safety	6,248	21,073	9.80
Labor	1,087	5,176	12.75
Transportation	15,118	38,643	7.48
Development	713	11,052	23.47
Conservation and Recreation	4,492	16,620	10.60

Source: NATIONAL PLANNING ASSOCIATION, in LOOKING AHEAD, May, 1969, at 11.

insurance include surety bonding for minority contractors and guarantee of equity investments in minority enterprise.[34]

6. *Direct Loans.* The government makes a significant amount of direct loan money available, particularly through SBA and EDA programs.

7. *Tariffs and Quotas.* The selective use of trade barriers has provided substantial opportunity for industrial development in a number of industries.

8. *Supply of Capital Equipment.* The government has often stimulated industrial development by allowing private firms to use or buy government-purchased equipment at reduced rates.

9. *Subsidized Markets.* The use of agricultural subsidies has provided a substantial impetus toward the creation of a highly efficient agriculture industry in this country.

This list indicates ways in which the federal government can use its powers to stimulate business development. However, minority businessmen have been almost totally excluded from such government programs. They have participated, if at all, only recently, and then primarily through the direct business loan.[35]

At present, spending by federal, state, and local government is approximately one-fifth of GNP, and is projected to increase during the period from 1967 to 1980 by an

---

[34] OEO's newly initiated Opportunity Funding Corporation (OFC) will attempt to determine the efficacy of using federal government guarantees in a wide variety of applications to stimulate minority business and capital base development. *See* OFFICE OF ECONOMIC OPPORTUNITY, OPPORTUNITY FUNDING: AN ECONOMIC DEVELOPMENT DEMONSTRATION PROGRAM (1970).

[35] A recent survey (by NACMBE) of SBA lending practices revealed that most loans to minority entrepreneurs were direct Equal Opportunity Loans (EOL) of $25,000 each, while those to non-minority entrepreneurs were considerably larger, averaging $56,000, and were guaranteed loans. The findings of the NACMBE indicated that minority businessmen have been almost totally excluded from most government business development programs.

average annual rate of 7.08 per cent (Table VI). The greatest increase in government spending will be for housing and community development, both of which are concerned with fulfilling social needs. In general, government expenditures will exhibit increased focus upon housing, urban renewal, and other social benefits. Large increases in government expenditures for health and hospitals, conservation, and recreation will occur, while spending on national defense is expected to show the slowest growth rate of government spending. Thus, much government spending for the coming decade will complement high-growth industry in such areas as housing, education and health care. All are areas which will also assist in community development and over which the community should be able to exercise some control in the letting of contracts and grants. Thus, minority enterprise could be given a substantial portion of this new, higher growth business.

IV

DEMOGRAPHIC-ECONOMIC TRENDS AND BUSINESS OPPORTUNITY

Population growth or decline by geographic area, together with growth or decline in the work force and the number employed by occupation, suggests increases in manpower resources to take advantages of emerging business opportunities, and in manpower to provide purchasing power. Such population changes constitute significant changes in business opportunities. Four sets of interacting population movements affecting business opportunities and markets can be identified: (1) regional population trends; (2) the movement from rural to urban areas; (3) the movement of city population to the suburbs; and (4) an exchange of population according to race.

In general, the greatest rate of job and population growth has occurred along the rim of the country—moving along the West Coast, through the Southwest, and over to Florida. Higher-than-average growth increases also took place in the South and the West. The West will show the fastest gains in population and income, and the Southwest will show the fastest gains in employment. Florida (Southeast), Arizona (Southwest), Colorado (Mountains), California and Nevada (West) will be the states spearheading the growth of their respectives regions.

There has been a substantial decline of rural populations, and an increase in metropolitan areas. Rural population increased from 61.4 million to 70.7 million in the 19 years from 1950 to 1969. At the same time, metropolitan population increased from 89.2 million to 127.5 million people.[36] Thus, while the rural (non-metropolitan) population was increasing by an annual average of .85 percent, the metropolitan population was increasing by 3.4 percent.[37]

There is also a geographical concentration present among the states experiencing the fastest growth in services. Of the six states experiencing the greatest increase

---

[36] 1969 BUREAU OF THE CENSUS CURRENT POPULATION REPORTS.
[37] *Id.*

in service dollars spent (Maryland, South Carolina, Georgia, Florida, Alabama, and Hawaii, in that order), the fastest growing five are in the Southeast. Moreover, the service field, compared to retail trade, is a highly concentrated market geographically. The two leading states in spending for services are New York and California. These two states do more than one-third of the nation's service business, although they contain only one-fifth of its population. Illinois, Pennsylvania, Texas, and Ohio are the other national leaders in service dollars spent. All of these states contain substantial minority populations which could benefit from the growth of these service industries if an appropriate national strategy were developed now to channel substantial amounts of this new business to minority enterprise.

Given the above facts, it is obvious that business and job opportunities do not necessarily lie either in the northern United States or in the large cities. Business opportunity is growing more rapidly in the South (where the minority population is concentrated) than the national average. Medium-size cities may have better business growth opportunities than the inner city areas of the large cities.

Finally, there have been surprising increases in the population of small non-metropolitan cities. In other words, the movement from the farms is not necessarily to the big city. This suggests that there are important nodules of business opportunity in cities of this smaller size, even in predominantly rural states.

It is important to realize that these population trends are not merely population movements, but are *opportunity* movements—opportunities for jobs and business—because they reflect an underlying growth of business and government in the fast-growing areas. This data gains importance when it is realized that the movement of the minority population is not in the direction of greatest opportunity. The movement of the minority population appears to be going in almost the opposite direction, although it must be cautioned that conclusions in this area are often impressionistic, since data on the movement of race is scarce. But an example which supports the hypothesis is New England. Its average annual employment growth rate during 1961-68 was next to the lowest of the regions, 2.3 per cent,[38] but its increase in non-white male workers was the fastest in the nation; and this increase is expected to continue to grow at a rapid rate in the 1970's.

During the past 25 years, the proportion of non-whites in the central city population has doubled, but it has declined in suburbia. In fact, between 1960 and 1966, the Negro population in American central cities increased 22.9 per cent. It declined by 1.8 per cent for whites.[39] Meanwhile, industry and manufacture have abandoned their old quarters, and have followed or even preceded the general movement of the more affluent population and business to the suburbs. The contrast is apparent: blacks go into the city while the jobs and businesses are moving away.[40]

---

[38] 1969 MANPOWER REPORT OF THE PRESIDENT 35.

[39] U.S. BUREAU OF THE CENSUS, DEP'T OF COMMERCE, CURRENT POPULATION REPORTS, SERIES p. 20, No. 181, Apr. 21, 1969, at 1.

[40] 1968 MANPOWER REPORT OF THE PRESIDENT 132.

The South has increased in population, but the net growth is accounted for by the white population; the blacks have moved to the North and to the big cities. In the 1950's, the South experienced a net loss of over 1.4 million non-whites. Estimates place the net outmigration from the rural areas during the 1960's at an average of more than three-quarters of a million persons a year.[41]

When total population movements are related to the population trends of minorities, it appears that there is increasing emigration of non-whites from higher-growth areas. This result suggests the need for a network to inform minorities of business opportunities based on demographic changes. At the very least, such information is needed to enable the minority entrepreneur to make realistic calculations about risks and opportunities. Rather than proposing a mass migration of minorities to higher-growth areas, it is proposed that some business opportunities for minorities be matched to specific areas of comparative advantage. Fortunately, there will exist in the 1970's not only expanding horizons for business growth in geographic districts which are rapidly developing, but also opportunities in the inner city and the large metropolitan areas. These are often considered *passé* by non-minority entrepreneurs who think in terms of economic and business growth opportunities.

V

CONCLUSION

It is clear that greater opportunities for business development must be made available to minority entrepreneurs in order to provide one important component of total community development. It has not been suggested that business development, without other facets of development, such as greater education and health care opportunities, as well as greatly expanded job opportunities in non-minority business, is a panacea. But minority business development must provide a significant element in building the capital base in the minority community, in providing success models, and in providing opportunities for self-development.

Present programs for minority enterprise development are largely focused on short-term goals, such as providing quantities of equity and debt capital to numbers of minority enterprises, almost without regard to the growth potential of these enterprises. If the vast bulk of minority business is investment in low-growth, low-profit potential businesses, then present programs may have the long-term impact of widening the gap between minority and non-minority businesses. It is, therefore, important that we attempt to make available to minority entrepreneurs the full range of business opportunities, with particular emphasis on higher growth potential opportunities.

It is possible to identify a number of areas of higher growth potential through a variety of indicators, such as projections of government spending, consumer de-

---

[41] Maitland & Nebel, *Rural to Urban Transition*, MONTHLY LABOR REV., June, 1968, at 28-32.

mand, socio-economic patterns, and demographic projections. All of these changes represent new and often important higher growth potential opportunities. It is important to identify these areas, make this information available to minority entrepreneurs, and provide necessary financing, management and technical assistance. Such a program of business development must include a broadly based strategy designed to meet the many development deficiencies in the minority community. Such a comprehensive program has recently been proposed by the National Advisory Council on Minority Business Enterprise (NACMBE), which includes more than seventy-five recommendations for new and expanded programs in business opportunities, education, community development, and finance.[42] Only a comprehensive program of this type will provide the human and technical resources needed to implement the business development strategy discussed in this paper.

The role of the federal government is crucial in the implementation of the proposed strategy. It may be desirable to delegate much of the actual implementation of the proposed strategy to the private sector, but only the government can provide the financial incentives, and create the markets needed to provide numbers of higher growth potential minority enterprise. The government can fill this latter role by: (1) the direct purchase of goods and services; (2) acting as a guarantor and subsidizer; (3) providing licenses; (4) acting as a risk taker; and (5) providing tax incentives or direct grants to motivate non-minority business involvement.

To summarize the proposed business opportunities analyzed, a comprehensive business opportunity strategy should concern itself with moving on all possible fronts. It must match community and individual resources with business opportunities. It must focus on higher-growth areas while performing a variety of community development functions, including employment, capital creation, and the production of needed goods and services. This mix of functions will provide a "staging area" for entrepreneurial development which can make a meaningful contribution to overall minority economic development.

---

[42] *See* 1971 NACMBE FINAL REPORT (1971).

GAMES THE GOVERNMENT PLAYS: FEDERAL FUNDING OF MINORITY ECONOMIC DEVELOPMENT

Otto J. Hetzel*

INTRODUCTION AND GAME PLAN

Little control or ownership of wealth-generating resources in the United States is in the hands of minority group members.[1] In an avowed attempt to increase participation in the economic mainstream,[2] a number of federal government programs have held out the hope of financial support for development of minority business enterprises. These programs have included those administered by the Office of Economic Opportunity (OEO),[3] the Department of Housing and Urban Development (HUD),[4] the Department of Commerce,[5] and the Small Business Administration (SBA).[6] In every instance, pronouncements of specific thrusts to develop innercity minority business have been widely heralded. Some programs have included development efforts for rural areas as well, thereby assisting Indians and Mexican-Americans. In each case, however, the "getting" has been far from easy, and the "using" has been equally frustrating. This article will attempt to illustrate that the government's administration of these programs often constitutes a series of "games" imposed on those minority group members who attempt to utilize the financial

---

* Professor of Law, Wayne State University, and Associate Director, Center for Urban Studies. The author wishes to acknowledge the valuable assistance of Thomas Werner, a student research assistant, in the preparation of this paper.

[1] Industry distribution showed that most minority ownership was of retail businesses with personal service businesses second. There was little minority ownership of construction and manufacturing concerns. Nearly all of the minority businesses were situated in urban areas. SMALL BUSINESS ADMINISTRATION, NATIONAL SURVEY OF U.S. BUSINESS 1, 2 (1969). The "typical" minority businessman operates a one-man personal service or retail shop in a central city area, and has annual gross receipts of $20,000 or less. The comparable figure for other businesses is $50,000. Only 3.25% of the nation's more than 5,000,000 small businesses are owned by members of minority groups, although such members comprise 15% of the nation's population. *Hearings on the Economic Opportunity Amendments before the Subcomm. on Employment, Manpower and Poverty of the Senate Comm. on Labor and Public Welfare*, 91st Cong., 1st Sess. 579 (1969) [hereinafter referred to as *Economic Opportunity Hearings*].

[2] The federal government has developed several thrusts to expand minority involvement in the SBA's programs. Under the Johnson Administration these efforts were entitled "Project OWN." The Nixon Administration renamed them "Operation Mainstream" to stamp them with its imprint. Dedicated as these titles seem, it must be remembered that it is effectiveness—not titles—that provides progress.

[3] The Office of Economic Opportunity distributed funds authorized under title I-D of the Economic Opportunity Act of 1964, 42 U.S.C. §§ 2701-2981 (1964), *as amended*, 42 U.S.C. §§ 2763-68 (Supp. V, 1970).

[4] HUD administers the Model Cities program, which is the colloquial name given the program authorized under the Demonstration Cities and Metropolitan Development Act of 1966, 42 U.S.C. §§ 3301-13 (Supp. V, 1970).

[5] The Department of Commerce's Economic Development Administration manages the program authorized under the Public Works and Economic Development Act of 1965, 42 U.S.C. §§ 3121-26 (Supp. V, 1970).

[6] Small Business Act, 15 U.S.C. §§ 631-47 (1964).

resources offered. A typical program may include some or all of the following games initiated by the government and often involving various gambits, variations, and other gamesmanship qualities which the government's bureaucracies have painstakingly, albeit unknowingly, constructed.

Initially the government begins the action with *Come Play with Me*, a game that generally follows a consistent form. The government brings forth its development program and through brochures, pamphlets, public speeches, personal sell, and other similar techniques attempts to interest minority group members in playing—that is, requesting financial support. Promises are made, expectations are planted, and minority businessmen become eager to play.

Once the government has attracted the minority group member, it initiates a second game, *See if You Qualify*. This is the first of a long series of frustrations for the now recruited applicant as he attempts to successfully complete his quest. Often *See if You Qualify* is a long game. The government makes it very difficult for a minority businessman to find out if he is eligible. Eligibility also can be complicated if the goverment decides to impose *Gotta Play with Those Guys* (even if they don't want to play with you). In *Gotta Play with Those Guys* the minority businessman is forced to acquire a partner before he can proceed. The partner may have to be a private lending institution, a local government body, or both. The partner will, of course, extract a price for its "cooperation." The game ends, along with any hope of federal aid, if the minority businessman is not willing to or cannot acquire a partner. Another game that arises in conjunction with *See if You Qualify* is *Gotta Bring Your Own Ball* (even if you don't have one). *Gotta Bring Your Own Ball* requires that the minority businessman acquire a certain amount of private capital before he can qualify for a loan or a grant of federal money. If he fails to acquire that capital either on his own or from his partner, the games are over and he loses.

Should the minority businessman be successful at *See if You Qualify*, the government continues to play other games with him, although the tactics used can vary depending upon the program involved. For instance, the government often imposes *Only One Game at a Time*, thus prohibiting the player from participating in several government programs simultaneously. While one government bureaucracy may ask for multiple program involvement, another will invoke *Only One Game at a Time*. This tactic forces the minority participant to choose only one program, and the player then can use no other program's aid during the game.

Perhaps the most frequently imposed game is *Change the Rules*. This comes in two segments: specific rules are set by the government[7] and agreed upon by the player; then, when the player begins to play under them, the government changes the rules. *Change the Rules* can result in the players' needing to renegotiate totally his relationships with government-imposed partners (often to his great detriment), to

---

[7] Rules can be set by statute, administrative regulations, policy issuances, guidelines, speeches, or contract.

change his internal organization, or to amend his business operation. If he refuses to change, the practical result is often that he is prevented from participating further in government programs.

Another favorite government game seems to be *No Mistakes Allowed*. The player is allowed to play until he makes an error, whether major or minor. Sometimes it is better to make a major error, because no bureaucrat likes to admit he approved of aid to an applicant who turned out to be a real "loser." After the error the government often moves against the player in a concerted effort to drive him out of the program.

No administration of a government program is complete unless it involves *Rig the Game*, with its many variations and gambits. *Rig the Game* occurs in three forms. One involves use of time controls by the government. When a player falls behind the imposed schedule and time runs out, the player loses. Government time delays are also part of this ploy: it can delay action at certain stages of the program for so long a period that the player is forced to quit the game and search elsewhere for aid. In a second variation of *Rig the Game*, government aid is designed so that no player has enough money at any time with which to succeed. Sooner or later, he goes broke and loses the business. The government may also *Rig the Game* by promising to supply managerial and technical assistance to its players. In most cases this aid either is not given or is insufficient to impart the knowledge necessary to make the business successful. Sometimes when the aid is effective, the government "rewards" the initial success by using the tactic *Withdraw the Aid* or by rendering it ineffective by other means.

The ultimate result of these games is to provide the government with an opportunity to play *You Fail*. In *You Fail* the player becomes so discouraged that the government assumes his role and closes off the program to him. Near the end of this game, all player influence is eliminated. The government continues the program with other applicants attracted by *Come Play with Me*—it seems to have an insatiable need for fresh players. Conversely, it is axiomatic that every administrator must have a program to administer.

During the development of the minority business the federal agency which has imposed the games acts as referee. Its decisions are final and no protest is allowed the player. Occasionally the player attempts to reverse roles and instigate a game called *Legal Review*. This game, however, usually results in further losses for the player, and little relief is obtained. There is usually an analogy here to "don't bite the hand that feeds you." The condition of servitude thereby involved can be a bitter pill to minorities using economic development to obtain their independence. Finally, even "success" in *Legal Review* comes far too late for the player who is out of business or, at the least, has lost control.

By attempting to work within the system, the minority businessman is required to play the government's games. When the minority businessman ultimately loses, he naturally feels embittered toward the system. If major improvements are not made in the government's attitude, and in its approaches to operation of its economic development programs, the economic condition of minority groups will become even more depressed. Traditional funding sources have not been adequate to give minority-owned or controlled business an opportunity to establish itself. The government must abandon its game playing, and take the initiative and the risks necessary to fund new ventures. Its current dependence upon the use of private lending sources, particularly as a way to escape taking risks, must be curtailed, for, in the area of financing, it is simply impractical to expect the private sector, which must be profit-oriented, to underwrite minority developmental effort.[8] Significant public resources must be made available before progress can occur.

I

SMALL BUSINESS ADMINISTRATION

A. In General

SBA's version of *Come Play with Me* involves loan programs as well as technical and managerial assistance. These programs have received special emphasis from the last two administrations. Under the Johnson Administration SBA embarked upon "Project OWN" which had as its goals "to insure free competition as the essence of American economic system of private enterprise, and to strengthen the overall economy of the Nation."[9] The Nixon Administration renamed the program "Operation Business Mainstream" and announced that its goals were: (1) to stimulate small business in deprived areas, (2) to promote minority enterprise opportunity, and (3) to promote small business contribution to economic growth and competitive environment.[10]

Currently SBA offers small business financial and management assistance in the form of lease guarantees,[11] management assistance,[12] aid in obtaining government contracts,[13] counseling services,[14] and more than 800 publications covering successful practices in every small business field. SBA also expressly helps victims of disasters[15]

---

[8] Even with guarantees, private sources must charge the costs—namely red tape—of doing business with the government. Admittedly, direct loan programs involve a budgetary impact which guarantees avoid. Nevertheless, in the end, direct government loans are less expensive and *should be* less complicated.

[9] SMALL BUSINESS ADMINISTRATION, SBA: WHAT IT IS, WHAT IT DOES 2 (1970) [hereinafter referred to as SBA: WHAT IT IS].

[10] SMALL BUSINESS ADMINISTRATION, SBA BUSINESS LOANS 2 (1970) [hereinafter referred to as SBA BUSINESS LOANS].

[11] SBA: WHAT IT IS, *supra* note 9, at 11.

[12] SMALL BUSINESS ADMINISTRATION, MANAGEMENT AND TECHNICAL ASSISTANCE 2 (1968) [hereinafter referred to as MANAGEMENT AND TECHNICAL ASSISTANCE]. Service Corps of Retired Executives (SCORE), Counseling at the Local Level (CALL), and Active Corps of Executives (ACE) are the best known management assistance programs provided by SBA.

[13] SMALL BUSINESS ADMINISTRATION, 8(a) CONTRACTING 2 (1970) [hereinafter referred to as 8(a) CONTRACTING].

[14] SBA: WHAT IT IS 24; MANAGEMENT AND TECHNICAL ASSISTANCE, at 2.

[15] SBA: WHAT IT IS 8.

and small business concerns which are displaced as a result of federally-aided contruction programs.[16]

The strength of SBA's role in *Come Play with Me* lies in its various loan programs. SBA can participate in, or guarantee, up to ninety per cent of a bank loan and, in certain instances, can make a direct government loan.[17] Through the Economic Opportunity Loans (EOL) program, a loan of $25,000 can be made to any resident in an area aided by SBA[18] who does not have adequate income to support the basic needs of his family and has been denied adequate business financing through normal lending channels.[19] SBA may also help finance small firms through privately-owned small business investment companies (SBIC's) by a loan or by a guarantee program.[20]

The SBA programs look very attractive to a minority businessman and he can easily be persuaded to tackle the other games played by SBA. *See if You Qualify* is a crucial game. To qualify, a business must be a "small business"[21] which, depending upon its categorization,[22] has sales of $1 million to $15 million and 250 to 1,500 employees.

Gotta Bring Your Own Ball is at the heart of all SBA programs. The applicant must meet general credit requirements which include the following:

(1) Have adequate capital prior to the loan, so that with an SBA loan he can operate on a sound financial basis;[23]
(2) Show that the past earnings record and future prospects of the firm indicate the ability to repay the loan and other fixed obligations out of profits.[24]

Specific percentages of required capital were dropped in 1970 in favor of the more vague standard of a "reasonable" amount of private equity.[25] However, a reasonable amount of private equity is usually $1 for every $9 loaned for a local development company (LDC)[26] and can be as much as $1 for every $5 loaned for other private businesses.

---

[16] *Id.* at 10.
[17] *Id.* at 4.
[18] *Id.* at 5, 6. The area of coverage is the United States, Puerto Rico, and Guam.
[19] *Id.* at 6.
[20] *Id.* at 15, 16.
[21] A "small business" is defined as "one which is independently owned and operated and which is not dominant in its field of operation." SBA BUSINESS LOANS, *supra* note 10, at 3. Gambling or speculative firms, newspapers, and television and radio stations are not eligible for SBA aid. SBA: WHAT IT IS, *supra* note 9, at 2.
[22] SBA: WHAT IT IS, *supra* note 9, at 2.
[23] SBA BUSINESS LOANS, *supra* note 10, at 4.
[24] *Id.*
[25] This "reasonable" standard is applied to businesses owned by minority group members. SBA National Directive 510-1A at 49 (Jan. 9, 1970) and app. 20, at 245 (Feb. 20, 1970).
[26] The extent of equity to be supplied by the LDC varies with the size of the town in which it is located. A community with a population exceeding 10,000 must contribute 20% of a project's cost in addition to the private equity investment so the leverage is not nearly as great as the 9 to 1 ratio implies. *See*, SMALL BUSINESS ADMINISTRATION, 502 LOCAL DEVELOPMENT COMPANY PROGRAM 2 (1968), for other LDC percentage involvement.

SBA invoked *Only One Game at a Time* when it stipulated, by way of an unpublished directive,[27] that government cash grants could not be used to furnish the required private share of the loans. *Only One Game at a Time* eliminates most uses for HUD, Model Cities, and EDA money in SBA games and, in conjunction with *Gotta Bring Your Own Ball*, has effectively prevented many minority businessmen from participating. This is true regardless of their personal ability, since eligibility is measured by an applicant's existing financial resources. However, capital is usually in short supply for development projects in inner city areas.[28] The requirement, therefore, causes many applicants to be rejected without consideration of other factors which may balance the lack of personal funds.

Even though there is no set amount of capital necessary for any certain amount of loan, it is assumed that there must be "reasonable" personal capital invested. There is no evidence that regional SBA directors have used this flexible standard to make more money available to applicants. In fact, given SBA's past record, one can expect that even more rigid standards may now be applied than were required before the "reasonable" standard was promulgated.

SBA should adopt a policy which not only looks at the capital which persons organizing the business have available, but, in addition, considers the type of business and its chances for success in the field, the skill possessed in management and technical capacities of the applicants, the personal ambition and self-pride of the applicants, and the business contacts and other expected financing prospects available if the business becomes viable. Here, again, SBA must be willing to take risks.

SBA also requires *Gotta Play with Those Guys* by imposing the requirement that a minority businessman include a private lending institution as a participant. Most of these loans require bank participation, and direct government loans are made only in a small number of cases where private support is not available.[29] Thus, SBA requires that:

(1) the bank and SBA participate together on a loan with a maximum SBA interest rate of 5½% and maximum SBA participation not in excess of $150,000 on any loan (the bank's interest rate is not to exceed 8% on the remaining amount of the loan);[30] or
(2) the bank accept an SBA guarantee of 90% (or $350,000, whichever is less) on a bank loan; interest is set by the bank.[31]

These programs often require SBA to adopt the lending practices of the bank because it cannot function without bank cooperation. Even with a ninety per cent guarantee many banks are hesitant to participate in SBA's minority loan program

---

[27] SBA National Directive 535-2 at 42.
[28] Note, *Community Development Corporations*, 83 HARV. L. REV. 1558, 1635-36 (1970).
[29] SBA: WHAT IT IS, *supra* note 9, at 3.
[30] *Id.* at 4.
[31] *Id.* at 4.

because of the perceived high risk[32] and red tape involved. In the participation program the bank is nearly as reluctant to loan money as it would be if it were the only source of the loan, for if a bank will not lend money to an applicant on its own, it usually is no more likely to do so even with SBA participation or backing. *Gotta Play with Those Guys* puts the program in the hands of the private lenders, who must agree to play with the minority businessman. Since such participation is difficult to come by, this game effectively eliminates many applicants. Thus, the minority businessmen who may need SBA most are excluded from the game, while others, who already qualify for private funding, are accepted and can receive more aid. This means SBA tends to help those businessmen who can help themselves, while denying help to those who really need government aid. This operating policy is in basic conflict with the philosophy Congress declared in creating SBA.[33]

The various versions of *Rig the Game* also seem very popular with SBA, and delaying tactics occur frequently in its early stages. Before SBA will make a loan on its own, the regional director must make a thorough investigation of the applicant's qualifications. Time and effort on the part of the applicant and the SBA staff in processing and completing a loan, however, is often excessive. It generally takes six to eight months from the time the applicant first expresses the desire for a loan and inquires about it to the time when the loan money is in his hand.[34] Even prior loan recipients who later request more money run into delay problems. For an on-going concern, or for someone who has expended his own money in expectation of going into business, these delays can be disastrous.

SBA attempted to curtail its use of the *Time Delay* tactic by recourse to a Simplified Blanket Loan Guarantee Plan (SBLG).[35] Under this program, the bank participating with the SBA prepares a simplified set of forms which become the core of the report submitted to the regional director. This new program, however, only disguises the *Time Delay*, for SBA measures time in a very singular way under SBLG. Time does not start until SBA accepts an application; but the application is not "accepted" until all of the forms are in order, so that the *final* report can be written. On one SBLG loan traced through SBA, *Time Delay* was played as follows:

—December 29, 1969—SBA receives letter and forms already completed by SBLG bank.

—February 11, 1970—Letter of December 29, 1969 marked "received, February 11,

---

[32] Interview with Ray Willis, former Controller of Citizens Urban Opportunity Fund of Detroit, Michigan, in Detroit, Mar. 1, 1971.

[33] "It is the declared policy of the Congress that the Government should aid, counsel, assist, and protect, insofar as is possible, the interests of small-business concerns in order to preserve free competitive enterprise, to insure that a fair proportion of the total purchases and contracts or subcontracts for property and services for the Government . . . be placed with small-business enterprises . . . ." 15 U.S.C. § 631(a) (1964).

[34] G. Britts, SBA Operation Mainstream: An Administrative Study 7, May 26, 1970 (unpublished paper delivered to the Seminar on Minority Economic Development, Harvard Law School).

[35] SBA National Directive 510-1A, Appendix 19, at 30 (Jan. 24, 1969); *See also* 13 C.F.R. § 122.20(b) (1970).

1970." A file was set up and the application was marked "accepted, February 11, 1970."

—March 18, 1970—Loan approved.[36]

SBA personnel play an important part in *Rig the Game*. The effectiveness of a lending program where profit is not the declared objective depends on the attitudes of the men involved and their willingness to get the job done. One man in the SBA network can adversely affect the progress of an application. A reluctant regional director could refuse many of the loans requested, and similar attributes in the assistant director for financial assistance could mean a drop in the number of loan recommendations made to the regional director.

Implementation of SBA programs varies greatly from city to city. According to a recent study, the effectiveness of some regional offices differed by a ratio of sixteen to one.[37] Where the decisions emanate from a sensitized Minority Enterprise Team,[38] the results have been much better. However, such a focus requires proper direction from the higher levels of SBA. Sensitive and effective employees all along

---

[36] Britts, *supra* note 34, at 8.

[37] Harris, *Compensatory Capitalism: A Description and Evaluation of Project OWN*, in *Hearings on the Organization and Operation of the Small Business Administration Before the House Select Comm. on Small Business*, 91st Cong., 1st Sess. A32-A35 (1969). The program submitted at fiscal year 1972 appropriations hearings showed the following data:

SBA LOAN APPROVALS*—MINORITY AND NONMINORITY
[In thousands of dollars]

Minority type	Fiscal year 1971 (March 1971)		Fiscal year 1970		Fiscal Year 1969	
	Number	Amount	Number	Amount	Number	Amount
Black	3,215	$ 87,424	4,083	$107,639	3,362	$77,135
Puerto Rican	662	13,334	846	16,925	610	10,133
American Indian	235	7,912	228	5,948	91	2,147
Spanish American	1,033	23,018	871	19,239	461	9,953
Asian	218	11,532	205	10,102	114	4,852
Eskimos and Aleutian	29	738	29	514	8	112
Subtotal	5,392	143,958	6,262	160,367	4,646	104,332
Undetermined	34	948	42	2,293	110	5,607
Other, including white	9,124	588,404	8,798	546,950	9,754	588,134
Total	14,550	733,310	15,102	709,610	14,510	698,073

* Excludes disaster loans.

Hearings on Appropriations for the Dept's of State, Justice and Commerce, the Judiciary and Related Agencies for Fiscal Year 1972 Before a Subcomm. of the House Comm. on Appropriations, 92d Cong., 1st Sess., pt. IV, at 629 [hereinafter referred to as *SBA FY 1972 House Appropriations Hearings*].

[38] The function of a Minority Enterprise Team (MET) is to (a) coordinate SBA programs to stimulate minority owned business through expansion of existing businesses or creation of new businesses, (b) identify potential minority entrepreneurs, (c) assist minority businessmen with loan applications to banks, and (d) assist in providing managerial and technical assistance as necessary. The MET works principally in the ghetto and can therefore develop a close relationship with its businessmen. For a complete discussion of MET, see *Hearings on the Organization and Operation of the Small Business Administration Before the House Select Committee on Small Business*, 91st Cong., 1st Sess., at A10 (1969).

the chain of decision might serve to eliminate some of the large regional differences. A sufficient number of employees to handle the volume of work is also necessary. It is irrational to establish a program which is heralded as the cure-all for eliminating problems in business opportunity and then staff it so inadequately that it can not accomplish its goals without maximum inconvenience to its applicants. Yet unless SBA takes such actions, it will continue to *Rig the Game.*

B. MESBIC Program

SBA plays another variation of *Rig the Game* with minority businessmen who apply for assistance in setting up a minority enterprise small business investment company (MESBIC). In 1969, SBA, in cooperation with the Department of Commerce, instituted the MESBIC program. MESBIC's were created by adopting the SBIC program, as authorized by the Small Business Act.[39] Through MESBIC's, the express purpose of SBIC's, supplying venture capital and long term financing, was to be directed toward minority small business concerns. All SBIC's are authorized to purchase stock or debt securities issued by small businesses and thereby provide venture capital and financing. The MESBIC's have usually been created as subsidiaries of large corporations, which in turn provide the necessary private capital for the MESBIC's operations. Since MESBIC's are treated as separate entities for SBA loans and for income tax purposes, they are an attractive investment for large corporations.

The opportunity for minority ownership of MESBIC's has been limited. MESBIC's are subject to *Gotta Bring Your Own Ball*, and the minimum private investment required is $150,000.[40] With $300,000 of SBA assistance, the MESBIC can accumulate $450,000 for investment. As large as this figure appears to be, it is far from adequate to establish a successful MESBIC. SBIC's which are capitalized for less than $1 million have rarely been successful, and three to five million dollars is a more realistic figure for success.[41] Since it is very difficult for a minority group to find financial backing of $1 million to $2 million size factors alone make the program inaccessible to minority businessmen and thus the game is "rigged."[42] Moreover, any firm the MESBIC invests in must make a 100 per cent to 500 per cent profit increase before the MESBIC benefits.[43] This is too much to expect from the overwhelming number of businesses which ask MESBIC's for investment capital.

---

[39] 15 U.S.C. §§ 681-87d (1964). Relevant SBA regulations are contained in 13 C.F.R. §§ 107.1-1411 (1970).

[40] SBA: WHAT IT IS, *supra* note 9, at 15.

[41] Rosenbloom & Shank, MESBIC Myopia: The Department of Commerce and Minority Economic Development, April 1970 (unpublished paper on file at the Center for Community Economic Development, Cambridge, Mass.). To encourage larger investments, SBA provides a three to one match for over $1 million in private investment.

[42] The MESBIC program is not that attractive to large corporations either, since they must subsidize a significant portion of early expenses. This additional drain on corporate resources deters many corporations from becoming meaningful sources of venture capital. Thus, minority groups are not the only ones subjected to SBA "games."

[43] Interview with James Hill, President of PRIME (Pooled Resources In Minority Enterprise), a MESBIC, in Detroit, Feb. 15, 1971.

Another SBA version of *Rig the Game* involves the requirement that investments by a MESBIC must be in a business owned or managed by at least fifty per cent minority personnel.[44] Such a business has less chance for success than other businesses, because of the special problems faced by blacks and other minorities.[45] All new businesses have limited chances for success, but the problems of an inner-city business are compounded. Additional problems stem from the historical lack of business experience among minorities.

SBA guidelines further inhibit a minority role in MESBIC operations. MESBIC's are required to have two full-time managers on their staffs before a license will be granted.[46] This requirement implies a permanent office and related expenses which can result in overhead of $35,000-$60,000 a year or more for even the smallest MESBIC. SBA further requires that such expenses be paid out of revenues, not invested capital.[47] It is absurd to believe that an investment company capitalized at from $450,000 to $1 million, and with its funds committed to newly emerging minority businesses, can generate this kind of cash from early operations. Often the sponsoring parent organization must maintain the MESBIC staff on its own payroll and pay the overhead expenses. The success story of AIC (the MESBIC of Arcata) illustrates the fact that a benevolent parent is the only reason the MESBIC has prospered.[48] In actuality a MESBIC can only operate as a subsidiary division of a strong, benevolent, and well-heeled parent and not as a separate business unit in any meaningful sense.

Another aspect of *Rig the Game* involves the size of the loans a MESBIC can make. Under SBA regulations a SBIC can not invest any more than twenty per cent of its capital in any single investment. Such a limitation may reduce the risk to the MESBIC from over-concentration, but it also eliminates ventures of significant scale and encourages only "Ma and Pa" tokenism. Moreover, because such businesses tend to be marginal, quantum change is inhibited. Ownership of such enterprises does little to give minorities any significant economic role, particularly if grocery stores and dry cleaning establishments are given preference over manufacturing firms and more extensive business which could employ many more times the number of people.

---

[44] SMALL BUSINESS ADMINISTRATION, MESBIC, MINORITY ENTERPRISE SMALL BUSINESS INVESTMENT COMPANY 1 (undated) [hereinafter referred to as MESBIC].

[45] Since so few minority businesses survive the SBA qualification games, it is not surprising that the SBA experience with minority businesses has been as good or better than with other types of businesses assisted by SBA. Interview with James Hill, *supra* note 43. The loss statistics, covering actual and estimated losses from March 1967 through fiscal year 1970, with respect to loans to blacks as contrasted with loans to whites reveal that for EOLS there were 9.88% losses on loans to blacks of $69 million and 9.94% losses on loans to primarily whites of $41 million. For regular 7(a) business loans there were 3.16% losses on loans to blacks of $66 million and 1.21% losses on loans to primarily whites of $972 million. *SBA FY 1972 House Appropriations Hearings* 630.

[46] Rosenbloom & Shank, *supra* note 41, at 5.

[47] *Id. But see*, MESBIC, *supra* note 44, at 2. That publication states that although government funds or grants may not be used to capitalize a MESBIC, such grants may be used to cover operating expenses if this is not specifically prohibited by the terms of the grants.

[48] Rosenbloom & Shank, *supra* note 41, at 3.

If SBA is to succeed, it must be willing to take more risks with its loan funds. A sincere commitment to minority economic development will require that Congress accept the concept that such loans are *inherently* risky. SBA should thus be authorized to expend funds consistent with this philosophy.[49] Only then, will SBA be willing to take chances and only then will existing self-protective SBA constraints be removed. As the program is now implemented, minority businessmen take all the risks in a game they cannot win.

As these game analogies indicate, a new and radically different approach must be taken by SBA if this program is to succeed. The present program seems to dictate that the profitable SBIC's will be of the least help to small businesses. The basic purposes of fostering minority enterprise will not be served unless the SBA program supports development of some large and efficient enterprises which can compete openly in the mainstream of American business. Some alteration of MESBIC size requirements and loan amounts must be made. Rules preventing initial operating expenditures to be paid from capital must be changed to allow the possibility of minority ownership of MESBIC's. Similarly, the ratio of SBA loan amount to private capital must be increased to permit minority ownership, despite their more limited capital sources. MESBIC's can benefit the minority community without "colonizing" such areas only where they are not dependent upon and not controlled by the same interests from which the community seeks to establish a degree of independence.

C. Local Development Company Program

SBA also has its games for the local development company (LDC) program.[50] *Come Play with Me* in this case involves attractive (nine to one) leveraging through LDC's for loans to finance small businesses. SBA can lend up to $350,000 to each small business assisted by an LDC.[51] The loans are intended to assist community development, as distinguished from solely individual entrepreneurs.[52] The LDC must have a minimum of twenty-five stockholders, and the operations of the LDC must be limited to a specified area, with at least seventy-five per cent of its voting control held by persons living within the operations area.[53] The LDC can make loans to businesses affiliated with or owned by the members of the LDC so long as none of the owners being assisted has more than twenty-five per cent voting control. The most effective use of an LDC is to employ it as part of the corporate shell for

---

[49] The SBA budget request for FY 1971 was $320,500,000. This figure represented an increase of $74,183,000 over FY 1970 appropriations. Of this amount it was proposed that $10,000,000 be used for the MESBIC program which is an increase of $5,000,000 over FY 1970 use. *Hearings on Appropriations for the Dept's of State, Justice, and Commerce, and the Judiciary and Related Agencies for Fiscal Year 1971 Before a Subcomm. of the House Comm. on Appropriations*, 91st Cong., 2nd Sess., pt. 4, at 802, 803 (1970) [hereinafter referred to as *SBA Hearings*].

[50] 15 U.S.C. § 696 (1964); 13 C.F.R. § 108.502 (1970). There is also a state development company program, but it is relatively inactive. *See* 13 C.F.R. § 108.501 (1970).

[51] SBA: WHAT IT IS, *supra* note 9, at 7.

[52] *Id.*

[53] *Id.*

a community development corporation (CDC) that carries on other economic development activities.

After interest is aroused, SBA's LDC program administration begins to play *Rig the Game*. The loans available from SBA have limited usefulness. Such loans apply primarily to the financing of plant construction, conversion, or expansion (including the acquisition of land).[54] This financing cannot be employed to support the full range of activities necessary for development of a small business. Extensive controls by SBA are involved in each loan which an LDC makes.[55] The applicant must be identified with a particular small business, and at both the time of approval and disbursement the LDC must show that the funds will be used by a small business.

The resultant *Time Delay* tactic complements SBA's playing of *Rig the Game*. The application and approval process for each loan can be long and tedious. Thus, the LDC will not have the flexibility to determine its own investment policy, and it will not have SBA funds available to take ready advantage of promising investments. The LDC acts solely as a loan packager, sponsor, and guarantor for SBA loans to a small business. In spite of the LDC's guarantee, SBA still scrutinizes each loan carefully and grants only those with very low risk of loss possibilities. The LDC seems to serve no meaningful purpose except as a "buffer" for SBA in locating loan applicants.

Rig the Game does not always lead to *You Fail*. However, such impediments often make the LDC program ineffective. Consequently, the best use for an LDC would be as a passive instrument, to be activated only when a section 502 loan is made. An LDC should not be perceived as an active corpus for community development.

D. The Section 8(a) Program

Come Play with Me, as applicable to section 8(a) of the Small Business Act of 1953, is the potential for SBA, as prime contractor, to enter into contracts with other federal agencies for supplies and services and to then subcontract the work out to small minority firms.[56] SBA is able to negotiate the subcontracts under this program, and the lowest bidder does not necessarily receive the job. SBA, thus, can direct the work to a small business. Firms awarded these contracts are eligible to receive free management and technical aid in their operations.

The section 8(a) program looks promising, but its implementation leaves much to be desired. The minority businessman is forced to participate in *Gotta Play with Those Guys*, in this case with other government agencies which do not want to play with him or SBA would not have had to exercise its powers under section 8(a). This situation seems a clear invitation for failure.

---

[54] *Id.*
[55] The principal difference between a MESBIC and an LDC is that a MESBIC handles its own loans, whereas an LDC must get each loan individually approved by the SBA. Also, an LDC may fund fixed assets, whereas a MESBIC can fund fixed assets and operating capital.
[56] 8(a) CONTRACTING, *supra* note 13, at 2.

The decision to enter into contracts with SBA is left to bargaining between SBA and the procurement officers of the respective government agencies. Therefore, the success of SBA under this program depends on the consent of another agency to apply its appropriations to this additional social purpose. If and when government contracts are granted, small businesses must tolerate low profit margins, rigorously-applied performance standards, legal complexities, vast amounts of paperwork, and other hazards typical of government involvement.

President Nixon's five-year plan to increase section 8(a) contracting may lead to more effective use of the program.[57] Until recently SBA had not extensively utilized section 8(a),[58] but if there is a sudden increase in section 8(a) contracts, the agency will have to expand its staff in order to handle the new volume of business.

SBA also plays a version of *Rig the Game* with the section 8(a) program which includes the standard *Time Delay* tactic and the limited nature of assistance available through SBA. The section 8(a) program also has suffered from the lack of experience of SBA personnel in the contracts they must administer. Further, often it takes too long for a government agency to work through SBA, and consequently contracts of an immediate nature are sent elsewhere. Finally, although the picture is improving, another aspect of *Rig the Game* for this program is the fact that the contracts are seldom of sufficient size to make much difference to minority firms.[59] Small contracts can be useful if there is sufficient volume, but this is unlikely to occur.

II

OFFICE OF ECONOMIC OPPORTUNITY—TITLE I-D

A. Special Impact Program

OEO's version of *Come Play with Me* concerns title I-D of the Economic Opportunity Act of 1964,[60] which provided for the creation of Special Impact programs to address the critical problems of "dependency, chronic unemployment, and rising community tensions" within those urban areas having an especially large concentration of low-income persons, and within those rural areas having substantial out-migration from eligible urban areas. Each program receiving OEO funding had to

---

[57] *See, SBA Hearings, supra* note 49, at 803. More emphasis will be placed on section 8(a) and more managerial and technical assistance will be provided to those minority businessmen receiving section 8(a) contracts.

[58] *Id.*

[59] The March, 1971, summary of section 8(a) contract awards showed:

	No. of Contracts	Total (millions)
FY 1968	8	10.5
1969	30	9.0
1970	196	22.25
1971 to date	351	29.5

Excluding one $5 million contract to Aerojet General, the average contracting was $70,000. If one assumes a 7-8% profit margin, that means only $4900 to $5600 profit to the firm.

[60] 42 U.S.C. §§ 2763-68 (Supp. V, 1970).

be "of sufficient size and scope to have an appreciable impact on the [community]."[61] The OEO grants in fiscal year 1969 generally went to community development corporations (CDC's) and averaged about $1 million each. This represents ninety per cent of a project's cost, the remaining ten per cent being supplied by the private sector.[62] Potentially these grants could have great flexibility and, if granted in large enough amounts, could have the impact intended.

The grant funds may be used for a variety of investment programs which will create jobs for poverty area residents, improve living conditions, develop managerial and entrepreneurial skills, and create opportunities for participation in ownership of production and commercial facilities by poverty area residents. Special Impact grants have also been made to venture capital pools.[63]

The Special Impact program has especially suffered from government game playing, particularly *Change the Rules* and *Rig the Game*. OEO has usually granted enough money for a minority group to begin operating but not nearly enough money for any group to become successful. Partly this was due to limited use of title I-D appropriations for community development corporations. In fiscal 1969, Congress alloted $11 million for OEO use;[64] for fiscal 1970, $30 million was allocated out of $36 million alloted. Of this, $20 million went for urban CDC's, and of that, $10 million went to just one, Bedford-Stuyvesant.[65] Second, the average $1 million grant given to each program is hardly enough to create a "substantial impact" in any large urban area. In fact, $1 million is a small amount of capital with which to begin a SBIC or other community organization of any magnitude whatsoever. Although the ten per cent, *Gotta Bring Your On Ball*, private contribution requirement is not too stringent, only fifty applicants raised such private funds and went through the rigors of *See if You Qualify* in fiscal year 1969. Only ten of these were accepted by OEO for funding.[66] It is doubtful that organizers will be able to maintain the requisite funds every year to qualify for the program when the chances are only one in five that federal aid will be forthcoming. But spreading the wealth to other applicants, of course, would only assure shortfunding of the first recipients.[67]

---

[61] *Id.* §§ 2763, 2764 (Supp. V, 1970).

[62] Federal grants to any program shall not exceed 90% of the cost of such program, including cost of administration, unless the director determines that assistance in excess of such percentage is required. 15 U.S.C. § 2768 (Supp. IV, 1969). Thus the standard is flexible, and the 90% limit is not an absolute barrier to qualified persons who cannot acquire the necessary capital.

[63] Office of Economic Opportunity, *Guidelines for OEO Special Impact Program Fiscal Year 1969*, at 5 (undated mimeo. on file at the *Harvard Law Review*) [hereinafter referred to as *OEO Guidelines*].

[64] *See Hearings on Appropriations for the Dept's of Labor and Health, Education, and Welfare, and Related Agencies for Fiscal Year 1970 Before a Subcomm. of the House Comm. on Appropriations*, 91st Cong., 2d Sess., pt. 8, at 336, 338 (1969) [hereinafter referred to as *OEO Hearings*]. $8.3 million went to 8 urban CDC's and $2.5 million to 7 rural CDC's. Letter to author from Joseph Halbach, Director, Economic Development Division, Office of Program Development, OEO, July 20, 1971.

[65] Halbach letter, *supra* note 64.

[66] *OEO Guidelines, supra* note 63, at 5.

[67] Of the $30 million in fiscal year 1970 only 5 of the 8 urban CDC's first funded were funded again; In fiscal year 1971, 7 of the first 8 CDC's were funded again; 4 of those funded for the first time in fiscal year 1970 were dropped and one new one added. Halbach letter, *supra* note 64.

B. Opportunities Funding Program

If the player is successful in obtaining title I-D funds, *Withdraw the Aid*, another version of *Rig the Game*, begins. Programs which receive funds one year and are on the verge of becoming successful may offend local interests, and funds for future years may be curtailed. In order to make the "substantial impact" required under its legislation, however, title I-D funding should continue for a number of years. Failure to do so because of political pressures or "spread the wealth" philosophies make the original investment worthless. Moreover, such action reinforces minority perceptions of white hypocracy.

A further problem in the administration of the I-D grants involves the pervasive controls imposed on recipients by grant provisions. OEO still requires specific approval of each investment project. Technical assistance seems appropriate, but little capacity will be developed in the grantee if every investment decision is subject to prior approval.

The Nixon Administration has instituted a significant version of *Change the Rules* for title I-D funds. This has involved administrative change-over for a portion of these funds to a new program, Opportunity Funding. Opportunity Funding takes a different approach than Special Impact with respect to emphasis on particular communities. Using the Special Impact funds, Opportunity Funding does not concentrate on an "impact" area, but attempts to stimulate *outside* businesses to invest in the inner city. Opportunity Funding has three principle goals:

(1) to determine the loss factor when private credit and capital are engaged in low-income area projects and to identify those situations where losses can be kept within tolerable limits;
(2) to determine whether the use of proven guarantee, banking, and incentive arrangements will substantially increase the flow of private capital and credit into low income communities;
(3) to determine whether the information resulting from these pilot projects furnishes a basis for legislation to help achieve economic growth in low income communities.[68]

It was OEO's opinion that these goals could be met with a resulting rise in the strength of the commercial banking and savings vehicles currently present in target communities.[69]

An Opportunity Funding corporation is composed of three units, an opportunity guarantee component, which considers capital and credit problems, a community development component, which handles the marketing of inner-city business securi-

---

[68] OFFICE OF ECONOMIC OPPORTUNITY, OPPORTUNITY FUNDING, AN ECONOMIC DEVELOPMENT DEMONSTRATION PROGRAM 1 (1970) [hereinafter referred to as OEO OPPORTUNITY FUNDING].

[69] *Id.* at 2.

ties, and an incentive simulator component, which attempts to encourage private business investment in low income communities.[70]

While the goals of the Opportunity Funding program cannot be questioned, there are grave questions about the means by which they are to be attained. The legality of the program is questionable, since it uses title I-D funds, which were designed to be used exclusively in selective poverty areas.[71] Opportunity Funding attempts to diffuse the funds into a large number of areas, a policy which frustrates the title I-D concentration policy. The program also has selected only one isolated element, capital flow, out of all the poverty area problems, while title I-D was explicitly conceived as a multipurpose, coordinated attack upon many levels of problems. The Opportunity Funding program uses funds for a research and demonstration program which seems contrary to the goal of "arresting tendencies toward dependency, chronic unemployment, and rising community tension" of title I-D.[72] Such administrative shifts leave little or no opportunity for the countergame of *Legal Review*, since former title I-D recipients may have questionable standing to sue and strong disincentives to challenging their funding source. Switching to Opportunity Funding, moreover, intensifies *Rig the Game* because it reduces the limited title I-D funds available to community development corporations.

Opportunity Funding forces the minority businessman into *Gotta Play with Those Guys*. To get assistance, he must go to the beneficiaries of Opportunity Funding, the banks, insurance companies, and other financial sources. Without more leverage or more desirable benefits available to these institutions, their aid will still contain the same restraints on low income investments that it did prior to OEO influence. OEO funds would be put to better use if Opportunity Funding concentrated more on making ghetto businesses better credit risks than on attempting to influence more lending institutions to lend money to risky, unstable ghetto businesses. *Change the Rules* also applies here since another level of bureaucracy has been added under Opportunity Funding. Special Impact funds are handled directly by OEO, but Opportunity Funding grants must go through OEO and then Opportunity Funding's component administrator.[73] This needless duplication swallows up more of the title I-D allocation in administrative expenses.

The Special Impact funding of CDC's has come to be recognized as the most fruitful program yet tried in a low-income community.[74] Opportunity Funding,

---

[70] *Id.* at 5, 6.

[71] 5 U.S.C. § 552 (1967). In fiscal year 1970, $3.9 million was diverted from title I-D funds for the use of the opportunity funding program; less was diverted in fiscal year 1971. Halbach letter, *supra* note 64.

[72] *Id.* A technical analysis of the insecure legal status of the Opportunity Funding Program is presented in a memorandum from Bert Griffin and David Madway to Donald Rumsfeld, OEO Director, April 2, 1970.

[73] OEO OPPORTUNITY FUNDING, *supra* note 68, at 3.

[74] For example, the Special Impact funding of the Bedford-Stuyvesant Section of Brooklyn has been widely heralded; *see* Highlight Memorandum, Special Impact Program (Title I-D) Grant No. CG-8532, A10. Specific accomplishments include a job creation program, community home improvement program,

however, proposes to use its funds for purposes at odds with or unrelated to such a community participation approach. Lacking OEO funding, CDC's will not be able to continue to build a community participation model for economic development.

Moreover, Opportunity Funding continues a form of *Rig the Game* by the very nature of its emphasis on loan programs. In simple terms, Opportunity Funding is directed toward supplying the minority businessman with debt capital. It is debt financing, however, that usually overloads a business and restricts its growth. The critical difference here is that Special Impact can provide desperately-needed equity capital without burdening minority businesses with the less attractive debt funding.

III

ECONOMIC DEVELOPMENT ADMINISTRATION

The Economic Development Administration (EDA) was created in 1965 as an agency of the Department of Commerce by an act which authorized a wide range of programs to help distressed communities attract new industry and permanent jobs.[75] These programs include grants and loans for development facilities, industrial and commercial loans, and technical planning and research assistance.

EDA plays an intricate form of *See if You Qualify*. Relying on data supplied by the Department of Labor, the Department of the Interior, and the Department of Commerce, it designates areas which may be considered for aid. Each designated area then must prepare an overall economic development program (OEDP) within six months after it has received notice of its designation.[76] If an area fails to submit an OEDP, it will become ineligible for consideration by EDA for two years.[77] If the OEDP is approved by EDA, the area will be officially designated as a "redevelopment" area and EDA will state which types of assistance are available to the area. Each specific project in an area is examined, and aid is given only to those projects which meet other EDA standards.[78]

Urban areas may qualify as "redevelopment" areas in four ways:[79]

(1) as areas of "substantial and persistent unemployment";
(2) as areas with "low median family income";
(3) as areas which have lost a major employer producing added unemployment;
(4) as areas designated Special Impact areas.[80]

---

community facility development, manpower development, and housing development. *See also Economic Opportunity Hearings, supra* note 1.

[75] Public Works and Economic Development Act of 1965, 42 U.S.C. §§ 3121-3226 (Supp. V, 1970).

[76] O'Connell, *Financial Assistance Available from the Economic Development Administration*, in 6 LAW NOTES 16 (1969).

[77] *Id.*

[78] These standards vary depending on the type of proposed project. Usually the amount of investment money available for the project plays an important role in its consideration. Note, *supra* note 28, at 1648. *See also* O'Connell, *supra* note 76, at 18, for an example of project requirements.

[79] 42 U.S.C. § 3161(a) (1966).

[80] For a discussion of the limited nature of this qualification, see p. 80 *supra.*

The minimum "area" size under the Act is either an entire city, county, or metropolitan area.[81] *See if You Qualify* has effectively eliminated almost the entire country. For most areas, the statistics do not accurately describe conditions in smaller portions within their boundaries. Therefore, the high unemployment and low family income of the ghettos are often hidden for purposes of EDA. Very few areas have been designated Special Impact localities under OEO, so this qualification does little to aid the expansion of EDA programs. Qualifications (1)-(3) are so severe and rigorous that only three major cities had by 1969 qualified under (1) and (2),[82] and sections of only three cities had qualified under (3).[83]

EDA's approach to economic development consists primarily of attracting strong businesses to locate in economically depressed areas.[84] As a result, minority businessmen are forced into *Gotta Play with Those Guys*. Large, established corporations and business are the associates a minority businessman must take. Another form of *Gotta Play with Those Guys* results from another EDA regulation, which provides that before any aid is given, both state and local government agencies for economic development must approve of the project. The applicant has no right to attempt to reverse state and local objections at the federal level.[85] This requirement gives state and local agencies considerable power over organizations interested in EDA aid.

EDA also plays a very rigorous game of *No Mistakes Allowed*. In its evaluation of the eligibility for assistance of a low-profit, marginal business, EDA places emphasis upon demonstrated and exceptional management competence.[86] EDA also permits little leeway in project design and retains tight supervisory control over all of its funds. Even minor programmatic changes must be approved, and no room is left for the use of discretion by project officials.[87]

EDA assistance comes with even tighter controls than financial aid from traditional sources. It definitely is not a program which will promote economic activity of any magnitude for minority firms. The number of areas qualifying for aid and the amounts available for distribution are too small. Everything EDA proposes to do can be done by other government agencies and private lending institutions with

---

[81] 42 U.S.C. § 3151(b)(4). Some exceptions have been made for labor market areas which are portions of cities. *See* note 83 *infra*.

[82] The cities are Newark, Oakland, and Cleveland. U.S. Dept. of Commerce News Release, EDA 69-290 at 3 (June 29, 1969).

[83] These were Brooklyn's Navy Yard area, and the Chicago and Omaha stockyard districts. U.S. Dept. of Commerce News Release, *supra* note 82, at 3.

[84] "Our objective is to assist such areas to achieve stable and independent job-creating economics by encouraging private businessmen to establish or expand facilities there." *Hearings on Appropriations for the Dept's of State, Justice, and Commerce, the Judiciary, and Related Agencies for Fiscal Year 1970 Before a Subcomm. of the House Comm. on Appropriations*, 91st Cong., 2nd Sess., pt. 3, at 61, Testimony of Asst. Secretary Robert Podesta [hereinafter referred to as *EDA Hearings*]. *See also* U.S. DEP'T. OF COMMERCE, EDA HANDBOOK 32 (1968).

[85] 42 U.S.C. § 3142(b)(2), (10) (Supp. IV, 1969); EDA HANDBOOK, *supra* note 84, at 36, 37.

[86] EDA HANDBOOK, *supra* note 84, at 35.

[87] Note, *supra* note 28, at 1645.

fewer restraints and less red tape. Although EDA has significant funds,[88] their use is so restricted as to be of little value for minority economic development.[89]

IV

DEPARTMENT OF HOUSING AND URBAN DEVELOPMENT

A. Model Cities

The Model Cities program was intended to provide "additional financial and technical assistance" above that available from existing federal grant-in-aid programs.[90] It has a broad mandate in slum areas to expand housing, jobs, and income opportunities; to reduce dependence upon welfare payments; to improve educational facilities and programs; to combat disease and ill health; to reduce the incidence of crime and delinquency; to enhance recreational and cultural opportunities; to establish better access between homes and jobs; and generally to improve the quality of life.[91]

Model Cities funds come from and are controlled by the Department of Housing and Urban Development (HUD). The program has wide-sweeping potential application in the field of urban economic development. Funds are supposed to be responsive to local determination and use.[92] There is an elaborate planning process built into the program.[93] Unfortunately, despite efforts to reduce federal control of local decisions,[94] the Model Cities program maintains extensive review procedures and close federal supervision of projects. When contemplating a new major federal program, one can hope its administrators would learn from previous mistakes made by government agencies and eliminate some of the games in the administration of the new program. But the contrary is more apt to be true: the Model Cities program displays its own version of most of the games which have previously been discussed.

One hundred and fifty cities were chosen to receive Model Cities grants.[95] In each selected city, a Model Cities area or neighborhood was outlined, and a city demonstration agency (CDA) was designated by the local government to concen-

---

[88] Appropriations for FY 1970 reached $271,000,000. Funding requested for FY 1971 is $263,000,000. *EDA Hearings, supra* note 84, at 58.

[89] During calendar year 1969, EDA made only 38 business loans which averaged about $1 million. *Id.* at 64, 75. Indications from the hearings are that this small number will drop even lower in the coming years. Evidence of this decline is illustrated by the fact that requested funding for FY 1971 is down $8 million from FY 1970 appropriations. *See* note 88 *supra*.

[90] Demonstration Cities and Metropolitan Development Act of 1966, 42 U.S.C. §§ 3301-13 (Supp. IV, 1969).

[91] 42 U.S.C. § 3303(a)(2) (Supp. IV, 1969).

[92] The Senate Committee report stresses that the "character and content of the program must be based on local judgment as to the cities' needs"; S. REP. No. 1,439, 89th Cong., 2d Sess. 14 (1966).

[93] *See* 42 U.S.C. § 3304 (Supp. V, 1970).

[94] *See* 42 U.S.C. § 3303(b)(1) (Supp. V, 1970).

[95] *Hearings on the Progress of the Model Cities Program Before the Subcomm. on Housing and Urban Affairs of the Senate Comm. on Banking and Currency*, 91st Cong., 1st Sess. 13 (1969).

trate and coordinate federal, state, and local public and private programs within the area.[96] *See if You Qualify* is played indirectly through restrictions imposed on the CDA, which in turn is to apply the rules to those requesting the CDA funds. Thus, recent HUD regulations indicate that to obtain Model Cities money one must play certain qualifying games.[97] One is a form of *Gotta Play with Those Guys*, where minority businessmen come under regulations which require that, normally, Model Cities funds be used in conjunction with private capital.[98] Consequently, Model Cities funds should not be used to provide loans to business enterprises in the absence of participation by other lenders or guarantors.[99] Since the local administering agency (CDA) and the local governing body (city council) must approve all projects funded by Model Cities, *Gotta Play with Those Guys* forces recipients to play with local government as well as private "partners." In a positive sense Model Cities attempts to prevent *Only One Game at a Time*. Use of funds from SBA, OEO, and EDA is encouraged.[100] The logic of Model Cities cannot be faulted, for government agencies must begin to coordinate their efforts. But, commendable as the idea is, Model Cities money cannot be used with that of the other federal program if other federal agencies will not cooperate.

Although HUD professes that major program decisions lie with local governments,[101] the Department has engaged in a spirited version of *Change the Rules* which severely restricts local initiative. It is often difficult for minority enterprises to determine what rules are in effect. For example, the recent HUD regulations on economic development only became "official" in November, 1970, while informal rules had been applied since July, 1969.[102] Previously, the area of economic development had been left to local discretion, aside from general HUD review of projects and local programs.[103] Administrators at HUD, nevertheless, did not hesitate to *Change the Rules* applicable to this program area when they desired.

---

[96] This was in accordance with the provisions set out in 42 U.S.C. § 3301 (Supp. V, 1970). The CDA was to work in conjunction with a citizen participation component, generally one elected by residents of the model neighborhood.

[97] The most recent HUD regulations were stated in HUD, CDA Letter 10c Transmittal Notice MC 3135.1 Supp. 2 (Nov. 1970) [hereinafter referred to as CDA Letter 10c].

[98] *Id.* at 3. It suggested that Model Cities funds not be used on a grant basis. Alhough these guidelines became official in November, 1970, the discussion of the Citizens Urban Opportunity Fund Program below will illustrate that these more stringent guidelines were in fact frequently used prior to that date.

[99] "Every effort shall be made to obtain the participation of private lenders in financing businesses." *Id.*

[100] *Id.*

[101] "The purpose of the Model Cities Program is to achieve, through the carrying out of plans developed by local governments and their citizens, substantial improvement in the quality of life of people living in blighted city neighborhoods." CDA Letter No. 1, at 1, Oct. 30, 1967. "Cities are encouraged to experiment with new program approaches. Each city should determine its own program emphasis. . . ." *Id.* at 2.

[102] *See* North City Area-Wide Council, Inc. v. Romney, 428 F.2d 754, 757 (3d Cir. 1970).

[103] The Secretary must determine under section 103(a) of the Act [42 U.S.C. § 3303(a)] that the program submitted by the city is eligible for funding pursuant to the criteria set forth in that section. Section 105(a) [42 U.S.C. § 3305(a) states: "The Secretary is authorized to approve comprehensive city demonstration programs if, after review of the plans, he determines that such plans satisfy the criteria . . . ."

B. Model Cities Case Studies

1. *Philadelphia*

HUD's imposition of *Gotta Play with Those Guys* and *Change the Rules* is illustrated by a recent case involving the Model Cities program in Philadelphia. In March, 1967, the city of Philadelphia applied for a planning grant from HUD for its model neighborhood in North Philadelphia. The citizen participation component of the program, the North City Area-Wide Council (AWC), was organized and funded. *Gotta Play with Those Guys* involved the city with AWC, and they jointly proceeded during the ensuing year to plan for the execution phase of the program. At the end of the planning period, on December 31, 1968, a comprehensive plan for the first year of execution of the program was submitted to HUD. The plan required $49 million, although only $25 million had been allocated by HUD for the Philadelphia program.[104] During negotiations with the city's representatives, in addition to suggesting the necessity to revise the request to fall within the targeted amount, HUD raised "concerns" because AWC, the operator of many projects in the plan, was also to evaluate its own effectiveness. HUD questioned the impartiality of evaluation under such circumstances.

A revision of the plan by the city in cooperation with AWC was made by way of a supplement sent to HUD on April 30, 1969. The supplement proposed a wide range of programs to benefit the model neighborhood which were to be implemented by the city agencies or existing private entities. The new plan also proposed that a large portion of the program be carried out by seven new nonprofit corporations, acting under contract with the city, with specific responsibilities for housing, land use, health, education, and (significant here) economic development. To enhance the citizen involvement in the corporations, a majority of the directors of four of the corporations and significant minorities for the other three were to be selected by the citizens of the model neighborhood through the AWC.

In May, 1969, HUD expressed reservations about the plan as now "supplemented" and reiterated its concern over AWC's dual involvement in the direction of the corporations and evaluation of the program. In response to the HUD objections, the city submitted a further supplementary statement to HUD on June 9, 1969, *without* the participation or approval of AWC or other residents of the model neighborhood. In that statement, the city agreed that only one-third of the directors of any corporation could be appointed by AWC, the remaining members to be appointed by organizations selected by the city with the "consultation" of AWC. The final decision was to remain with the city. The city also reserved the right to appoint such additional government representatives as directors as the city deemed appropriate.

Even this supplementary plan was apparently not sufficient for HUD, which on July 3, 1969, found the city's latest proposal "acceptable" only if (1) citizens were

---

[104] Brief for Plaintiff at 2, North City Area-Wide Council, Inc. v. Romney, Civil No. 691909 (E.D. Pa., Nov. 10, 1969).

forbidden to nominate as a director a member of AWC and, (2) after the first year, board members were selected by some method other than nomination by AWC.[105] To emphasize its desire to control these matters, HUD only approved $3 million of the $25 million, thus providing funds solely for administration activities pending resolution of the dispute. Although the city offered to continue to contract with AWC as the citizen participation component for the program, including $41,000 for AWC's monthly operating budget, AWC tried to fight HUD's tactic of *Change the Rules* and instituted the countergame, *Legal Review*. AWC's suit charged that HUD had violated its own published regulations and its statute since the Act required "widespread citizen participation" and an "emphasizing of local initiative in the planning, development and implementation" of the program.[106] AWC also asked that its funding be continued and that the city be enjoined from using HUD funds to aid any other citizen organization during the pending litigation.

The federal district court held that the Council lacked standing to maintain a legal action and that even if requisite standing existed, neither HUD nor the city had violated the regulations. On appeal the key issues before the Third Circuit were: (1) Did AWC have adequate standing to sue? (2) Were HUD's actions a legitimate exercise of departmental discretion and thereby not subject to judicial review? and (3) Were the restraints imposed upon AWC consistent with statutory emphasis and other legal precedent?

In a brief opinion[107] the court of appeals reversed the district court, holding that (1) AWC had standing to sue by virtue of the decisions in *Association of Data Processing Service Organization, Inc. v. Camp*.[108] and *Barlow v. Collins*;[109] (2) "[u]nless the language or structure of a particular statute precludes judicial review, there is a presumption that administrative action is reviewable";[110] (3) the implementation of the statute requires the constructive involvement of citizens in the model neighborhood area; and (4) the city government is responsible for seeing that the citizens are fully involved in policy making, planning, and execution of all program elements.[111] In this case neither the requirements added on June 9, 1969, nor the requirements added on July 3, 1969, involved any citizen participation.[112] The court acknowledged that a veto power in the neighborhood citizens is not necessary, as was "full citizen participation" not required for minor decisions. For major decisions which may influence the basic strategy of the program, however, consultation with

---

[105] North City Area-Wide Council, Inc. v. Romney, 482 F.2d 754, 757 (3rd Cir. 1970).
[106] 42 U.S.C. § 3303(b)(1) (Supp. V, 1970).
[107] 428 F.2d at 754.
[108] 397 U.S. 150 (1970).
[109] 397 U.S. 159 (1970).
[110] 428 F.2d at 757. The court also noted: "Moreover, the issue here does not concern, as claimed by the Government, 'agency action . . . committed to agency discretion by law.' (5 U.S.C. § 701(a)(2)). Instead, it concerns the question whether the administrative agency has conformed with the statutory requirements, and this question is a proper subject for judicial review." *Id.*
[111] *Id.* at 758.
[112] *Id.*

the citizens' group is, in the court's view, essential. Thus, the court found the unilateral actions by the city and HUD involving major modification of the program a violation of the Act. The case was remanded to the district court and hearings were held. The district court has subsequently ruled that despite the circuit court opinion, AWC would not be reinstated and the revisions would stand.[113]

From this case one may fairly question the advisability of fighting "city hall" by recourse to the countergame of *Legal Review*. AWC has been without funds since July, 1969, and the corporations have not been active or effective in the areas originally planned for them.[114] The lesson here may be that the minority businessman must acquiesce to the government's often changing rules if he expects *any* federal aid to be given. Particularly frustrating to AWC, however, was that once having adjusted to a particular set of rules, and having been successful in playing by them, the AWC found that its success in self-determination was to be denied because of the federal, not the city, bureaucracy. City revisions were clearly the direct result of HUD's refusal to approve the program until supplementary changes were made. Under a reasonable reading of the statute, HUD had limited authority to request these changes.[115] It had even less basis to make changes without regard to the procedural due process set forth in the Administrative Procedure Act which requires publication of new or revised regulations.[116] The experience of AWC, however, illustrates that the courts may be rather limited vehicles for protecting the rights of groups who are attempting to work within the system. Only if the admin-

---

[113] Opinion and Order, No. 69-1909, July 9, 1971. The district court seems to have failed to comprehend that there was a rule change by HUD, *see* note 138, *infra*; that the new rule should not be applied retroactively; and, that any changes in the city's program, even absent a change in rules, should have required consultation with the then citizen participation organization, AWC. Admittedly it was a difficult case since a finding for AWC on any of these points would require reinstating AWC and negotiations over program content. This would effectively stall the program for an additional period.

[114] Telephone interview with Austin Norris, Director of Administration, Philadelphia Model Cities Agency, Apr. 28, 1971. Of the seven proposed nonprofit corporations, only two have been organized: the Urban Education Institute and the Economic Development Corporation. The former is operative, but the latter has still to appoint its directors. The principal corporation is a section 501(c)(3), Model Cities Community Foundation. There are two related corporations in the economic development complex for the program, each with contractual relationships with the Foundation. One is the Model Cities Economic Development Corporation, which as a stock issuing corporation will be an operating arm of the Foundation. The other is an Urban Venture Capital Corporation, which is profit-making. One-half of its 200,000 shares will be purchased by the Foundation and the remainder sold to model neighborhood residents, thereby providing paid-in capital in addition to the $7 million to be made available to the Venture Capital Corporation for investment in inner-city businesses.

As a result of the law suit, Philadelphia delayed reorganization of a citizen participation component until the initial successful result in the district court. HUD funds during the interim were also limited. Sixteen local councils were organized. There was also a central body called a "Continuation Committee." At present, a 47-man Citizens Advisory Committee provides the citizen participation component for the program. In addition to two representatives from each local council, there are 15 persons appointed from the phase-out Continuation Committee. The basis for appointments of directors to the economic development corporations are apparently substantially the same as set forth in the June 9th supplementary statement to the city's Model Cities Program.

[115] *See* 42 U.S.C. § 3303(b)(1) (Supp. V, 1970).

[116] 5 U.S.C. § 552(b)(1)-(3) (Supp. II, 1967); *See also* 5 U.S.C. § 553 (Supp. II, 1967); Skoler, *Legal and Quasi-legal Considerations in New Federal Aid Programs*, 56 Geo. L.J. 1144, 1155, & n.40 (1968).

istrators of these programs feel bound by essential elements of fairness in applying and living within their rules, as well as in the process of changing such rules, can a wholesale and possibly violent challenge to our existing government be averted. When some come to realize that the government is indeed "playing games" with them, the reaction may become extreme.

There may have been valid reasons to question the potential for economic development as envisioned by the newly-created and inexperienced corporations in the Philadelphia program. But, if they constituted the agreed-upon program of the city and AWC, once having raised these doubts, the federal bureaucracy was obligated (as the circuit court determined) to abide by local decisions. In fact, difficulties with federal control of local decisions have been one of the strong arguments for some form of federal revenue sharing or bloc grants to localities.[117]

2. *Detroit*

In Detroit the effect of *Change the Rules* along with *No Mistakes Allowed* has resulted in the demise of a promising and innovative program closely related to economic development activities in the city's Model Cities program.[118] Detroit's program, Plans for Progress, called for the establishment of a Citizens Urban Opportunities Credit Bank which would provide grants, loans, and loan guarantees for various personal objectives. As set up in 1969 by contract with the city, the Citizens Urban Opportunity Fund (CUOF), as it was renamed, incorporated the concepts of "grants and loans to provide individual and community options and incentives toward self-improvement." The program was to function as a "gap-filling revenue." It was also to serve as the depository for funds to be distributed to other contractors and to handle the disbursement and accounting for such other funds. There was to be a ceiling upon grants, and variable interest was permitted on loans. In most cases recipients were given vouchers exchangeable for goods. CUOF then redeemed the vouchers from the merchant selected by the recipient. The Citizens Government Board (CGB), the citizen participation component in the Detroit program, had responsibility for the implementation of CUOF in "partnership" with the CDA.[119] They were jointly to appoint a board of directors for CUOF, selecting both public and

---

[117] "The major difficulty is that States and localities are not free to spend these funds on their own needs as they see them. The money is spent instead for things Washington wants and in the way Washington orders." Message form the President Relative to Revenue Sharing, Feb. 4, 1971, H.R. Doc. No. 92-44 at 4, 92nd Cong., 1st Sess. (1971). AWC's problems with respect to economic development activities are not uncommon in the Model Cities program. In Fresno, California, one major difficulty was the attempt to overcome SBA's *Only One Game At A Time* rule, so as to use Model Cities funds to provide the initial capital to match SBA funds for SBIC. *See* Note, *supra* note 87, at 1558, 1606 & n.86. SBA still seems to be adamant about refusing to allow flexible use of Model Cities funds along with SBA funded programs. *See* notes 27, 44 *supra*.

[118] This program, Citizens Urban Opportunities Credit Bank (as it was first known), seemed to be one of the more innovative approaches taken by Model Cities in developing new financing techniques to overcome obstacles to full opportunities for development for both individuals and organizations. *See* Hetzel & Pinsky, *The Model Cities Program*, 22 VAND. L. REV. 727, 743 (1969).

[119] COMPREHENSIVE DEMONSTRATION PROGRAM, CITY OF DETROIT, CITIZEN'S URBAN OPPORTUNITY CREDIT BANK, PROJECT DESCRIPTION 351 (1968).

private representatives for the sixteen positions. CUOF's proposed budget was for $1 million plus administrative costs, and the Fund also was disbursement agent for almost $5 million in additional program funds.[120]

Under the contract with the CDA, CUOF was to provide grants, loans, and loan guarantees "to any person or group, for any purpose, for any amount, and under any terms consistent with the provisions of this Agreement."[121] The CGB was to select four directors, one from residents in each model neighborhood sub-area, and one from each of five additional CGB standing committees that would be concerned with CUOF's operations. The other seven directors were to be appointed by existing organizations, both private and public, including a faculty member from a local law school, a member of a commercial bank, and one from the staff of the model neighborhood agency. Limits were set on grants and loans to individuals ($1500) and groups ($15,000), unless higher amounts were approved by a two-thirds vote of the directors. The contract was finally approved on February 3, 1970, with certain standard HUD provisions attached. These included the requirement that "unearned payments under the contract could be suspended or terminated upon refusal to accept additional conditions that may be imposed by HUD at any time...."[122] There were also provisions permitting the CDA to terminate for cause or, with proper notice, for convenience.

Rig the Game was also present there in the form of time delays. Seven months elapsed between the time the city approved the plan and receipt of the funds by the CDA. Another six months passed between receipt of the money by the CDA and the signing of the CUOF contract on February 3, 1970. Following the contract approval in February, intense pressure was generated to get the project operational and to distribute the funds.[123] Nationally, HUD was under criticism for the small amount of money which had actually been expended in the Model Cities program. The pressure resulted in an acceleration of CUOF's activities to get the money to the people that needed it. A foreseeable result of that process was the potential for minimal adherence to administrative procedures, and, as a result thereof, there was failure to conform to safeguards for the handling of money.

A new city administration took over in Detroit after the signing of the contract, and the necessary result was a change in CDA directors.[124] CUOF had been required to take the CDA as a partner under the contract.[125] Having adjusted to *Gotta Play with Those Guys* for one CDA staff, CUOF was required to readjust and accept

---

[120] *Id.* at 55.
[121] Contract, City of Detroit Model Neighborhood Agency and CUOF, Inc., at 1(b), Scope of Services 1. (Feb. 3, 1970) [hereinafter referred to as CUOF Contract].
[122] Model Cities Administration, Supplementary General Conditions for Contracts with Operating Agencies and Contractor (Incorporated by reference into CUOF Contract, Part I, 6, 2), MCGR 3100.8 Appendix 6, page 2 (July 1969).
[123] Detroit News, Sept. 27, 1970, § B, at 6; Detroit Free Press, June 15, 1970, § A, at 3.
[124] With election of a new mayor, the resignation of the CDA Director was accepted. A new Director was appointed and took over about February, 1970.
[125] CUOF Contract, *supra* note 121, at 1.

new personnel from its required partner. The necessary adjustment, as it turns out, was unsuccessful. The new director for the CDA imposed tight administrative control of the program.[126] According to some reports, he evidenced concern over the operation of CUOF.[127] Then came the same *Change the Rules* problem which AWC experienced in Philadelphia.

Although discussions apparently were initiated between the CDA and HUD as early as August, 1970,[128] on September 21, 1970, a memorandum from HUD the Regional Office in Chicago enunciated certain conditions for continued requisitions of funds to CUOF. In brief HUD's concerns were:

> "(1) CUOF seemed to have been making only grants and needed to develop some ratio of grants to loans consistent with the understanding HUD thought it had with the CDA some eighteen months earlier;
> (2) some grants had gone to members of the board of directors, which HUD implied created possible conflicts of interests;
> (3) some of the grants seemed to be for purposes other than those for which CUOF had authority;
> (4) adequate reports on the use of the funds had not been provided the CDA and HUD."[129]

On the same day the CDA director set forth additional requirements in a letter to CUOF:

> The membership of the Board of Directors must conform to a July 29, 1970 "statement of policy" which was "promulgated" by HUD which restricts CGB members from serving on the CUOF Board and reduces the number who may be appointed by the CGB to CUOF.[130]

At the same time, this letter affirmed a unlilateral CDA reduction of $750,000 in the grant amount to CUOF, purportedly made in August, 1970.

From the above commentary by HUD and the CDA (and it is not clear whether the federal response was at the request of the CDA or vice-versa) both seemed to have imposed, along with appropriate requests for a firming-up of CUOF procedures, new requirements which had not been agreed to by CUOF. As in the situation faced by AWC, basic changes in the board of directors of CUOF were to be required without any federal issuance of formal regulations. Moreover, these requirements were clearly contrary to the specific provisions of the CUOF contract with the CDA.[131] After attempts at negotiation, including a proposed agreement of

---

[126] *See* sources cited in note 123 *supra*.
[127] *Id*.
[128] *Id*.
[129] Memorandum from Alan Goldfarb, Regional Administrator to Sylvester Angel, Jr., CDA Director, Sept. 21, 1970.
[130] Letter from Sylvester Angel, Jr. to Ralph Richardson, Sept. 21, 1970. It should be noted that the only policy statement "promulgated" by HUD was CDA Letter 10c, which was not issued until November, 1970.
[131] CUOF Contract, *supra* note 121.

understanding which seemed to resolve almost every issue,[132] CUOF went to court to prevent the CDA cut-off of funds.[133] Disbursements were halted both by the CDA and temporarily by the court. Attempts were then made by the CDA to go through CUOF's transactions, and CUOF acceded to these requests. Based upon a superficial examination of the books and review of some transactions, the CDA went before the City Council to ask termination of the contract with CUOF.[134] The CDA director, however, failed to present any evidence of impropriety before the Council, and it refused to terminate the contract.[135] The investigation by the city of CUOF's books and records, nevertheless, continued. The CDA again went before the Council with some tentative audit findings. After heated debate and a threat by HUD to cut off all Model Cities funds to Detroit, the Council voted five to four to terminate the contract.[136]

It should be noted that by the time that the September HUD memorandum came, CUOF had been operating only six months under contract and had been actually issuing funds for only two of those months. Thus, the CDA and HUD pressure were illustrative of the game *No Mistakes Allowed*. It is difficult to see why the CDA and HUD instead could not have halted funds for CUOF and required a revision of procedures sufficient to assure that funds were not used improperly. The agreement proposed by CUOF during negotiations on September 24, 1970, was sufficient to have assured this result. In that proposal CUOF offered to establish a policy for loan-grant ratios, although it had no knowledge of any agreement between HUD and the CDA in that regard. Second, pending resolution of the conflict of interest issue raised by HUD, CUOF offered to abide by the federal interpretation. With respect to the purposes for which loans or grants could be made, CUOF offered to review such criteria with the CDA and HUD, although it had thought that under its contract with the city the type of loans or grants were in its sole discretion. Finally, CUOF agreed to a review of certain grants it had made. It further agreed to limit for the present its expenditures of funds to one-half of the original amount set forth in the contract, $500,000. The question of the composition of the board of directors was left to negotiation between the CGB and the CDA.[137]

These offers seem reasonable and perhaps would have resolved many of the deficiencies which concerned HUD. From all of the circumstances, CUOF concluded that the issue of citizen control seemed central in the dispute.[138] In part, that

---

[132] Agreement of Understanding Between CUOF and MNA, Sept. 24, 1970. See also Detroit News, *supra* note 123, at 6-B.

[133] CUOF v. City of Detroit, et al., Civ. No. 165676 (Cir. Ct. Wayne County, Mich., Sept. 22, 1970).

[134] Detroit News, *supra* note 123. This must have seemed to CUOF like bad faith since the ostensible purpose of the review was to determine what had occurred and what changes were needed, not to provide a basis to terminate the program.

[135] Detroit News, Oct. 5, 1970, at 1.

[136] Detroit Free Press, Oct. 30, 1970, at 2.

[137] Agreement of Understanding, *supra* note 132. Over $330,000 had been committed at that time.

[138] Detroit News, *supra* note 123. The CDA was seemingly only reflecting the change in policy of HUD. In an address on July 8, 1969, Robert Baida, the Deputy Assistant Secretary, Model Cities Administration, said: "Unfortunately, this administration inherited a philosophy in many areas of the country

conclusion is reinforced by the recourse of HUD and CDA to the game *No Mistakes Allowed*. This game effectively prevented CUOF from making the necessary adjustments so that it could proceed in a more orderly fashion. Conceding that mistakes had been made, the failure by the CDA and HUD to permit reorganization seemed to CUOF to reflect the policy change toward limiting citizen participation in the Model Cities program which had been made in Washington with the change of administrations.

The difficulty was not the change in policy, so much as the way in which the change was handled. Admittedly, the initial HUD regulations were not necessarily a full recitation of HUD's authority to set the role of citizens and their control of operating agencies for Model Cities projects. Nevertheless, there was a failure to accord any consideration to outstanding contract commitments (of which HUD had notice) and an attempt at *ex post facto* imposition of the new policy. Moreover, this was done prior to issuance of the new regulations. This type of agency action was described in the article, *The New Sovereign Immunity*,[139] where it was characterized as "sovereign lawlessness."[140] That article also documents similar action taken by the government in one of the OEO programs. In that case also the game of *No Mistakes Allowed* was played to a similar conclusion for the recipient of the federal funds.[141]

The analogy to *ex post facto* imposition of new regulations seems appropriate here since it was not until November, 1970, that HUD formally issued its regulations. Even then, they were not published in the *Federal Register* as is arguably required by the Administrative Procedure Act.[142] Although the Model Cities program is relatively new and still developing, significant changes in policy should not be arbitrarily or informally imposed. This is the clear import of that part of the decision in *North City Area-Wide Council v. Romney*[143] in which the court comments that the Secretary acted illegally in imposing additional significant terms of his own without citizen consultation.[144]

Where there are existing contracts setting forth the rights and obligations of the grantee city and sub-recipient CUOF, these provisions are subject to a yearly review and could be revised or terminated at that time. The contract should not be abrogated at the whim of the administering federal agency. This is not to say, however, that changes in policy and procedures should not be made—especially where they may reflect additional wisdom in administering complex and novel programs. What it does imply is that due process must be followed in making such changes. In

---

dedicated toward extensive citizen control. Because of this, many first and second round cities are in difficulty with their programs, and in some cases we have found it necessary to require substantial revisions prior to the tender of planning or execution contracts."

[139] Cahn & Cahn, *The New Sovereign Immunity*, 81 HARV. L. REV. 929 (1968).
[140] *Id.* at 930.
[141] *Id.* at 930-34.
[142] *See* note 114 *supra*. The concept of due process of law would seem to require no less.
[143] 428 F.2d 754 (3d Cir. 1970).
[144] *Id.* at 758.

addition, in keeping with the innovative spirit of the program, the operators of projects should be counseled concerning their decisions, but allowed to make their own mistakes. It is totally unrealistic to expect either perfection or immediate success from newly developing corporations. Given the lack of effectiveness of most existing efforts, new institutions responsive to self-determination needs are required, and it is certainly not clear that all wisdom lies in Washington concerning the development of local projects.

A final word should be uttered concerning the November, 1970, regulations. They clearly involve the imposition of some of the games similar to those played by other federal funding agencies. For instance, they require that grants not be used to finance a business[145] (*Gotta Bring Your Own Ball*); that there normally be participation by private lenders or guarantors before HUD funds are loaned[146] (*Gotta Play with Those Guys*); and that for new corporations no more than one-third of the directors be selected by the citizen participation component[147] (*Change the Rules*). Other regulations contain restrictions on more than one member of CGB-type boards serving on the new corporations' boards of directors.[148]

Clearly some rules are needed to give direction to the economic development aspects of the program. It is also apparent that waiver of these rules is possible in appropriate circumstances.[149] These Model Cities rules are much less restrictive than those of other federal programs. Unfortunately, however, there is insufficient recognition of the potential of flexibility in providing venture capital for economic development activities. Such flexibility seems not only consistent with but mandated by a bloc grant program such as Model Cities. But the critical need is for venture capital to start businesses. If controls are to be imposed, they should be related to the capacity and potential of the minority entrepreneur development organization. Due regard should be given to the need to provide appropriate technical assistance to assure the best opportunity for the enterprise to succeed. Most loans involved here are essentially grants, given the high potential for failure.[150] There seems little reason to hold *two* Swords of Damocles over the minority businessman's head. Failure itself should be enough without the threat of long term debt or the need for recourse to bankruptcy. If there is to be risk, the government is in the best position to assume it. The regulations should not be there so much to protect the money as to try to assure that the endeavor has the optimum potential for success. If any measuring standard is to be used, it should be this one.

---

[145] CDA Letter 10c, *supra* note 97, at 3.
[146] *Id.*
[147] *Id.* at 6.
[148] HUD, CDA Letter 10d, MC3135.1 Supp. 3 (Nov. 1970).
[149] The Deputy Assistant Secretary of the Model Cities Administration indicated some flexibility by stating that use of existing corporations was required, "except in unusual cases." Baida, *supra* note 138.
[150] Because chances for repayment of high risk, inner-city business or personal loans are often not great, such loans should be viewed as grants. One might wonder about why there was so much concern expressed in CDA Letter 10c and in the CUOF case over use of grants rather than loans.

Conclusion

The referencing of various federal rules and regulations to a series of games should not prevent recognition of the necessity for appropriate controls over use of federal funds for minority economic development. Since funds are limited and their utilization should maximize their effectiveness, recipients should evidence a reasonable possibility of success in the endeavor to be undertaken. Projects should be feasible, reasonable documentation of the use of funds should be required, and technical assistance should be available from both the public and the private sector. What has evolved for most programs, however, is a set of restrictions which have become so complex that they do not function as controls but take the appearance of a succession of games to be imposed upon the intended beneficiaries.

There are understandable reasons for the development of the mass of constraints which are applied to these programs. Perhaps the primary one stems from the fear of reaction by Congress when exercising its oversight function, particularly by the applicable appropriations subcommittees. Presentations to these committees for continuation of program funding often emphasize criteria insufficiently related to the purpose for which the legislation was enacted. In its appropriate overseer's role, moreover, Congress is especially sensitive to misapplication and malfeasance regarding these funds. Since most programs have had limited success, Congressional expectations for program effectiveness are not high. Therefore, mismanagement (in terms of legislative objectives), inefficiency, delay, and ineffectiveness are seemingly only of secondary concern to Congress. New criteria should be considered when reporting to Congress—those which have some tangible relationship to program objectives. Many of these are high-risk programs, a fact which should be clearly and openly stated to these subcommittees. Success should be measured by the number of opportunities provided rather than the number of safe loans made. Similarly, an honest estimate of the lead-time necessary before attempting to measure success should be the rule, not the exception, in testimony before committees. As thus described, the problem is one which must be mutually ascribed to Congress and the agency administrators. In the last analysis, however, the administrators can do much to sway the congressional attitudes if they take forthright positions concerning necessary changes.

There is a related cause of much of the recourse to gamesmanship in the executive branch, often denoted as "bureaucratic tendencies." Success is measured by not making mistakes, by delaying decisions, by recourse to the private sector to make the determination, and by careful, extended consultation to spread the risk of failure. Such problems are endemic to bureaucracies generally and are not limited solely to economic development programs.

The majority of these economic development programs are administered locally. It is fitting that responsibility for the program should be placed on those persons at the local level who must operate it. Advice and counseling should be provided, but success in development activities can be built in only if local administrators and minority businessmen are allowed more freedom. In most circumstances, the federal administrator *may* delegate responsibility to the recipients of the funds. In effect, Congress has asked that program administrators force "the horse to drink," whereas, it should be sufficient if they simply "bring him to the water."

Inherent in the enactment of all of these federal programs is the fact that the private sector has not been able to revive the depressed economic condition of the inner cities. There seems little to be gained by *forcing* private involvement. If there must be budgetary "tactics," a 100 per cent guarantee along with a small incentive fee should serve that purpose, while placing the risk with the government, which in the final analysis is the only body which can and should take it. By acknowledging this role and proceeding to make the effort as successful as possible, the government can obviate, or at least reduce, the elaborate system of games that now exists.

At a minimum, the following list of rather simplified recommendations should be considered in testing the appropriateness of program requirements:

(1) controls should relate to increasing opportunities for participation and success, not solely to safeguarding funds;
(2) mistakes should be permitted and assistance in correcting them should be provided (the government makes many of them);
(3) minority businessmen should be allowed independence and not be forced to take "partners" unnecessarily;
(4) sufficient funds to permit success should be provided if financial support is given;
(5) quantum changes should not be expected overnight;
(6) success in administration of programs should be judged on the effectiveness the program has had in accomplishing statutory objectives;
(7) persons who administer programs should where possible have applicable experience (perhaps the best use of the SBA SCORE program would be to advise the SBA administrators first, and applicants second);
(8) an applicant for financial assistance should be judged on his capacity, not on the amount of funds he has accumulated to date;
(9) the number of reviews (and resulting delays) should be drastically reduced by reliance on post-audit procedures;
(10) where the rules must be changed, proper procedures should be used and the changes applied prospectively;
(11) flexible use of funds (including pyramiding of support) should be possible; **and**
(12) the government should be the risk-taker of last resort.

A TAXPAYER'S CHOICE INCENTIVE SYSTEM: AN EXPERIMENTAL APPROACH TO COMMUNITY ECONOMIC DEVELOPMENT TAX INCENTIVES

ROBERT S. ROBIN*

I

THE TAX INCENTIVE DEVICE IN THE POVERTY CONTEXT

There is currently no reliable evidence of the value or the cost of any community economic development tax incentive, and because of this, it seems preferable to experiment with broadly applicable tax devices before enacting or even proposing legislation. Any one-track tax incentive system which benefits only a narrow band of businesses will not produce a wide reception among those whose diverse needs are not covered by it.[1] Broad participation in an actual or simulated program can be obtained, however, under a tax incentive system which, within an overall limit, permits individual businesses to select a mixture of tax benefits which matches the demands of the operation involved. A multi-track, taxpayer-choice incentive system may become more narrow as facts are developed relating to taxpayer-use frequency, economic results, and government costs, but breadth and scope are needed initially in any experimental system to induce use of it. Actual simulation of highly experimental tax incentives is one way to create businesses and jobs in ghettos. And it is the only way to produce evidence of which tax incentives, if any, helped or hindered the effort.

One factor which forces experimentation rather than legislation is the realization that no one, in or out of government, can develop a factual case supporting the value or the cost of *any* poverty area tax incentive. Community economic development tax incentives are a new, strange, and misunderstood phenomenon. No one really knows what to expect of them because they have never been used in this country before.[2] Indeed, such incentives must draw business into ghettos in the first place, a task not normally assigned to such devices.[3] Because these kinds of incentives

---

* [The author, one of the draftsmen of the tax sections of the Community Self-Determination Act of 1968, is engaged in the private practice of law in Chicago.—Ed.]

[1] Part II of this article provides an example of how a one-channel tax incentive system can provide significant tax benefits but illustrates that these are available only to a taxpayer willing to sell his facility to a community corporation. Such a program dictates the types of businesses to be provided to ghettos and the methods of providing them and is precisely the type of narrow program to be avoided.

[2] Such tax incentives have been used extensively by numerous developing nations overseas. *See* Robin, *Developing Nations Eager for U.S. Investors*, J. COMMERCE, March 2, 1964. Some principles of foreign economic development tax incentives were utilized in the preparation of the tax incentives discussed here and those which were part of the Community Self-Determination Act of 1968.

[3] Several companies, such as IBM, Eastman Kodak, and Mattel Toys, have tried ghetto operations in the past two or three years. However, the ghetto operations of some companies have special support in terms of loans, guarantees, out-put contracts, and gifts of senior managerial talent. The creation and continued sponsorship of such ghetto operations, although laudible, cannot be regarded as motivated by normal hard-nosed business considerations.

are new and strange, there is considerable difficulty in thinking clearly about them, and this is the reason why no one, especially in government, can produce enough of an illusion of certainty about their effect and their cost to justify proposing a definite incentive program to Congress.

Rather than wasting another three years waiting for nothing to happen,[4] it is time to recognize that the government has three choices with respect to poverty area tax incentives: (*a*) it can forget about them; (*b*) it can recognize that no one has the evidence necessary to soundly predict the value to the taxpayer or the cost to the government of any incentive, but ask for tax legislation anyway (and let all parties wink at the absence of facts); or (*c*) it can recognize that no one has the facts and say so, but proceed with a more pragmatic search for a solution through tax legislation simulation. The purpose of this article is to explore this last alternative.

This new approach should include a realization that the purpose of any incentive is to change a taxpayer's mind about the financial attractiveness of a particular activity. Thus, it is necessary to discover what risks bother him, and to attempt to quantify those risks as he would. Instead of asking for tax legislation without examining what incentive might induce a change of mind, the government should actually simulate the incentives by cash payments which allow each cooperating taxpayer to choose the incentives he thinks best for him. This approach should provide a basis for determining which tax incentives, if any, provide the necessary conditions and inducements to persuade a businessman to bring his capital, know-how, and jobs to the poor. Then, if an incentive, or a group of them, actually produced desired action at a sensible cost, legislation should be proposed. Evidence of the workability of the incentive should be convincing to Congress.

The first step toward clearing up present misunderstandings is to start over again and ask the right questions. The traditional governmental approach to economic development tax incentives by-passes the right questions about taxpayer motivation and substitutes assumptions instead. The doctrinaire government tax specialist, a "hard line Revenuer," unencumbered by the facts as he is, adopts the silent assumption that any tax incentive automatically provides a taxpayer with a sufficiently increased chance for profit to justify his acceptance of any and all other risks, whatever they may be. With that proposition firmly established (resting, as it does, on "all taxpayers are crybabies" theory), our man in Washington further assumes the maximum use of the incentive by the broadest class of potentially eligible taxpayers (which in our case means every sizeable business in the country plus a few nasty promoters. Reliance on these unstated perceptions causes planners to miss completely the issue of taxpayer motivation. Moreover, these perceptions result in an overstatement of the cost of poverty area tax incentives to the government. It is especially unfortunate that reliance on an unspoken faulty assumption not only smothers the problem, but also loads the answer to the wrong question.

---

[4] Nothing has been proposed since August, 1968.

These assumptions do not surface in the intense discussions, in and out of government, relating to tax incentives. But the term "cost effectiveness" always does. The phrase "cost effectiveness" is designed to raise the issue of whether the government will receive what it regards as effective action in exchange for the loss of tax revenues resulting from enactment of a particular incentive. Calculation of the loss of tax revenues must be based on some judgment of how much less money taxpayers will be paying because of their use of a tax incentive. Sometimes this issue is analyzed. Often it is not. Often it does not have to be. In business operations in which the Treasury or the Internal Revenue Service has years of experience, a sensible estimate of the dollar amount of noncollected taxes resulting from the use of an incentive by taxpayers can be made. However, in the unexplored area of private sector ghetto operations, no one, in or out of government, can provide real evidence of which tax incentives will be accepted and used. Indeed, no one knows for sure what the extra risks will be, and *a fortiori*, no one can determine the costs to be cut (by whatever legislative mechanic) in order to provide the possibility of a profit. Because these answers are unavailable, the right question, at this stage, is not and cannot be "cost effectiveness." The right questions are whether and to what extent tax incentives will be used by taxpayers.

In order to forecast the dollar cost of those tax incentives which will encourage a taxpayer to act, one must understand why a taxpayer is not now acting. Government must understand the risks perceived by business if government is to exercise effectively its power to (1) reduce risks or (2) trade tax benefits for acceptance of unmeasurable risks. Government action, whether by legislation or experimental simulation, is useless if it does not deal directly with the pitfalls which businessmen actually see or think they see in the undertaking of an untried and unwanted project.

It must be accepted that the taxpayer for whom the incentives are to be designed presently sees very little business reason for locating his plant in the ghetto or for hiring the untrained. The raw economics of running most profitable businesses simply does not justify ghetto operations. A plant put in a ghetto is subject to more risks than one located elsewhere. Employment of a large group of the hard-core unemployed is thought to subject a business to more risks and costs than it faced previously. And as of now, such increased risks are not matched by the possibility of profit. Moreover, several of the substantial risks are not of a business nature and, thus, are harder to measure. This means that the corporate and professional experts who specialize in risk measurement and profit potential projections are not equipped with the skills or experience required to forecast a dollar exposure or profit return on a ghetto investment. When a corporate board of directors reviews any business plan, it is the risks which they see. Thus, when a ghetto business plan is reviewed, a board will want to know its risk potential. What will be obvious to the board and what will cripple any chance of approval of a scheme is the absence of a dollar exposure forecast based on experience. To such a board, approval of a ghetto business or employment plan would be tantamount to signing a blank check. No businessman will do this. Businessmen want as much certainty as possible. They will take risks if they can measure those risks. But they will not spend money—even if they will get part of it back from the government—without some idea of whether the spending will produce profits.

Although incentives can be created to meet a variety of circumstances, the perceived risks which presently inhibit action by the private sector in the poverty area seem to be common to most types of businesses. A businessman, in the privacy of his own office, might analyze the risks he sees or thinks he sees this way:

"1. If I put hard-core employees in my plant, I must set up, and pay for, special facilities to train them. I can get all the workers I need now to perform the functions which the hard-core employees *might* be able to perform after training, so I see no reason to spend the extra money to assure myself of a supply of employees I don't presently require.

"2. By introducing such a group of employees into my plant, I risk the hostility of other employees on all levels. I create labor union representation problems, and, at worst, I may be confronted with protection and violence problems.

"3. If I put my plant in a ghetto, there is the risk that it will be burned down or become a pawn in a political or social dispute. The issues which can trigger such events are not business issues and thus I have no control over them nor do I have any expertise in my organization to deal with them. I cannot buy insurance to cover any such catastrophy. I don't want the publicity which would derive from such a situation or the controversy leading up to it. And besides all of that, there is no business reason for my plant to be in the ghetto in the first place.

"4. If, despite all the foregoing problems, I would still be willing to undertake such tasks, I cannot get anyone in my already thinned-out middle management level to take charge of a training program or a ghetto plant because he will feel he is sidetracked from his main career, which is moving up in the mainstream of this company.

"5. I can discharge my responsibilities to the poor with much more facility and with no intereference in the operation of my business by making a charitable contribution to some foundation which does what it can. This will enable me to say 'I gave at the office.'"

Can fiscal incentives be developed to overcome these risks and difficulties which the taxpayer sees as inherent in transferring jobs, facilities, and know-how to an underdeveloped community? They can be, if initially we understand the substance of tax incentives, the necessity for a system of incentives (and why one or two big ones won't work), and the manner in which a taxpayer looks at an incentive package. With this understanding, one will conclude that there are a lot of different ways to get the job done.

When the technical convolutions of the tax code are stripped away, it appears that there are only two types of tax "breaks" available: tax deferral or tax forgiveness. Tax deferral means that the taxpayer pays the same amount of tax he otherwise would have to pay, but the payment of all or part of the tax is postponed until a future time. The time to which payment is postponed is supposedly tied to an event which will produce cash, thus making it easier to pay. That event is usually the sale of something which presumably will produce cash to pay the taxes which, but for the incentive, should have been paid earlier. The event which triggers the payment of postponed tax can be almost anything. It can even be some date in the future at which nothing actually happens, but by which time something might have happened. In other situations, the event is merely the passing of a determinable period. Tax forgiveness, on the other hand, is just that; the taxpayer is relieved of an obligation to pay particular taxes.

Of course, it is not all that easy. Tax deferral or tax forgiveness or a combination of the two principal tax incentives are always set in a complex structure of technical requirements designed to limit the cases to which the incentive can apply and thereby prevent abuses. It is with respect to these technical rules that a draftsman has great flexibility to tune and tinker the tax incentives to accomplish his objectives and to minimize the risks perceived by the taxpayer.

What kinds of tax incentives can produce the desired action? The answer to this question requires consideration of the twin issues of how large a single incentive must be to motivate taxpayer action and whether an incentive of the requisite size is too large to be passed by Congress. For example, there has been much talk of a tax credit (partial tax forgiveness) which is geared to wages paid by companies to train undereducated employees. The credit stops when employees reach the level at which they can function on the production line, whenever that is. The cost of the extra training is said to be about $3,000 per hard-core unemployed worker. Further, the turnover rate is said to be 50% higher than normal for hard-core factory labor. As discussed in detail later, extra costs over the first three years of extra training and recruitment for a 120 man work force, half of whom are hard-core unemployed, is $396,000. A 10% tax credit yields an actual annual cash savings of $39,600. This is hardly enough to motivate management to set up a program which trains workers they think they can do without and which exposes the company to extra risks which it feels it cannot handle. A tax credit of significantly more than 10%, *by itself*, would hardly have a chance of becoming law. And a tax credit of 10% (even one which does not distinguish between training and productive time and which thus eliminates the inevitable Internal Revenue Service bargaining audit) would not be used by a taxpayer because it is not big enough. Thus, dead ends will always exist at both the enactment level and the taxpayer-use level if single tax incentives, even good ones, are considered by themselves. These impediments are avoided by a tax incentives package which has a chance of both being enacted and being used.

Development of a tax incentive system for actual use will mean that a taxpayer also has some work to do. He must guess as to the likelihood of the occurrence of events which trigger tax savings, identify and quantify extra risks, add up his extra costs resulting from extra risks, compare the profit producable by those costs to the extra tax savings, isolate the nonbusiness open-ended exposures, and see if it all makes sense. The fact that he will have to make all these judgments and assume the risk of the occurrence of tax-significant events will *not* stop him. Indeed, this is the basis of all tax planning. For example, if a taxpayer buys a building and takes accelerated depreciation, he knows now that at a particular point in the future, the depreciation deduction will run out and his cash flow costs will increase because, at that future time, he will have used up his depreciation allowance. He knows that he will have to sell the building nine or ten years from now or start investing cash to make up for the tax benefits which have run out. Or, he will have to buy another building and take fast depreciation on it to make up for the loss of depreciation on the first building he bought. At the time he undertakes the plan, he knows that he is on the depreciation treadmill and that the whole structure will fall apart if he does not buy a second building or sell the first one in time. Thus, an analysis involving prediction of facts and events in order to analyze a tax package is nothing new. This is precisely how sophisticated taxpayers think. This is the way tax incentives should be created because this is the way tax incentives will be used, if used at all.

II

How a Taxpayer Quantifies Risks and Determines the Value of Tax Incentives Designed to Share Those Risks

In 1968, the Community Self-Determination Act was jointly introduced in the House and Senate.[5] Buried in that legislation was a set of tax incentives, part of which applied to community corporations and part of which applied to outside companies. The outside company was the established business which had jobs to give, had a plant to locate in the ghetto, had the know-how to do both, and of equal importance, had the experts who could try to advise it of the consequences. The policy decision behind the Act was that the outside company should set up the plant, provide the training and the jobs, and then *sell* the plant to a community corporation which was to be a "neighborhood conglomerate" designed eventually to own businesses. The Act set up this institutional acquiring entity owned by the "people," provided funds to make such acquisitions possible, and gave the outside company a package of tax incentives which would offset all the risks if the plant were successful and if the plant were actually sold. The key tax breaks, those which would provide most of the cash to make the outside company whole and give it a profit on its risky investment, were tied to the sale of the plant.

---

[5] S. 3875, 90th Cong., 2d Sess. (1968).

Naturally, a complex statutory "infrastructure" was thought to be required to make this program work: (1) each poor man was to own a piece of all the companies eventually purchased—hence the "community corporation"; (2) the poor were to be provided enough money to buy the plants—hence "community economic development banks" and nationwide government guaranteed bond issues; and (3) with all this money and power, measures were to be taken to prevent abuses—hence ninety per cent of the Act. Enactment of the whole institutional framework seems unlikely, at least for now. However, some of the tax incentives designed to benefit the outside company will be considered here because the program illustrates how a taxpayer assesses the value of an untried tax package in an unexplored area of business activity.

In order to quantify the risks perceived by the taxpayer and, at the same time, examine tax mechanics designed to share some of those risks, this section of the artcile will examine the actual dollar impact of the incentives on the taxpayer for the purpose of determining how he will fare if he enters the poverty business. Also considered is the issue of whether a tax incentive program in which the tax break is tied to the sale of a successful business will work without an elaborate "infrastructure." In part III of this article, the focus is whether there are events other than the sale of a business to which tax benefits can be tied in order to attract taxpayers who are *not* willing to sell their plants.

Assessment of the dollar impact of a tax incentive package which contemplates eventual sale of a facility to a poor community necessitates a discussion of several interrelated tax benefits, which, although individually insufficient, produce a substantial return in the aggregate. The tax program of the Community Self-Determination Act, stripped of much of its infrastructure, sets up these incentives:

1. Physical plant facilities will be permitted rapid tax amortization depending upon the degree to which the community is underdeveloped. If some development index indicates that the community is at the maximum level of economic underdevelopment, physical facilties *including* real estate may be amortized in as short a time as thirty-six months.

2. The old investment tax credit relating to certain machinery and equipment will be resurrected. There will, however, be no tax credit recapture upon the sale of a facility to a "community group."

3. An additional tax credit, called the human investment tax credit, will be available in an amount equal to ten per cent of the wages and salaries paid by the taxpayer to employees. No distinction is to be drawn between training and production activities of such employees for purposes of utilizing this credit.

4. The profits received by the taxpayer upon the sale of a factility to the "community" are normally subject to a capital gain tax. Such capital gains tax would not then be payable so long as and to the extent the proceeds of the sale are reinvested in another similar operation or in low interest-bearing deposits in a bank

which provides extremely liberal financing to poor communities, including financing to the "community" to buy the facility.

5. Upon the occurrence of a sale of a facility, there will be no recapture of rapid amortization benefits, investment tax credits, or human investment tax credits so long as and to the extent the profits of the sale are reinvested in another similar project or in special bank deposits.

6. Following the sale of the facility to the "community," the taxpayer-seller will receive a sustained profitability tax credit which is equal to fifteen per cent of the profits generated from the operation of the facility for each of five years *after* sale.

Prior to any sale, a plant engaged in ghetto operations will be owned by a taxpayer who, it is assumed, will have other income. A taxpayer having other income will thus be able to utilize the tax benefits accruing prior to the sale without regard to the profitability of the facility. The rapid amortization deduction, the resurrected investment tax credit, and the new human investment tax credit—all of which operate prior to a sale of the facility—can be applied by the taxpayer against its taxable income from other sources. Carry-forward and carry-back provisions enable complete utilization of these tax benefits by the taxpayer. The question in the taxpayer's mind is what all these benefits are worth in hard dollars.

A specific example will illustrate the operation of these provisions.

In calculating dollar savings to the taxpayer, a conservative view has been taken. As indicated, tax savings take two forms. First, there is tax forgiveness through the tax credit mechanism. In this case, dollar savings are calculated as the gross amount of tax forgiven. Second, there is deferral of the collection of taxes which is achieved either by permitting accelerated deductibility or by actually delaying collection of a tax. The savings from tax deferral is calculated at seven per cent of the amount deferred. This represents either the interest charge the taxpayer would incur if he had to borrow the money to pay the deferred taxes or, if he has the money available, the interest he would earn if invested for the period of deferment.

A particular type of die casting plant can be started for approximately $600,000. If and when profitable, it will produce pre-tax earnings of $300,000 on gross sales of approximately $4,000,000. Direct labor costs will run about $300,000 per year in the casting operation, foremen's salaries will run approximately $135,000, and indirect labor costs will be about $155,000. Depreciable assets comprising the physical facility will have a cost basis of approximately $200,000, representing approximately $100,000 in equipment and $100,000 in real estate.

Several assumptions are necessary: the plant becomes a "community" facility; the outside company which owns and operates the plant has other income and files a consolidated return and, thus, can utilize all special tax benefits available to it; and the community in which the facility is to be located is in the lowest level of economic development, thus entitling the taxpayer to the maximum tax benefits to be provided. What do the tax provisions yield in saved dollars to the taxpayer?

Rapid amortization within 36 months of real estate and equipment (total $200,000) will produce annual deductions to the taxpayer of $66,666 for each of three years. The resurrected investment tax credit of 7% applicable to section 38 property[6] will apply to the equipment in the plant ($100,000), yielding a direct credit against taxes payable by the taxpayer in the amount of $7,000. The human investment tax credit will apply to the wages of those persons in the facility. Assuming that *only* one-half of the combined direct and indirect non-administrative wages are paid to qualified employees, a first level calculation will produce a human investment tax credit of $29,500 (10% of one-half of the sum of $300,000 and $135,000 and $155,000). If it is assumed that an annual limitation of $25,000 is applicable to such tax credit, the maximum human investment tax credit for one taxable year of operations will be $25,000 plus 50% of the excess, or a total of $27,250. The $2,250 unused excess credit for each year is not lost; it can be carried back three years or forward seven years.

Assuming consistent levels of employment and equipment utilization, the above tax deduction and credit calculations apply to each of the first three years of full operation of the facility. The savings to the taxpayer who has other income sufficient to permit full utilization of is as follows:

(1) The annual rapid amortization deduction is $66,666. The provision speeds up the deductibility of a fixed amount, but does not increase the amount deductible. The benefit is basically one of cash flow in early years. The greater the amount deductible, the less cash will be needed to pay taxes. And at the very least, fewer dollars will be needed to cover the cost of borrowing money to pay taxes, or, if cash is available, more dollars will be earned upon investment. It should be recognized that the amount of "normal" depreciation deductions vary according to the type of asset depreciated. Likewise, land value, as such, is not depreciable. However, in order to facilitate illustration, it will be assumed that there is a combined plant and equipment life of ten years and that the amount of the yearly deduction does not vary. Under these assumptions, the normal available deduction for each of ten years would be $20,000. On the other hand, the casting plant established under the Act may be depreciated over three years, thereby producing an extra deduction of $46,666 per year for each of the first three years. Assuming total elimination of the surtax and one surtax exemption utilized to cover other income, the tax rate is 48%. The tax due on $46,666 is $22,400. It is collection of this tax which is deferred to the future. When calculated at 7%, the minimum dollar value of not having to pay this amount is $1570 per year for each of three years.

(2) The investment tax credit is $7,000. This is available in only one year, but is not subject to eventual recapture. The human investment tax credit, which is enjoyed annually, is $27,250. An unused portion to the extent of $2,250 may be carried forward.

Thus, the savings during the first year is $35,820. The second and third years

---

[6] INT. REV. CODE of 1954, § 38.

yield a net dollar saving of $28,820, or a total, over three years, of $93,460. It should be emphasized that the minimum savings of $93,460 over three years is enjoyed by the taxpayer irrespective of whether the facility is profitable. The $600,000 investment required for the project can be highly leveraged by long term borrowings. The annual benefits, except for rapid amortization, continue to accrue to the taxpayer prior to sale.

Now assume that the facility is sold in the fourth year of operations and that the encouraged transplantation of know-how has been effective so that the facility earns a profit in the fourth year of *half* of its full profit potential—$150,000 before taxes. The tax rate for year four is 48% less one surtax exemption. The computation includes the tax payable upon income *not* matched by a depreciation deduction because all depreciation deductions were utilized in the first three years. At this point, a tax of $75,100 is owing. The amount of net after-tax cash retained by the taxpayer is $74,900, representing after-tax profit and depreciation adjustments.

The facility may be sold to any community group within the statutory definition on any basis which the parties are able to negotiate. Assume a classical earnings-multiple sale price formula is applied and that the multiple for this facility is 10. A critical issue is whether the specially reduced post-tax earnings of the facility which applies once the plant is in the hands of the community should be used in calculating the sale price. Normally, the multiplicand is post-tax earnings. The reason for this "normal" post-tax calculation is that the purchase price is based on payment of taxes on earnings of a facility in the hands of the acquirer. This normal rule may be applied to the casting plant with modification. When a community group is an acquirer, its tax rate will be lower than normal because of both a surtax exemption of up to $200,000 and the lower tax rates which will be in effect when the tax becomes due.

The issue is illustrated in our example. The above model facility, when and if completely successful, will earn $300,000 pre-tax profit per year. Assuming that the acquiring community group is in a severely underdeveloped community, taxes payable by it on such earnings can only be $3,000 ($300,000 less a $200,000 surtax exemption equals $100,000; 00% of the first $50,000 and 6% of the remainder yields a $3,000 tax).

It has been posited, however, that the model facility is sold at a time when it has reached only half its earning potential, namely $150,000. Applying a special surtax exemption to earnings of the facility after its acquisition by the community group, no taxes will be then owing. If the sales price is negotiated on the basis of earnings at the time of sale less taxes payable on those earnings by the transferee, the earnings multiplicand will be $150,000. Given an earnings multiple of 10, the sale price will be $1,500,000.

If the classical multiple earnings formula for arriving at a sales price were applied to the ghetto facility, the acquiring community entity, because of its special low tax rates, would pass on some of its special tax benefits to the outside taxpayer in the form of a much higher purchase price. The community group would pay more money for the facility than would a private sector purchaser subject to regular tax rates, a result which is not necessarily unintentional.

The tax payable by the seller on the transaction can be computed from the sales price. Normally, the tax will be 30% of the gain plus an amount which reflects tax recaptures. Assuming that the cost of the plant is $600,000, utilization by the taxpayer of maximum 90% leverage, and an equity basis of $60,000, his gain is $1,460,000, and his tax is $438,000. It is the collection of this tax which is delayed if the taxpayer utilizes the sales proceeds to enter into another arrangement covered by the statute or if he invests the proceeds in low interest-bearing accounts in a bank which offers special loans—including the loan to buy the plant—to community groups. At the very least, the deferral of collection of such taxes can be viewed as an interest-free loan from the government, and at 7%, represents actual dollar savings of $30,660 per year. Even after the facility is sold, the outside taxpayer may have the benefit of an additional tax incentive. For each of five years following sale, the sustained profitability tax credit offsets the taxes payable by the seller to the extent of 15% of the pre-tax income of the facility. A steady profit of $150,000 per year will produce a tax credit of $22,500 per year, or a total credit of $112,500 over five years.

Thus, assuming maximum leverage (90%) is utilized by the outside taxpayer to set up the $600,000 facility, and assuming that all facts have worked out as indicated, the taxpayer's $60,000 investment has produced (1) a tax benefit of $93,460 in excess of what would be available if the facility were sited elsewhere than in the community, (2) a postponement of collection of capital gain tax of $438,000 which is worth $30,660 per year, (3) a sustained profitability tax credit of $22,500 per year for each of five years following sale, (4) a capital gain of $1,460,000 less repayment of total start-up loan of $540,000 and less capital gain taxes of $438,000 eventually payable, and (5) net profit less tax in year four of $74,900. The taxpayer maximizes his benefit from the incentive over a nine year period: investment in the first year, profit by and sale of the facility in the fourth year, sale proceeds invested in tax deferral-producing investments or deposits in the fourth year with deferral of taxes upon sale proceeds until the ninth year. The net after tax cash return on the $60,000 investment can be calculated as follows:

Investment $60,000

Return on investment in the ninth year	$1,460,000
Post-tax income in the fourth year of operations	74,900
less (1) tax on sale proceeds in year nine	(438,000)
(2) recaptures	-0-
(3) repayment of initial loans	(540,000)
	$ 556,900

plus:

(1) minimum dollar value of deductions (rapid write off, section 38 tax credit; and human investment tax credit in the first three operating years)   93,460

(2) minimum dollar value of postponement of collection of tax on sale proceeds for five years   153,300

(3) minimum dollar value of sustained profitability tax credit   112,500

(4) carry forward or carry back of unutilized human investment tax credit   6,750

(5) minimum dollar value of absence of recaptures on rapid write off and section 38 tax credit assuming constant value of underlying assets (difference between ordinary income tax on $207,000 and capital gain tax on $207,000)   37,260

    403,270

    $ 960,170

The minimum actual dollars produced by this tax incentive program are $403,270. The amount of gain realized upon the sale of the facility is also affected by the tax results in that the sales price formula is calculated on the basis of post-tax earnings of the purchaser. The absence of taxes upon the income of the community group increases the sales price. The sales price of $1,500,000 to the "community" was calculated at ten times earnings of $150,000 after application of the special tax treatment afforded the community group. A non-community acquirer would pay tax in an amount equal to that payable prior to the sale. The tax on $150,000, without the special tax incentives, would be $72,000, yielding a sales price of $780,000. The sale to the community increases the selling price by $720,000. Thus, considering the minimum dollar benefits produced by this tax package, the availability of significant debt financing, and the likely sales price increase, the total dollar return induced by a facility in an underdeveloped community requiring a $60,000 equity investment is $960,170 net after all taxes and loan repayments.

In order to determine whether the special tax features will have the desired result of prompting taxpayer action, it is necessary to determine whether this sum is sufficient to offset the dollar cost of risks he perceives. This inquiry requires identification of the extra risks involved in setting up a facility in a ghetto. The primary risk is the cost of hiring and training the hard core unemployed. Estimates of this cost range from $1,500 to $5,000 per employee and include the costs of recruitment, training, and decreased productivity. If the turnover rate is 50% higher than the normal 40% rate, a 60% annual increase in the basic re-recruitment and retraining costs would be experienced. Our sample facility employs approximately 120 people, half of whom are, by assumption, considered to be hard-core unemployed. Assuming an average training cost of $3,000 per worker, the cost in the first year would be $180,000. In the second year, 60%, or thirty-six, of the hard core employees will leave, yielding a second training cost $108,000. The same result will occur in the third year. Thus, for the first three years of operation, the extra recruitment and training costs totals $396,000.

In light of this cost, the extra tax benefits yield conservative dollar savings of only $35,820 in the first year and $28,820 in the second and third years, or a total of $93,460 for the three years. Obviously, the tax savings at this point (which accrue to the taxpayer whether or not the facility is profitable) are insufficient to meet the increased special costs of ghetto operations. It is also necessary, however, to assess the impact of attainment of profitability in the facility. On the above facts, this is achieved in the fourth year and is immediately followed by the sale of the facility to the community. If it is assumed that the facility earns an average of $150,000 annually over the five years after acquisition by the community, the minimum dollar value of all tax savings to the taxpayer is $403,270, an amount which is only $7,270 in excess of the perceived extra costs.

Thus, this tax incentive program is designed to return to the taxpayer, on approximately a dollar-for-dollar basis, the extra costs involved in putting the facility into an underdeveloped community—and then only if the positive actions taken by the taxpayer produce the desired result of the transplantation of a profit-producing capital facility to a poor community.

All that has been done to this point is to attempt to offset the predictable extra costs. It is also necessary to provide a profit to cover the unpredictable, open-ended, non-business risks. The bonus lies in the purchase price for the profitable facility. As set forth above, this will exceed the price which would have been paid by a non-community acquirer because the community's tax load following acquisition is less. The amount of this profit is a matter of negotiation between the community and the taxpayer, subject to governmental review. The existence or amount of the profit, as it is in all acquisitions, is negotiable and as such is subject to all of the sophisticated credit techniques which can be used to "split the difference," such as increases in the purchase price following sale dependent upon increased actual earnings.

Thus, on a basis of minimum dollar savings produced by the above tax incentive package, a company which transmits its know-how and facility to the poor is made whole following a successful effort and has an opportunity to negotiate a profit for doing so. Following this successful effort, the community has acquired sixty well-paying jobs which it didn't have before, and those jobs belong to the people in the community. Further, members of the community group own a business which is actually producing $150,000 in annual earnings. Added to this would be the 5 to 1 multiplier effect on new jobs produced by reinvestment of earned business profits in other ventures.

On the other hand, if a taxpayer uses this tax package to unload out-dated facilities or fails to establish a new facility at viable profit-producing level in the competitive market, he will not benefit. Likewise, if a poor community group does not initially present to the taxpayer a stable organization, it will not attract an outside company in the first place and the desire for continuing jobs and profitability will not be satisfied.

III
Taxpayer-Selected Tax Incentives

The tax package analyzed above presents a fairly rigid scheme. It places the taxpayer in a tight factual grid in which the government's power to trade tax money for acceptance of open-ended risks comes into play with significant tax dollars only when a plant is sold to a community group. In order to qualify for the tax benefits, the taxpayer must use *his* money *first* on a roughly 10 to 1 ratio and maintain that level of expenditure for approximately four years. Moreover, he must assume the risk of being able to find a community group to purchase his plant, and he must rely on their ability, not his own, to run the plant after the sale. If any one significant event misfires, the benefits of the program evaporate and the taxpayer loses a significant amount of money. Few taxpayers would regard this tax package as overwhelmingly attractive. At best, a taxpayer would regard it as a nice gamble, and only because of the big pot of tax benefit gold at the end of a nine-year rainbow.

The policy decisions reflected in the tax package have fixed the dollar flow of tax benefits to a trickle in the early years. The tax incentive dollars produced in these years come nowhere near what the taxpayer is then paying out. As compensation for the mismatch of dollar benefits to dollar exposure in the early years, a huge tax break occurs upon sale and continued profitability of a plant. A large reward for a successful undertaking of a huge long-term risk is the basis of this tax package. But only *this* risk is rewarded by this tax system. A more attractive alternative incentive system may exist.

To find that alternative, it is not necessary to review a whole series of tax incentive packages and decide which one is best. An attempt to find the tax incentive package which is "best" merely compounds the error of trying to guess what incentives will encourage a taxpayer to act. By selecting one tax package which rewards only one rigid risk mix, a legislature would merely be speculating as to what will work in a highly complex and largely unexplored area. Moreover, selecting a "best" program would cancel out use of all of the imagination available in the private sector.

The task of a tax incentive program is to provide the taxpayer with a reason for doing something or, negatively stated, to minimize the risks which heretofore inhibited his desire to act. But, at the same time, a tax incentive program which is to operate in the unknown area of community economic development should not be designed or accidentally drafted in a way which dictates either the types of businesses to be provided or the methods of providing them. A tax incentive program which works only for highly labor-intensive investments and which does not encourage action by businesses with a reverse mix of labor and capital goods excludes industries of the future. Moreover, a program which works only if a taxpayer is willing to sell his plant to others will most likely exclude companies having proprietary products—those companies will not transfer their patents or whatever to companies which they do not control. A system which excludes from its benefits any significant type of business or which limits too greatly the method of providing meaningful career jobs to the poor may be less desirable than no incentive program at all. It is, again, over-promising. A one-track tax incentive program which freezes the kinds of economic development and narrows the methods for achieving development is especially unwanted in cases where those who develop the structure are not the businessmen who will have to take the risks.

A crucial question concerns the likelihood that a system of tax incentives for ghetto operations can be developed which will provide a taxpayer with different sets of benefits chosen by *him* to meet the risks *he* sees in a specific business opportunity. Moreover, it must be asked whether a system can be developed which will appeal to both the taxpayer who is willing to take only small risks, even at the expense of affecting the size of eventual benefits, as well as the taxpayer who is willing to assume a large risk if it would potentially yield a significant return. Of course, it is possible to permit such flexibility, and there are probably several mechanical ways to do it.

One workable multi-track community development tax incentives program would utilize all of the substantive tax incentives outlined earlier, but instead of fixing the amount of the benefit, the program would adopt several modifications. (1) The *amount* of the incentive would be variable within an established range. (2) The taxpayer would be permitted to choose the amount he wished to assign to a particular incentive. (3) The taxpayer could choose to attach a larger benefit to one tax incentive with the effect that this would limit the size of the benefit he could obtain under another incentive. (4) The *total* amount of benefits chosen by the taxpayer would be controlled by use of a limitation expressed in terms of either dollars or points assigned to particular benefits.

A simple example will illustrate the effect of this type of multi-track tax incentive program. The program which included the following benefits might utilize the following value allocation:[7]

1. Rapid write off of physical facilities.
    (a) Write off covering the physical plant but not real estate.
        (i) in 36 months—X points

---

[7] The use of the symbol X instead of a number is intentional. By doing so, a discussion of the value of any particular incentives is postponed until a detailed system is worked up and tried out. What is important now is the principle of and experimentation with a taxpayer's choice incentive system.

(ii) in 30 months—X plus 2 points
(iii) in 24 months—X plus 4 points
  (b) Write off of both physical facility and real estate
    (i) in 36 months—X points
    (ii) in 30 months—X plus 2 points
    (iii) in 24 months—X plus 4 points

2. Physical facility investment tax credit.

    at 7%—X points
    at 8%—X plus 2 points
    at 9%—X plus 4 points
    at 10%—X plus 6 points

3. Human investment tax credit.

    at 10%—X points
    at 11%—X plus 2 points
    at 12%—X plus 4 points
    at 13%—X plus 6 points

4. Postponement of capital gain on sale; non-re-capture in event of sale; sustained flexibility tax credit effective after sale.
   (a) If elected—X plus 20 points
   (b) If not elected, then double the amount of benefits otherwise elected may be chosen

A multi-track incentive system, such as that suggested above, would permit the taxpayer to select a package of tax incentives tailored to: (a) the precise type of business which the taxpayer is considering for ghetto operation, (b) the peculiar risks he perceives in the project, and (c) a flow of tax benefits in which the amount and timing of the tax advantage is inversely proportionate to the risks accepted by the taxpayer. For example, a taxpayer considering labor intensive operation which requires a relatively small investment in physical facilities would choose the highest human investment tax credit available. He would not be particularly concerned about tax benefits relating to physical facilities whether such tax benefits took the form of rapid right-offs or physical facility investment credits. By selecting the highest possible percentage of human investment tax credit, he would not only be selecting a benefit with particular application to his business, but he would have also decided that he wanted the cash flow resulting from the selected tax benefit to match as closely as possible the time at which he is required to spend money on the hard core unemployed. The human investment tax credit is an example of partial tax forgiveness which occurs in the year of the qualifying expenditure, rather than at some later time at which the risk of the occurrence of some event must be accepted by the taxpayer. Because the human investment tax credit is available in the year of expenditure and is available to the taxpayer upon the occurrence of an event controlled by him, namely paying his hard core employees, he not only has selected a tax benefit which applies to his kind of business and received the benefit in the year he paid his money; but he has also made receipt of the benefit a certainty, or at the very least, highly predictable. In exchange for receiving tax benefits concurrently with the expenditures which produce them, the taxpayer gives up a larger tax benefit contingent upon future events which would have subjected him to more risk. If the tax package of the Community Self-Determination Act is based upon a policy of providing a taxpayer with a large reward for undertaking a large risk, the tax incentives selected by the taxpayer in this example show the operation of a tax system which exchanges a smaller tax benefit for a smaller risk.

Under a flexible system, there are legion combinations of tax benefit packages which can be designed by a taxpayer for his specific operation to compensate for the number, type, and degree of risks he is willing to accept. The permutations available under a multi-track tax incentive program are exactly what is required to encourage the experimentation necessary to provide evidence of the type of incentives which actually encourages private sector investment in the ghetto. It is only at this point—the point in time when the evidence is in—that will be possible to determine which combination of incentives, if any, were successful and, then, whether the government got its money's worth.

IV

SHOULD TAX INCENTIVES BE USED AT ALL?

Many thoughtful men in government, in law schools, and elsewhere have spent much time and effort considering the viability of tax incentives as a means of encouraging taxpayer action. Opinion differs widely. Some take the position that utilization of tax incentives is a misuse of the taxing power, a distortion of the symmetry of the Code, and an evil which provides the opportunity to achieve artificial transactions in order to benefit the rich who are fortunate enough to be able to hire tax advisers. Others suggest that a new start be made with the tax code and that we reduce the tax rate significantly and eliminate all of the gimmicks. Although over one thousand pages of tax code may not be a desirable thing, it does exist, and it is the author's view that this should be dealt with as it is, not as it might have been.

Unbridled faith in the utilization of tax benefits is a position taken by others. It is true, for example, that the use of a 10% tax credit achieves the result of having a taxpayer spend $9 for every dollar the government is willing to spend to achieve certain action. Obviously, this represents a first level $9 savings to the government if it were in the position to spend the $10 in the first place. There are very few who would suggest the multiplier effect resulting from the use of incentives is not an important factor to consider.

It does seem, however, that there may be certain risks for the private sector in community economic development which cannot be solved by tax incentives, no matter how big they are, no matter how much taxpayer choice there is, and no matter how lenient the Internal Revenue Service is willing to be on audit. It has been pointed out that incentive legislation enables the government to exercise its power to either reduce risks or trade incentives for acceptance of unmeasurable risks which currently inhibit desired action by the private sector. To the extent that a risk is a business risk—that is, one which is calculable in dollars and of a type familiar to the taxpayer—tax or other fiscal incentives are probably applicable. On the other hand, if a risk is a non-business nature—unmeasurable by application of currently available business skills—one ought to have second thoughts about using tax benefits to overcome it.

For example, a non-business risk which appears to be in the minds of many businessmen is the fear that their plant, whether in the ghetto or elsewhere employing the hard core unemployed, will become the subject of a political or social dispute. This is the kind of risk which businessmen do not know how to measure. And worse, they find it difficult to sense the occurrence of an innocent appearing set of facts which might give rise to a situation in which their plant becomes a pawn in a social battle. The tax incentive designed to meet this problem would, in effect, become income interruption insurance. A total loss coverage tax incentive would never become law. But this problem may be the proper subject of a special government insurance program in which private sector insurance companies develop a pooled risk program with government participation.

The risk that a plant may become involved in a political dispute is not a new problem to American businessmen who have operated overseas in underdeveloped nations. In such cases of overseas economic development, the risks of war and civil disturbance are often present to varying degrees. Congress approached this problem years ago, and legislation was created to meet the risks preceived by American businessmen.[8] Under an investment guarantee program an American company could buy "political risk insurance" from the government which covered some of the risks of war, rebellion, and civil commotion. It was provided that the insurance would not be available unless it was the very issuance of a guarantee which "encouraged" the company to make the investment. Thus, the legislation creating the investment guarantee program specifically acknowledged that it could be used only by a company which was otherwise unwilling to act because of its perception of certain risks. It is not suggested, however, that the foreign investment guarantee program could be applied directly to business activities in domestically underdeveloped areas. The analogy is not sufficiently complete to permit the transposition.

The example should indicate that it is possible to develop a workable incentive system which would offset measurable business risks. But it seems equally clear that

---

[8] Foreign Assistance Act of 1961, 22 U.S.C. § 2351 (1964).

tax incentives cannot offset certain risks of a non-business nature which cannot be measured in dollars and the occurrence of which cannot be successfully forecasted. A program combining a multi-track tax incentive program and a "domestic investment guarantee program" should be developed. If successful, it would likely be cheaper, from the government's point of view, than either the undertaking of community economic development by the public sector or the symptomatic control of the social problems of the ghetto by expanded police and riot control forces.

V

A Noble Experiment

If a program involving a multi-track taxpayer's choice tax incentive system and an investment guarantee insurance pool (or insurance company tax incentives) is to be tried, it seems that Congress is entitled to some evidence that such program will work before it legislates such matters into the Internal Revenue Code. The current fad is to develop "models." It is always possible to select facts, select a group of tax incentives, and program a computer so that it will apply such facts and incentives to each other in order to produce pro forma or actual operating financial statements of a "model" company and "model" tax returns to show what would happen if a particular "model" program would have been in effect at the time. Even this much is helpful because it is more than has been done before. However, computers are only able to add, subtract, multiply, and divide; they are not able to judge. An artificial attempt to computerize unquantified risks in an unexplored area is a guess on a print-out sheet; nothing more. Indeed, such an attempt is nothing more than what was done in part II of this article and both efforts are subject to criticism if they are represented as anything more than guesses. A great deal more experimentation is required than can be provided by a nude computer or law review articles. Only by intentionally introducing the human element into the equation is it possible to provide a sampling of actual taxpayer use of incentives. And it is only that kind of evidence which ought to justify the creation of new sections in the tax code or the creation of a government insurance program of the type which will work.

I suspect that somewhere in the federal government there are funds available to actually simulate the effect of tax and/or insurance incentives on more than a six month or one year basis and that there is someone in the government to decide which agency or inter-agency pidgeon hole should receive the project. The mechanics are not the issue, for the success of the experiment depends on other factors. The question is not so much the availability of funds to simulate such a program, or the style of the simulation, but, as is true in most cases, the key is the human beings who administer such a program. We are dealing with questions of taxes. We are dealing with business people and we are dealing with a relationship of a taxpayer to the Internal Revenue Service and to eventual audits performed by it.

It seems that an attempt to experiment with possible tax laws before they become laws would have its best chance of being successful if guided by the toughest, most suspicious, no-nonsense tax specialists and hard-line Revenuers the government has in its shop. If nothing else, this would at least make people available who can speak a businessman's language. But there is something else: having tax people in the act minimizes the very human bias which propels any man to sink a project if he, the expert, was not in on it in the first place.

This is not to say that the Office of Economic Opportunity or the Model Cities office or parts of the Commerce Department or parts of the Labor Department or, indeed, counselors or advisers at the White House should not get involved in such programs. They are all, in one way or another, in the poverty business; and since tax incentives or an insurance program are designed to add an additional tool for the achievement of their goals, it would certainly be a mistake to exclude such people. To formulate and to simulate tax incentives without tax people, however, would invite disaster.

Tax experts know that if the problem were to aid the growth of a specific industry, there would be a half-century of tax incentive tradition and evidence available so that exhaustive experimentation would not be necessary. In such cases, the analysis would be carried along within predictable and acceptable lines emanating from a defined and proven source. But the task faced now is to aid *any* kind of business, not as an end in itself, but as a *means* to provide a self-supported future to poor people. This task assigned to tax incentives is new in this country, without tradition and without factual evidence of its viability. The work done now is the source. The issue is: the source of what? The thinking, the testing, and the theories we struggle with are more than games for the amusement of lawyers and professors. To experiment is to produce evidence, and a simulation may produce a method, other than welfare, to help change the grim reality which makes life so brutalizing for so many. Of course, the evidence may point the other way. If the end result of the simulation is that neither tax incentives nor insurance programs will encourage private sector participation in poverty areas, so be it. At least we will have tried something useful and we will know more then than we know now.

MINORITY ECONOMIC DEVELOPMENT: THE PROBLEM OF BUSINESS FAILURES

WILLIAM A. STRANG*

In theory, the private enterprise system offers individuals the opportunity to achieve respect, power, and financial success through business ownership, limited only by their personal capabilities. During the 1960's the nation became painfully conscious that economic opportunities were in fact very limited for our minority populations. Past discriminations have placed them in a weak competitive position in terms of capital, experience, and entrepreneurial motivation. One of the most glaring deficiencies in the system was the lack of business ownership opportunity for minority people.

I
THE SCOPE OF MINORITY ENTERPRISE
A. Minority Business Today

The evidence is irrefutable that minority business is a pitifully insignificant part of our total economy.[1] Of approximately 5,000,000 businesses in the country, only 45,000 are black-owned.[2] Yet black people comprised more than eleven per cent of the total population in 1969.[3] The lack of black business ownership in cities where black populations are large is one explanation of ghetto unrest.

> Newark . . . has approximately 400,000 people, of whom more than half are black. Of the 12,172 licensed businesses in the city, a little more than 10 per cent are Negro-owned. . . .[4] Of the 800,000 residents of Washington, D.C., Negroes are a majority of 63 per cent. Yet, out of 11,755 businesses in our nation's capital, Negroes own only 1,500—less than 13 per cent.[5]

The statistics are even more striking when the small size of most black businesses is taken into account. Theodore Cross has pointed out that "only a dozen Negro businesses in Manhattan employ ten or more people . . . ."[6] And Andrew Brimmer has shown that black-owned businesses in Washington, D.C., are concentrated in retail trade and services, primarily barber and beauty shops, dry cleaning establish-

---

* Assistant Professor, Graduate School of Business Administration, University of Wisconsin.
[1] Because of the availability of data, the discussion will focus on black business. The situation is undoubtedly similar among Spanish-Americans and Indians.
[2] McKersie, *Vitalize Black Enterprise*, HARV. BUS. REV., Sept.-Oct. 1969, at 88, 89. While this figure may be disputed, there is no argument that the number of minority businesses in the country is small relative to minorities' share of the population.
[3] U.S. DEP'T OF COMMERCE, BUREAU OF THE CENSUS, CURRENT POPULATION REPORTS: POPULATION ESTIMATES AND PROJECTIONS 5 (Series P-25, No. 441, 1970).
[4] T. CROSS, BLACK CAPITALISM: STRATEGY FOR BUSINESS IN THE GHETTO 60 (1969).
[5] *Id.* at 60-61.
[6] *Id.* at 60.

ments, and food stores.[7] A 1968 survey conducted by the National Business League revealed similar situations in seven different cities with substantial black populations.[8]

Even when black businesses operate in areas of greater potential, such as those in manufacturing and insurance, they tend to be small-scale operations heavily dependent on the ghetto environment.[9] For example, North Carolina Mutual, the largest black life insurance company has assets of approximately $96 million, but the combined assets of all the black-owned life insurance companies still equal only 0.2 per cent of the industry total.[10] Two successful black business ventures often held up as examples of black capitalism at its best are the Johnson Publishing Company and Park's Sausages, with sales of about $12 million and $7.5 million, respectively. These successes are dwarfed by competing corporate giants, such as Time, Incorporated, with sales of more than $600 million, and Swift, with sales over three billion dollars. Howard Samuels, former Undersecretary of Commerce, has stated that the black community controls only one-tenth of one per cent of the total business investments in the nation.[11]

Without question, black businesses are few in number, small in size, and limited in potential for growth.

B. The Rise of Black Capitalism

Faced with intense pressures from minority groups, government (primarily the federal government) and private business responded to a campaign idea of President Nixon. The idea was black capitalism, and it was enthusiastically embraced by the white community, although acceptance was mixed in the black community. As a result of the black capitalism concept, a number of programs were initiated to encourage and assist minority businesses. An Office of Minority Business Enterprise was established in Washington, D.C., to coordinate various governmental programs related to minority business. The most important of these involved the Community Development Corporation,[12] MESBICs,[13] and the Small Business Administration's Loan Guarantee and Economic Opportunity Loan programs.[14] In the private sector, groups such as the Urban League, the National Business League, and the Interracial Council for Business Opportunity began to work actively toward minority business development. Several large corporations, including IBM, General Foods, and Xerox, attempted individually to assist minority businesses, often by purchasing from minority suppliers. Universities became involved, as schools of business around

---

[7] Brimmer, The Economic Potential of Black Capitalism 11 (paper presented at the 82d annual meeting of the American Economic Association, Dec. 29, 1969).
[8] NATIONAL BUSINESS LEAGUE, PROJECT OUTREACH (1968).
[9] Brimmer, *supra* note 7, at 11.
[10] CROSS, *supra* note 4, at 62 n.24.
[11] Daily News Record, May 7, 1969, at 1.
[12] Sturdivant, *The Limits of Black Capitalism*, HARV. BUS. REV., Jan.-Feb. 1969, at 122.
[13] Rosenbloom & Shank, *Let's Write Off MESBICs*, HARV. BUS. REV., Sept.-Oct. 1970, at 90.
[14] 13 C.F.R. §§ 119.1-120.3 (1970).

the country established scholarship programs for training black managers and consulting programs to provide advice for minority businesses.[15] In some schools, MBA students themselves organized minority consulting operations outside the framework of the institution.[16] At others, the consulting became part of the academic program.[17] It is clear that a great many people, from government, business, and universities, are deeply involved in efforts to develop black business.

Almost as soon as programs for minority business development began to emerge, criticism of the concepts of black capitalism arose. The most publicized was by Andrew Brimmer, but others flooded the academic journals.[18] Critics felt that the potential impact of black capitalism on the black population was limited, that its goal was to create a few more black millionaires or, conversely, to perpetuate "mom and pop" retail and service establishments, and that the realities of the economic environment precluded success on a significant scale. The term *black capitalism* itself, symbolizing an economic system that historically had denied opportunity to black people, came under attack. Some critics even believed that the system of free enterprise was incongruous with the needs of minority groups.[19] Among groups actively participating in and benefiting from the system, there were many who were irritated at the thought of special advantages being offered to black people. And others were concerned by the thought of new competition.

Many of the criticisms of black capitalism were clearly justified. The ghetto environment *is* difficult for business. The short-term impacts of increased minority business ownership *will be* small relative to the potential gains possible through the eradication of discrimination in employment. And most gains in minority business, in terms of the number of businesses, *are* likely to come among small retail and service establishments, while the bulk of the nation's economic power will likely remain concentrated in the large corporations.

Yet, despite the critics, government, business, and universities continue to expand and improve their minority business development programs. Why?

The response from within the black community has clearly demonstrated that many blacks have strong desires to participate in business enterprise. Whites, particularly white businessmen, realize that it takes time to build business enterprises, that most black businesses will be small just as most white businesses are small, and

---

[15] U.S. DEP'T OF COMMERCE, OFFICE OF MINORITY BUSINESS ENTERPRISE, HIGHER EDUCATION AID FOR MINORITY BUSINESS: A DIRECTORY OF ASSISTANCE AVAILABLE TO MINORITIES BY SELECTED COLLEGIATE SCHOOLS OF BUSINESS (1970).

[16] Glasser, *Student Consultant—Ghetto Client: A Developing Rapport*, MBA, Oct. 1969, at 30.

[17] W. STRANG, CONSULTING FOR BLACK ENTERPRISE—A CHALLENGE TO THE BUSINESS ESTABLISHMENT (1970). *See also* Seldin & Kokus, *Management Aid for Black Entrepreneurs: The American University Program*, J. SMALL BUS. MANAGEMENT, July 1970, at 13-15.

[18] Brimmer, *supra* note 9. *See also* MacDowell & Vorzimer, *Black Capitalism: Opportunity or Myth?*, U. WASH. BUS. REV., Summer 1970, at 24; Boggs, *The Myth and Irrationality of Black Capitalism*, REV. BLACK POL. ECON., Spring/Summer 1970, at 27; Booms & Ward, *The Cons of Black Capitalism: Will This Policy Cure Urban Ills?*, BUS. HORIZONS, Oct. 1969, at 17.

[19] Boggs, *supra* note 18.

that accomplishments will always seem insignificant on a year-to-year basis. But they have a basic faith in the free enterprise system. They understand the importance to individuals of having the opportunity of business ownership available to them and the psychological value, particularly on the local level—where we all live—of seeing living examples of successful businesses operated by citizens of the community. Being pragmatic, they see the end goals of minority business development as the sum of the successes of individual minority-owned business ventures. Thus, the key questions about black capitalism are: How many black business ventures can be developed? What is the market potential of these ventures? Will they succeed or fail?

This article is based on the thesis that the reasons for the success or failure of small businesses, particularly those pertinent to minority businesses, can be identified and that steps can be taken to reduce the failure rate.

II

THE PROBLEM OF BUSINESS FAILURES

Most business ventures fail. Dun and Bradstreet, probably the nation's most informed source on the subject of business failures, has stated that "only one out of two [businesses] will survive as long as eighteen months and . . . only one out of five will still be in business in ten years . . . ."[20] Because Dun and Bradstreet studies include only those failures involving court proceedings or voluntary actions likely to end in creditor losses, overlooking marginal businesses that survive without success, the true failure rate is likely to be much higher.

The problem of business failures is especially important to the black business community. Any business failure is a traumatic experience for the man who loses his capital and sees his efforts wasted. But, in the white community, failures are accepted as a characteristic of the system; and as one venture fails, another begins. In the black community, where the goal is to *increase* the market share of black business, business failures cannot be so easily accepted. Each individual failure is a blow against the achievement of the community goal.

A. The Causes of Business Failure

Businesses fail for many reasons. Stories of individual business failures never cease to be interesting, because of the variety of explanations offered for the failure. Yet behind these explanations, certain basic causes of failure appear and reappear.

Dun and Bradstreet studies have identified the most frequent causes of business failure. As shown in Table 1, their studies have indicated that incompetent management is by far the most frequent cause of business failure. Including the closely associated reasons of unbalanced experience (strength in some functional areas, but not others), lack of managerial experience, and lack of experience in the line,

---

[20] Wyant, *Business Failures*, DUN's REV., Oct. 1968, at 145.

TABLE 1

CAUSES OF BUSINESS FAILURE, 1969

Underlying Cause of Failure	Percentage of All Failures
Incompetence	45.6
Unbalanced experience	19.5
Lack of managerial experience	13.7
Lack of experience in the line	8.7
Neglect	2.8
Disaster	1.4
Fraud	1.2
Reason unknown	7.1
Total	100.0

Source: DUN AND BRADSTREET, THE FAILURE RECORD THROUGH 1969, at 11.

TABLE 2

OPERATING PROBLEMS RESULTING FROM POOR MANAGEMENT

Cause of Failure	Percentage of Failures Due to Mismanagement
Inadequate sales	42.2
Competitive weaknesses	22.9
Heavy operating expenses	12.1
Receivables difficulties	10.1
Inventory difficulties	4.5
Excessive fixed assets	3.9
Poor location	2.8
Other	1.5
Total	100.0

Source: DUN AND BRADSTREET, THE FAILURE RECORD THROUGH 1969, at 12.

management weaknesses account for almost ninety per cent of all business failures. Fraud, neglect, and disaster are relatively infrequent reasons for failure.

Table 2 is presented to show the operating difficulties that arise most frequently because of poor management. The most common operating difficulty leading to failure is inadequate sales; this is followed by competitive weakness. Both of these indicate a lack of marketing ability. Other operating problems frequently causing failure, in order of importance, are heavy operating expenses, receivables difficulties, and inventory difficulties, all suggesting a lack of controls within the business. The latter two could also be due to a lack of adequate capital within the firm.

Dun and Bradstreet attributes almost all operating difficulties to inadequate management, apparently assuming that competent managers could solve the problems that arise and thus keep the business afloat. This may be a bit harsh. One can certainly visualize totally unforeseeable situations that could arise to crush a business. In addition, it is possible to understand how a good manager denied adequate capital resources might choose to attempt his venture in spite of the high risk artificially created by the lack of capital. But other sources confirm the judgment that poor management is the principal cause of business failure. Frank L. Tucker has stated,

> In various studies and surveys for the purpose of determining the causes of failure of small firms the principal problems seem to be deficiencies in capital and management. In my opinion, if a company has good management, it is not likely to have financial problems. . . . I suspect that the most usual causes of chronic shortages are poor planning, recklessness, and a desire to maintain maximum equity control. This reasoning brings the spotlight to rest on management as the critical variable in small business success.[21]

Wilford L. White, with years of experience in counseling small business concurs, adding that the principal reasons that small firms fail to grow are a lack of experience, the lack of a customer point of view, a hesitation to hire others, an unwillingness to delegate authority with responsibility, the fear of the strange and new, and a fear of growth.[22]

Paul J. Fitzpatrick, in his study of business failures during the period 1920-1929, recognized several external factors, which are generally beyond the control of business executives and which often lead to business failure,[23] and he pointed out that during the depression period of the 1930's the external factors predominated over the internal factors. The internal factors that he identified more than thirty years ago are probably applicable to the causes of business failures today:

1. Overinvestment in fixed assets, especially in the short period of a year;
2. Excessive advances to, and/or investments in, affiliated and subsidiary companies;
3. Overinvestment in inventories;
4. Overinvestment in receivables;
5. Insufficient working capital;
6. Weak cash position;
7. Excessive good will and other intangibles;
8. Unbalanced financial or capital structure;
9. Excessive current or short-term obligations;
10. Excessive funded or long-term obligations;
11. Inadequate and declining net sales;
12. Insufficient net profits or earnings;
13. Unusual and unexpected losses;
14. Excessive interest and other fixed charges;
15. Excessive operating expenses;

---

[21] Tucker, *Foreword* to L. ALLEN, STARTING AND SUCCEEDING IN YOUR OWN SMALL BUSINESS at xi (1968).
[22] White, *Introduction* to *id.* at xv-xviii.
[23] P. FITZPATRICK, THE PROBLEM OF BUSINESS FAILURES 67 (1936).

16. Inadequate reserves for depreciation, contingencies, and other necessary purposes;
17. Excessive and unearned dividend payments; and
18. Economically unwarranted existence of the enterprise.[24]

He suggested that management, in most instances, was responsible for the above conditions.

Although businesses fail for many reasons, the predominant belief is that the owner-manager's ability to avoid or solve problems is the key to the success of a business enterprise. Because most businesses fail, it is apparent that the standards for success are high. The strong and the talented survive at the expense of the weak.

B. Minority Business Failures

Before evaluating the causes of minority business failures, it is first necessary to determine the criteria to be used for success. Normally, the evaluation of business success or failure is based on financial factors, such as profitability. There has been some consideration given to the idea that the criteria should be different for black business. The goal of black business may be to build community pride, to provide service where none existed before, or to provide employment. In addition, financial success is difficult because a ghetto operating environment is severe, raising costs and prices for a market that cannot afford to bear them. Thus, in the short to medium term, it may be desirable to evaluate minority businesses on goals other than profit, providing financial subsidies of one form or another to allow the "successful" firms to continue. But in the long run, so long as the free enterprise system endures, success must be measured in financial terms. Pride will come only when the minority business establishment can be compared on equal terms with the white business majority. In addition, minority business, if it is to grow and prosper, must compete in the larger, more wealthy markets outside the ghetto. To successfully accomplish this end, minority business will eventually have to accept the standards of the majority and to compete for men, money, and capital on the basis of the ability to manage resources.

III

A Survey of Minority Businesses

In an attempt to discover the factors leading to the success or failure of minority businesses, the author conducted a survey in September 1970 of organizations and individuals actively involved in assisting minority businesses. Mail questionnaires were sent to seventeen organizations and individuals. Five were found to be just beginning their assistance programs; of the remaining twelve, seven responses were

---
[24] *Id.* at 67-68.

received. The respondents were working with 792 minority businesses in different areas of the country, and the data returned related to forty-eight of these businesses.

The businesses being served were young, averaging 2.3 years since their inception. They were primarily retail establishments (forty-six per cent) and service organizations (thirty-three per cent), but there also were some manufacturers (ten per cent), contractors (seven per cent), and wholesalers (four per cent). The consulting agencies had been working with these firms for an average of eleven months, almost half of their business lives.

On a rating scale of 1 to 7, with complete failure at point 1 and complete success at point 7, the respondents were asked to evaluate the *financial* success or failure of the firms with which they were working. (Respondents who had worked with more than twelve firms were asked to select the six most successful and the six least successful for evaluation). Fourteen firms were rated as successful (5, 6, 7) and twenty firms as failures (1, 2, 3); ten received neutral ratings. The mean, mode, and median ratings of success/failure were approximately 3, below the neutral point. In other words, the minority firms that the respondent organizations and individuals had been working with had met with mixed success and on the average had not succeeded. The most successful types of firms were retail establishments (4.5), followed by

TABLE 3
FINANCIAL SUCCESS OR FAILURE OF ASSISTED FIRMS

Consultant Evaluation	Percentage of Firms Evaluated					
	Retail	Service	Construction	Manufacturing	Wholesale	Total
Successful............	50	20	—	25	—	32
Failure...............	35	47	67	50	100	45
Neutral results........	15	33	33	25	—	23

Source: Bureau of Business Research & Service, University of Wisconsin, Survey of Minority Enterprise Consulting Organizations Sept. 1970).

service organizations (3.5); manufacturers (2.8), contractors (2.0), and wholesalers (1.0) rated as complete failures financially. The results of the ratings are presented in Table 3.

The respondents were asked to suggest the reasons for the success or failure of the firms they had assisted. The reasons for success are presented in Table 4. Because the number of successful firms was only fourteen, the percentage results in Table 4 should be interpreted with caution. The most significant column is the total firm column.

Strong motivation was the most frequent reason given for the success of the minority businesses studied. This was not surprising. Although it is no guarantee of success—many businesses go down fighting—it is one of the essentials. One of the characteristics of a new business venture is that problems seem to arise continually. It takes a highly motivated manager to resolve them day after day.

Consistent with the Dun and Bradstreet findings about business failures nationally, factors related to managerial ability (experience in the line, managerial ability, business education/experience) were also important explanations for the success achieved by the firms under study. Among the operating strengths resulting in success, marketing seemed somewhat more important than others (good market potential, good marketing effort), but formal controls and planning, location, businesslike attitudes, capable employees, good credit management, and good inventory management were also mentioned. It was interesting that relatively few firms appeared to succeed on the basis of strong financial capacity, confirming the thought that capital is secondary to management as a determinant of success.

A study of the firms that failed, or were failing, brought forth some interesting differences. As shown in Table 5, lack of motivation was a relatively infrequent reason for failure. Apparently, most of the minority businesses that were studied had motivated managers. The findings suggest caution in approaching potential entrepreneurs. Convincing them to begin their own businesses if they do not have strong motivation is doing them a disservice, because of the serious consequences of failure. The most significant fact about the finding, however, is that only three of the thirty-four firms rated as successes or failures suffered from a lack of managerial motivation.

The most frequent causes of failure related to a lack of managerial ability, business education, and experience, again consistent with the Dun and Bradstreet findings. However, while only twenty-six per cent of the nation's business failures were attributed to reasons associated with a lack of formal controls, sixty per cent of the minority firms encountered these difficulties. Although differences in data

TABLE 4

REASONS FOR SUCCESS

Reason	Percentage of Firms Mentioning			
	Retail	Service	Other	Total
Strong motivation	60	100	100	71
Experience in particular line of business	70	33	100	64
Managerial ability	70	67	—	64
Good market potential	50	67	—	50
Business education/experience	50	33	—	43
Good marketing effort	30	33	100	36
Good formal controls and planning	30	67	—	36
Good location	40	33	—	36
Businesslike activities	20	67	100	36
Capable employees	20	67	—	29
Good credit management	30	—	100	29
Good inventory management, good buying practices	40	—	—	29
Strong cash flow, adequate working capital	30	—	—	21
Earnings returned to the business	10	—	—	7

Source: Bureau of Business Research Services, University of Wisconsin, Survey of Minority Enterprise Consulting Organizations (Sept. 1970).

TABLE 5
REASONS FOR FAILURE

Reason	Percentage of Firms Mentioning			
	Retail	Service	Other	Total
Lack of managerial ability	57	86	67	70
Lack of business education and experience	86	43	67	65
Lack of formal controls and planning	86	43	50	60
Insufficient cash flow or inadequate capital	43	43	83	55
Inadequate marketing effort	43	57	33	45
Inadequate capital at inception of business	29	43	50	40
Employee lack of experience, lack of skills	14	43	50	35
Lack of experience in particular line of business	43	—	33	25
False attitudes toward business	14	43	50	25
Inventory mismanagement, poor buying practices	71	—	16	30
Inadequate management counseling	—	—	67	20
Lack of motivation	14	29	—	15
Poor credit management	—	29	—	10
Lack of market potential	14	14	—	10
Other	28	—	17	15

Source: Bureau of Business Research and Service, University of Wisconsin, Survey of Minority Enterprise Consulting Organizations (Sept. 1970).

make a direct comparison between the two studies difficult, the survey of minority businesses suggests that basic bookkeeping and planning are important needs to be met if the rate of minority business failures is to decline.

Although not the most severe problem, inadequate capital (insufficient cash flow, inadequate capital at the inception of the business) was an important reason for failure, and capital seemed to be a more serious problem for minority businesses than it was for the total business community. Marketing problems were also mentioned often enough to be of concern. Insufficient cash flow problems may often have been a function of inadequate marketing. It is interesting that only ten per cent of the failures attributed their difficulties to a lack of market potential. Apparently, the basic ideas for the businesses were usually sound. The difficulties arose in organizing resources to achieve the potential.

The response "false attitudes toward business" embraced a number of things, but it primarily indicated a lack of understanding of the need to work hard, to meet competition, and to achieve by satisfying market needs. In one-fourth of the minority business failures, this was a problem.

In view of the managerial weaknesses indicated by several of the other answers, it was surprising that only twenty per cent of the failures were attributed to inadequate management counseling. One explanation may lie in the fact that the respondents evaluating the failures had been providing counseling. It is difficult to imagine that adequate counseling on a continuing basis could not have helped to solve such basic problems as a lack of formal controls, planning, inadequate marketing effort, and others.

In summary, it appears that the managers themselves, their motivation and abilities, were the key to the success or the failure of the minority businesses studied.

IV

Minority Business Failures: Some Examples of the Problems

A. Management Weaknesses

The major cause of business failure in both the white and black communities has been attributed to management weaknesses. In the black community, where past discriminations have prevented blacks from holding positions of significant responsibility, the problem of lack of experience is especially devastating. Indeed, the lack of opportunity to work for others has often been the primary motivation for starting a business.

Managerial weakness is usually soon revealed by the operating problems that arise. One of the most frequent difficulties is in the area of controls. The examples are endless: the Wisconsin construction company that lost $55,000 in its first two years (and showing a loss *before* operating expenses), because it had no idea of its job costs; the roofing contractor who kept his bills and accounts receivable in a single box, seldom referring to it, and who accidentally discovered that he had owed a supplier $1,700 for three months; the Milwaukee meat wholesaler who did not understand how to use his cash register and did not even know his sales volume. Correcting problems of this kind is relatively simple in theory. An accountant might donate his services and spend four or five days, part-time, to bring the books up to date and then take a few hours to present an ongoing bookkeeping system to the owner-manager. In truth, of course, the problem is much more difficult. The need is to convince the owner-manager of the importance of keeping records and to teach him how to do it. Generally, it takes several months of repeating instructions, checking and rechecking, and using the output of the records in decision-making before the business has an accurate and useful system.

Marketing problems are among the most frequent causes of failure for small businesses generally. If revenues are flowing into the business, time is usually available to solve other operating problems; but when sales do not produce revenues, a business can die quickly. In many cases, the minority entrepreneur is a craftsman, who knows how to produce a good product or service. He assumes that it will be bought and is terribly discouraged to discover that his sales estimates are not realized. There is the example of the Milwaukee printer, who resisted advice to market his services, because he did not want to grow too fast. As a result, his sales never reached the break-even point, and he survived only by never paying himself a salary. A Wisconsin manufacturer of aluminum screen doors and windows was disturbed at his inability to make a profit, but when he developed a marketing program, his sales quickly moved past the break-even point.

Some black businesses expect that black ownership itself will be enough to generate local sales to support the business. The danger of this assumption is revealed by the statement of a black businessman, "Now I believe that nearly all black people have reached a point where they don't resent coming to a business run and owned by a brother."[25] Not only is black ownership not a guarantee of success, but prejudices within the black community have had to be overcome. American Dream Soap was launched on the strength of black loyalty, but the bulk of its sales have been to upper-class blacks and to whites.[26] In contrast, sales to black consumers based on a differentiated product rather than loyalty to black business have met with unqualified success.[27] Supreme Beauty Products was successful in promoting the natural look in black hair styles; black dolls have also found a ready market.

On balance, it probably is true that black owners can expect to achieve some loyalty on the basis of race, so long as they offer a good product and reliable service. "Rather than facing unique problems, the black merchant may have a unique advantage in black areas; just as the white merchant has in white areas .... Some members of P.D.A. (Progressive Development Association in Philadelphia) are successfully operating stores that were failing under white ownership."[28] But black patronage due to black ownership should be viewed as an opportunity, not as a guarantee of success.

Another frequent problem is the accumulation of too many assets. A small black printer had purchased about twice as much equipment as was justified. A $7,000 mailing machine had been purchased a year earlier, and it was producing only about $200 of sales revenues annually. A black modeling and charm school, with very weak revenues, purchased an expensive television taping unit that was used only a few times a year, and even then was not essential to the running of the business. A roofing contractor neglected to pay his accounts payable, allowing them to rise to a dangerous point, while he purchased used trucks, a bus, and other equipment of dubious value to his company. Discussions with the businessmen revealed that they felt more secure putting their money into tangible equipment than building up working capital or reducing their debts. In addition, having had little before beginning their business, their equipment was to them a visible display of their success. The danger of such practices is evident.

A fourth operating problem that occurs frequently enough to mention is high operating expenses relative to the ability to pay. Many minority businessmen, starting from a weak financial position, discover too late that they have been too free with

---

[25] *Success*, BLACK ENTERPRISE, Aug. 1970, at 29.
[26] G. BERKNER, BLACK CAPITALISM AND THE URBAN NEGRO 25 (1970).
[27] *Id.* at 26.
[28] McLaughlin, *Black Enterprise: The Philadelphia Experience*, J. SMALL BUS. MANAGEMENT, Apr. 1970, at 39.

their expenditures. Common situations involve high pay for employees who are paid on the basis of what they "deserve" (rather than what they can contribute to the firm), "draws" for the owner above what the firm can afford, and the purchase of unnecessary services.

Pricing problems are also frequent, particularly with manufacturing companies, which are usually job shops, and construction companies, which have to estimate costs and submit bids to obtain orders. A black businessman in Milwaukee was asked to submit a bid to do some electronic servicing and installing. He was elated with the prospect of making substantial profits, only to have an MBA consulting team show him that he would have lost money on the job—that the bid should have been approximately four times as high. Unfortunately, in spite of the fact that estimating procedures can be laid out, bidding competitively is almost an art and can best be learned through experience. Minority businessmen, who have never had the opportunity to participate in bidding before, can be expected to make mistakes as they learn. The danger is that their firms may fail before they have gained the needed bidding skills.

B. Lack of Capital

One of the most common complaints of small businessmen is that they were never provided enough capital to sustain them. Minority businessmen often feel that they have been denied access to capital because of their race. Undoubtedly, this has been true historically, and it is probably true in many situations today. For obvious reasons, many minority businessmen were unable to accumulate capital before they went into business. Thus, when they do undertake a business venture, they have little or no equity capital and they have little collateral.

Efforts have been made to supply capital to black businessmen on bases that put aside the standard criteria for providing loan or equity money. The federal government's MESBIC and Economic Opportunity Loan programs offer one source for financing. The Rochester Business Opportunities Corporation, Progress Enterprises in Philadelphia, the Harlem Commonwealth Council, and the Bedford-Stuyvesant Restoration Corporation, are examples of groups formed to provide capital to minority entrepreneurs. In addition, a number of large corporations, such as Phillips Petroleum, Johnson's Wax, and Westinghouse Electric, have taken steps to provide capital to business ventures begun by minorities. It is difficult to argue with the fact that a number of financial sources have been developed to serve the minority businessman.

At the same time, there are problems. A businessman who bought a theater in a Los Angeles ghetto area was denied SBA funds, "because of his job and an excellent credit rating," which theoretically enabled him to get financing through more conventional channels; but the banks turned him down.[29] A fast-food fran-

---
[29] *Failure*, BLACK ENTERPRISE, Aug. 1970, at 31.

chiser, who would operate in ghetto locations and would franchise to blacks, was unable to raise "a nickel of equity capital" from any of over 200 establishment sources contacted, despite a superior plan and an equity base. The company started without the extra financial support and was operating profitably within a month.[30]

It may be just as bad to provide too little money as no money at all. A Milwaukee plastics manufacturer began with a loan of $10,000 and no equity capital. Sales proved expensive to obtain (because of travel expenses) and slow to materialize. The $10,000 was quickly used up and the loan extended to more than $17,000, a few thousand dollars at a time. The business has great potential, and it appears that sales contracts are coming from such large firms as General Motors, Chrysler, IBM, and Western Electric. Contracts have been already received from United Airlines and American Motors. This firm has progressed well, but there are some doubts as to its survival because of inadequate initial financing. A plastics manufacturer consulted about this project suggested that it takes $30,000 to $50,000, and three years, to establish a firm in plastics.

Capital *is* a problem for the minority entrepreneur. Hopefully, the financing programs underway will continue to grow and, one way or another, the needed financing will be made available.

C. The Ghetto Environment

A problem of significant proportion for black-owned businesses is that the ghetto environment is difficult for any kind of business. While many black-owned businesses, especially those seeking to compete in the total market, will be and should be operated outside the ghetto environment, it is reasonable to expect that a large number of black-owned businesses will be established in ghetto areas. The major difficulties of operating in a ghetto are a lack of skilled employees, a relatively poor market, a reluctance of white customers to enter the ghetto, high insurance costs, and danger from losses due to fire and theft. The examples of the high cost of operating a business in the ghetto are abundant: the fast-food franchiser who lost $11,000 over a period of several months because his employees were stealing from his cash register; the theater owner who saw his business fail because of vandalism by youths;[31] the dress-making company that found that the skills of its employees did not match their enthusiasm.[32] Establishing black-owned business in the ghetto is one approach to improving the environment, but the disease may be stronger than the medicine.

V

REDUCING THE FAILURE RATE

Black enterprise, while encouraged by a number of resounding successes, continues to suffer from a high failure rate. If meaningful success on a national level

---

[30] Shiriak, *Letter to the Editor*, HARV. BUS. REV., Nov. 1970, at 31.
[31] *Failure*, BLACK ENTERPRISE, Aug. 1970, at 36.
[32] *I Started with $1,000*, BLACK ENTERPRISE, Aug. 1970, at 36.

is to be attained, the ratio of successful individual business ventures to failures must rise. How can this best be accomplished?

The prescription for a successful minority enterprise development program seems to have four major facets:

1. *Encourage potential minority entrepreneurs to undertake business ventures.* Aside from the difficulty of identifying potential entrepreneurs, there is the very important problem of avoiding overencouragement to those who really do not want to go into business. Because strong motivation is a necessity for success, it would be a mistake to encourage persons who lack the drive to make their businesses succeed. It is probably best to publicize the opportunities for business success and at the same time be clear about the risk and personal demands involved.

Finding potential minority entrepreneurs may be less difficult than one would suspect. Because of past discriminations that have discouraged minorities from entering business, a large pool of persons who have a desire to own their own business, but who have been held back, exists in the minority community. Minorities, dubious of their chances for advancement working for others, may also be more interested than the average person in controlling their own destinies. Also encouraging is the finding that, historically, entrepreneurs have tended to have relatively low levels of education, fathers who were farmers or laborers, and relatively difficult childhood circumstances.[33] They have had to overcome problems throughout much of their life, and it is the problem-solving skill that becomes important to the success of the business they form.[34]

2. *Provide business opportunities for minority entrepreneurs.* Often the minority entrepreneur will have developed his own business opportunity. However, in many instances, the potential minority businessman, having had limited contact with the business establishment, will have difficulty visualizing a role for himself. Rather than waiting for individuals to develop good ideas, the process of black business development can be speeded up by aggressively seeking out business opportunities. In some instances this may mean developing franchising opportunities, and essentially taking advantage of somebody else's good idea. In other cases, it may mean contacting established businesses to attain purchase agreements for the supply of goods or services. The community development corporation has often been effective in identifying community needs and the resulting business opportunities.

3. *Provide the needed start-up financing and continuing lines of credit.* Many funding programs are already in existence and they seem to be growing in scope. Minority business development can succeed by using these capital sources effectively, but continued pressure is needed to ensure that these programs continue to expand and be made available. There is some danger that financing may disappear well before the end goal of increasing the market share of minority business

---

[33] O. COLLINS & D. MOORE, THE ORGANIZATION MAKERS: A BEHAVIORAL STUDY OF INDEPENDENT ENTREPRENEURS 15-38, 49-62 (1970).
[34] *Id.* at 38.

is accomplished, simply because the current enthusiasm may diminish. Continued effort should be made to make use of traditional capital sources as well.

4. *Provide the management counseling and training needed to raise minority entrepreneurial skills to a level that is competitive.* The key to a successful business is the owner-manager. In most instances, the business succeeds or fails depending on his ability to manage the resources at his disposal. Minority businessmen have often had little business experience of significant value, and therefore they are often less prepared to manage than their competitors. Certainly, many important entrepreneurial skills are life skills that are difficult to teach, and many minority entrepreneurs need little or no management help. But on the whole, the need for competent, dedicated counseling help is enormous. More than any other factor, such help can dramatically reduce the failure rate of minority business to less than that for white business.

Ideally, counseling should begin with the planning of the business idea and continue until the minority manager has raised his skill level to a point where it is equal to or better than that of his competition. Counseling is interrelated with all other facets of an effective minority business development program. It is useful in helping potential entrepreneurs to evaluate their personal potential; it is well-suited to the task of evaluating business opportunities; and it is capable of making full use of financing programs that might seem incomprehensible to the potential minority entrepreneur.

But it is probably most important in providing guidance to the entrepreneur as he begins to manage his resources. The consultant can instill basic skills, such as bookkeeping, provide advice about marketing, and help to make the business contacts that so often spell the difference between success and failure.

Accomplishing the transfer of business management knowledge is a difficult task. It requires tact, so as not to belittle the entrepreneur, who may feel insecure about his own abilities; it calls for training as well as advice, so that the entrepreneur can gain independence; and it requires many hours of consultant effort, made available on a flexible basis. Taking two hours to discuss an individual problem or evaluating the financial statements monthly is not enough. The effective consultant must be an extension of the business, the partner who is not a partner. The minority entrepreneur must have confidence in his consultant to the point where he wants to pick up the telephone and ask for help when he is confused or uncertain. Of all the resources needed for minority business development, the consultant is the most needed.

VI

THE OUTLOOK FOR MINORITY BUSINESS DEVELOPMENT

The outlook for minority business enterprise is bright, despite the fact that its impact on the total economy will not be great for a long time.[35] Minority business

---

[35] I recognize that this article has not dealt with the major task of opening entrepreneurial opportunities

will grow, because of an eager desire in the minority community to participate in business and because resources have been made available and are expanding (despite a national shift to environmental concerns).

Minority businesses operating in ghetto environments will probably require subsidies of various forms, such as tax advantages, job-training grants, and low-cost capital. But the transfer of management skills, offered freely, is the most important "subsidy" that the business establishment has to offer. The transfer of these skills will require many hours of person-to-person contact in each of several thousand individual minority business ventures. On a national level, the problems of minority enterprise development may seem overwhelming. But, with energetic application of our efforts to meet the needs of individual minority entrepreneurs, the national goal seems more attainable.

---

in the more dynamic sectors of the economy. In my opinion, significant shifts of minority enterprise into technologically-oriented industries of rapid growth potential will not be possible for several years. Certainly every opportunity to accomplish this shift should be taken advantage of as it arises. Hopefully, as minority people gain experience as employees in research positions, they will be able to generate important ideas for businesses that have the potential to grow more rapidly than the economy. One current example of a technology-based, black-owned company that shows great promise is Interface Technology, Inc., in Sacramento, California.

PROFIT MOTIVATION AND MANAGEMENT ASSISTANCE IN COMMUNITY ECONOMIC DEVELOPMENT

JOHN E. OXENDINE* AND ALVIN N. PURYEAR[†]

In July 1968 a community development corporation (CDC) in one of New York City's depressed minority communities initiated an economic development program which was designed to encourage local residents to initiate business ventures. After two years, it had provided financial and management assistance to over thirty minority entrepreneurs. The purpose of this paper is to present the findings of a study which examined the importance of profit motivation and management assistance in determining the success or failure of twelve of these businesses.

I

THE ASSISTANCE PROGRAM

The CDC in this study is a non-profit, community-based corporation which supplemented its economic development activities with housing, community development, and employment projects. Its economic development program emphasized the establishment and expansion of business enterprises owned and operated by local residents. With respect to financial aid, the CDC gave loans of approximately $2 million which, in turn, stimulated banks and private investors to provide a nearly equal amount of capital to these businesses.

The CDC felt that the creation and expansion of locally owned businesses was not a unique feature of community economic development. It believed that the more challenging task was to provide the means for insuring that local businesses would maintain their existence and grow into financially sound firms capable of generating economic returns for the community. While the CDC recognized that there was a need for management assistance, its approach in meeting this need differed from that of many other organizations. The dominant view in other assistance programs was that management assistance could best be accomplished through a system of volunteers, usually from outside the effected community. While recognizing that volunteers can play a very effective role in assisting local business development, the CDC questioned whether volunteers should be the primary instrument of assistance. As a consequence, the CDC decided not to use a "canned" program

---

* Consultant, Frye Consultants, Inc., San Francisco, California. Former Management Assistance Consultant to Bedford-Stuyvesant Restoration Corporation.

[†] Associate Professor of Management, Bernard Baruch College of the City University of New York. Former Deputy Executive Director of Bedford-Stuyvesant Restoration Corporation.

which might have worked for others, adopting, instead, a "contact man" system for its management assistance effort.

Under this system each businessman was designated the client of a CDC contact man who was given full responsibility for helping that client until a successful business operation was established. The contact man was expected to provide a wide range of services to the client. Initial assistance was often in the form of guidance to the client in his preparation of a request for funds. Typically, the contact man then assisted the client in negotiating with a bank, obtaining a business location, and selecting equipment and machinery. In effect, he provided all services which were needed to help an entrepreneur who was starting or expanding a business. Once the doors of the business were open, the contact man increased his efforts. It was then his responsibility to insure that the enterprise would be a success and add to the economic growth of the community. Obviously, the contact man, regardless of his skills, could not solve all problems and often had to go outside of the CDC to seek specialized skills. However, under this approach, even outside assistance, whether from volunteers or paid consultants, was secured under the direction of the contact man.

II
The Determinants of Success

In order to determine the ingredients necessary to insure a successful small business operation in a depressed community, we examined thirty-two firms assisted by the CDC and then selected twelve for an intensive study. Of the twelve, two were franchise operations, six were retail and service firms, and four were manufacturing companies. In the first category were a transmission franchise and a fried chicken franchise. The retail and service firms included a uniform guard service, a photo studio, a radio and television service store, an electronics store, a men's shoe store, and a moving company. The manufacturing concerns included a plastics manufacturer, a metal fabricator, a dress manufacturer, and a handbag manufacturer.

The twelve cases suggested that many factors influence the ultimate success or failure of a new business. In order to focus on the primary determinants of successful business development, we isolated five key factors which the case studies indicated were most important. The five were: (1) the technical competence or experience of the entrepreneur; (2) the capitalization of the business; (3) the amount of risk incurred by each entrepreneur; (4) the motivation of the entrepreneur; and (5) the ability and willingness of the entrepreneur to accept management assistance.

A. Technical Competence: A Panacea

At the beginning of its economic development program, the CDC believed that one key to successful community economic development was to assist individuals possessing technical competence or experience. The following factors supported this rationale: (1) the entrepreneur would know how to provide the products or services; (2) the entrepreneur would have a working knowledge of the industry's problems and practices; (3) the entrepreneur would know the sources of supply for raw materials and methods of distribution; and (4) the entrepreneur would be able to work out start-up problems in a shorter period of time. Consequently, the majority of the persons assisted by the CDC possessed a relatively high degree of technical competence. Many of these entrepreneurs had acquired their technical experience through employment in similar enterprises or through operating marginal businesses. All six of the service and retail trade entrepreneurs had some experience in their respective fields. Of the four manufacturers, only the plastics manufacturer lacked extensive experience before receiving CDC assistance.

While the CDC believed that technical competence was essential, it also made loans to a few persons who did not have experience in their new business fields. For example, it assisted the operators of the tranmission and fried chicken franchises because it felt that these were standardized operations and that franchisor management support greatly increased chances for success. Its loan to the plastics manufacturer was to continue the business that his cousin had started. In this instance, it felt that he would be able to hire persons possessing the necessary technical competence.

If the CDC's theory about technical competence was correct, one would expect that the businesses having owners with this competence would be more successful than those without. That is, the nine businesses in which the owners had technical experience would be successful, while those three in which the owners did not have experience would be less successful. Yet, the case examples did not allow us to draw such a conclusion about the value of technical experience. We saw that only four of the businesses in which the owners had technical competence were successful. These were the uniform guard service, the radio and t.v. service store, the metal fabricator, and the handbag manufacturer. At the same time, the other five—the photo studio, the electronics store, the men's shoe store, the moving company, and the dress manufacturer—were failures. Looking at the businesses in which the owners lacked technical proficiency, we found that two of the three—the transmission franchise and the plastics manufacturer—were failures, while the third—the fried chicken franchise—was entrenched solidly in success. Thus, while the CDC believed that technical competence was the key to creating successful businesses, the facts did not support this belief. Instead, the experiences of these entrepreneurs showed that technical competence was not a panacea, and that certain other ingredients would have to be present if success was to be achieved. In this regard, we examined the role of capital investment since many persons theorize that adequate capital is a necessary supplement to or substitute for technical competence.

B. Money: An Enigmatic Experience

Studies of community economic development indicate that minority entrepreneurs can seldom marshal enough capital to start a business. Our analysis of owner's equity showed that twenty-seven of the thirty-two CDC assisted businesses had owner's equity of less than $5,000. More important, the average capital invested by the owners of the twenty-seven was $1,750 or only 3.6 per cent of the average capital required of $48,000. While three of the thirty-two businesses had owner's equity between $5,000 and $15,000, the owner's average capital contribution was $9,500 or only 5.3 per cent of the average capital required of $179,500. Finally, the CDC assisted two businesses which had capital contributions greater than $15,000 and whose stockholders raised amounts which represented a relatively high sixteen and thirty-three per cent of the total capitalization required. Except for these two, however, it is significant that the entrepreneurs of the other thirty businesses were able to contribute less than five per cent of the total capitalization their businesses required.

It should come as no surprise to the reader that depressed minority communities have a severe shortage of internal capital. While one might expect outside capital to be available for ventures which show good economic promise, this has not been the case. In fact, the absence of external capital is as acute as the absence of internal capital. So the ghetto businessman must turn to the shylock for financing, or if he is lucky, to a community development corporation.

As indicated earlier, the CDC in our study had approximately $2 million which it utilized with the owners' small equity investments to partially capitalize the businesses. At the same time, it leveraged its funds by pursuing bank participation on each venture. Consequently, its $2 million coupled with the owner's investment and bank loans provided sufficient capital for the thirty-two businesses. The initial capital positions of the twelve case studies indicate the distribution and importance of this funding.

The two franchises had a total capitalization of $97,400, $36,400 of which came from the CDC, $57,500 from other lending institutions and only $3,500 from the owners. In both cases this was ample funding for the two operations. Yet one failed, while the other succeeded. The six retail and service firms also had adequate capitalization, although primarily because of assistance from the CDC and lending institutions. Of the total funding of $232,352 for the six firms, the CDC provided $172,900, lending institutions $51,252, and the owners but $8,200. In three cases—the uniform guard service, the photo studio, and the radio and t.v. service store—the CDC provided $89,500 or ninety-six per cent of the total capitalization, a very high figure. Regardless of the "funding mix," the fact remains that each of the six was financed adequately, and that four of the six failed, while only two succeeded. Finally, a similar pattern existed with the manufacturing operations. While the lending institutions provided $162,338 to the four operations, the CDC was the primary financier, supplying $594,530 or about seventy-five per cent of their total funds. Again two of the four were unsuccessful despite the fact that they received adequate funding from the CDC and the lending institutions.

Thus, although the CDC had limited funds, it was able to generate sufficient funds for all of the businesses it assisted. Yet of the twelve businesses, seven failed, including five of the nine in which the owners were also technically competent. While the CDC, the community, and the entrepreneurs believed that money could solve almost all problems, they learned that money and technical competence are not enough in themselves to guarantee success.

C. Risk: The Unconscious Persuader

In deciding among business alternatives in which to invest, it is important that funds not be given too freely, lest they defeat their primary purpose—to generate profits. Economists argue that the level of profits should be commensurate with the level of risk. In the absence of risk, one may no longer be concerned with profitability and funds may be used injudiciously for non-economic goals, thereby decreasing scarce pockets of capital. However, despite acceptance of this principle, the CDC did not include a risk factor in its financial assistance program. The evidence indicated clearly that most of its financial assistance was given consciously on a risk-free basis.

So far we have seen that the entrepreneurs of the six service and retail firms possessed a relatively high degree of technical competence and had sufficient funds to create profitable businesses. Furthermore, three of the four owners of manufacturing firms also had technical experience and sufficient funding. Finally, though the owners of the two franchises and one of the manufacturing companies did not possess this same degree of technical competence, they, too, received sufficient financial resources. Therefore, the question remains, Why did seven of twelve fail? Moreover, what accounts for five failures in cases where the entrepreneurs received sufficient financial assistance *and* had technical competence? Perhaps the failures of both the technically proficient and non-proficient can be explained by an *absence* of financial risk.

The case studies showed that only two of the nine entrepreneurs who had technical competence assumed any measurable amount of financial risk in starting their businesses. In this regard, it should be pointed out that all of the CDC loans were made to corporate entities, with the owners of the corporations having no legal obligations for the loan repayment. The best examples of absence of risk are found in the owners of the uniform guard service, the photo studio, and the radio and t.v. service store, all of whom not only received interest-free CDC loans, but in addition, had no bank financing for which they were liable personally. Equally important, they all had marketable skills which guaranteed them employment in the event that their businesses failed.

A step removed from these with respect to degree of risk were the partners of the moving company, the handbag manufacturer, the dress manufacturer, and the metal fabricator. Although they were liable personally for bank loans, there was little risk since each of the four firms had collateralized loans secured by equipment, the value of which more than offset the owners' personal liabilities. Finally, only two of the technically proficient entrepreneurs were vulnerable in that their bank loans were not covered fully by capital assets. The owner of the electronics store had borrowed from a commercial bank to supplement his CDC loan. Though he had repaid some of this obligation before his store closed, the equipment which remained did not offset fully his liability to the bank. Similarly, the men's shoe store owner did not have sufficient assets to offset his $21,500 bank loan. As a matter of fact, the store's fixtures and inventory were valued at only $5,000, thereby placing a relatively large amount of risk on the owner.

Of the three entrepreneurs who did not possess technical competence at the outset, only one—the plastics manufacturer—was completely free of risk. While he received $29,500 from lending institutions, it was more than offset by $100,000 in plant machinery. The other two owners in this category—the transmission franchisee and the fried chicken franchisee—both had risk. Because the bank loan to the former was not offset fully by the value of the machinery and equipment remaining in his transmission shop, he stood to suffer from a business failure. The latter, because of heavy debt financing, was also in a very vulnerable position. Not only was he personally liable to lending institutions for $40,000, but in addition, his chicken shop had little in capital assets as offsetting security. Thus, only three of the twelve owners faced a degree of risk likely to cause them to sustain personal financial losses.

In several of the cases, we found that lack of risk permitted or even *encouraged* the entrepreneurs to be unconcerned about the futures of their enterprises. Such cases illustrate clearly what happens to entrepreneurs who have sufficient money and technical competence, but who have nothing at stake in the event of failure. Had these entrepreneurs been liable for their investments to the extent of their personal and future assets, they might have exercised more protection for the assets of the business. Or they might have chosen not to go into business at all, in which case the risk factor would have served to select individuals committed totally to running successful ventures.

The case study revealed, however, several instances in which owners *did not* neglect their entrepreneurial duties even though they made small investments and had no personal risks. Do such cases indicate that in lieu of risk, entrepreneurs will be successful if, for example, they are willing to work long hours as did the handbag manufacturer and fried chicken franchisee? Certainly long hours are laudable, but do they explain success? Probably not, since it seems unreasonable to define *risk-free, but successful*, entrepreneurs in terms of hard work alone.

III

The Roles of Motivation and Management Assistance

A. Motivation: Mover of Men

Motivation is an intangible quality which makes an individual want to succeed, no matter what the cost. One might view it as a creative dissatisfaction which forces a man not to accept his lot but to seek new levels of achievement. Regardless of a definition of motivation, it became clear from the twelve cases that it was a key ingredient in business success. Unanswered was how "motivation" is translated into successful business operations. "Wanting to succeed," "wanting to go into business," or "seeking levels of achievement" does not insure success. The evidence in the cases suggested that if the entrepreneur was to be successful, his motivation had to be directed toward business goals. And the most basic of all business goals is profitability. Therefore, essential for the successful development of a business are entrepreneurs characterizd by a high degree of *profit motivation*. The twelve cases illustrated that profit motivation was present in the operators of the successful ventures, and absent in the operators of the failures.

The contrast in the two franchisees, for example, was most evident in their respective views of the ultimate objectives of the businesses, and accounted largely for the success of the fried chicken franchise and the failure of the transmission franchise. While the owner of the former committed himself totally to making his business a financial success, the owner of the latter spent insufficient time at his enterprise, did not utilize the management advice he received, and demonstrated that he was not interested in making his enterprise financially successful. The case for profit motivation was also evident in the experiences of the six service and retail firms. Although all of these entrepreneurs possessed sufficient experience and capitalization, only two of the six were successful. As with the franchise operations, it was clear that an essential element in determining the success of each was their owners' high motivations toward the goal of profits. The importance of profit motivation was made clear again in the case studies of the manufacturers assisted by the CDC. The metal fabricator and the handbag manufacturer possessed a high degree of profit motivation, while the unsuccessful owners reached their goals by "being in business," not by showing a profit. The divergence between these two views is wide enough to show that the profitability goal was a key determinant of success.

Thus a significant difference between the two groups—the successful and the unsuccessful—was the level of their commitment to the goal of profitability. This was reflected in the entrepreneurs' willingness to put forth the effort necessary to guide their firms to profitable positions, regardless of other—often personal—considerations. The cases illustrated that while technical proficiency, money, and risks contributed toward success, they had to be supplemented by profit motivation. Yet, all of these were useless without a vehicle to give them proper direction. This vehicle was managerial skill.

B. Management: The Essential Ingredient

In the twelve case studies we found that a variety of conditions existed with respect to each business and each entrepreneur. This was especially true in correlating success to technical ability, financing, and risk. Though all twelve firms were funded adequately, the degree of success of each was not related directly to the experience of the entrepreneur or the potentiality of a personal loss to him. In fact, the only consistent ingredient with respect to success was that the five successful entrepreneurs had a high degree of motivation toward achievement of profitability, while it was absent in the seven unsuccessful owners. Implicit in the cases was the notion that, in addition to profit motivation, the successful firms were also characterized by a pattern of good business management.

The CDC's experience showed that management may take one of two forms, enlightened or unenlightened. The unenlightened manager was incapable of giving overall direction and coordination to his business. Moreover, he was unable to see the necessity of supplementing his abilities with the skills needed to develop a profitable enterprise. Of even greater significance, the unsuccessful manager was not *motivated* sufficiently to even accept the management assistance provided through the CDC's "contact man" system. Thus, the unenlightened manager did not recognize the need to supplement his skills even when the assistance was available and given within an organized structure.

In this regard, an analysis of the twelve cases indicated clearly that the seven unsuccessful owners, in addition to lacking profit motivation, were also unenlightened. In looking at the management experiences of the five technically proficient owners who failed, one might have argued that their prior experiences should have prepared them to operate a business. This was not the case since their technical experiences could not overcome their management deficiencies. More important, these entrepreneurs also refused to accept any management assistance from the CDC. And the refusal to accept management advice does not limit itself to entrepreneurs who possess technical proficiency. Unfortunately, the owners of companies without this technical experience were also unreceptive. The transmission franchisee and the plastics manufacturer failed because they were deficient in both technical competence and management skills. In both cases the entrepreneurs did not accept the free management assistance made available by the CDC and others.

Despite such instances, there are cases—including the five successful firms in this study—where the CDC management assistance effort bore fruit. However, it should be recognized that in such cases, the owners were *motivated* to accept and use fully such assistance. Thus, the *enlightened* manager's capacity to give overall direction and coordination to the business resulted from his supplementing his management skills with the management assistance of an outsider who provides council.

If a businessman practices good management skills, or if he is willing to utilize fully a good management assistance program, it matters little that he might not possess the optimum amount of technical expertise. This fact is borne out in this study where the five owners who were motivated toward profit achievement did well regardless of their prior experiences. Of greater significance, these five cases also demonstrated that the entrepreneurs with this profit motivation were willing to accept, and, indeed, often sought CDC assistance in solving management problems.

Conclusion

Our analysis of the twelve case studies indicated that a variety of complex variables are important in determining how successful community development corporations will be in introducing economic development programs in this country's depressed areas. While one cannot say that these twelve examples are illustrative of all such minority business enterprises, it should be clear that—at the very least—they do introduce several factors which must be considered relevant for successful community economic development.

The analysis showed that while technical experience is useful, it does not insure success. This point is especially pertinent when the experience is not related directly to the management aspects of business. Also apparent was the fact that adequate capital investment is a necessary ingredient to successful community economic development. However, the familiar cry for dollars must be offset with the knowledge that funds invested without adequate direction will bring no return. Even the widely accepted view that investment capital must be accompanied by a reasonable degree of risk is ot sacred. For as our study showed, risk does not guarantee that the entrepreneur will direct himself toward the business goal of increased profits. Finally, at least two other ingredients must be present if the CDC is to promote successful economic development programs. First, the entrepreneur must have a high degree of profit motivation. That is, he must see profits, and not "going into business," as *his* primary goal. Second, good management is essential. However, because most businessmen assisted by CDC's do not possess management backgrounds and training, they must be exposed to a good program of management assistance. We have seen that the profit motivated entrepreneur will avail himself of such management assistance.

COMMUNITY ECONOMIC DEVELOPMENT

Part II

FOREWORD

The following articles continue the discussion begun in part I of this symposium on community economic development. While the contributors to this issue discuss different specific problems, the underlying controversies confronted here are the same as those treated in the prior issue. It is recognized that a matter of fundamental concern is the sources and types of financing available to development groups in low-income communities. Of equal importance is the extent to which the unique background and objectives of business ventures in underdeveloped communities necessitate special planning efforts. Finally, there is a need to define the appropriate role of government regulation in the planning and operation of community development efforts.

Government funding has been the major source of financial support for ghetto business development. The substantial risk which attends ghetto investment and the major role which social objectives play in community development suggest that the predominance of the government role is likely to continue. Charles E. Olken discusses the integration of economic development activities into the Model Cities program. An advantage of this type of funding is its potential for relating economic development to other aspects of community development. Another recent governmental program, the Opportunity Funding Corporation, attempts to provide publicly-financed incentives for private capital investments in low-income communities. The objectives and structure of the new program are discussed by Professor Samuel I. Doctors and Sharon Lockwood.

The status of the community development corporation under the Internal Revenue Code has a significant effect upon both the types of funding which will be available to it and the types of activities in which the CDC will be likely to engage. The impact of the provisions of the Tax Reform Act of 1969 relating to private foundations is analyzed by Jordan D. Luttrell.

It is clear that even with adequate initial funding, additional planning is needed to insure that minority business enterprises develop as viable economic units. The difficulties encountered in starting a small business place significant demands on the energies of the minority entrepreneur. Programs for managerial assistance to the minority operator may provide the advice necessary to insure the orderly growth of the business. However, the success of such efforts depends upon the achievement of a durable working relationship between the consultant and his client. Professor Thomas P. Ference discusses the difficulties encountered in structuring an effective program. He describes a model program which is designed to anticipate potential conflicts. Because the minority business operates in an environment distinct from that typically found in other sectors of the economy, many of the traditional approaches to business development must be modified. The effect of the location and objectives of the minority business upon its marketing activity are analyzed by Professor Carl E. Block. While planning for community economic development has concentrated on the establishment of traditional business units, there is increasing realization that housing development by community organization may both stimulate significant economic activity and satisfy an immediate social need of the community. Paul G. Garrity outlines the considerations which will affect the formation of a community-controlled housing program.

The presence of extensive public funding provides the occasion for an interaction of community goals and the institutional policies of government. The two are often not compatible and a means of accommodation is needed. Geoffrey Faux discusses the manner in which governmental controls have been employed in some programs to achieve the political and philosophical objectives of program administrators. Another aspect of the relationship between community development and government policy is treated by Stewart E. Perry. The author examines the institutional and philosophical origins of the community development corporation and suggests the need for insuring that national policy formulations take account of the political and social significance of this organizational form.

February, 1972   JOHN C. WEISTART

MANAGERIAL ASSISTANCE: PROMISES AND PITFALLS[*][†]

THOMAS P. FERENCE[**]

I

THE DIMENSIONS OF MANAGERIAL ASSISTANCE

Minority owned and managed businesses are the keystone in any serious attempt to foster community economic development. While it is true that minority group members are likely to spend most of their working careers in the employ of others, just as do their white counterparts, the importance of minority enterprise as both a symbolic and a social force cannot be denied.[1] One of the primary forces for integration and cohesion in a developing community is the existence of a flourishing business community. This sector provides not only the jobs and the sources of capital that the larger community needs for further development, but it also provides the leaders, the symbols of success, and the stability needed to insure continued motivation towards further development. While the primary function of this business sector may be the provision of services, particularly retail services, to its own community, it is also essential that it participate fully in the larger market place. This insures the complete interaction of the minority community with the larger economic system.

It is too often true in our cities at present that the economic subsystem represented by the minority community is asymmetrically related to the larger economic system. The flow of funds (working capital) out of the minority community greatly exceeds the flow of funds into it from the larger system, and the minority community consumes proportionately a greater share of the goods and services proffered by the larger system than the system consumes of the goods and services proffered by the minority community. This results in two phenomena, the first of which is widely recognized and easily demonstrated, the second of which is more subjective but in the long run more invidious. The first is the provision of funds to the minority community by means of various government programs such as welfare and unemployment insurance. While this maintains the level of consumption behavior

---

[*] I would like to thank George A. Fraser, Robert Lenzner, and Hoke S. Simpson for the guidance and insight derived from many conversations over the past four years, and Albert White for assistance in researching this paper.

[†] The preparation of this paper was made possible in part by a grant from the Faculty Research Fund of the Graduate School of Business of Columbia University.

[**] Assistant Professor of Business, Graduate School of Business, Columbia University.

[1] It is not claimed that small business development is a solution to all of the economic ills of minority communities. Those who might rely solely on such a solution overlook the realties of the economic system. As will be seen below, the focus of this piece is on those small businesses which provide symbolic evidence of the capabilities of minority businessmen and which can further the participation of the minority community in the larger economic system.

in the minority community, it has no multiplier effects for the economic subsystem. Thus, while in static terms the system is stable and closed, in dynamic terms, there is no contribution to the economic growth potential of the minority area. This leads to the second phenomenon—the long-run decay of the economic subsystem of the minority area. Without either an influx of working capital to the minority community or retention of such capital as exists in the community, the long-run effects of the cycle described above result in an ever-widening gap between the two systems. This process highlights the need for a strong, indigenous business sector which acts as a manager of capital and provides the necessary linkage between the minority community and the larger capital markets.

The need for either injections of capital or more efficient use of existing capital in minority areas has long been recognized by proponents of community economic development.[2] It has become increasingly apparent, however, from the experiences of the various lending and capital financing programs the past decade, that the mere influx of capital is not sufficient to meet the needs of the minority communities. In fact, capital alone may do more harm than good. Capital provided for starting new businesses or bolstering existing businesses is usually accompanied by considerable publicity and the raising of great expectations that the long-term process of decay and disenfranchisement from the economic system is being reversed. Capital represents, however, only the promise of participation in a business and in the economic system; capital must be managed properly if it is to fulfill this promise. Thus, in recent years, the critical need for managerial assistance in minority economic development has been recognized. It is the purpose of this paper to examine the many aspects of managerial assistance as they interact with the long-run goals of community economic development.

A. Distinguishing the Forms of Assistance

Managerial assistance is an umbrella-like term covering many forms of interaction between majority businessmen and representatives of government agencies with minority entrepreneurs and members of community organizations. In its broadest sense, it is concerned with improving the performance of minority organizations which are engaged in economic activity. Such organizations may include individually-owned businesses, consumer cooperatives, and various forms of nonprofit community corporations. The nature of managerial assistance provided may extend from review and criticism of proposals through participation in management seminars through on-site consulting to actual physical participation in the operation of the business. The duration of the interaction also may vary considerably from with-

---

[2] *See, e.g.*, T. CROSS, BLACK CAPITALISM (1969); E. FOLEY, THE ACHIEVING GHETTO (1968). For a more comprehensive analysis and proposal, see McLaurin & Tyson, *The Gheddiplan for Economic Development*, in BLACK ECONOMIC DEVELOPMENT 126 (W. Haddad and G. Pugh eds. 1969). For a more complex treatment of the barriers to minority economic development, see L. DURHAM, BLACK CAPITALISM (1970).

drawal by the majority participants once the business or organization is initially established to continued participation over several years.

Initial differentiation of the many possible forms of managerial assistance may be achieved by distinguishing between efforts on the part of individuals and programs which exist under the auspices of some controlling organization. Many majority businessmen, government officials, students, and others have on an individual basis contributed generously of their time and effort to assisting minority businessmen and community organizations. The greater amount of managerial assistance, however, is provided through organized programs rather than by individual practitioners. Since this is likely to continue to be true in the future, the remainder of this paper will focus on organized programs. Much of what is to follow in terms of critique and prescription for organized programs could, of course, also be profitably applied to individual efforts.

In describing various programs of managerial assistance, there are two primary dimensions which must be considered. First, there is the nature of the assistance to be provided, and here there are two polar types. The first involves the importation of management, as where a corporation provides a managerial work force on either a loan or permanent basis to operate a plant or other facility in a minority area. The duties of this managerial work force usually include both the efficient operation of the facility in normal business terms and the identification and training of minority group members who would then gradually take over the management positions.[3] The second polar type involves the provision of consulting services to new or existing minority businesses. In these cases, operating responsibility is vested in the minority manager who has available for consultation experts in the various functions of business drawn from participating corporations and other organizations. There are also a variety of intermediate positions along this dimension including various types of seminar and classroom training programs for minority businessmen conducted either by university faculties or participating businessmen.

Consultation itself may be provided under many guises. Among the more familiar of these are (a) *the nonprofit agency*, such as the Interracial Council for Business Opportunity (ICBO) which serves as a clearing house, bringing together volunteer business executives and minority entrepreneurs; (b) *assistance provided as a condition of financing*, either under the auspices of venture capital corporations or through commercial banks; and (c) *university programs*, which use graduate business students and faculty as consultants, often on a fee basis. It is not within the scope of this paper to attempt to review and discriminate among the myriad of programs now existing or being planned across the country; a comprehensive com-

---

[3] If normal business standards are not used in estimating the viability of minority enterprises, then the survival of such enterprises will be dependent on continued subsidies from the sponsoring organizations. This runs directly counter to the symbolic and growth potential goals of minority economic development.

pendium of managerial assistance programs has been developed by the Department of Commerce.[4]

In addition to the distinction between importing a management team and providing consulting aid to indigenous managers, the second major dimension is the choice between programs aimed at providing assistance to existing minority enterprise and those concerned with establishing and assisting new enterprise. To some degree these two dimensions are correlated, for the possibility of importing management teams is probably greater in new enterprises than it would be in the fortifying of existing enterprises. This is particularly true when we consider that much of the currently existing minority-owned business in the country falls into the category of small retail or service-type businesses. It is possible, however, to conceive of assistance programs which provide management teams for existing businesses which are at a critical growth stage or which provide consulting services to new businesses.

It is probably inappropriate to attempt to argue that one or another of the possible combinations of types of assistance and types of business is the most preferable or the most desirable in a program of community economic development. These several combinations represent different aspects or starting points in the same process. Thus, if the goal of managerial assistance programs is to foster the fuller involvement of minorities and minority areas in the economic system, then each of the possible combinations of importation, consultation, and new and established businesses may be desirable, but their desirability may be determined by differing circumstances.

1. *Importing a Management Team*

Several desirable characteristics can be identified in a program which relies on the importation of a management team and the establishment of a new enterprise. First, the importation of a management team generally occurs when an existing corporation has decided to "adopt" a minority enterprise and has made a commitment to its future. The new enterprise may be engaged in producing a product which is needed by the parent corporation, or the parent corporation may in some manner be acting to guarantee the market of the minority enterprise, at least during its formative years.[5] To the extent that the parent corporation's prestige and self-image are committed to the success of this project, the prospects for the minority enterprise may be quite bright.

---

[4] U.S. DEPARTMENT OF COMMERCE (Office of Minority Business Enterprise), PRIVATE PROGRAMS ASSISTING MINORITY BUSINESS (1970). *See also* B. FLOWER, BUSINESS AMID URBAN CRISIS (Studies in Public Affairs #3) (1968); NATIONAL INDUSTRIAL CONFERENCE BOARD, THE ROLE OF BUSINESS IN PUBLIC AFFAIRS (Studies in Public Affairs #2) (1968); Cohn, *Is Business Meeting the Challenge of Urban Affairs?*, 48 HARV. BUS. REV. 68 (1970).

[5] It is essential that there be a real growing market for the products of the minority enterprise. New ventures into marginal product areas, even if subsidized, are not likely to succeed. *See* L. DURHAM, *supra* note 2.

A second desirable characteristic of the adoption process is that it connects employees and managers drawn from the minority community into the larger organization. This creates a spin-off of jobs for minority residents and brighter prospects of career development for the emerging group of minority managers. Thus, importation programs offer guaranteed short run success, are generally larger in scope than individually started business enterprises, and can provide more jobs for the minority area. These jobs can incorporate training and development programs and provide links to larger career paths for minority employees and managers.

These are, of course, ideal conditions, and there are many pitfalls in the path of such programs. First, the willingness of corporations to engage in such programs is clearly tied to the leverage that they have available to them as a result of economic conditions. It is unlikely, at the time that this is being written in late 1970, that the market place for such new business ventures would be as favorable as it was only a few years ago.

A second problem in the realization of the full potential of such programs is the possibility of distrust in the minority community itself. It is not always true that the potential for job training and upgrading of management has reached fruition. Much of the criticism of job placement and manpower training programs for minorities has been leveled at the lack of upgrading and career possibilities. A final problem is that the end efforts of the imported management team may be to amplify the dependency of the minority employees and managers-in-training on this team. If the successful adopted minority enterprise is seen as being successful only because of the efforts of the majority participants, then the enterprise will make only a minimal or perhaps a negative contribution to the development of the minority business sector. Since one of the major concerns in developing a minority business sector is to provide success models and leadership for the minority area, successes in minority enterprises which are attributable mainly to majority participants are of little value. Thus, importation programs for developing new enterprises are likely to contribute to minority economic development only under favorable economic conditions which will stimulate the participation of large corporations, only when these corporations follow through on the promise of training and upgrading, and only when there is a true transfer of responsibility, authority, and control to the minority management.

2. *Consulting with Existing Businesses*

A second combination is the program which provides consulting services to existing businesses. Attention will be focused on management consulting activities which are directly relevant to the ongoing operations of the business. These would include direct advice on such things as inventory planning and control, bookkeeping and accounting systems, promotional displays, and customer-employee relations. Off-job aspects of managerial assistance programs which are concerned with broader issues of the minority businessman's managerial development, such as seminars, extension programs, and other educational efforts, will be considered below.

In contrast to the "importation-new business" combination described above, programs emphasizing direct consultation on the ongoing problems of existing businesses are less grandiose in prospect, but probably more in tune with conditions and possibilities in minority areas. First, the target population for such programs already exists. Such businesses are generally beset with many problems including survival, financial and physical, and an overworked owner-operator. Further, the scale of operations of such businesses normally facilitates the assessment of these problems and the establishment of priorities for their resolution. Since programs of consulting to established minority businesses generally function by means of direct contact between one consultant or a team of business experts with the minority entrepreneur, it is generally possible to move directly to programs and proposals for improving the performance of the business. The small scope of operations—in terms of total volume, number of employees, and structural complexity—and the consequent availability of immediate feedback on the effects of actions, make it possible for the consultant to become immediately involved in the operating process of the business. The impact of the consultant is tangible and has immediate consequences.

It may also be true, of course, that the impact of successfully consulting with an individual businessman on the economy of the minority area may be less than the long-run impact of a successful new venture established under a parent corporation's protection.[6] A successful program of consultation to established businesses, however, has several desirable characteristics which tend to counteract this possible disadvantage. First, the impact of successful consulting efforts with local businessmen is likely to be immediate and readily observable to the community at large. Secondly, such programs are relatively insensitive to short-run fluctuations in economic conditions in the larger system since sizeable long-run commitments of capital and manpower are not necessary in order to get such programs functioning. The fact that the small businesses involved are already operating provides a further insulation from fluctuating economic conditions since the emphasis of the program is on performance of an operating enterprise and not on locating surplus capital and manpower which could be invested in a new project.[7] A third characteristic is that the program is "wired in parallel," that is, the failure of one of the small businesses involved in a program of consulting in a minority area does not directly affect the

---

[6] Again, the emphasis on small business does not imply that it is an end in itself, but a vehicle for fostering more extensive and significant economic development.

[7] To the extent that the problems of a particular small business revolve around acquiring capital either to support current operations or to expand, general economic conditions will clearly mediate the business' access to the capital markets, whether or not the business has available expert consultation from a managerial assistance program. The point is that consultation with small businesses represents a continuing process and does not, therefore, depend on the making of recurring judgments which are sensitive to economic conditions.

probabilites of success of the other businesses involved. Thus, consulting programs can accumulate successes while not being seriously debilitated by failures; programs which rely on the importation of new business generally only have one shot at success or failure. Finally, the symbolic impact of a series of success stories of small businessmen who maintained operating control and responsibility throughout the managerial assistance phase of their business history is probably greater and more responsive to the self-image needs of the minority community than would be the impact of a new business which was controlled and operating primarily by majority participants during its critical development stages.

There are, however, several serious pitfalls in the "consulting-existing business" route. These include the volatile nature of small business and the difficulties in developing and maintaining adequate systems for monitoring the interactions of individual consultants with their businessmen-clients. The client-consultant relationship is critical to the success of such a program, and yet it is highly susceptible to many kinds of breakdowns. The lifespan of most small businesses is rather short and the failure rate of new ventures is quite high. There is no reason to expect that the experience of small business in minority areas would be any more favorable. Thus, serious and diligent effort by a competent consultant is no guarantee of the eventual success of the business. The possibility that consultants may be less than ideally serious and diligent underscores the need for an efficient monitoring system.

B. Critical Elements in Choosing an Approach

It should be clear from the two combinations developed above that the remaining possibilities—consulting to new business ventures and importing management to operate existing businesses—are really special cases in the general process implied in the two examples given. Summarizing these examples, it becomes clear that the critical elements in evaluating or examining managerial assistance programs or in making the preliminary decision of what type of program is most appropriate at a given time and a given area include the following:

(a) the existence of opportunities to initiate a managerial assistance program; these might include the presence of an indigenous small business sector or the matching of favorable economic conditions and corporate needs with the possibilities of establishing a new venture;
(b) the probabilities that the enterprises receiving assistance will be successful;
(c) the nature of the interaction between minority and majority participants;
(d) the symbolic impact of the program on the minority community;
(e) the contribution that the program makes to improving the participation of the minority community in the larger economic system.

The following discussion focuses on assistance programs which involve consulting to existing businesses. This approach was chosen for detailed consideration because it speaks most directly to the immediate, short-run needs of the minority community, is best insulated from fluctuations in general economic conditions, and provides immediate, active contact with the existing minority economic system.[8]

Part II of this article will develop the notion of a "consulting to existing business" program further by examining the various levels of approach which fall into this classification. Part III will develop criteria which might be used in selecting and formulating a specific program and will examine some of the decisions which must be made in the preliminary planning stages. The application of this model to the establishment of a specific program will then be described in part IV. Part V will examine in somewhat greater detail the operating experiences of this particular program and will attempt to develop general guidelines for avoiding serious pitfalls in fulfilling the promise of managerial assistance to minority economic development.

II

An Overview of Consulting Programs

A. The Sources of Support

1. *The Federal Government*

The notion of programs of consulting to small business covers a wide range of specific formulations, which vary widely among themselves. While an exhaustive listing is probably not possible, a brief description of some of the more common types might be useful. The federal government, as well as many state and local governments, provides a wide range of managerial assistance to small businesses. These include an entire catalogue of brochures, pamphlets, and other "how to" materials designed to aid the businessman in establishing, incorporating, putting into operation, and managing his business. Other governmental services include the maintenance of agencies and local offices which can provide a wide variety of assistance to businessmen who come in with their problems. The best known of these programs is the Small Business Administration (SBA).[9] Assistance may involve the provision of loan funds, the insuring of loans obtained from commercial sources, or several types of operating assistance. In most cases, programs which involve the government as a participant in a loan arrangement have required the participating businessman either to accept consulting assistance from the government agency itself or to acquire it through some other source. In recent years, such special programs as MESBIC and Model Cities, which are discussed in detail by other authors in this symposium, have had required managerial assistance as an integral part of their formulation.[10]

---

[8] For another discussion of these issues which reaches a somewhat different conclusion, see L. Durham, *supra* note 2.

[9] An extensive listing of government programs is given in Department of Commerce Handbook for Small Business (1969).

[10] This new emphasis on managerial assistance may stem in part from a recognition that much, if not all, of the problems of a small businessman are problems of operating management and not of financing *per se*. The recognition that the infusion of funds is, at best, usually a stop-gap measure which

2. The Business Community

The participation of the business community has also taken many forms. Most commonly, corporations have permitted, or in many cases encouraged their employees to devote some of their time to working with minority businessmen.[11] For those employees who choose to serve as consultants, the relationship or the contact with the businessman is generally not made through employers but through some other organization or agency. In many cases, individual consultants make their own contacts but the use of an organizational mediator is more common. These mediators include nonprofit community organizations established primarily for the purpose of providing managerial assistance, such as Interracial Council for Business Opportunity (ICBO), government agencies such as the SBA (which utilizes retired executives in its SCORE program and active managers in its ACE program),[12] local economic development agencies, and, in some cases, university operated programs. In most cases, business consultants normally serve as volunteers on their own time although there are instances where the company permits the individual to set aside a certain amount of his working time for managerial assistance activity.[13]

Another source of managerial assistance has been the recent institution of organizations intended to provide financial and operational assistance to minority entrepreneurs. In New York City, for example, the Urban Coalition has founded the Coalition Venture Corporation whose task it is to provide, or serve as an intermediary in the securing of, capital funds for new and established businesses. Coalition Venture also provides a consulting service for its clients. There are several other organizations similar to Coalition Venture which seek to couple financial assistance with ongoing management consulting. Other examples from the New York area include the Bedford-Stuyvesant Capital Corporation and Capital Formation, Inc.[14]

3. New Consulting Firms

On the profit-making side, there have emerged in recent years a small but growing number of consulting firms, largely black-owned and operated, whose principal business activity is the provision of consulting to minority entrepreneurs.

---

does not speak to the real needs of minority entrepreneurs is substantiated by the experience reported in part V of this paper.

[11] For illustrative examples, *see* Cohn, *supra* note 4; B. FLOWER, *supra* note 4.

[12] SCORE (Service Core of Retired Executives) and ACE (Active Corps of Executives) are described in HANDBOOK FOR SMALL BUSINESS, *supra* note 9, at 176.

[13] In some instances, notably in the banking industry, the nature of the corporation's activities bring it into direct contact with minority entrepreneurs and, in these cases, the employee may be serving as a consultant directly under the auspices of his corporation.

[14] *See* PRIVATE PROGRAMS, Assisting Minority Enterprise, *supra* note 4, at 178, 181. In all, forty-two private programs of managerial assistance are listed for New York City. In comparison, eighteen programs are listed for Washington and twelve for Chicago. Questions of redundancy and possible benefits of coordination have not been seriously examined to date.

While these firms occasionally have individual businessmen as clients, the more common arrangement is with a businessmen's association or community development organization, often with the financial support of a government loan or grant program. While the future of these firms is yet to be decided because of their relative youth, their existence is an encouraging sign if we interpret it as an indication of the growing strength and vitality of minority enterprise.

4. *The Universities*

Finally, there are a number of existing consulting programs under the auspices of universities, particularly urban universities. These programs are generally located in the graduate business school and use graduate students (MBA's) as consultants with back-up support and guidance from the faculty. As these programs have grown, alumni, particularly those who were consultants during their student days, have also begun to participate in the programs. Such programs have no loan funds of their own and are normally involved in consulting on operations, although assistance to the businessman-client in the preparation of loan applications is also a major activity. The author has worked closely with a program of this type over the past three years; the experience of this program will be used (in part IV) as a vehicle for exemplifying the principles of a good managerial assistance program to be described in part III. The following sections consider a general managerial assistance program and describe the critical characteristics of such a program. It is recognized, however, that of necessity there will be many variations in the theory and in the practice of managerial assistance programs depending upon the area, the identity of the sponsors, and the particular needs and characteristics of the local business community.

B. Supplementary Development and Training Efforts

The above description of the classes of managerial assistance programs has focused primarily on the direct provision of consulting services to a businessman-client in his place of business. That is, the primary concern was with assistance aimed at improving day-to-day operation of the small business and at solving the immediate, pressing problems of such businesses. In addition to this primary focus at keeping the small businessman in business and making the enterprise profitable in the short run, most of the programs described above subscribe to the parallel goal of developing the small businessman's general abilities as a manager. This means that the consultant is not only concerned with solving the immediate problem of the small businessman, but also with improving the businessman's ability as a problem solver. This may entail helping the businessman come to a clear perception of his role as manager; it may also involve encouraging him to participate in job training programs. Most programs recognize that their efforts to solve pressing problems of their small business clients are stop-gap measures and that it is not enough to keep these businesses alive; they must also become self-sustaining. For this reason, most programs of consulting to small businesses incorporate some notion of off-job training generally in the form of attendance at conferences or seminars designed to increase the businessman's technical competence and general managerial ability. As with the types of consulting assistance, there are many off-job educational programs currently in operation. These range from intensive seminars or conferences of one or two or three days duration which focus on a particular issue such as advertising, franchising, or factoring of accounts receivable, through ongoing workshops which meet regularly over several weeks, to rather full-scale educational programs which attempt to provide a complex introduction to managerial training.

For example, AUCOA, in New York City, regularly conducts a course in the preparation of bids and other specific competitive problems of small contractors.[15] On a more elaborate level, ICBO runs throughout New York City and several other parts of the country the Business Opportunities Workshop program which provides an intensive fifteen session course in the several major facets of small business operation. These are only a few examples of the possible programs in continuing education which might be conceived as concomitants to consulting on operations. The remainder of this paper will concentrate on the criteria and issues involved in the establishment and operation of programs of direct consulting on current operations. The necessity of accompanying such programs with efforts to enhance the specific technical competences and ability of the minority entrepreneur, perhaps through formal training programs, should be evident from this discussion.

III

Determinants of a Successful Program: A General Model

A. Basic Criteria

We turn now to a consideration of the characteristics that should be incorporated in an efficient program of providing managerial assistance to minority enterprises. Focusing on programs which provide consulting assistance to existing businessmen, it is evident that at least four overriding criteria must be met if the program is to succeed.

(a) *Acceptance.* Planning and conception, the manner of introduction, the identity of the sponsoring organization, its consultants and the target population, and the operating procedures of the consulting organization are critical factors in determining whether or not the consulting effort will be accepted by the minority community. Note that if the program is to have maximum impact, it must be accepted not only by the minority business clients, but also by the rest of the minority community.

(b) *Empathy.* This is an intangible quality, but the consulting organization and its field representatives, the consultants, should have a sensitive prior understanding

---

[15] AUCOA (Association of United Contractors of America) is a non-profit organization of minority contractors in New York City.

of the conditions and circumstances of small business, should be flexible in recognizing and responding to the needs of their clients, and should be capable of finding grounds for effective exchange of information.

(c) *Knowledge.* Small business is a specific example of business in general; it is also a unique activity. Application of general business knowledge to the specifics of small business requires a careful and conscious translation process which is often overlooked by the providers of managerial assistance. To the extent that there are unique characteristics in the operation of a minority enterprise, an equally sensitive and conscious additional translation must be made.

(d) *Reliability.* Organizations and individuals who enter into consulting arrangements with minority businessmen must be completely reliable in fulfilling these commitments. Emergencies in the home office for the volunteer businessman, exams for the student, and special meetings for the government official may all be perfectly valid reasons from their viewpoints for missing a meeting with the minority clients. From the minority perspective, however, this can and frequently is viewed as one more piece of evidence that the majority participants are not sincere in their efforts. Another aspect of reliability is that the consultant frequently will be leading his client out on to what is shaky ground for the client. Programs initiated by the consultant often exceed the current competence of the client. Without adequate follow-up by the consultant such programs may do more harm than good.[16]

It is probably true that a variety of well run and well conceived programs could satisfy these four conditions, regardless of whether the program was under the auspices of government, business, community, or university sponsors. The underlying premise of managerial assistance programs—that they contribute to the long-run growth and development of the minority business community—suggests some further considerations which might guide the choice among possible sponsoring organizations.

Economic development programs can do harm as well as good, particularly if they are not in tune with the needs and perceptions of the community being served or if the lifespan of the program does not coincide with the period needed for individual businesses to reach maturity. This consideration suggests that desirable programs should be instituted under the sponsorship of organizations which are in close and continuing contact with the community, that the sponsoring organization must recognize that its commitment must be relatively permanent, and that the program must be reasonably well insulated from exogenous decisions. As has been suggested, empathy, acceptance, and reliability are at least as important as knowledge in motivating a successful program. Further, the stipulation of freedom from exogenous decisions suggests that the long-run success of the program depends on its freedom

---

[16] A related aspect of reliability is the problem of consultant turnover. In terms of impact on the minority businessman, there is a considerable difference between a continuing association with a managerial assistance program and a continuing association with a specific consultant. Frequent changes in the consulting team can greatly deter progress.

from concern over random fluctuations in the larger economy as well as relative freedom from the need to search continually for operating funds from external agencies.[17] This analysis would suggest that programs initiated by community-based organizations or by other organizations who have their permanent roots in the minority community would be preferable, particularly if they are on a "pay-as-you-go" or endowment basis.

B. Specific Operating Characteristics: The Model

The problem is to define requirements which will make the program acceptable to the community, capable of providing the specific technical business services that it promises, and capable of eliciting the continuing commitment of the sponsoring organization. A program which satisfies these requirements would have to have the following characteristics:

(a) The program must be seen by all parties involved as serving their own self-interests.
(b) The program must be responsive to individual and communal self-image needs.
(c) The program must overcome normal barriers to communication.
(d) The program should avoid the consultation-community participation morass.
(e) The program should take care to keep expectations from outpacing results.
(f) The program should provide and extend the legitimacy for parties involved.[18]

1. *Shared Self-Interest*

Perception of shared self-interest is a necessary precondition to establishing any program which will exist over time. Institutions will become involved in black economic development only to the extent that they are convinced that it serves their own self-interest. Programs initiated on a self-interest basis are, of course, capable of servicing social goals. It is not necessary to assume that the self-interest of the various sectors are mutually exclusive. The intricate relationships between the minority economy and the larger economic system have been outlined. It should be obvious that the health of the minority economy necessarily contributes to the health of the total economy. On the local level, moreover, many institutions and organizations find themselves in a position where their future markets, manpower

---

[17] For example, many managerial assistance programs are started with seed money provided by a foundation, the federal government, or some other institution. These funds enable the assisting organization to begin operation and to create expectations in the minority community. Frequently, however, funds run out just as the organization is beginning to function effectively, and the organization must then divert its efforts away from its businessmen-clients to the task of fund raising. When such an event occurs, it does harm to the direct consulting relationship and also to the trust and confidence vested in the program by the community and the clients.

[18] An expanded development of this model and of the history of MBA Management Consultants, Inc. is given in Ference & Fraser, *White Involvement in Black Economic Development*, 15 J. Soc. & Behav. Sci. (1969). See also Casten, *MBA Management Consultants: Blueprint for Student Involvement*, MBA 3, 1969; Sloane, *Management Aid for Harlem Business*, N.Y. Times, May 3, 1969 (Business and Finance), at 1, col. 4.

sources, and political environments are concentrated in a growing minority community.[19] Perceptions of shared self-interest provide insurance of participation by the sponsoring organization. Further, the perception by the minority community that the consulting program is providing a benefit to the sponsoring organization is a more readily understandable and acceptable motive for the sponsoring organization than is a vague sense of social responsibility. Shared self-interest also provides some guarantee that the decisions and actions of the assistance program and the specific advice and suggestions of consultants will be guided by realistic, hard-nosed business criteria and not by wishful thinking. Thus, the perception by all parties that they have "a piece of the action" insures that the regular rules of the game are being used.[20] All too often, majority consultants forget the rules and procedures that they use to make decisions in their own business when advising their minority clients. This frequently leads to unsound decisions, which in turn weaken the survival chances of the minority business. Self-interest and strict adherence to the rules of the business game are socially responsible as well as economically defensible.

2. *Self-Image Needs*

Responsiveness to individual and communal self-image needs implies that programs cannot be developed and initiated by the sponsoring institution acting on its own. Moreover, programs cannot be promoted as helping the minority businessman to better himself if they do for him things that he cannot do for himself. Such a paternalistic posture usually hampers any useful coming together of the sponsoring organization with the local business group or the larger community. Such an approach effectively prevents the minority businessman from developing his own potential as a manager and from expanding his market beyond his immediate community. An acceptable managerial assistance program, therefore, will take the form of a rational partnership wherein all parties contribute and derive from the activity. By recognizing shared self-interest, with tangible *quid pro quo* for all parties, all parties can retain the freedom to initiate or reject proposals and to terminate the relationship. This assures that responsibility for program adoption and for subsequent success is shared fully by the minority entrepreneur. Programs which are consistent with this premise contribute to the symbolic and practical development of self-sufficient minority enterprise.

3. *Effective Communications*

Circumventing communication barriers is essential if managerial assistance programs are to move beyond stylized interactions which currently typify majority-

---

[19] This has been particularly true of many of the major power companies and of large urban universities, which might explain why these institutions have been among the first to become active in community development programs.

[20] The "piece of the action" for many sponsors of management assistance programs is by way of an investment in the entire minority area rather than a commitment to a specific business. For some organizations, however, the piece of the action is just that—an equity share—a minority business.

minority relationships. Emphasis is usually placed on points of difference as the participants act out ingrained social roles such as that of the militant, philanthropist, superior, or subordinate. In all of these roles, there is no assumption of a commonality of interests. The minority businessman is a petitioner humbly or aggressively seeking the benefits from the majority controller of resources. Attempts to communicate within these roles are not likely to produce any revisions of thinking nor effective movement toward improved operations of minority enterprises. It is necessary, therefore, to focus on similarities in the relationship such as common interests and practical experiences in business, expertise in particular functions or aspects of business, and adherence to the value of business as a way of life. The majority consultant brings to the relationship his knowledge of sound principles of general management while the minority entrepreneur brings practical experience and expertise in the technology of a particular enterprise; both bring a particular view of reality based on their experiences. The consultant is likely to have as difficult a time in adapting his knowledge to the peculiar conditions of business in the minority community as the minority entrepreneur will have in absorbing the advice and reasoning of the consultant. In order for programs of managerial assistance to get off the ground and to succeed over time, the sponsoring organization and its representatives must continually demonstrate their respect for and dependence on the special knowledge and skills of the minority entrepreneurs with whom they work.

4. *Community Involvement*

In terms of transforming a program of managerial assistance from an idea to reality, many well-intentioned programs have foundered on the issue of community participation in the planning and initiating of the program. Consulting the community on matters that effect it is an intuitively appealing principle on both moral and political grounds. Those organizations which have attempted to achieve a community consensus before initiating their programs, however, have often found the process to be counterproductive. Adherence to a criterion of shared self-interest would seem to preclude engaging in the tedious and politically dangerous process of consultation. It is impossible to reach an accord with every community group, particularly since the groups in any given community are likely to have sharp disagreements among themselves. A program of consulting to existing businesses seeks to avoid the potential dangers of community participation by establishing direct relationships between individual entrepreneurs and the consulting organization. One specific implication of this position is that programs initiated at the behest of minority businessmen are more likely to be successful because the consulting organization has been invited into the area.

5. *Controlling Expectations*

A major pitfall facing all community oriented programs is the possibility that the expectations generated by the announcement of the program will continually outpace the results produced by the program. This is particularly true, of course, if the announcement of the program occurs months or years before the program is actually put into operation. Well-intentioned programs can founder for many reasons, including conflicts of interests, unreasonable projections of impact, and the simple passage of time between inception and results. When this occurs, expectations are thwarted and the underlying mistrust of majority intentions is reinforced in the minority community. Two specific implications follow from this point. First, programs which can be inaugurated with a minimum of publicity are preferable. Second, publicity should follow upon actions and should reflect accomplishments of the program. Programs of consulting to minority businessmen can fulfill both of these ambitions, particularly if publicity concerning the program is held to a minimum until after the program is well into operation and evidences of success in specific consulting-client relationships are available.[21]

6. *Preparing for the Future*

Consulting to minority business is a necessary first step in drawing the minority economy into proportionate participation in the larger economic system. It follows that programs of managerial assistance ought to provide extended legitimacy for the parties involved. The participants in the program must be consciously aware of the need to link their efforts to a larger process of change and development. Observance of the preceding conditions imply that programs of consulting to small business will initially have a fairly limited potential effect. In order to have significant impact on the economic conditions of minority areas, programs will have to affect larger numbers of people, providing concrete results and leverage for future programs. The logical next step will evolve out of experience with programs aimed at individual businessmen, but only if the participants in those programs consciously attend to the need to look for the next steps.

IV

MBA MANAGEMENT CONSULTANTS, INC.: THE MODEL APPLIED

A. Developing the Program

The Columbia Graduate School of Business, for a variety of reasons, sought in 1968 to become involved in the economic development of Harlem. Columbia University is physically situated in Harlem, a factor which provides sufficient reason for concern about the economic development of the area. Other factors, such as the interests of students and faculty, overtures from the business community, and a desire to demonstrate the school's capabilities, were also operative. It was recog-

---

[21] It would be charitable to say that institutions which seek much advanced publicity are naive with regard to the relation between expectations and performance. It is probably more often a case that such institutions are as much concerned with their public image and their troubled consciences as with the people that the programs are supposed to help. By avoiding publicity, sponsoring organizations should be able to disassociate themselves from this past history and programs of questionable motivation.

nized that a massive influx of people from the School of Business into Harlem or the masterminding of major development programs would feed upon the feelings of suspicion and antagonism which Harlem had developed toward Columbia. It was decided that the school would not initiate programs on its own but would constitute itself as a skills broker in the managerial assistance field, providing the services of faculty and students to whatever groups or individuals sought them. Skills brokerage is on the surface a passive concept. In practice, existing word of mouth communication networks were utilized as a means of encouraging requests for assistance from the community. Thus, the school provided speakers for many occasions, acted as organizational design consultants for some community action groups, conducted a blue ribbon seminar in minority business development, and met with a broad spectrum of business-oriented groups. These exchanges provided many leads, but only those which offered a reasonably high probability of success were pursued beyond the information exchange stage. This decision was based on a recognition of the school's limited resources and on the perception that association with ineffective projects would hinder acceptance as a participant in other efforts.

The school decided to focus upon providing consulting to existing minority entrepreneurs. This choice was prompted by several factors. First, the small business sector seemed most likely to provide a steady flow of relationships; there are three to four thousand minority-owned businesses in Harlem, most of them small. These independent entrepreneurs provided a viable point of entry into the community. Second, the business students had been looking for opportunities to make some contribution to community development. It seemed that exposure to small, operating concerns would be a reasonable vehicle for tapping their skills without getting them in beyond their capabilities. Third, relations with individual businessmen would be roughly independent of those with other clients. None of these affiliations would be large enough initially to attract a great deal of attention. This would provide the program with a chance to succeed or fail on its own merits. Finally, the school had received specific overtures from a reasonably successful entrepreneur who was seeking whatever managerial assistance might be available. This initiation provided an ideal entry for establishing the program.

Out of these considerations emerged what is now MBA Management Consultants, Inc.[22] Two or three member teams of graduate business students serve as consultants to individual businessmen. The student team also has access to a faculty advisor. MBA began as a student activity but has recently become a nonprofit membership corporation. Membership in the corporation is held by the minority entrepreneurs who are the clients and the students who are their consultants. The corporation is governed by a fifteen-man board of directors, elected by the membership. Seven members of the board are businessmen, four are drawn from the Graduate School of Business, and the remaining four are representatives of the New York

---

[22] *See* Ference & Fraser, *supra* note 18; Sloane, *supra* note 18.

business community. Daily operations are managed by a full-time director and a staff of five student officers who work part time. Student consultants are compensated for their services from funds donated for that purpose. The original funding of the program was provided mainly by the Urban Center of Columbia University and Arthur D. Little, Inc. Future plans for financing the corporation include the transferral of part of the financial burden to the clients, perhaps on a fee basis, and an enlarged fund raising program. After two and one-half years of existence, MBA is now actively engaged in consulting with forty separate businesses and utilizing the services of approximately ninety students and about twenty-five faculty and advisors.[23] In some cases, alumni of the school who had participated as consultants during their educational program have continued to work with their clients on a voluntary basis.

B. The Consulting Relationship: The Model Implemented

The student-businessman relationship is structured in terms of the typical managerial consulting relationship. It is a typical business arrangement. The businessman contracts for the consulting service. He is not obligated to accept the consultants' suggestions and he retains the right to reject a particular consultant or team at any time. Thus, the student-consultants are in the "employ" of the businessman. The businessman-client gains access to the specialized knowledge of the students but retains the discretion of applying this knowledge to his own operations. The student-consultants earn a reasonable wage (three dollars per hour) and derive the benefits of the client's years of practical experience. The consultants' experience in the job market at graduation has shown that this exposure to the real world is a readily marketable commodity. Thus, at the individual level, the consulting relationship represents a clear case of shared self-interest and avoids threatening the self-image of either party. It is particularly clear that the student gains as much from the interaction as does the businessman.[24]

The management consulting relationship also speaks directly to the need to circumvent communication barriers. The consultant-client relationship does not challenge the intelligence or ability of either party; it asserts that they have different types of competence. The client is a practicing businessman, immersed daily in all the problems of running a business. His knowledge, while often intuitive and unsystematic, is comprehensive. His concern with keeping afloat from day-to-day has most likely prevented him from doing much planning or from examining the deficiencies of his activities. The student-consultant is receiving specalized training in a variety of formal techniques and approaches. He can serve as a technical

---

[23] In its three-year history, over two hundred students have participated as consultants to over sixty businesses.

[24] From the school's perspective, there is also a sharing of self-interests. The school is likely to remain in close physical proximity to Harlem and, thus, involvement in the economic development of the area represents an investment in long-run survival and stability. The consulting experience is also a valuable addition to the student's education, and one which would be impossible to simulate in the classroom.

specialist in the solution of specific problems. He also fills a broader role, that of an objective outside observer. He thus can provide both the incentive and the justification for the client to take a careful look at his enterprise. Exchanges between consultant and client allow both parties to examine their activities and try out new ideas. A consultant provides the lever necessary for the client to develop his skills as a manager and planner. The client in turn provides a sounding board for examining the practicality of the ideas and theories of the consultant. Each is, therefore, both student and teacher. This common ground can act to break down communication barriers while protecting the integrity of the individuals involved.

Of the remaining considerations, the needs to avoid publicity and the political difficulties of community consultation are fulfilled by basing the program on affiliations with individual businessmen. The final premise—that of legitimizing future programs—should follow from satisfaction of the above premises. It can be seen that a program conceived along the lines of MBA Management Consultants, Inc., satisfies the basic requirements of a successful managerial assistance program that were outlined in part III. The continued existence and growth of MBA demonstrates that these requirements are valid. This is not to say that MBA has experienced no difficulties. In fact, the problems that it has experienced relate directly to the primary criteria of acceptance, empathy, reliability, and knowledge identified above.

C. Operating Problems: Failures to Satisfy the Model

The problem of general acceptance has been the most readily resolvable. The student's motives are seen as a mixture of the desires to perform some socially beneficial work and to gain some useful experience (and also, in some cases, to earn a modest income). These motives are acceptable to the minority businessmen and go a long way toward easing fears of exploitation.

On the level of the individual enterprise, however, the most serious practical difficulties in the program have been in developing adequate rapport between specific clients and consultants and in satisfying the participants in the program that the program is really benefiting the clients. There is no question but that the student-consultants have reaped great benefits and that the image of the business school in the community has been enhanced. But the assessment of the impact on the community and on the individual clients is much more difficult to ascertain. The problem of rapport is treated in part V; the problem of assessment of impact deserves further consideration here.

Frequently, programs of managerial assistance assume that their very existence will provide a "good" to the community and to the individual businessmen who participate. There are many possible pitfalls in such programs. First, there is the issue of whether the managerial assistance program is speaking to the true needs of the minority entrepreneurs. An emphasis on short-run capital financing when the true survival concerns revolve around managerial behavior is likely to do more harm than good and dissuade both the community and the sponsoring organizations. Second, most programs of this type utilize expressions of greater knowledge, better communication, or feelings of improvement as measures of success of the program. While these subjective criteria are undeniably important, an assessment of normal business parameters must be made before judging the worth of the program.[25] Unfortunately, minority businessmen are often unwilling to make the necessary data available for examination and record keeping purposes. Without some measure of profit, gross revenue, sales volume, or other pertinent indicator of economic performance, it becomes extremely difficult to assess the impact of any given program. Finally, managerial assistance programs face the need of obtaining the resources necessary to continue in operation. Frequently, such programs are funded for a specific time either by the government or by some other sponsoring organization. When the funding period expires, or the money runs out, the program must seek renewal or search for new funds. It becomes extremely difficult to justify requests for new funds without performance measures. Yet, the benefits derived for both majority participants and the minority community from a successful managerial assistance program can be lost rather rapidly if the program goes out of business before its job is completed. Thus, lack of adequate performance measures greatly exacerbates the second major problem of MBA Management Consultants, Inc., and most other managerial assistance programs—the continued availability of operating funds.

MBA has been funded for specified time periods by two major grants and by smaller contributions from several corporations. It is apparent that the continued operation of MBA will hinge upon the willingness of corporations and other funding agencies to provide working capital. As was suggested earlier, this dependence on exogenous decision makers is not the most desirable situation. It would be preferable if MBA could receive a sufficient endowment to guarantee its long-run existence or if it could establish itself on a "pay-as-you-go" basis. Under present circumstances, neither of these conditions seems likely to be realized. Thus, in the future, as it has in the past, MBA will be engaging in an effort to secure funds from corporate and government sponsors.

A final problem experienced by MBA has been that in many cases the needs of the businessmen often go beyond the specific competencies of the student-consultants. The students can provide assistance at a reasonably sophisticated level across the general range of business problems. However, for the businessman who has particularly thorny problems in bookkeeping, inventory control, or some other issue, the need for an expert in that area is often great. MBA is currently attempting to elaborate on its present consulting technique by establishing teams of experts, composed of either student or alumni specialists, who will serve as consultants on specific problems within the area of their expertise.

---

[25] An approach to assessing the viability of minority enterprises as targets for managerial assistance and development is given by L. DURHAM, *supra* note 2.

D. A Look to the Future: Redesign and Expansion

These four problems—rapport, assessment of impact, funding, elaboration of technical competence—indicate instances where MBA has yet to fully realize the requirements of the general model outlined in this paper. At the present time, the organization is attempting to evolve to a slightly modified form which will be better suited to resolving these difficulties. In general, this form will include teams of experts in particular areas who will join with the general management consultant. It will also include the establishment of a fee for clients in order to place at least part of the funding of the organization on an independent basis. It will utilize a more formal set of performance measures so that MBA can get a better insight into its impact.

One further development in the growth of MBA which is worthy of note is that the organization is beginning now to move beyond its concern for the operation of individual businesses toward acting as a body on issues of concern to all businesses in the community. For example, MBA is currently planning an effort to improve the access of minority businessmen to burglary and fire insurance. Other programs in developmental stages include participation of the organization in community planning activities, the establishment of a summer job program for high school students, and the utilization of experienced clients as consultants to other minority businesses. It is this last set of programs, indicative of the continuing growth and strength of MBA, which go farthest toward justifying this approach as a means of fostering economic development in minority areas.

V

MBA MANAGEMENT CONSULTANTS: THE FIELD EXPERIENCE

A. The Small Businessman

The consulting relationship basically begins with the problem of establishing rapport between client and consultant. The consultant, by virtue of his training, is oriented toward formal accounting systems, delegation of authority, long-range planning, and quick, decisive action. The client, for a variety of reasons, is likely to be intimately involved in every aspect of his business. The client is an expert—although a self-taught one—in his particular field, be it shoemaking, boiler maintenance, or building rehabilitation. He may be uncomfortable with delegating authority to subordinates and accustomed to performing all the functions of the business himself. He is likely to want to oversee every sale, purchase, and inventory decision personally, and to be reluctant to think of himself as a manager with executive responsibilities. He may be lax in separating his personal and business finances and may resist efforts to formalize his bookkeeping practices. He is likely to be too busy to indulge himself in long-range planning and is probably more comfortable with daily receipts as opposed to forecasts. This thumbnail sketch is typical of MBA businessmen-clients and points out some of the major obstacles to realizing an effective consulting arrangement. Examination of these characteristics of the small business will identify the areas in which assistance is most frequently needed as well as the types of behavior required of the consultant if he is to be successful.

The small businessman, minority or otherwise, is a uniquely American species, having opted to go it on his own. While it is dangerous to generalize about so diverse a group, MBA's clients share many of the following six attributes:

(a) *Ambivalence toward authority.* Most clients were led to set up their own businesses by a desire to avoid taking orders from someone else. At the same time, they resist delegating responsibilities to their employees. The client typically supervises all of his employees directly and requires that all decisions be cleared by him. The impetus for establishing a small business often comes from earlier failures in the larger economic marketplace. The client gains considerable gratification from the association with the entrepreneurial tradition and usually feels that his continued presence is essential to the survival of the business. The consultants, who view the development of a managerial definition of one's role as the critical stage in transforming a small business into a corporate entity, have found their most difficult task to be assisting the client to adopt a managerial perspective.

(b) *Boundless personal energy.* Clients often express the fear that the managerial role would be dull, overly limited, and "out of touch." These individuals thrive on personal contact, on immersing themselves in the rush of daily activity, and on the challenge of keeping their heads above water in the face of conflicting pressures and demands. This drive and tenacity is a major source of strength for the businessman. It is, however, a potential source of difficulty in developing the organization and individual employees.

(c) *Susceptibility to the gambler's malaise.* Most clients believe firmly in the golden opportunity—the big score. They are frequently engaged in several marginally related enterprises. Each time a new deal presents itself, they cannot resist taking a flyer because "this one may be the big one." This dilution of the manager's effort and of his working capital often gets in the way of taking actions which would insure the growth and stability of the organization.

(d) *A static short-run view of time.* Most small businessmen do not engage in much planning, mainly because of the pressures on their time coming from the daily flow of events. Appointments may not be kept; deliveries, bills, and taxes may be late or overlooked. Work is frequently not scheduled, but rather is done as pressure from customers requires. This static viewpoint often interferes with the attempts of consultants to establish control systems.

(e) *An undifferentiated view of one's business and personal life.* The small businessman often runs his treasury out of one pocket and his personal finances out of the other, with frequent transfers in both directions. He may not pay himself a regular salary but will draw cash for his personal needs from the cash register.

Clients frequently see their most pressing need as one of obtaining working capital. The consultants cannot normally begin to work on this issue until they have been able to separate the client's business from his personal life.

(f) *Adherence to a conspiracy theory*. The client frequently views the main barrier to his personal success as a lack of capital and discriminatory treatment by the banking and credit systems. These problems are intimately related and contain considerable truth. Historically, minority businessmen have experienced considerable difficulty in obtaining loan funds, in getting accounts receivable factored, and in obtaining and paying for insurance and other services. This precludes a comfortable cash flow and creates problems in maintaining inventories and providing credit. This situation often leads the businessman to see the solution of these financial problems as providing the entire key to his success. This focus on financial issues very often interferes with the resolution of the very real managerial problems described above.

These six characteristics provide some indication of the variety of issues and problems which have emerged in the client-consultant relationship. It is evident, first of all, that the consultant must realize that the client does not necessarily share his view of what is rational. A main problem in consulting to minority businessmen is to find some mutually agreed upon set of operating procedures and systems which are necessary to the continued functioning of the business. Systems seen as crucial by the consultant frequently have little immediate appeal to the client. The consultant must not only concern himself with translating the work of his proposals to the client, he must also look to the development of the client's personal competence.

B. Pitfalls for Consultants

A particularly seductive and dangerous pitfall in managerial assistance programs is the fostering of a dependency relationship between client and consultant. The consultant must be continually aware that his role is just that, a consultant, and not a functioning member of the business. His legitimate functions are to investigate and analyze, advise and advocate. Thus, the consultant may develop and propose programs and then act as an advocate, but it must be the client who decides whether a proposal is to be adopted. To the extent that the client becomes dependent upon the consultant for direction, decisions, and approval, the underlying goals of managerial assistance programs have been thwarted. If the consultant is setting policy and making operating decisions, the goal of fostering an independent, viable minority business community is not being realized. In addition, the potential for developing the client's managerial abilities and self-confidence will have been lost. Also, the potential symbolic contribution of flourishing minority business will be jeopardized and possibly even lost if the community perceives that these businesses are being sustained primarily through the efforts of outside parties. The danger of allowing dependency relationships to emerge is considerable, since the consultant often first encounters the businessman at a time when the the businessman is undergoing a crisis, and the consultant is easily seen as the only means of survival available. Dependency is also fostered by the initial differences in sophistication and technical competence between client and consultant.[26] The consultant must be aware of the potential for dependence and must carefully guide his own actions so as to maximize the client's acquisition of competence and self-confidence. It is relatively easy for the consultant to fall into the trap of "doing it himself," rather than taking the extra time which might be necessary to explain a new idea fully to the client and to allow the client the time to reflect upon and practice it.

In addition to avoiding the formation of a dependency relationship, the consultant must also be constantly aware of the difference in accountability between himself and the client. What to the consultant may be a laboratory for the testing out of new ideas is to the client his livelihood, his identity, and perhaps his only chance for success. The consultant, in his advocate's role, has the obligation to evaluate risks from the client's perspective. The consultant must remember that he is not engaged in an intellectual exercise wherein he may test pet theories or experiment with alternative procedures; the client is engaged in a business activity where profit and loss, success and failure, have immediate impact. This means that the consultant must adapt his proposals to the realities of the client's situation. Very frequently what is sound in terms of management theory or has been effective in large corporations is not directly applicable to the running of a small business in a minority community. The consultant must learn to be sensitive to the client's assertion of what will not or cannot work for him. He must recognize that the client's unwillingness to embark upon grandiose expansion efforts or visionary programs may represent a realistic appraisal of possibilities in his market as well as an aversion to risk.

A final pitfall to be avoided on the consultant's side is the frequently voiced assumption that all of the problems of minority business can be explained away by an infusion of sufficient funds. The client himself may frequently express such an opinion, but the consultant through careful observation often comes to realize that this financial insolvency is a symptom of broader deficiencies in managerial capacity. Thus, while much of the effort of MBA consultants has been directed to financial matters, particularly in the establishment of bookkeeping and other control systems, they have also dealt extensively with questions of executive responsibility and delegation, planning, and the development of information systems. In many cases, the consultant never quite gets around to dealing with the specific problems that led the client to seek assistance from MBA. For example, in assisting a client to put

---

[26] In psychological terms, the consulting relationship is a supportive one, much like therapy. As in therapy, the critical task is to transform the relationship to one where the support provided by the consultant is minimal and limited to specific areas of differential expertise. This transformation can be impeded either by the client's unwillingness to accept increased independence or by the consultant's unwillingness to encourage it.

his business in order so as to be able to apply for financial aid, a consultant will often be led to deal with and resolve a number of operational and managerial problems, the resolution of which may greatly decrease the need for additional funds. It is imperative that both consultant and client look beyond the quick adoption of simplistic panacea for the ills of small business—such as short-term capital inputs— and look toward establishing the systems, plans, and managerial practices needed for long-run stability and success. The avoidance of these pitfalls—dependence, use of the small business as a laboratory, identification of cure-all solutions—depends primarily upon the consultant. This implies that consultants should have a realistic view of the role of small business, a willingness to view themselves as technicians or experts in specific areas of competence, and an openness to learning from association with small businessmen. The success of any program of managerial assistance hinges critically on the competence, adaptability, and sensitivity of the consultants who will work with the small businessmen.[27]

VI

Some Concluding Remarks

This paper has presented a broad description and analysis of the role of managerial assistance programs in minority economic development. The analysis focused first on a delineation of the several ways that managerial assistance might be packaged and then on a discussion of the broad criteria and operational considerations which are critical to the success of such programs. The path to success for minority economic development efforts has many crucial elements—motivation of the participants, selection of ventures, design and implementation of the program, perceptions and behaviors of the parties involved—and there are many pitfalls which threaten even the most well-intentioned programs.

It has been shown that the interrelation of economic systems may provide the motivation for serious efforts to generate fuller involvement of minority areas in the national economy. Thus, majority participants can appeal to self-interest in supporting managerial assistance programs. The thrust of the argument, moreover, is that only those programs which are undertaken with a recognition of self-interest are likely to be successful. A sense of social responsibility, admirable as it may be, is a rather ephemeral star on which to pin the hopes of a community.

The selection of economic development ventures is particularly crucial. Minority enterprises must be judged on their potential for independence, growth, and performance; that is, the regular "rules of the game" must be used. Enterprises which

---

[27] This also underscores the importance of the consultant's commitment. A successful effort with a minority businessman hinges on building a trust relationship between client and consultant. This cannot be done if consultants are unreliable or have unrealistic expectations about the nature of small business in minority communities. These factors lead to high turnover of consultants and can destroy the program. See Ference & Fraser, *supra* note 18.

require a continuing subsidy to survive or which deal in products which have limited or declining markets should be avoided.

There are many choices to be made in the design and implementation of the program: sponsor—government, business, community agency, university; target—new or existing businesses; type of assistance—importing a management team, consulting to minority businessmen, seminars and training programs. While it is recognized that any of the possible combinations of these factors may produce a successful program, this article has focused on the "consulting to existing businesses" approach, using a university-based program as a specific example. In addition to economic viability, successful design and implementation were seen to depend upon satisfaction of four criteria: acceptance, empathy, knowledge, and reliability. These criteria were then used to develop an operating model; the components of the model reflected efforts to avoid the major pitfalls in the institution of managerial assistance programs. Briefly, these pitfalls include the recognition of shared self-interest as motivator and guarantor of continued participation, responsiveness to self-image needs and communication barriers, avoidance of the political dangers of community participation and of the temptation to exaggerate expectations through excess publicity, and incorporation of individual programs in a larger perspective of continuing development.

The eventual success of programs flowing from this or similar models ultimately rests on the perceptions and behaviors of the participants. In describing the organization and operating experience of MBA Management Consultants, Inc., the characteristics of clients and consultants and the nature of the consulting relationship have been stressed. Small businessmen—minority businessmen—are individuals, but individuals who share many characteristics and perceptions. The consultant must be sensitive to these; he must also be sensitive to the temptations of fostering dependence, to the different stake that the client has in the success of his business, and to the deceptiveness of "cure-alls" such as capital infusion.

To summarize, managerial assistance is essential to effective minority economic development, but its provision cannot follow any simple, automatic formula. Minority business is still business and, in the end, the rules of the game will take their toll of poorly conceived, designed, or monitored programs. Minority enterprise must be economically viable if it is to survive, and managerial assistance programs must be acceptable, emphatic, knowledgeable, and reliable if they are to fulfill their promise. Anything less than full observance of the sense and importance of these criteria by majority or minority participants will not suffice.

MARKETING TECHNIQUES FOR THE COMMUNITY-BASED ENTERPRISE

Carl E. Block*

Introduction

Prior to making any attempt at addressing the theme of this paper suggested by the title, it is imperative to establish a conceptual base with respect to the fundamental nature of community-based enterprises. This is particularly important because of the lack of a consensus among interested parties concerning such basic questions as "What is a community development corporation?" and "How should its objectives ordinarily be framed?"

To establish this point of departure, two steps are taken. First, a set of assumptions is offered to lay the major portion of the conceptual base referred to above. And no doubt there may be considerable disagreement on these issues. Nevertheless, this is a necessary first step. Then, attention is given to more specific instances evidencing attempts by community development corporations (CDC) to carry out their perceived responsibility. Following these introductory sections, the remainder of the paper will be devoted to a discussion of the marketing aspects of the community-based enterprise's operation. In this latter part, specific attention will first be given to the marketing considerations which must be examined in the servicing of the local constituency in light of its particular characteristics and modes of life. This orientation toward the immediate neighborhood will be followed by an emphasis on the advantages of and problems associated with trying to reach out to serve a broader market.

The initial assumptions regarding community development corporations are as follows: (a) the private profit system has not sufficiently nurtured the growth and development of private enterprises which are capable of meeting the needs of low-income communities for goods and services; (b) there is considerable interest on the part of residents of economically depressed areas to cooperate in a community controlled venture in an attempt to free themselves from public dependency; (c) the community development corporation, offering neighborhood participation, is a viable type of organization for facilitating the drive for independence; (d) the CDC is a locally-based organization that conducts revenue-generating business with the primary purpose of fostering economic development of the immediate area; (e) the CDC can provide many essential goods and services for local residents while still contributing to the development of a desirable economic base in the depressed area it is serving; (f) since the primary objective of the CDC is to contribute to

---

* Associate Professor of Marketing, School of Business and Public Administration, University of Missouri-Columbia.

economic development, trade-offs will occasionally be necessary between providing for the immediate social needs of the residents and economic growth; in such cases the latter will be favored; (g) the skill potential of the poor, that is, their innate capacity to learn, is sufficient that such persons can acquire the necessary know-how to participate actively in community-based enterprises; (h) there is sufficient interest on the part of society generally to commit substantial catalytic resources for economic development of depressed areas and this support is a product of an interest that can be relied upon over an extended period of time; (i) it is not the purpose of the community development corporation to foster a particular level of racial integration or separatism; and (j) the plight of most depressed areas is so great, that no one organization, agency, or legislative act can be expected to resolve all economic problems; at best, progress will be made in phases with each new effort being built upon the experiences of earlier endeavors.

I

CDC Experience

Community development corporation business action to date can be categorized as either essentially catalytic—directed toward encouraging the formation and/or growth of private business—or more typically, as participatory—taking form through direct organization involvement in revenue-generating business. No matter which orientation has been the focal point of a particular CDC, the immediate neighborhood has been the market of greatest interest.

A. Catalytic Action

Much has been said about the catalytic effects of the community development corporation on the development and revitalization of private minority enterprises. So far none of the CDC's have acted in a strictly catalytic manner, although a number proclaimed this to be their major function.[1] The catalytic action that has been taken by CDC's can be classified as direct, or overt, action and indirect, or secondary, action.

Probably the most effective organization in direct catalytic action has been the Inner City Business Improvement Forum. ICBIF, an all-black financial organization through which the Detroit power structure is channeling its assistance, had utilized almost $1,000,000 of its funds for loans or investment in eighty-six black businesses by early 1970. In addition, ICBIF had participated with Detroit banks and the Small Business Administration in loan packages worth $3,700,000. While ICBIF cannot claim to have solved the capital problem for minority enterprises, it has engendered a growing confidence of Detroit banks in the black business community. The six Detroit banks with SBA guarantees increased minority business loans from $703,000 in 1968 to $5,600,000 in 1969. In addition to financing private

---

[1] As an example, Hough Development Corporation's strategy of business was to ". . . act essentially as a catalyst, using its funds as leverage rather than as direct investment whenever possible." The Hough Development Corporation, Harvard Business School Case, 1969, p. 7. (xeroxed).

black businesses, the ICBIF has made other direct catalytic efforts. Several campaigns have been organized by ICBIF and the Economic Development Corporation to bring potential black suppliers together with purchasing executives of Detroit corporations. Also, the ICBIF operates a computerized accounting service that furnishes free financial services for budding minority entrepreneurs. ICBIF does have direct interest and control in several projects. It is worth noting that ICBIF, while it is an all-black corporation, has not established as a goal community ownership or control.[2]

Another example of direct catalytic action is the Progress Plaza shopping center developed in 1967 by Zion Investment Associates, Inc., of Philadelphia.[3] Of the sixteen store spaces in the center, ten were available to operations with poor credit ratings.[4] In addition, Zion was able to require that outside-owned businesses employ only community residents for all positions. Zion has received funding to assist in establishing similar ghetto shopping centers in other cities. Other CDC's, such as that in Cleveland's Hough area, are planning their own shopping centers, while still other community-based organizations, like Watts Labor Community Action Committee, are involved in providing community services such as vocational training; although this latter example is more appropriately classified as indirect action.[5]

Much more difficult to perceive and measure are the effects of indirect catalytic action by CDC's. Generally there appear to be four categories of effects:

—development of business "infrastructure"
—creation of new markets
—community involvement
—momentum

Development of business infrastructure includes providing for manufacturing and office space, the training and motivation of potential minority entrepreneurs, development of desirable work habits among ghetto residents, and the establishment of lines of communication. Also important to infrastructure is the development of a minority equity market. Logically, the manufacturing operations started by CDC's will create a new demand for materials and services, which can potentially be supplied by the individual entrepreneur. Perhaps equally important is the potential creation of demand for goods and services complementing those produced by the CDC enterprise. Finally, it is obvious that community involvement and momentum are vital to the goals of minority economic development.

It can be reasoned that the major impediment to the accomplishment of direct catalytic action by CDC's in most instances is direct community ownership or control of the corporation. This goal is in conflict with the goal of the individual entre-

---

[2] Scott, *Report from Detroit*, FORTUNE, Feb. 1970, at 71-72.
[3] Note, *Community Development Corporations: Operations and Financing*, 83 HARV. L. REV. 1558, 1562-67 (1970).
[4] All ten were leased by minority entrepreneurs, eight of whom were not in business prior to the shopping center development.
[5] Ackerson, *supra* note 3, at 1577.

preneur to run his business to maximize personal profit; however, it may be improper to categorize the entrepreneur of the depressed area according to classic entrepreneurial definitions. Another potential impediment is that the CDC may react to the temptation to achieve short-run success and proceed to marshal its limited talent and money into one unit.

B. Participatory Action: Direct Operation of Businesses

Although CDC's have acted as a catalyst in fostering the growth of private business in depressed areas, their primary mode of operation is that of conducting revenue-generating business as a means of producing substantial economic and social progress in their immediate environment. While CDC direct involvement has covered a variety of business ventures, all of the CDC's appear to have selected their businesses on the basis of at least one of two selection criteria. The operations are either labor-intense or they fill a pressing need for merchandising and service establishments which will broaden the patronage opportunities of the neighborhood residents. To a large exent, businesses meeting these criteria were plentiful in the area at one time, but for one reason or another, were no longer servicing the local community.

Such business selection on the part of CDC's gives what appears to be visible evidence of progress to both the impatient ghetto populace and program sponsors—evidence which in each case may be a prerequisite to continued support. In addition, business ventures selected on the basis of the two identified criteria foster immediate social benefits, such as reduced unemployment and the lessening of consumer exploitation, while the slower process of developing economic resources takes place.

Several CDC's have started with a venture intended not to return a significant profit, but rather to provide for certain pressing social needs. Zion Investment Associates of Philadelphia, one of the most successful CDC's, started in 1964 with this approach by building a housing project called Zion Garden Apartments. Since this initial project was completed, Zion has become involved in the aerospace and garment industries and has developed a local shopping center.[6] Action Industries, Inc., a CDC in Venice, California, has been operating a number of small merchandising and service establishments with rather limited success.[7] The Hough Development Corporation, a Cleveland CDC, has followed a similar strategy of business involvement. For instance, in 1969 the Hough CDC had the following businesses at various stages of consideration: a supermarket, dry cleaner, automotive center, donut shop, home maintenance service, taxi service and credit union.[8]

By contrast, there are few examples of successful on-going manufacturing facilities or wholesale distributorships operated by CDC's in depressed areas, even though these forms of business represent a more viable means of bringing wealth

---
[6] *Id.* at 1564-65.
[7] T. Cross, Black Capitalism: Strategy for Business in the Ghetto 227 (1969).
[8] The Hough Development Corporation, *supra* note 1, at 226-28.

into the local community since they would serve a broader market beyond the economy of the neighborhood. To a large extent CDC's have established business enterprises which offer an opportunity to maximize "social profits" with relatively little attention given to maximizing long-run "economic profits" through gaining control of capital.

II

Market Orientation

It is apparent that CDC's at best have followed a traditional orientation to business management where emphasis is placed on developing and financing the physical plant and production facilities. This is in sharp contrast to most progressive firms today which are market-oriented organizations emphasizing such activities as marketing research, promotion, and dealer-customer relations as central, not peripheral, aspects of their management.[9] Consequently, to be competitive in at least some of the markets that appear most promising for CDC cultivation, a very basic change is necessary. The CDC must broaden its perspectives so that substantial management attention is given to such activities as marketing, research, and promotion. Any meaningful discussion concerning the development of logically sound and operationally feasible marketing strategies for CDC use must include suggestions dealing with servicing the consumer of the immediate neighborhood, but not neglect the broader market beyond this depressed environment. A part of the conception of a broader market for the CDC involves reaching out to serve various governmental divisions as well as private businesses.

A. The Consumer Market

Research evidence shows that the typical consumer goods marketer today is increasingly facing a younger, better-educated, more perceptive and more affluent market than ever before. During the next 10 years, median family income will probably increase by more than fifty per cent to at least $15,000 per year. At the end of World War II, less than ten million people had at least some college education. At the close of 1969, there were twenty million with this level of attainment. And by 1980, there will be close to thirty-three million with at least some college training. In 1965, there were 41.5 million families with household heads under thirty-five years old. Now there are nearly forty-five million. As a result of such changes firms are being forced to modify the assumptions upon which their marketing strategies are based.[10]

Old fears regarding the consequences of breaking with tradition in such areas as store patronage, brand selection, and credit arrangement have all but been abandoned by consumers. Therefore, marketers have had to sharpen their skills in the

---
[9] L. Preston, Markets and Marketing: An Orientation 79-80 (1970).
[10] *Selling to the Hottest Market Ever*, Bus. Wk., Oct. 17, 1970, at 124-31.

ever challenging process of monitoring current behavioral patterns while simultaneously attempting to forecast future demand.

Apart from this dynamic environment there is what Michael Harrington has called the "Other America."[11] Although not restricted to the depressed ghettos of our major cities, poverty is increasingly becoming an urban problem. Many of the poor living in these congested areas are black and suffer from racial discrimination as well as economic deprivation. Large numbers of these same poor are members of families that moved from the rural south to more northern cities where jobs appeared plentiful and public assistance was better.[12]

As a group they were studied intensely during the 1960's and, therefore, identified and classified, although not necessarily fully understood. In this process the poor in the United States have been characterized in economic terms by dollar thresholds to poverty. By recent standards, a nonfarm household of four would be considered poor if their combined annual income were $3553 or less, while a two member household would not be classified as poor if their income exceeded $2262.[13] Nevertheless, poverty is much more than this, as the Mayor's Commission of Cleveland indicated. "It is attempting to sell blood to buy a child toys at Christmas and being turned away for being anemic. It is a child wearing $1.00 tennis shoes through the winter. It is selling food stamps to buy sanitary napkins and toothpaste. It is covering one's mouth to hide missing teeth."[14] To a large extent, this represents the populace of the areas where CDC's are located and, therefore, their most immediate market.

However, despite their sharing a common experience of economic deprivation, the poor are not a homogeneous group.[15] Therefore, the constituency of one CDC may well vary from that of another serving a different area. Or one CDC may itself be dealing with several identifiable groups. For example, even though poverty is fast becoming an urban problem with twenty-five per cent of all poor white persons and forty-two per cent of all poor black persons in this country residing within the central cities of our metropolitan areas, nearly half of all poor persons still live outside urban areas.[16] The variation in congestion alone may dictate a different business mix for the CDC in a rural setting as compared to its counterpart servicing an urban environment.

Despite these and other dimensions of deprivation which demonstrate something less than perfect uniformity within the ranks of the CDC constituency, there are identifiable similarities. And after a cautious warning about too much generalization

---

[11] M. HARRINGTON, THE OTHER AMERICA: POVERTY IN THE UNITED STATES 1-7 (1962).

[12] Daniel P. Moynihan, *Poverty in Cities*, in THE METROPOLITAN ENIGMA: INQUIRIES INTO THE NATURE AND DIMENSIONS OF AMERICA'S URBAN CRISIS 337-39 (James Q. Wilson ed. 1968).

[13] BUREAU OF THE CENSUS, CURRENT POPULATION REPORTS: CONSUMER INCOME, POVERTY IN THE UNITED STATES 11 (1969).

[14] THE CRISIS IN WELFARE IN CLEVELAND: REPORT OF THE MAYOR'S COMMISSION 3 (H. Stein ed. 1969).

[15] COMMITTEE FOR ECONOMIC DEVELOPMENT, SUPPLEMENTARY PAPER NUMBER 26, A. DOWNS, WHO ARE THE URBAN POOR? 16-17 (1968).

[16] BUREAU OF THE CENSUS, *supra* note 13, at 7.

regarding likenesses among the poor, the emphasis must be placed upon several clusters of similarities which can be used to help most CDC's develop market strategies for servicing the local residents. What follows is an attempt to identify some of the characteristics that people of the low-income areas typically served by CDC's have in common. Included here is an indication of what marketing implications these similarities offer. This represents a strategy of identifying the local constituency through the use of secondary sources of marketing information. Also, it suggests that CDC's need not have marketing research experts at their disposal, but that considerable data is already available with respect to their most immediate market.

B. Predominant Life Styles of Neighborhood Residents and Their Marketing Implications

The day-to-day behavioral patterns of the lower socioeconomic class which makes up most of the CDC's local market can be characterized by several distinctive themes, all of which are apparently related to a deprived, alienated position in society. The more salient themes include that of fatalism, an orientation to the present, authoritarianism, and concreteness.[17] To a large extent the market behavior of the local residents, including their general receptiveness to CDC-run businesses, will be shaped by these themes.

This behavioral field is substantially different from that of the more general consumer population and, therefore, varied marketing techniques may be required if the low-income consumer is to be served effectively. For example, the fatalism of the poor appears to be a result of a genuine powerlessness they experience with respect to so much of their life. They feel controlled by external forces rather than being in control themselves. This attitude acts as a definitive brake on occupational and educational aspirations. It also retards their interest in such critical problems as health care. In addition, it may nurture a tendency to limit one's shopping scope or willingness to negotiate favorable terms when making a purchase. When either of these latter propositions is true, established local business has a distinct advantage in gaining consumer patronage, a competitive market advantage which the community-based enterprise must recognize. However, it is possible that the unique nature of the CDC as a broadly based *community-owned* entity, once understood by the constituency, will alleviate some of the feeling of complete helplessness. If so, this could represent a major contribution to facilitating a significant change in the attitude of the poor. And furthermore, it may enhance the possibility of realizing a successful relationship between CDC-operated businesses and their local market.

An orientation toward the present goes hand in hand with fatalism. The poor generally feel that it is fruitless to anticipate the future, when fortune and chance

---

[17] Irelan and Besner, *Low-Income Outlook on Life*, in LOW-INCOME LIFE STYLES 7-9 (L. Irelan ed. 1968).

are considered its basic determinants. Also, when so much of one's personal resources must be expended simply to survive in the present, there is little time left to consider the future. This predisposition precipitates a lack of interest in planning for future needs and a general feeling of insecurity. As a result, a family frequently lives from one crisis to another.

This behavioral pattern can have various marketing implications for the community-based enterprise. For example, major durables may well be purchased on the basis of a short search experience following the realization of a need—possibly one resulting from the breakdown of an automobile or refrigerator. The need to replace such an item within a short period of time, coupled with other constraints on search behavior, will frequently lead the low-income shopper to go no further than his neighborhood dealer. Having an appropriate CDC-run business readily accessible within the immediate area will greatly enhance the probability of gaining local patronage.

This is not to suggest, however, that the poor are confined to the immediate neighborhood for their shopping. Many go outside to make selected purchases and, therefore, the community-based enterprise must view its competitors as including most of the major retail outlets in the surrounding area.[18] This will at least require merchandising policies that offer benefits to the local residents similar to those available at alternative retail outlets. Particular attention should be directed to customer servicing policy. Evidence from several studies shows that variation in personal aspects of customer servicing are particularly important in gaining the patronage of the low-income consumer. For example, both Caplovitz and Rainwater discovered a discomfort in working class women shopping in downtown stores, apparently a result of a lack of empathy among clerks toward the problems of the less affluent.[19]

A third theme by which the poor live is that of authoritarianism. Generally, this is a belief in strength as the source of authority and in the rightness of existing systems. This perspective arises in part from the limiting, mundane life experiences to which those living in poverty have become accustomed and also from the constant subordination of the poor to the rest of society.

Such a predisposition has particular marketing implications. First, it is likely to reduce one's interest in aggressive shopping. A role of subordination to the local merchant may be accepted as a continuation of a more general subordination in society. In order to combat such ready acceptance of merchant domination in the customer-dealer relationship, the community-based enterprise must promote the utilization of collective action as a means for equalizing bargaining strength. In addition, CDC businesses may offer an equitable relationship between buyer and seller. This will of necessity have to include flexible credit terms to meet both the special needs of the local residents and the competition from the merchants who

---

[18] D. CAPLOVITZ, THE POOR PAY MORE 54-57 (1967).
[19] L. RAINWATER, R. COLEMAN, AND G. HANDEL, WORKINGMAN'S WIFE 182-89 (1959).

remain in the area or who selectively solicit the residents' business through their door-to-door representatives.

The availability of favorable credit terms is generally a critical consideration to local consumers when buying appliances and home furnishings.[20] In fact, the principal competitive advantage may well accrue to the merchant who can offer "easy" credit. As a result, low-income market retailers frequently specialize in granting credit to consumers who may not have any credit references or who may have a poor credit rating by normal standards. The CDC will also have to deal with another phase of the local merchant's credit business. It is the practice of encouraging customers to make weekly payments in person, which further exposes them to the enticing wares of the merchant. Upon an expression of interest in new merchandise, the local retailer frequently responds with a willingness to provide the consumers with the desired goods at no increase in weekly payments, thereby further extending the number of visits the residents must make to the established store.[21]

A final life theme of the poor is that of concreteness. It reflects a life-pattern of placing greater emphasis on material goods than intellectual things. It has evolved quite logically among a group of people preoccupied by material problems—such as keeping a roof over their heads and food on the table. Concreteness becomes evident in verbal patterns, in the distrust of intellectualism, and in occupational values. As a result, the life of the poor includes fewer generalizations, relies less on the conceptual process than on observation, and is more tied to the world of immediate happenings and momentary sensations. In a purchase experience, such an orientation may lead to placing most importance on the breadth of product features, convenience of operation, and brand name, rather than on more long-run considerations including durability, economy of use, and frequency of repair.[22] Here again, strong overt effort will be necessary on the part of the CDC to overcome the consequences of a predisposition toward concreteness. Nevertheless, if the local consumer can be reached through advertising and direct contact with the CDC businesses and is made to realize the benefits of altering his previous behavioral tendencies, much greater consumer satisfaction should result. And of equal importance, customer loyalty to the community-based enterprise should be enhanced.

C. Marketing Information and the Poor

So far emphasis has been placed upon understanding the fundamental nature of the low-income consumer's predispositions toward life and in interpreting these in a marketing context. However, once these behavioral tendencies are identified and

---

[20] In Washington, D.C., the Federal Trade Commission found that as a group, low-income market retailers who sell durables made 93% of their sales through installment credit. Federal Trade Commission, *Economic Report on Installment Credit and Retail Sales Practices of District of Columbia Retailers*, in THE GHETTO MARKETPLACE, 81 (F. Sturdivant ed. 1969).

[21] Huber, *The Poor in the Market Place*, in POWER, POVERTY AND URBAN POLICY, 167-68 (W. Bloomberg, Jr. and H. Schmandt eds. 1968).

[22] Richards, *Consumer Practices of the Poor*, in LOW-INCOME LIFE STYLES, *supra* note 17, at 75.

the product and service mix of the businesses properly adjusted so as to take maximum advantage of this insight, attention must be given to the subject of communication. The objective of this communication should be to foster an effective flow of pertinent consumption facilitating information from the business source to the low-income consumer user.

One recent study showed that when given sufficient time to deliberate the problem of making a major purchase, the poor respond similarly to our model of economic man in search of product information. There is a recognition of the need for product information generally considered most relevant, even though in an actual buying situation the poor may not make an exhaustive search for such information.[23] A sample group of low-income consumers was asked to identify the type of information which should be secured before a large purchase is made. Three times as many respondents requested product-oriented information as desired dealer-oriented data. This latter finding may in part reflect the limited flexibility that the poor have with respect to dealer choice. Such constraints on their shopping scope are exemplified by the fact that only twenty-three per cent of the 350 households studied had access to an automobile and forty-two per cent stated they were limited to shopping within walking distance of their home.

Given the general plight of the poor, a very basic question concerning the availability of consumption facilitating information might be raised: Are these people as deprived of information dealing with the selection of goods and services as they are of the goods and services themselves? There is evidence to indicate that the mass media do reach the urban poor in significant numbers. Furthermore, television and newspapers appear to be the two most effective modes of communication for reaching the poor. In fact, over seventy per cent of the St. Louis respondents were found to be regular television viewers and approximately two-thirds of the interviewees read or at least looked at a newpaper almost everyday.[24]

Newspapers and television were also found to be the two most useful sources in helping these individuals choose a product, that is, help them to obtain the most for their money. Although personal contact may appear to be a very desirable means of communicating with economically deprived consumers, they themselves do not place as high a value on this type of exchange as one might expect. Also, they do not place as much emphasis on personal sources as do more affluent consumers interested in making similar purchases.[25] The poor of the ghetto areas of St. Louis consider newpapers the best single source of product information with television the next best source. Advice from friends followed television as a source of product

---

[23] C. Block, Prepurchase Search Behavior of Low-Income Households, Nov. 12, 1970 (a paper presented to the Southern Marketing Association Meeting, Atlanta, Ga.). This paper reports the findings of a study of the general prepurchase search behavior of 350 low-income households living in St. Louis in August, 1968.

[24] Block, *Communicating with the Urban Poor: An Exploratory Inquiry*, 47 JOURNALISM Q. 4-9 (1970).

[25] Udell, *Prepurchase Behavior of Buyers of Small Electrical Appliances*, 30 J. MARKETING 51 (1966).

information, while radio was ranked fourth, store window signs fifth, advice from sales clerks sixth, magazines seventh. Advice from social workers was considered the least desirable source of product information.[26]

Given the evidence, community-based businesses will probably find it impossible to depend upon personal word-of-mouth informational flow to communicate the virtues of their product and service offerings. In fact, it may be imperative that persuasive promotional messages be carried to the neighborhood constituency through the local media. In additon, some may find other techniques helpful as did the St. Louis grocery merchants serving the depressed areas. They found that mass media promotional efforts could be effectively supplemented by using home delivered advertisements—some of which were simply hand-printed memos promoting weekly specials.

C. Selected Demographic Dimensions of the CDC Constituency and Their Marketing Implications

Poor families tend to be larger than non-poor families. For instance, about five per cent of the families above the poverty line have seven members or more, while nearly sixteen per cent of all poor families have seven or more members.[27] This attribute has a number of specific marketing implications. The desire for labor-saving durable goods is particularly strong among the poor, and this group is no less vulnerable than others to promotional messages emphasizing the features of these products. A serious consequence of this interest in labor-saving durables is that the high unit cost of any such purchase has a significant impact on an already overburdened budget. Given this evidence, it would seem desirable for some CDC's to develop a business service line responsive to the need for reducing the investment of family labor in tasks such as washing clothes. A chain of self-service laundries might be the type of investment that would satisfy this particular need while at the same time operating as a profitable enterprise. Assuming that an appropriate business venture could be initiated, another social benefit would be realized; a substantial decline in the need for consumer durables among the poor would reduce one of the major sources of consumer exploitation in depressed areas.[28]

Age distribution is another important dimension of the constituency of CDC's. Among the poor, there is a large concentration of persons under 25 years old, many of whom are dependent children, and an equally important concentration of senior citizens.[29] It is not unusual to find large numbers of persons in this latter group who did not experience poverty until retirement.[30]

This bimodal age distribution suggests the existence of special needs. These include the need for a multitude of health-related products and services. One business

---

[26] Block, *supra* note 24, at 7.
[27] BUREAU OF THE CENSUS, *supra* note 13, at 4.
[28] Federal Trade Commission, *supra* note 20, at 81-84.
[29] Orshansky, *The Shape of Poverty in 1966*, 31 SOC. SEC. BULL. 16-18 (1968).
[30] H. BROTMAN, A PROFILE OF THE OLDER AMERICAN 1-15 (1968).

investment that could facilitate the satisfying of these needs, while still presenting a viable business venture, is the discount drug outlet. Another is an establishment supplying various equipment for the ill or injured on a rental basis.

Provision for service to older neighborhood residents must be structured to reflect other features. Not only are some of the elderly experiencing poverty for the first time, but their plight seems even more permanent than that of others. These aging persons recognize that they have passed the time when they were active participants in their community and that they are in a period of decline that may ultimately end in complete dependency. Furthermore, like most low-income groups, the aging spend proportionately more of their income on food, shelter, fuel, and medical care than the average American.[31] Consequently, the senior citizen is best served by a marketing strategy that stresses convenience of access with respect to sources of goods and services and which provides economy in a setting which preserves the dignity of the consumer.

III

The Market Beyond the Immediate Neighborhood

If the community development corporation extends its operations to markets outside the economically depressed area, it must confront the issue of its relative competitive position. There are two general alternatives to the issue. First, the CDC can enter competition through the marshalling of its own resources or through the acquisition of a firm already established in the selected field. In either case, the CDC is likely to face competition from other established competitors and from potential competitors, if the market or product involved is lucrative. Under this strategy, the CDC does not have any real differential advantage available to it that is not also available to any other competitor within the framework of a capitalistic structure. The second alternative for the CDC is entry into selected areas where some differential advantage might exist, either through artificial or natural market forces. The discussion here will concentrate on the later approach since it is likely to be the more promising.

A. The Governmental Market

The federal procurement program contains several provisions highly favorable for any firm, controlled or owned by minority persons or located in a labor surplus area, which desires to serve the government market. The Small Business Administration was authorized by the Small Business Act to negotiate with other federal agencies and departments the conditions under which certain procurement needs for property, services, maintenance, repair, construction and research and development are set aside, either totally or partially, and bidding is restricted to small businesses.[32]

---

[31] *Id.*
[32] For definitions of small business concerns, see Federal Procurement Regulations, Subpart 1-1.701. In general, it can be assumed that all CDC's are small businesses at this time.

In the case in which bidding for an individual item or an entire class of items is totally restricted to small business concerns, the CDC firm would be bidding against other established small businesses. Since the definition of a small business is rather liberal (e.g., in manufacturing the maximum employee limitations range from 750-1500), the CDC would probably meet some vigorous competition. Where only a portion of an individual item or a class of items is set aside, the CDC firm does have some advantage, in that the highest priority is given to firms located in sections of concentrated unemployment. However, that advantage is offset by two factors: the unit price contracted on the unexempted portion of the procurement agreement is the ceiling on the set-aside portion and preferential treatment for labor-surplus area concerns are disallowed in defense procurements. From 1961 through 1967, federal procurement set-asides for small business ranged from 4 to 6.3 per cent of total federal procurements, with the greatest absolute amount being $1.9 billion in 1967.[33]

Of greater benefit to the CDC is the provision under section 8(a) of the Small Business Act which authorizes the Small Business Administration to provide assistance, through a subcontracting program, to small business concerns owned and operated by economically or socially disadvantaged persons. Through cooperation between SBA and government procurement agencies, the SBA acts as prime contractor for specific items and subcontracts to one or more minority-owned small businesses. The section 8(a) program was first begun in late 1967, with the SBA subcontracting about $50 million by early 1970 in more than eighty subcontracts.[34] The SBA had set a goal of $100 million in commitments through the section 8(a) program by July, 1971, and it appears that this goal will be reached and perhaps slightly exceeded.[35] The section 8(a) program does have some serious weaknesses, however, which might make the market less attractive to the CDC than other alternatives. First, the SBA, as late as April, 1969, had only five people working directly on this program, with no apparent plans to add more.[36] Considering the amount of coordination and administration inherent in these subcontracts, there would seem to be a practical limitation of $25-$30 million per year for *all* minority small businesses. Another important drawback is the fact that most of the subcontracts have been for defense procurements, including such products as tents, wooden pallets, wooden and metal boxes, bakery products, and military clothing, and such services as repair or modification of electronic equipment

---

[33] *Hearings on the Position of Small Business in Government Procurement Before Subcomm. No. 2 on Gov't. Procurement and Economic Concentration of the House Select Comm. on Small Business*, 90th Cong., 1st Sess. 23 (1968).

[34] 1968 SBA Ann. Rep. 25-26; 1969 SBA Ann. Rep. 23; Office of Minority Business Enterprise, Building Minority Enterprise 23 (1970).

[35] *Hearings on Federal Minority Enterprise Program Before the Subcomm. on Small Business of the Senate Comm. on Banking and Currency*, 91st Cong., 1st Sess. 6 (1970).

[36] *Hearings on the Department of State, Justice, and Commerce, The Judiciary, and Related Agencies' Appropriations for 1970 Before a Subcomm. of the House Comm. on Appropriations*, 91st Cong., 1st Sess. 327 (1969).

and modification of T-33 aircraft.[37] A market of this nature is vulnerable to such things as a "reordering of priorities."

A preferential procurement policy for municipalities and state governments would open similar opportunities. While none exist at present, the Ghediplan, or Ghetto Economic Development and Industrialization Plan, as formulated by Dr. Dunbar S. McLaurin might serve as a basis for future action.[38] Basically, the Ghediplan calls for New York City to set aside ten per cent of its "other than personal services" procurements in a manner similar to the section 8(a) federal program. According to Dr. McLaurin, New York City alone could provide a $50 million "guaranteed market" for minority firms in its own depressed areas.[39] A local government program such as this would probably be more effective and of more value to a CDC for several reasons. First, the CDC would be in a much more effective bargaining position in dealing with a municipal government rather than with a federal agency. Second, the general confinement of the geographical market would ease communications and aid coordination of some of the functional aspects of the community enterpirse. Third, the market would be non-defense oriented and thus could better prepare a new firm for entering the regular marketplace. Fourth, and possibly most important, the municipal government should be more sensitive to a CDC's needs than a federal agency could be.

B. The Private Business Market

Should the CDC find that government contracting is either undesirable or unavailable in a sheltered form for the product or service it has decided to furnish, a viable alternative is to seek sheltered markets through private corporations. While numerous community-owned enterprises have been started on the basis of a procurement commitment from a large corporation, it is difficult to determine the exact extent to which these commitments have sheltered the infant firm. In a few cases, the procuring firm has admittedly paid a premium—in effect a subsidy—for goods or services readily available from other sources. Procurement commitments have been made for as long as three years. These long-term commitments often serve as the basis for stimulating financing not otherwise available. Occasionally, the procuring firm will provide management support and services to assist the minority-owned firm in fulfilling the contract. In most cases of sheltered corporate markets, the sheltering corporation is accepting a risk in dealing with an unstable firm, which would probably not be undertaken using conventional economic criteria.

Zion Investment Associates, Inc., has used sheltered markets to start two of its relatively successful ventures.[40] In 1968, General Electric gave Zion's Progress Aero-

---

[37] 1968 SBA Ann. Rep. 26; 1969 SBA Ann. Rep. 23.

[38] *Hearings on Economic Development Opportunity Before the Senate Select Comm. on Small Business*, 90th Cong., 2d Sess. 233-475 (1968).

[39] *Id.*

[40] Note, *Community Development Corporations: Operations and Financing*, 83 Harv. L. Rev. 1558, 1563-65 (1970).

space Industries, Inc., a $2.5 million order extending over an eighteen month period, in addition to planning and management assistance in starting the venture. When Zion later decided to form a venture for garment manufacturing, called Progress Garment Manufacturing Enterprises, the Villager Corporation gave purchase contracts and management assistance. Renmuth, Inc., a Detroit metal stamping operation started in part by catalytic action of the Inner City Business Improvement Forum, was headed by two former Ford employees and began operations with a three year purchasing commitment from Ford.[41] The total cost of procuring some twenty-one parts from Renmuth will reportedly cost Ford several hundred thousand dollars more than if Ford continued making the parts, as it had in the past. There are other publicized corporation shelters. Xerox guaranteed $500,000 in purchases for two years to Fighton, a new manufacturer of metal stampings and small transformers located in Rochester. Eastman Kodak helped set up Camura, a camera repair shop, and became its first customer. Eastman also gave P.A. Plastics, Inc., its plastic mold shop and a $150,000 contract. S.S. Kresge retained a black-owned insurance company to underwrite group life insurance for over half its employees.[42]

Minority groups, including community development corporations, can sometimes use economic and social leverage to bring about sheltered markets. After sixteen weeks of boycotting and picketing, Operation Breadbasket in Chicago forced an agreement with A&P to market minority produced products.[43] Within six months after the agreement was reached, A&P was marketing the products of twenty-five minority manufactures in its stores located in minority populated areas. As market strength is developed by the individual manufacturers, their products will be distributed by all 260 A&P stores in the Chicago area. Several are now in this stage. One of these, Argia B's Food Products, has grown to a sales volume in six figures and now has a 10%-15% market penetration in the Chicago area for its one product, barbeque sauce.[44] Since Operation Breadbasket made its original agreement with A&P, a total of eight food store chains in the Chicago area have made similar arrangements. Whether Operation Breadbasket is a case of a forced shelter or simply the opening of a competitive market which was otherwise closed to minority manufacturers is open to speculation.

Private sheltered markets offer several advantages to a CDC. First, corporations generally have more flexibility than governmental agencies. Second, the private sector seems to offer a much broader market for possible products as compared to the federal procurement program which appears to be limited primarily to nonessential defense goods. The level of technology which an infant CDC operation can achieve may be relatively high, primarily because of the procuring firm's commitment to accept a risk and its ability to provide the new firm with managerial

---

[41] Scott, *supra* note 2, at 72.
[42] Brower and Little, *White Help for Black Business*, 48 HARV. BUS. REV. 6 (1970).
[43] BERKNER, BLACK CAPITALISM AND THE URBAN NEGRO 18-19 (1970).
[44] McKersie, *Vitalize Black Enterprise*, 46 HARV. BUS. REV. 92 (1968).

and technical assistance in an effective manner. There are risks for the CDC, however. It is possible that a corporation would be willing to provide a sheltered market because that product was unprofitable, or to put itself in a better negotiating position with other suppliers of the same product. Also the new firm may become dominated by the procuring firm and end up as a "captive" operation, but since many new enterprises start under similar conditions, this would not be a problem unique to a community-controlled firm. Probably the greatest shortcoming from the CDC's point of view is the conflict which might arise within the supporting corporation between socially oriented goals and traditional capitalistic goals.

Another alternative available to the community development corporation seeking some form of market shelter is franchising. If the franchisor has an effective marketing program, both locally and nation-wide, and grants an exclusive area franchise, the franchise holder has in effect a quasi-monopoly of a localized nature. Hough Area Development Corporation has operated a McDonald's Restaurant unit for some time and the Conservative Vice Lords in Chicago hold a Tastee Freeze franchise.[45]

In recognition of the potential in franchising for the minority entrepreneur, the Small Business Administration and Office of Minority Business Enterprise have jointly instituted a program designed to increase the availability of franchise opportunities. Franchisors are invited to Washington in groups of twenty-five, where they are solicited to provide at least twenty-five new franchise opportunities to minority entrepreneurs over a two year period and to modify equity requirements consistent with the financial status of minority entrepreneurs.[46] Upon enrollment the franchisor is screened by the Small Business Administration to determine his capability to fulfill the agreement. If the franchisor is found to be eligible, the SBA makes a blanket loan guarantee on all loans by the franchisor to the minority entrepreneurs. By early 1970, seventy-two franchisors were enrolled of which fifteen were auto-related, twenty-five were food-oriented, and the remaining thirty-two provided a variety of other services.

In a related move, the Department of Commerce got a pledge from eighteen oil companies to increase the proportion of minority-held service station franchises.[47] Specifically, the Department of Commerce set a goal of a proportion of minority-held franchises equal to the minority proportion of the population.

Franchising has some specific advantages to offer the minority businessman, including management training and consultation, financial assistance, national advertising, brand image, and the localized quasi-monopoly position referred to earlier. Unfortunately, where a CDC is involved, the disadvantages are major. First, the great majority of franchises are retailing or service oriented. The franchisor retains

---

[45] Note, *Community Development Corporations: Operations and Financing*, 83 HARV. L. REV. 1558, 1658 (1970).

[46] OFFICE OF MINORITY BUSINESS ENTERPRISE, *supra* note 34, at 31.

[47] *Id.*, at 33.

a relatively high degree of control in the form of detailed operational restrictions, constant supervision, and the threat of termination of the franchise. Furthermore, the management training that is provided by the franchisor is mostly of a low level nature and often for the sole purpose of enabling the franchisee to carry out the franchisor's instructions and rules. Most franchisors will only deal on an individual basis, not with a corporation, particularly one with a social orientation such as the CDC. The most serious drawback is the fact that while the franchisee may have a quasi-monopoly, the franchisor has rather complete control over his franchisees. This power can be exerted in the form of continuing charges for advertising and consulting, and required use of franchisor-supplied goods or services.

Franchises differ, of course, and each must be judged on its individual merits. In general, however, it would appear that franchising is not a viable long-term strategy for a community development corporation to follow in its direct business ventures, either in serving the economically-depressed area or the broader consumer market. This does not mean, however, that franchises should be entirely overlooked by the CDC. Indeed, a franchise program might be the most effective manner in which a CDC can act as a catalyst in matching the franchise opportunity and the minority entrepreneur and assisting the entrepreneur in setting up his operation.

Conclusion

The business practices of CDC's have not typically resembled the market-oriented posture of the modern business firm. Probably of necessity, community-based organizations have placed most emphasis on financing their infant operations and on establishing the physical facilities for servicing the local residents. However, in order to realize the greatest possible impact on the economic conditions in the low-income areas which they serve, CDC's must now become market-oriented entities. This is particularly important because their primary consumer market is made up of people who are more suspicious and less well informed than those who populate the more affluent consumer market existing outside economically depressed areas.

The low-income area resident is to a large extent a captive consumer in that his shopping is effectively restricted to his immediate neighborhood. He is, however, by no means a captive of the CDC business. While convenience of location is probably a necessary condition for gaining his patronage, it does not guarantee his support. In fact, it appears that without a forceful marketing effort, the community-based enterprise is likely to lose out to established businesses because these firms are familiar to the local residents and are likely to continue to be aggressive in attempting to maintain their market position.

The CDC cannot fail to consider the potentially profitable opportunities beyond the neighborhood economy, for these may provide the means of gaining the greatest economic advantage presently available. Special arrangements offering a quasi-monopolistic position to the CDC seem to be the most viable ventures. These opportunities include the section 8(a) program of the Small Business Administration and the proposed program for developing a preferential procurement policy for state and local governments. Other opportunities exist in the private business market. Varying forms of preferential treatment have provided the major market impetus for several organizations. Also, CDC's might turn to franchising as means of gaining the desired quasi-monopoly market position. Each of these approaches, however, will involve the CDC with private or governmental institutions from outside the depressed area which it serves. While the economic benefits of such associations are attractive, the controls which these agencies impose may conflict with the social goals of the CDC. In its movement toward greater involvement in markets beyond the neighborhood, the CDC will likely be required to reassess the compatability of its social and economic goals.

COMMUNITY ECONOMIC DEVELOPMENT AND LOW-INCOME HOUSING DEVELOPMENT

PAUL G. GARRITY*

INTRODUCTION

Although the ideologists of community economic development disagree among themselves as to the significance, meaning, and objective of the "community" part of the equation,[1] both they and the practitioners seem to approach near unanimity in equating economic development with business development.[2] Even so, questions must be answered. How did this agreement come about? Does this consensus as to business development (whatever that means) as a strategy for achieving community economic development exclude or reject alternative or additional methods? Would low-income housing development be an effective and efficient alternative or additional way to bring about community economic development?

The following analysis will respond to these issues and will also discuss some of the problems of "community" that should be considered when the decision, however arrived at, is made to develop housing for low-income individuals and families.

I

THE TERMINOLOGY OF DEVELOPMENT

A. *Defining Community Economic Development*

To attempt to construct a dictionary-like definition of a term such as "community economic development" invites obfuscation and redundancy. The two elements of the term, "community" and "economic development," can be interpreted only in relation to specific contexts, and the context under consideration is rather unique both historically and contemporaneously.

1. *A Suggested Historical Perspective*[3]

The historical method to a large extent involves comparative factual analysis, and there have been many scholarly narratives published concerning the grim urban life of immigrant ethnic groups over the past 100 years.[4] There is substantial doc-

---

* Assistant Professor of Law, Boston College; Urban Fellow, Harvard Law School.
[1] *Compare* the more radical view proposed by Rosenbloom, *Corporations for Urban Development*, in SOCIAL INNOVATION IN THE CITY 161 (R. Rosenbloom & R. Marris eds. 1969), *with* the traditional approach espoused by Allen, *Making Capitalism Work in the Ghettos*, HARV. BUS. REV., May-June 1969, at 83.
[2] For a catalog listing what the practitioners are doing, see U.S. DEP'T OF JUSTICE, COMMUNITY RELATIONS SERVICE, NEW MINORITY ENTERPRISES (1969) [hereinafter cited as NEW MINORITY ENTERPRISES].
[3] The term "suggested" is employed so the reader will not regard the views offered as conclusive. The few observations are, of course, superficial, although they have been gleaned from extensive readings in this area.
[4] *See, e.g.*, THE CITY IN AMERICAN LIFE (P. Kramer & F. Holborn eds. 1970).

umentary evidence to support the facts that institutional discrimination against and economic repression of such groups continued until, by virtue of the size of the vote that could be mustered, they seized or participated in political power.[5] Political power, then as now, has its rewards to those wielding it, including not inconsiderable pieces of the employment, housing, and other municipal services action. Although there have always been urban racial ghettos, only with the mass migrations during and after World War II have blacks, by virtue of their numbers, constituted a potentially significant political force in cities.[6] Moreover, this potential did not become realized until the 1960's when militants and poverty program organizers created in black neighborhoods a sense of racial identity and community, which had not existed in ethnic ghettos, and liberals urged recourse to the ballot box.[7] Unfortunately, by that time the pay-offs generated by political control had declined in quality and quantity. Civil service legislation had insulated much municipal employment from the spoils system, and the pork barrel was fiscally lean. Most cities were nearly bankrupt and too impotent politically to tap the resources of the white suburban rings or to share in the revenues of the federal government which had pre-empted the field for municipal tax gatherers. There had occurred an imbalance, aggravated to an acute degree in the inner cities, between resources and human, physical, and social needs which, to many community leaders, meant developing an indigenous economic base to satisfy these needs.[8]

2. In Terms of Goals and Strategy

What are these needs? Any comprehensive study considering the "urban crisis," such as the *Kerner Report*, restates the problems and rephrases the solutions.[9] In the final analysis, any cycle of poverty and deprivation—and that is the inner-city "crisis"—can be broken with money. It takes money to provide high paying employment, to devise an adequate income-maintenance program, to furnish adequate housing, education, and social services, and, of course, to develop a community

---

[5] Oscar Handlin has observed with respect to the Irish immigrants in the 1850's: "They faced exhausting difficulties in making a place for themselves in the city's economic life. . . . The degree of their penetration into any trade varied inversely with its desirability. . . . Generally, the only opportunity for aliens to figure in commerce or finance grew out of the patronage of their own communities." Handlin, *Boston's Immigrants: The Economic Adjustment*, in *id.* at 82-84.

[6] REPORT OF THE NATIONAL ADVISORY COMMISSION ON CIVIL DISORDERS 115-20 (1968) [hereinafter cited as the KERNER REPORT].

[7] *Id.* at 104-12.

[8] ADVISORY COMMISSION ON INTERGOVERNMENTAL RELATIONS, URBAN AMERICA AND THE FEDERAL SYSTEM 7-11 (1969). *See also* L. ECKER-RACZ, THE POLITICS AND ECONOMICS OF STATE-LOCAL FINANCE 195-211 (1970). However, many community leaders argue that the only path to power is the political one and that economic development is diverting and divisive.

[9] The confirmed cynic would concur with Dr. Kenneth Clark, who, in testimony before the Kerner Commission, observed: "I read that report . . . of the 1919 riot in Chicago, and it is as if I were reading the report of the investigating committee on the Harlem riot of 1935, the report of the investigating committee on the Harlem riot of 1943, the report of the McCone Commission on the Watts riot. I must again in candor say to you members of this Commission—it is a kind of Alice in Wonderland with the same moving picture reshown over and over again, the same analysis, the same recommendations, and the same inaction." Quoted in KERNER REPORT 265.

economically. One very obvious method or strategy of making money is business development, and, not surprisingly, Black Power became Green Power.[10] The theory seems to be that with the development of business will come more and improved employment opportunities, increased income, and profits which can be rolled over into more business development or community services unobtainable from municipal treasuries. The extent of community involvement in the direction of this process would depend on communities themselves. With few operating exceptions, this is what community economic development has come to mean in practice.[11]

B. An Analysis of Inner-City Business Development

1. *In Operation*

The slogans adopted by inner-city business developers include "Black Capitalism," "Minority Entrepreneurship," and "Community Economic Development." One current federal assistance program contemplates the establishment of minority enterprise small business investment companies (MESBIC's),[12] and possible federal legislation is entitled the Community Self-Determination Act.[13] With two exceptions,[14] however, federal financial assistance is in the form of direct loans or loan guarantees and is allocated to the development of minority-owned *small* businesses. To be sure, there exist other federal efforts which respond to the non-money needs of inner-city entrepreneurs, but such programs rely primarily on the voluntary participation of the private sector.[15] One exception, called title I-D Special Impact

---

[10] *See* DeLorean, *The Problem*, in BLACK ECONOMIC DEVELOPMENT 7, 10-12 (W. Haddad & G. Pugh eds. 1969).

[11] NEW MINORITY ENTERPRISES, *supra* note 2. The Center for Economic Development, 56 Boylston Street, Cambridge, Massachusetts, maintains a comprehensive and up-to-date inventory of the activties of economic development ventures, and the records at the Center confirm this fact.

[12] As of August 1970, there were 16 MESBIC's licensed and in operation. OMBE OUTLOOK, Aug. 1970, at 11.

[13] S. 3875, 90th Cong., 2d Sess. (1968). The most astute analysis of this legislation is contained in Miller, *Community Capitalism and the Community Self-Determination Act*, 6 HARV. J. LEGIS. 413 (1969).

[14] The Public Works and Economic Development Act of 1965, 42 U.S.C. § 3121 (Supp. II, 1967), and programs funded under its authority, should not be considered an exception since few ghettos, when combined for eligibility purposes with outer-city areas, are not sufficiently underdeveloped to receive such program grants and loans. However, technical assistance funding has been provided to ghetto entrepreneur assistance groups under this legislation.

[15] For a complete listing, consult U.S. DEP'T OF COMMERCE, OFFICE OF MINORITY ENTERPRISE, SPECIAL CATALOG OF FEDERAL ASSISTANCE PROGRAMS FOR MINORITY BUSINESS ENTERPRISES (1969).

[16] This program, administered by the Office of Economic Opportunity, has been described as "a new experimental program designed to promote community-based economic development as a means of making a measurable impact upon chronic unemployment, dependency and community tensions in urban areas of high concentration of poverty and rural areas of high out-migration. This program provides substantial grants to development corporations representative of special impact areas. These grants may be used for a variety of investment programs which will create jobs for poverty area residents, develop managerial and entrepreneurial skills, and create opportunities for participation in ownership of production and commercial facilities by poverty areas residents. Community corporations can guarantee loans and provide technical assistance to new and existing businesses and can themselves participate in an enterprise on an equity basis." *Id.* at 81.

program,[16] furnishes substantial, but inadequate, funding for broad economic development purposes to community groups which, in most cases, have engaged in small business development. The other exception involves community development corporations being established and operated as component programs of local Model Cities agencies, and they have followed the pack in channelling their activities into small business development.[17]

2. *A Critique*

Inner-city business development is obviously not the most direct method of generating employment and profits or of increasing incomes. The optimum strategies would perhaps be job creation by subsidies, income maintenance programs, and grants for municipal services, but ghetto leaders view this approach, and accurately so, as politically and fiscally unattainable. However, what of the efficiency of the indirect strategy of business development and, in this case, *small* business development, in achieving these goals?[18] As contrasted with numbers of businesses established, how much minority employment is created, say, for each million dollars of SBA appropriations allocated to minority entrepreneurship ventures? What is the quality and duration of such employment? How much leakage is there—that is, employment of those already adequately employed or of non-minority group members? How much profit is actually generated and what portion of it benefits others in addition to the entrepreneur himself?[19] It has been pointed out that the environment of inner-city neighborhoods is improved by the establishment of, for example, a pharmacy where there was none before, but is this improvement neutralized if in fact the black pharmacist must maintain prices at high levels to compensate for the increased insurance and other costs of doing business in the ghetto?[20] In sum, if the process of economic development must be accomplished indirectly, is small business development the way, or even a way, to go about it?

One alternative strategy for small business development would be the location of larger business, probably industrial and commercial, in the inner city. Here, the pay-offs to the community are more ascertainable and substantial.[21] Unfortunately, the capital and expertise required for such undertakings are not usually available to minority entrepreneurs and require government and private sector assistance. Moreover, the federal government is usually not interested in large enterprise development unless some (other than minority) national interest is at stake and in-

---

[17] Demonstration Cities and Metropolitan Development Act of 1966, 42 U.S.C. § 3301 (Supp. II, 1967).

[18] For an appraisal along these lines, see S. Levitan & R. Taggart, Developing Business and Entrepreneurs in the Ghettos, Apr. 17, 1969 (unpublished paper prepared for the Community Self-Determination Steering Committee).

[19] *Id.* at 32.

[20] The problems of ghetto pharmacies are outlined in *The Ailing Drugstore: Looking for a Cure*, BLACK ENTERPRISE, Jan. 1971, at 28. The harsh facts of ghetto business life are catalogued in F. COLES, AN ANALYSIS OF BLACK ENTREPRENEURSHIP IN SEVEN URBAN AREAS (1970).

[21] However, there are pitfalls with this approach. *See* S. SETHI, BUSINESS CORPORATIONS AND THE BLACK MAN; AN ANALYSIS OF SOCIAL CONFLICT: THE KODAK-FIGHT CONTROVERSY (1970).

sufficient state and local incentives are available to offset the economic risks to large corporations establishing a ghetto subsidiary.[22]

II

THE STRATEGY OF LOW-INCOME HOUSING DEVELOPMENT

Although the housing development industry as such is fragmented and has at times been characterized as "chaotic,"[23] it is certainly a "business" to those who engage in it. Yet it is considered by many observers as something unto itself, and this sentiment is reflected in federal policy and programs.[24] How does "housing development" compare with "business development" as a strategy of community economic development?[25]

A. Financial and Impact Leveraging

The general goal of economic development presupposes that inner-city communities are undeveloped or, more likely, underdeveloped. There are insufficient local financial resources, and the strategy of business development takes this into account by leveraging government and private sector monies to secure most of the expenses of business development.[26] However, in most cases the ghetto entrepreneur must and should[27] furnish an amount of venture capital, although some private organizations have been formed to furnish the usual owner's investment. Because of tax shelters available with housing development, it is quite possible and desirable to arrange for outside infusions of venture capital and, depending upon the arrangement worked out between a community sponsor and equity investors, to have the venture capitalist pay for the privilege of investing.[28] Moreover, the sources and amounts of government and private financing for low-income housing development are greater than those available to small business developers under current and foreseeable federal priorities.[29]

---

[22] See Tabb, *Government Incentives to Private Industry to Locate in Urban Poverty Areas*, 45 LAND ECON. 392 (1969).
[23] See G. BEYER, HOUSING AND SOCIETY 225-26 (1965), where the author contrasts the automobile and homebuilding industries.
[24] For example, SBA loans cannot be used for real estate investment.
[25] Some community economic developers are interested. See Morey, *Housing and High Leverage Innovating Financing as a Start-Up Point for Community Economic Development*, Apr. 1970 (unpublished paper prepared for the Center for Community Economic Development).
[26] See generally McNeish, *Where Does the Money Come From?*, in BLACK ECONOMIC DEVELOPMENT, *supra* note 10, at 85.
[27] Interpret "should" from the perspective of having one's own stake in the business and because of the reality that excessive debt may very well spell business failure.
[28] For the details, consult Gabinet & Coffey, *Housing Partnerships: Shelters from Taxes and Shelters for People*, 20 CASE W. RES. L. REV. 723 (1969). Surrey, *Tax Incentives as a Device for Implementing Government Policy: A Comparison with Direct Government Expenditures*, 83 HARV. L. REV. 705 (1970), and Ritter & Sunley, *Real Estate and Tax Reform: An Analysis and Evaluation of the Real Estate Provisions of the Tax Reform Act of 1969*, 30 MD. L. REV. 5 (1970), both present convincing critiques of the efficiency and appropriateness of the tax shelter in producing housing—but housing is produced where none might be otherwise.
[29] Another complete listing is contained in Welfeld, *A New Framework for Federal Housing Aids*,

With housing development, the beneficial impact on the community as a whole is potentially greater than with business development. Employment related to housing development and resulting job skills will be generated, the incomes of those paying less for better housing will in effect be increased, and predictable profits, which can in turn be allocated to any number of community purposes, will occur.[30] Moreover, one possible goal of business development would be to obtain profits for improved housing; when emphasis is directed at housing development, this result can occur at an earlier stage.

B. The Certainties of Housing Development

Perhaps the main advantage of housing development contrasted with business development is that its variables can be calculated with reasonable certainty, including the effects of both inflation and government red tape. The costs of land, construction, and maintenance can be determined in advance, and these expenses—and the funding possible under government subsidy programs—can be fed into a computer to obtain feasibility and other desired information.[31] Moreover, not only is there a relatively certain demand for the product, but the dream of most fledgling businessmen, a sheltered market,[32] would be more than fully realized; for the market in which the low-income housing developer operates is also a subsidized one.

C. Possible Activities by Community Development Groups

Most non-private sector low-income housing development has been accomplished by not-for-profit sponsors,[33] (in many cases religious organizations) with varying degrees of community participation, but rarely has a community group as such functioned as a developer. Most community organizations formed to carry out "housing" activities usually do just that, and their focus is predictably tenant-oriented in the sense of organizing and counselling tenants rather than working on development. A few "community economic development" organizations engage in housing development in addition to their business development activities.

A certainly unique example, but relevant as a model, of a community development organization conducting low-income housing development would be the Bedford-Stuyvesant Restoration Corporation (BSRC), which also makes loans and provides management assistance to minority entrepreneurs.[34] BSRC operates at several housing

---

69 COLUM. L. REV. 1355 (1969). Although the current administration has included mobile homes within the statistics of housing produced to meet announced goals, the target levels have not been cut back.

[30] *See* Gabinet & Coffey, *supra* note 28, as to the predictability and amounts of "profits" available.

[31] Comprehensive computer analyses are contained in R. O'BLOCK & R. KUEHN, AN ECONOMIC ANALYSIS OF THE HOUSING AND URBAN DEVELOPMENT ACT OF 1968 (1970).

[32] A cause of many inner-city entrepreneurial failures, guesting rather than assessing "the market," is now being remedied by groups conducting sophisticated market studies. *See, e.g.*, CENTER CITY, BUSINESS AND INVESTMENT OPPORTUNITIES IN CENTRAL BOSTON (Boston Urban Foundation, 1969).

[33] Apparently there has been little success by such groups. The story recounted in P. NIEBANCK & J. POPE, RESIDENTIAL REHABILITATION: THE PITFALLS OF NON-PROFIT SPONSORSHIP (1968), is all too typical.

[34] The author spent nine weeks during the summer of 1970 on the legal staff of BSRC as part of an urban legal studies fellowship program.

developments levels. It acquires deteriorated properties, rehabilitates them, arranges financing, and resells these properties to residents. It assembles sites and develops new housing to be managed by tenant groups. BSRC also functions as a general contractor and furnishes training and bonding for minority subcontractors. Where BSRC does not possess an in-house development competency—for example, to put together detailed architects' plans—it farms out such work to experts managed by or staffed with blacks. Unfortunately, BSRC is a showcase operation, and few community development groups have such expertise or, more importantly, the access to resources to approximate its activities.[35]

III

IMPEDIMENTS TO LOW-INCOME HOUSING DEVELOPMENT

Aside from what could be included under the catch-all term of "risk," the two most significant obstacles to successful inner-city entrepreneurial development are difficulties in obtaining financing and the fact of less than adequate managerial skills. It is important to understand how much of a problem these two factors present as well as to recognize some additional difficulties peculiar to the development of low-income housing.

A. Financing

As with other business development, for-profit housing development requires equity investment, or a down payment, usually calculated as a percentage of funding expected to be made available by financing sources. Housing development also demands certain start-up resources, which have come to be known as "seed money."

1. *The Need for and Sources of Seed Money*

Housing development seed money is usually necessary to pay for organizational expenses and determinations of feasibility—in sum, to package a "deal" eligible for financing.[36] This process is analogous to that in which a minority entrepreneur would engage prior to and while preparing his application for a business loan. With the small businessman, however, there are fewer factors to consider and less detail to document, perhaps because the detail is not ascertainable. Moreover, the entrepreneur is not required to enter into commitments both to determine and to control costs—such as expenses for architects' drawings and site options. The alternatives available to a housing development group seeking seed money are quite limited. Limited financing from private sources may be available. In some cases, especially with not-for-profit sponsors, the funding comes in the form of charitable contributions. Another possibility is entering into a joint venture with a private developer who will

---

[35] For a summary description of BSRC's organization and activities, see Note, *Community Development Corporations: Operations and Financing*, 83 HARV. L. REV. 1558, 1650 (1970).

[36] *See generally* Berger, Goldston & Rothrauff, *Slum Area Rehabilitation by Private Enterprise*, 69 COLUM. L. REV. 739, 749 (1969).

make advances but not without some *quid pro quo*. A third alternative, which may be available to community groups funded under the Model Cities or Special Impact programs, is to request government monies to pay for these start-up expenses.

2. *The Need for and Sources of Equity Investment*

With housing development, the amount of equity capital required is usually proportionately less than that necessary with business development, perhaps because of the existence and nature of the security available in all cases. There are techniques available for reducing it still further. With private sector housing development, the developer either furnishes the equity himself or solicits investment from private sources. Ghetto groups retain this option and also have the possibility of soliciting funding from community residents as one way of assuring participation and a stake in the outcome. Another alternative available to community groups is seeking equity funding from the National Housing Partnership.[37] The Partnership was formed for a variety of additional purposes, including providing seed money and technical assistance, but the primary reason for its existence is to furnish equity funds for federally-assisted, low-income housing development. However, this equity investment is not "free" and may have to be considered as a private source, depending upon the bargaining stance the Partnership assumes as to a proper return on its equity investment.[38]

3. *The Need for and Sources of Financing*

In the private housing development industry, financing is classified as construction or mortgage, and quite often the same source provides both types. With low-income housing development, the source in both cases depends upon government assistance, and the problem is not availability, even if the existence of this assistance is assumed, but rather feasibility. The solution is to piggyback as many government programs as possible to reduce consumer costs to within governmental assistance eligibility limits and thus make a project feasible.[39] In other words, government insurance and purchase of a mortgage may induce a commercial lender to make financing available, but, because of high construction costs, interest subsidies alone may be insufficient to reduce rents to within limits administratively allowable for low-income families, and rent supplements would be required. The developer must then determine whether there are sufficient governmental appropriations for *all* of these housing programs since failure to qualify for only one of them may destroy the entire project's feasibility.

4. *Incidental or Indirect Sources of Funding*

In some locations, low-income housing is simply not feasible even with sufficient

---

[37] Housing and Urban Development Act of 1968, 42 U.S.C. §§ 3931-40 (1970).
[38] In other words, will the Partnership drive as hard a bargain as a private investor?
[39] Welfeld, *supra* note 29, at 1360 n.19.

"direct"[40] federal assistance by way of mortgage insurance, interest subsidies, rent supplements, and the like. There are, however, "indirect" ways of reducing costs to make impossible projects possible and to lessen expenses for possible developments. For instance, an obvious tactic commonly used is to secure land which has been reduced or written down in price with urban renewal funds. In addition, Department of Labor grants might be obtainable to subsidize construction costs as well as to influence hiring of minority construction workers. Department of Justice funding could be sought to provide security to a construction site, reducing that cost and perhaps lessening insurance expenses. To summarize, other government programs, quite unrelated to housing, might be piggybacked depending upon the ingenuity of the community sponsor and the malleability of the federal bureaucrats.

B. Technical Expertise

As with financing, the technical aspect of housing development might be subdivided into three areas which could cause problems for a community group engaged in producing low-income housing.

1. *Development Skills*

Perhaps the best way to characterize this nebulous competence would be to denote it as the ability to put together deals. It is very similar to the necessary skill termed management ability, but yet it is something more. It comprises a series of non-technical abilities and, more importantly, experience—something community groups do not possess vis-à-vis housing development. More specifically, it requires know-how in making detailed assessments of the nature of the market demand for a particular housing development, coordinating all of the professional inputs required, unravelling bureaucratic red tape, obtaining sites, financing, judging construction contractors, and performing a myriad of other activities too numerous to list.[41] One consideration of concern to private and community developers alike is whether to contract out for the various skills required or to retain in-house staff attorneys, accountants, financial analysts, and the like. Most community group developers have followed neither route but instead have relied on volunteer experts while forming staffs of community organizers. This has resulted in conflicts of interest, which will be discussed in detail in part IV.

2. *Construction Skills*

Very few private developers are so vertically integrated as to have operating subsidiaries which actually function as general contractors in the building of housing developments. Usually they and the community groups developing housing

---

[40] The most direct federal housing assistance would be providing income to the poor. *Id.* at 1373. However, would this result in more housing, or just higher prices for existing housing?

[41] *See* Moses, *Rental Housing for Low-Income Families Under Section 236*, in PRIVATE CAPITAL AND LOW INCOME HOUSING 28 (1969), for an excellent description of the developing process.

delegate to others this phase of development. From the standpoint of feasibility, how much delegation can be accomplished in an inner-city setting? Ghetto communities are justifiably antagonistic to the construction trades because of their well-publicized discriminatory hiring and apprenticeship policies, and the picketing by residents of such desperately needed municipal service centers as new hospital facilities, as well as housing construction sites, is not unknown. Moreover, existing construction industry building practices reflect a resistance to technological change, and in some cities this source of savings may be the only hope of bringing housing developments within allowable cost limits.[42]

3. *Management Competence*

Once a low-income rental housing development is ready for occupancy, what management role should a community group assume? It is quite obvious that the interests of the manager and tenants are somewhat conflicting. Would full disclosure of this fact and its ramifications to the tenants help here, or should community groups simply decline housing management responsibilities? Some equity investors and mortgagees may be unwilling to invest financially in a low-income housing development unless some community group acts as a buffer to assuage some of the basically economic tensions implicit in the landlord-tenant relationship. Such a prospective investor may require that a community group assume certain defined responsibilities to identify and resolve possible community "problems" which cannot themselves be defined with any precision. Thus the group may actually have no choice about participating in management.

C. The Uncertainty of "Community"

In the case of business development, the inner city is an inhospitable locus for investment, especially when contrasted with alternative investment possibilities. However, as was noted previously, at least with low-income housing development, investment factors such as costs, the market for the product, and the return on investment can be calculated rather precisely. What cannot be estimated in advance in terms of cost, and can only be vaguely articulated, is the significant risk which might come under the heading of community antagonism. An insensitive observer, without acquired insights into the frustrations and reactions caused by promises made to ghetto residents but never kept, would term it "irrationality."

By way of illustration, why do community groups continue to espouse the cause of rent control? By now, the evidence is overwhelming that rent control is totally counterproductive to an increase in and an upgrading of the existing stock of low-income housing and thus frustrates a resolution of the housing problems of inner

---

[42] Although savings obtainable from cheaper and more efficient construction methods are potentially not that significant in relation to total development costs, they may be the difference between feasibility or non-feasibility. Moreover, if more efficient methods result in savings in time, financing costs will of course be reduced.

cities.[43] Yet, sophisticated and well-intentioned ghetto leaders continue to lobby for rent control. More in point might be, for example, a demand by a community constituency for a day care center to be provided for each twenty-five units of housing, although the inclusion of such an amenity might result in the project being not feasible and no housing being built. Such a situation might arise at the beginning of planning or, to the dismay of a private developer, perhaps after significant amounts of seed money had been paid out. When this or a similar demand is voiced the issue usually assumes political ambiguities, and negotiations would proceed in a vacuum without reference to the economics. What role should a community group assume in such a case?

IV

COMMUNITY GROUP DECISION-MAKING AND LOW-INCOME HOUSING DEVELOPMENT

The purpose of this portion of the analysis is not a catalog of "how to do low-income housing development by community groups." Such an exposition is best left to the handbooks, of which there are several. There are differences between the development of low-income and other than low-income housing but, for the most part, the experience of developers of housing for the more affluent is relevant for community groups. The technical processes of packaging, site selection, financing, and construction vary little from luxury apartment development to low-income rental housing. Moreover, as soaring costs necessitate governmental assistance in the production of housing for those in higher income brackets, the differences will become insignificant.

There are, however, some issues, as contrasted with the technical processes once a project is underway, which require a community consensus of some sort when low-income housing development is being considered. How to achieve the consensus and who should participate in educating and being educated as to these issues—the community leaders, prospective tenants, or others—are questions best decided by individual communities themselves.

A. Should a Community Group Develop Low-Income Housing?

From the perspective of money profits to a community group, the answer is obviously yes. There are, however, other considerations. This issue requires some analysis of the interests involved in low-income housing development. The financial investors, the providers of the equity, the mortgage banker, and the party who subsidizes it all, the government, are variously concerned with the return on and the security of their business investment. The tenant, who perhaps tolerated previous housing which was substandard and expensive, does not view himself in a business context as the purchaser of housing but rather regards his occupancy as a right

---

[43] *See* RENTAL HOUSING IN NEW YORK CITY: CONFRONTING THE CRISIS 12-14 (I. Lowry ed. 1969).

of sorts; and he can be readily organized, for example, to participate in a rent strike even if justifiable rent increases are proposed.[44] And without the participation of a third group, low-income housing will not be developed. This group is the community leadership, which operates the community organization the approval of which will be a prerequisite to outside investment. What the outside investors desire is a joint venture between themselves and the community leadership group, the latter's function being to resolve the uncertainties of the particular community. The community group will be reimbursed for its efforts from the profits of the venture, and it might, for example, allocate these monies to rent reductions. In effect, the community group represents two potentially conflicting interests. The problem is exacerbated if the community group, assuming available financing and expertise, proceeds to develop housing on its own. It may be impossible for a community group which develops housing to retain the confidence of the community at large, there being a conflict of interest between "getting the project developed successfully" and being an advocate of perceived community interests. It is questionable whether such a problem can be resolved simply through community-oriented structures such as a board of directors elected at-large from the community and overseeing the activities of the solo or joint sponsors.

The remaining alternative is having a truly representative community leadership group canvass a community in advance or in response to a proposal by private developers and draft acceptable specifications for low-income housing development ratified by the community at large. The problem of specifications changed in the negotiations could then be resolved by another resort to community approval.

B. Where to Locate?

Perhaps it has been implied by this analysis that a low-income housing development should take place in the inner city. This may not be the most appropriate choice from the perspectives of costs and other equally important social factors. Sufficient land at a reasonable price may not be available in the ghetto. Real property taxes may be too high to bring rents within acceptable levels. Adverse environmental factors of extensive physical blight, high crime rates, and poor municipal and human services may make it unwise to develop in a section of an inner city where a completed project will sink to the level of its surroundings in a few years. In other words, it may be unwise to be the first one in. The bulldozer may be the only viable alternative short of increased Model Cities appropriations. Most importantly, the dilemma and results of continuing segregated residential patterns should be seriously considered.

Is it possible to locate a low-income development in suburbia? The first problem with this approach is that there is a need, and thus a political demand, for low-

---

[44] For a general study of tenant attitudes, see TRANSITION NEIGHBORHOODS IN NEW YORK CITY: THE PEOPLE'S VIEW OF THEIR HOUSING ENVIRONMENT (Vera Institute of Justice, 1969).

income housing for those poor already residing in the suburbs.[45] Moreover, multi-family rental housing, which may be the only feasible way to proceed at reasonable cost, might be blocked by restrictive land use practices. And rural or new town development, exemplified by the "New Communities" approach, appears doomed to failure unless employment, transportation, and other services are first provided.

Perhaps the most feasible choice, after all, is to build in an inner-city location, while undertaking measures to attract white, middle-class residents. What has come to be known as rent skewing might be the answer. It would be more ideologically acceptable to some ghetto leaders if for every white occupant relocating to such a development, a low-income resident displaced from possible occupancy could move to the area from which the white resident relocated.

C. New Construction or Rehabilitation Projects?

A factor, in addition to the obvious ones of cost and feasibility, bearing on the decision to engage in new construction or rehabilitation is the dilemma of relocation. In some municipalities, new construction costs may be prohibitive. However, rehabilitation expenses have been known in some instances to exceed costs of new construction, and the chief factor in holding such costs down appears to be rehabilitation projects sufficiently large to achieve economies of scale—and this causes relocation problems. Perhaps the only solution to relocation problems in such a case is reserve housing, which is probably unrealistic, or rehabilitation which is conducted sequentially.

D. Home Ownership or Rental Housing and Tenant Management?

With more recent federal programs, government-assisted home ownership for low-income families is possible even in the context of multi-unit developments.[46] The question then becomes one of determining what the prospective occupants of the intended housing prefer. If only multifamily development is feasible, do the low-income consumers desire ownership of such housing, or are they thinking of something else, perhaps in suburbia?

Assuming a decision is made to proceed with multi-unit rental housing, the community group must must still consider the desirability of performing management functions.[47] The possible problems here are quite similar to those hypothesized when a community group develops housing. The final decision will revolve upon whether the tenants or the community groups desire to be the managers and whether one would be more appropriate in that function than the other.

---

[45] *See* THE STATE AND THE POOR (S. Beer & R. Barringer eds. 1970), for convincing evidence that many suburban communities have in the aggregate more resident poor than the inner cities they surround.
[46] It is by no means established that low-income families would prefer home ownership. TRANSITION NEIGHBORHOODS IN NEW YORK CITY, *supra* note 44, at 84.
[47] In a survey conducted in New York, as many tenants preferred the city as landlord as preferred a community group landlord. *Id.* at 95.

Conclusion

It seems that low-income housing development is at least an effective and efficient additional strategy to achieve community economic development. The economic certainty contrasts most favorably with the financial risks inherent in inner-city business development. To be sure, the community "risks" are formidable and the accommodations that must be worked out are complicated.

ECONOMIC DEVELOPMENT IN THE MODEL CITIES PROGRAM

CHARLES E. OLKEN*

INTRODUCTION

The Model Cities program,[1] begat in the Great Society, altered and redirected under the New Federalism, and victimized by a continuing love-hate relationship with virtually all the politicians, bureaucrats, and community people who touch and are touched by it, continues to exhibit one key strength. It is the most highly-endowed source of non-categorical funds for urban development available in this nation; and Model Cities funds are now being used on a regular basis to support virtually all functions involved in community economic development, including economic planning, feasibility and market studies, venture capital on both equity and loan (including subordinated and low-interest) bases, land purchases and options, staff costs for business packaging and management assistance, management training, industrial promotion, direct loans, revolving loan and loan-guarantee pools, and bonding pools for minority contractors. Although the program may never achieve its widely heralded goals of breaking the poverty cycle in the chosen model neighborhoods and rationalizing governmental funding processes, the fervor with which it is being pursued and the relative flexibility of its resources attract the attention of those concerned with the urban scene in all aspects, including economic development by community development corporations.

It is important to note that the Model Cities program, unlike most other sources of funds relevant to economic development, asks that problem analysis and project-activity programming be approached on a comprehensive basis.[2] Cities are expected to develop strategies which are appropriate for the observed local pathology, emphasizing those factors most in need of change if the urban condition is to be improved. Thus, while comprehensive problem analysis is essential, the program initially undertaken to treat a given neighborhood's ills must concentrate on the *key* local variables. The theory followed here suggests that if strategic barriers are eliminated first, the other barriers to social change can fall more easily and in a more controlled manner.

The early Model Cities experience indicated that the depth of economic deprivation was widely recognized. However, the first plans also revealed that fewer cities than might have been expected were adopting strategies built around economic development, even though this generic area was given a high priority rating in terms

---

* Economic Development Advisor, United States Department of Housing and Urban Development, San Francisco Regional Office.
[1] 42 U.S.C. § 3301 *et seq.* (Supp. V, 1970).
[2] *Id.* § 3301.

of need for programming and was, in fact, receiving some attention in most plans. In most cases, the underlying problem was a lack of knowledge regarding economic development, which led to reluctance on the part of residents, CDA staff, and city councils to program heavily in this area. Our recent experience suggests a gradual increase in emphasis on economic development.

I

BACKGROUND AND SUBSTANCE OF THE MODEL CITIES PROGRAM

In October 1965, as part of his attempt to supplant the New Frontier with his Great Society, President Johnson appointed a special Task Force on Urban Problems headed by Robert C. Wood, then chairman of the Political Science Department of Massachusetts Institute of Technology.[3] The efforts of that group produced the basic concept of a new administration thrust, first heralded in President Johnson's January 1966 *State of the Union Message*.[4] His call for added public and private efforts to eliminate urban blight was supplemented by a special message to the Congress two weeks later entitled *City Demonstration Programs*.[5] On the next day, legislation to implement the President's proposals was introduced as H.R. 12341 and S. 2842, the Demonstration Cities and Metropolitan Development Act of 1966. After lengthy hearings and deliberations, the bill became law on November 3, 1966.[6]

Title I of the act authorized HUD to provide grants and technical assistance to cities to assist them in planning and carrying out local programs. According to HUD, these programs must provide "for a comprehensive attack on social, economic, and physical problems in selected slum and blighted areas through concentration and coordination of Federal, State, and local public and private efforts."[7]

Admission to the program required an application for a grant to plan a comprehensive program. The essential elements of such a plan, upon which specific projects are based, are a probing analysis of conditions and causes, a statement of long-range goals and program approaches, and an indication of the underlying strategy for attacking problems in a comprehensive manner. According to HUD, comprehensive programs should "encompass all of the deep-rooted social and environmental problems of a neighborhood."[8] HUD's working definition of "comprehensive" derives from the legislative purposes stated in section 101 of the Act, where the call for improvements in housing, income opportunities, education, health, criminal justice, transportation, and living conditions is manifested.[9]

---

[3] Other Task Force members were Kermit Gordon, Charles Haar, Ben W. Heineman, Edgar Kaiser, William Rafsky, Walter P. Reuther, Abraham Ribicoff, and Whitney Young.

[4] H.R. Doc. No. 321, 89th Cong., 2d Sess. (1966).

[5] H.R. Doc. No. 368, 89th Cong., 2d Sess. (1966).

[6] Demonstration Cities and Metropolitan Development Act of 1966, Pub. L. No. 89-754, 80 Stat. 1255.

[7] U.S. DEP'T OF HOUSING AND URBAN DEVELOPMENT, IMPROVING THE QUALITY OF URBAN LIFE 1 (1967).

[8] *Id.* at 3.

[9] 42 U.S.C. § 3301 (Supp. V, 1970).

A. Citizen Participation

The community is guaranteed an active role in model cities by virtue of the enabling legislation, which requires "widespread citizen participation in the program . . . ."[10] Although the Republican Administration has chosen to de-emphasize this aspect of Model Cities, Secretary Hyde and his chief aides continue to demand that cities clearly define and set forth the responsibilities of citizens in such a way as to insure their continuous and meaningful involvement. At the same time, it has become abundantly clear that this Administration makes a sharp distinction between citizen participation and citizen control and will not tolerate the latter in the planning process, whether it arises from either city indifference or effective community political action.

The early evaluation of this stance indicates a mixed bag of new opportunities and dangers for community-based economic development. HUD's position was not intended to discourage, and has not prevented, citizen control of new operating agencies, such as development corporations. But city councils, which have the final say in choice of program activities, have succumbed to Chamber-of-Commerce-type pressures against economic development by substituting less threatening (frequently manpower training) projects. The unanswered question is whether this kind of tampering with citizen initiative in economic development will increase or decrease as the Model Cities program matures. Hopefully, there is nothing so powerful as an idea when its time has come.

B. The Early Model Cities Response to Economic Issues

The Model Cities program was born at a time when the primary economic considerations in social planning were income levels and job training. Interest in community economic development had not emerged as a focal point in urban rhetoric, nor had the usefulness of the development concept been given any kind of careful examination. While it was possible to observe in 1969 that "job training cannot be compared with [community] economic development on an either/or basis,"[11] the 1966 view was clearly in the manpower tradition, even though the questions being asked by the new HUD team and the congressional mandate suggested a much wider focus. Then, in late 1967, HUD indicated that the comprehensive development program resulting from the initial-years' planning should provide (in the economics area) for projects and activities designed to achieve additional sustained employment opportunities and new careers in the public and private sectors. Without fully recognizing its potential, HUD also opened the door for community-based economic development by suggesting that manpower objectives might be met through the adoption of incentives designed to stimulate the expansion of commercial and industrial employment opportunities available to model neighborhood residents, add-

---

[10] *Id.* § 3303(a)(2).
[11] Green & Faux, *The Social Utility of Black Enterprise*, in BLACK ECONOMIC DEVELOPMENT 21, 23 (W. Haddad & G. Pugh eds. 1969).

ing rather lamely that it may be necessary to encourage the development of "private enterprises" in or accessible to the model neighborhood.

It was not long thereafter that HUD acquired staff capability in the economic development area and separated that resource from its manpower function. In addition, the regional staff function was expanded to include economic development under the aegis of a manpower and economic development specialist. Thus, by the middle of 1968 HUD had developed a recognition of the development field and exhibited a limited ability to respond to locally-expressed desires and explore the concept of "Green Power." To provide the correct historical prospective, it must be noted that the first group of model cities (seventy-five, in all, chosen from 193 applicants) had just begun the planning phase of their programs, and thus, a correlation existed between the staffing available to service local needs and the recognition of those needs. The nature of HUD's response and the staff's role in enhancing the potential for economic development in the model cities during the coming decade have both greatly expanded as the communities in the program have matured.

C. The Present HUD Stance on Economic Issues

It is fair to say that HUD was dragged kicking and screaming (although not entirely unwillingly) into a new definition of economic issues and a more realistic view of the role that economic development might play in local Model Cities programs, and it now realizes that the cities recognize Model Cities funds as the most flexible and versatile source of government financing for economic development programs. The Department's current response is a positive one, designed to enhance community desires to attack economic issues at the development and control level. Staff competence has been upgraded and the number of people working directly or indirectly on economic development has been expanded. In addition, HUD has hired two consultants, one to provide general economic development technical assistance to a number of communities who are or appear as though they will be "getting it on," and the second to train local staff in the intricacies of community economic development and business packaging techniques. Thus, HUD's position may be described as generally supportive, with top staff not entirely convinced while mid-level staff, which is charged with the responsibility for economic development, is moving ahead in assisting communities to plan and implement strong programs of local design.[12]

II

ECONOMIC DEVELOPMENT IN THE MODEL CITIES PROGRAM

Having explored the Model Cities program, its genesis and HUD's response to economic issues as they affect economic development, we can now logically turn to

---

[12] Attached to this article as an appendix is the HUD *Policy Statement on Economic Development*, which states the administrative parameters within which economic development may be carried out in the Model Cities Program.

the unique potential of economic development within local programs. The flexibility of the Model Cities program, its special relationship to federal and local resources, and its broad perspective create opportunities for economic development at the community level that do not exist to the same degree in most other programs and activities. That many of these avenues have not been extensively tapped to date is less important than the fact of their existence, for, in addition to the large financial resource that the Model Cities program makes available, these special opportunities are most exciting.

It has already been observed that local Model Cities programs are involved in a wide variety of traditional and not-so-traditional economic development activities, many of which are provided to the community through the CDC vehicle. The majority of these activities are similar in nature to programs being run all over the country and offer little that can be said to advance the state of the art. They are significant only because they rely on Model Cities funding for much of their financial resource and thus have been able to begin operations with at least one major hurdle aside.

The first part of the Model Cities planning year is geared to producing an in-depth problem analysis of the neighborhood, including such information as income and employment statistics, business participation rate, economic base analysis, a limited view of the goods and services available in the neighborhood and who controls (profits from) them, ongoing social and physical development programs, and the extent to which the neighborhood is involved with or bypassed by the area economy and its infrastructure. Thus, because it is a component of a Model Cities program, the economic development function begins life with a built-in pathological analysis of the community it is to serve.

In addition to the analysis of the symptoms of economic deprivation, the model cities are expected to pinpoint specific causes which have created the observed conditions. Although these causal factors tend to be somewhat similar in every location, each community is plagued by any number of unique elements which separate it even from its closest neighbor. One need only look at such communities as East Los Angeles (heavily Chicano) and Watts (primarily black) to realize that the problems are sufficiently different from neighborhood to neighborhood as to demand different stategies and direction for each. The advantage possessed by those who would pursue economic development in the Model Cities program is that they are able to tailor their activities from the outset to best meet the conditions of their individual communities.

This is not to say that economic planning and analysis ends when the city moves into its first action year. The city is expected to continue its analytical activities and to extend the range and depth of its studies to provide the full scope of information necessary to make program evaluation and funding decisions a rational process. HUD expects this kind of activity and examines cities' problem analyses, goals, and objectives to see that project funding patterns are consistent with stated measures and direction.

The outcome expected after all this planning and analysis is a logically-constructed program with a well-reasoned purpose and sense of direction. To promote economic development, the typical model city will move to set up some kind of development corporation, and one of the niceties of the Model Cities program is the relative ease with which such corporations can be organized. Community political hassles which frequently accompany the establishment of an acceptable development effort are often avoided in the model neighborhoods because of the recognition that the Model Cities program has received and the ongoing organizational activities that have necessarily occurred due to the existence of the local program.

The development company's credibility, while dependent in the long run on its ability to make positive accomplishments, in the short run, at least, is subject to less suspicion than many similar efforts. In addition, the local Model Cities program has usually made contact with other organizations that have a specific stake in the neighborhood or may be doing or considering economic development. HUD strongly encourages this kind of interaction and monitors local programs to see that existing institutions and organizations are utilized to their fullest. Thus, in Seattle, Washington, the Model Cities program, rather than setting up its own captive economic development arm is funding the United Inner City Development Foundation to carry out its development objectives.

Control of development corporations and programs is one of the most difficult issues that must be faced in the establishment of a new economic development activity. Again, when done as part of a Model Cities program, the politics become more easy to handle, although no less critical. In the first place, the community has a major role in the selection of corporation members and the board of directors. HUD policy limits the neighborhood citizen participation body to direct appointment of one-third of the corporation's governing body and allows only one joint membership (for conflict of interest minimization). However, it is silent on the method to be utilized in designating the remaining two-thirds, and presumably the procedure to be followed will at least be satisfactory to the citizen board even though it plays no direct role in the final selection of the larger group. In any event, the policy does require that the corporate governing body be broadly representative of the community within the model neighborhood area while also providing that participation be sought from the wider city community in an attempt to provide specific expertise and access to the necessary management and financial resources controlled from without the model neighborhood.[13]

In contrast to nearly all other economic development funds (OEO I-D,[14] EDA,[15]

---

[13] *See* Policy Statement on Economic Development § 7 (1971), infra app. A, at 225.

[14] This is the so-called Office of Economic Opportunity Special Impact program developed pursuant to 42 U.S.C. § 2763 *et seq.* (Supp. V, 1970).

[15] Economic Development Administration program regulations are set forth in 13 C.F.R. § 301.1 *et seq.* (1970).

SBA,[16] OMBE,[17] foundation, churches, and so forth), which come directly into the community from the funding source, Model Cities funds may be viewed as local funds, because HUD disburses the funds to the city for distribution to the selected operating agencies. There is, therefore, a local contract with the development corporation, the contents of which are specified locally. As a result, the community, through the Model Cities process, can exert extensive control over the existence and actions of the development corporation. Many cities use the contract to provide direction and emphasis for their development programs, using controls on the type and amount of investment funds as well as criteria for their spending (job/capital/wage relationships), earmarking funds for specific projects (industrial parks, shopping centers, land acquisition), regulating staffing patterns and salaries (business packaging specialists, industrial recruitment specialists), and describing the expected focus of the program (small business/medium and large enterprise, service/manufacturing/retail, neighborhood emphasis/larger economy).

Community influence and control accrues in a number of additional ways. The Model Cities staff is the most common prime mover in pulling together all the organizational elements—choice of board members by those so enfranchised, articles of incorporation and by-laws, and contract with the corporation after its formation. Setting eligibility criteria for financial assistance is a local responsibility. Employment of model neighborhood residents in the jobs created by the development effort is a programmatic requirement and is included in the contract with the corporation. Regular reports, monthly and quarterly, are required from the corporations and these are reviewed by the community, which may choose at any time to seek suspension or termination of the contract with the corporation. In addition, the local programs carry on extensive evaluation programs, which provide data that is used in the yearly refunding process. Suffice it to say that in the Model Cities program, local control over economic development is substantial and may well exceed that afforded in programs where funding comes directly to the project from Washington, New York, or any other locus of development money.

For those communities designated as model cities, the program may be a source of funds second to none other available to them in carrying out their economic development programs. Annual expenditures of Model Cities moneys are approaching $600 million. It is not unreasonable to expect that some eight to ten per cent of this amount, or $45 million to $60 million, will be allocated annually for a variety of economic development activities as the program matures. While $60 million is not an impressive figure when measured against the needs of the model cities, it compares favorably with other sources of funding for community economic development and establishes the Model Cities program as a full member in the movement.

---

[16] Regulations governing Small Business Administration programs appear in 13 C.F.R. § 101.1 *et seq.* (1970).

[17] Office of Minority Business Enterprise programs are administered under the Department of Commerce. *See* Exec. Order No. 11,458, 34 Fed. Reg. 4937 (1969).

What is perhaps more exciting is the flexibility of Model Cities funds in supporting nearly every stripe and hue of development. Aside from a number of restrictions imposed to avoid conflict-of-interest situations, HUD proscribes only one absolute constraint in the use of funds: Model Cities funds may not be extended to a for-profit enterprise to finance that enterprise on a grant basis.[18] There is also a general proscription against the use of Model Cities funds on a direct-loan basis in the absence of participation by other financial institutions.[19] It is the HUD position that even the softest of proposals, if it has a reasonable likelihood of financial success, can attract some "outside" financing if the Model Cities funds are used to advantage to bring in outside financing. In addition to possessing insufficient funds to assume the banking function, the Model Cities program (like other socially-oriented programs) has a stated legislative goal and an obligation to change our major institutions, but not to supplant them.

III

PROGRAM FINANCING

The list of uses for economic development funds that the Model Cities program will support is much too lengthly to be examined here. Of interest is the leverage that a community can achieve in using its Model Cities financial resources to attract the large financial injections necessary to support a broad-based economic development effort. The widely-recognized need for venture capital is satisfied by very few sources of development funds. In the Model Cities program, this use of funds is encouraged. Loans may be made on a subordinated basis at favorable interest rates with advantageous repayment terms. Moreover, equity positions are frequently taken by the development corporations in return for their financial participation.

Another interesting use of Model Cities funds on a front-end basis is in providing the local matching share for capital facilities financed under the SBA section 502 program.[20] Most packages brought to the SBA by section 502 Local Development Corporations associated with the Model Cities program have been considered eligible for ninety per cent loan financing, thereby requiring the community to supply only ten per cent of the total fixed facilities cost. Of course the community also benefits by its ability to retain ownership of the land and plant, which it leases to the assisted business concern at rates equal to or greater than the corporation's cash flow obligations on its section 502 borrowings.

Model Cities funds may also be risked for purposes other than the provision of front-end capital. Loan guarantees (usually on some kind of levered basis), interest subsidies, and other financial advantages such as deferred payments are frequently provided in conjunction with the deposit of Model Cities funds. A typical example involves an economic development corporation, funded by Model Cities, which was

---

[18] Policy Statement, *supra* note 13, § 5a.
[19] *Id.* § 5c.
[20] *See* 13 C.F.R. § 108.502 (1970).

confronted with a number of small businesses needing loan financing. The banks were interested in considering each small package ($500 to $5,000) on an individual basis provided that SBA guarantees were obtained. The development corporation, clearly seeing the inevitable frustration of carrying a large number of marginal packages through a complicated process, offered $100,000 of its funds to guarantee a $200,000 revolving loan pool provided by the bank to fund the corporation's small loan needs. It was further proposed that any loan recipient demonstrating a satisfactory earnings record over a two-year period be removed from the guaranteed pool and treated as an ordinary bank loan, since a seasoned loan no longer exhibits the element of risk that required the development corporation to act as guarantor at the time of financing. Such a procedure obviously would expand the funds available for other potential small business borrowers.

One of the constraints that most community development efforts must overcome is the need to provide a local matching share in order to receive federal funds and, in many cases, church or foundation funds. Any number of well-conceived programs have been delayed, abandoned, or have proceeded without adequate financing because of "buy-in" requirements imposed by funding sources. As troublesome as underfinancing has been for social service programs, it could well be fatal in economic development. Hopefully, this situation will be avoided in Model-Cities-related efforts. In the first instance, the Model Cities legislation specifically provides that funds "may be used and credited as part or all of the required non-Federal contribution to projects or activities, assisted under a Federal grant-in-aid program . . . ."[21] Second, the programmatic emphasis on the use of existing agencies would enable viable community agencies to enhance their relationships with funding sources since the local-share hassle will be eliminated by virtue of Model Cities support. Unfortunately, there is one major government program which does not accept Model Cities funds as the matching share. In the year or so that OMBE has been merchandising its *Wunderkind*, the Minority Enterprise Small Business Investment Company (MESBIC), a number of Model Cities agencies cleared the bureaucratic hurdles and set aside the initial capital necessary to receive a license to operate as a MESBIC. In each of these early cases the format differed, thus presenting OMBE and SBA with a choice of mechanisms by which a community with Model Cities backing could be allowed to function as an SBIC. Fresno, California, through the Fresno West Development Corporation, made application to be the sole source of financing for and sole owner-operator of a MESBIC which would become an integral part of its broad economic development program. The models proposed by Winston-Salem, North Carolina, and Atlanta, Georgia, were different in organizational structure but retained Model Cities funds as the source of their paid-in capital. Each plan was rejected as not meeting the legislative mandate that SBIC's be financed by substantially private capital.[22] If the HUD operatives in Washington led by Assistant

---

[21] 42 U.S.C. § 3305(d) (Supp. V, 1970).
[22] *See* 42 U.S.C. § 682 (1964).

Secretary Floyd H. Hyde and his economic development advisor, Norman De-Weaver, are not successful in their efforts to dissuade SBA from its restrictive interpretation of the SBIC legislation, the local Model Cities programs will have to develop less direct, more complicated strategies to obtain the obvious benefits derived from community control of the MESBIC mechanism.

One gambit that has been tentatively approved by SBA suggests the use of Model Cities funds to pay the operating costs of a MESBIC, the capitalization of which is provided by acceptable sources. This, of course, means that the Model Cities development agency must become involved in a search for funds from foundation, church, or private financial sources or by sale of stock. Not answered, at this time, are the questions of ownership and control of the board of directors. One can only guess that ownership would not be allowed to pass to the community, and, on the other hand, that SBA would not prevent community representation on the board of directors and community participation in selecting the staff and in determining the operating policies of the MESBIC.

The opportunity to undertake large-scale economic development, through enterprises capitalized in the hundreds of thousands of dollars, requires substantial financial resources. Many development efforts simply cannot function in these terms, because their funds are too limited and their leverage with the wider financial community almost nonexistent. Here again, programs linked with Model Cities have a built-in advantage. Many are expressly funded to attempt development of large-scale enterprises. Those that are not so funded are able to turn to the local model cities progam if they have reasonable prospects of putting together a substantial package.

In addition, Model-Cities-related efforts have both the financial and technical resources necessary to react quickly and responsibly to targets of opportunity that present themselves at random intervals. A typical situation, for which no rational planning is possible, would be a spin-off opportunity presented by a large corporation. Howsoever motivated, whether out of guilt, public self-interest, profit, or true belief, the corporate liberal demands quick action and, frequently, substantial monetary commitment in exchange for his setting up a captive enterprise in the community. Very few Model Cities need allow opportunities of this nature to go untapped. If the conjecture is true that uses of the spin-off technique will expand rapidly from the thirty or forty that have been attempted in the last few years, and if the best strategy for success involves an active partnership with the community in planning and creating the spin-off corporation, then Model Cities development agencies ought to be in a unique position to assist their communities in initiating as well as exploiting spin-off opportunities.

Much of the benefit suggested above can accrue to any community development effort that possesses adequate, flexible financial resources. Notwithstanding the fact that most of the new enterprises are required to run the gauntlet of private financial interests in order to reach fruition, economic development in the Model Cities program begins with the not inconsequential advantage of having adequate funding to make the best of any opportunities that it stumbles upon or generates.

IV

Opportunities Available to the Model Cities

Even with the critical problem of financing reduced to more manageable proportions, the actual establishment of viable businesses that will achieve the multifaceted goals of creating meaningful, well-paying jobs for large numbers of people, increasing the numbers and skill levels of middle management in the community, providing the community with greater control over the economic fortunes that govern people's lives, and creating new institutions that provide the community with substantial capital and capital-generating instrumentalities together with the skills to use that capital remains a problem in the Model Cities program as in any other community development activity. The suggestion that development efforts associated with Model Cities have an advantage in achieving these goals is not made lightly. The creation of viable enterprises is recognized by all as being a tough, tricky business in which the risk of failure is high. Because of their special relationship to the total community improvement effort of the Model Cities program, and because the Model Cities program is one of the federal government's major urban programs—and certainly its most comprehensive urban program—a number of unique opportunities exist to interface economic development programs with a wide variety of federally- and locally-initiated programs and activities of a more narrow scope. A number of these advantages which accrue in the Model Cities program are examined below, not so much in a how-to-do-it exposé, but rather with an eye toward increasing public recognition of them. Each might legitimately be the topic of a lengthy treatise, and the space devoted to them below is hardly indicative of their importance in this area.

A. Core Strategy Concept

The first of these, the core strategy concept, is almost totally unique to Model Cities. As noted above, each city participating in the program is expected to identify its specific problems, set goals and objectives that have local relevance, and develop a strategy to achieve those goals and objectives. A city whose community leaders and administration fully recognize the devastating effect of prolonged economic deprivation might well elect to concentrate its efforts on economic development. The legislative purposes of the program—"to rebuild or revitalize slum and blighted areas; to expand housing, job, and income opportunities; to reduce dependence on welfare payments; to improve educational facilities and programs; to combat disease and ill health; to reduce the incidence of crime and delinquency; to enhance recreational and cultural opportunities; to establish better access between homes and jobs . . . ."[23]—all can be defined in economic terms and, therefore, could lead many

---

[23] 42 U.S.C. § 3301 (Supp. V, 1970).

communities to attack these conditions through a program emphasizing economic development as the core strategy. This is not to suggest the absurd result that schools, hospitals, parks, and other social services delivery systems be established on a profit-making basis; rather, the enhancement of these systems will provide opportunities for development of real capital, through construction and related operational activities, as well as for the development of human capital to enable the community to participate fully in the economic gains that are being made.

An economic-development core strategy dictates that in addition to funding new business development, other Model Cities projects provide supporting services which enhance the community's ability to make economic progress. Thus, public improvement projects can be designed to increase the desirability of the neighborhood as an industrial location. Local contractors would receive technical assistance, enabling them to take on larger, more complex projects, as well as financial backing, which would provide operating capital for bonding and interim cash flow needs. Affirmative action programs, stated quantitatively and incorporated into the project bid specifications, would insure that area residents received the construction jobs generated. Manpower training projects would be keyed to the program's skill requirements, the majority of which ought to be identifiable during the planning period and would thus prevent skills training for nonexistent jobs. The primary thrust of educational programs would be the development of business management, professional, and technical skills needed to make the neighborhood self-sufficient in terms of its ability to run its own enterprises without resorting to imported labor. Housing development, a high priority desire of many Model Cities programs, would be related to the core concept through assistance to local contractors' affirmative action programs, the funding of nonprofit housing sponsors, and attempts to generate real estate development enterprises. The funding of housing activities would be timed to meet the demand created by the cash flows brought into the neighborhood through the economic development program.

Central to the economic development core strategy concept, of course, are the financial relationships among its various elements. Each must be funded in such a way as to produce a result which supports the other elements in the program. Funding for economic development would necessarily anticipate the cash and management assistance needs of the businesses generated by economic leverage derived from the social and physical sections of the program as well as from larger-scale, externally-focused business development.

Although the economic development core strategy concept is utopian rather than real at this point, a number of cities have achieved a moderate level of programmatic integration between economic development and other aspects of their Model Cities action programs. Inasmuch as the majority of model cities will not opt for the core strategy but will attempt *some* kind of economic development, it becomes important that programmatic linkages be achieved wherever possible.

B. Manpower Training

Clearly, the most obvious linkage is the relationship with manpower agencies. Any aggressive economic development program should be creating businesses and jobs.[24] Although the percentage will vary from program to program, a large number of these new jobs will require skill levels not possessed by most unemployed and underutilized community residents. By using its manpower funds to provide the training necessary to place residents in the new jobs, the Model Cities agency is guaranteed a maximum return on its expenditure, since training is provided for jobs controlled by the Model Cities program; and, at the same time, the model neighborhood's desirability as an industrial location is enhanced, since any new business is guaranteed a trained labor force at no expense.

In spite of the plethora of manpower training funds being spread over the land by an overwhelming variety of agencies, manpower resources paid for or controlled by the Model Cities program may be better suited for the community and, at the same time, more supportive of economic development than one normally expects. The key is flexibility to match people to training resources and guaranteed jobs. Model Cities development programs have, in some instances, been geared to providing job opportunities for the hard-core unemployed. The need for extraordinary training, counselling, and support is obvious. As a result, many existing manpower training programs cannot meet the high costs and will not tolerate the high frustrations of working with the hard-core. Naturally, Model Cities training resources have been required in these instances. Although the program is too new to provide definitive data, early results have suggested that placing the hard-core unemployed in local businesses, possessing more community orientation than is typical of private enterprise, can help overcome work hang-ups[25] experienced by the poor.

The use of Model Cities funds to train higher-income community people for the more highly skilled jobs—foreman, steward, and so forth—again insures any business locating in the model neighborhood of a supervisory force which is not only already trained but which is also likely to be more acceptable to the labor force than imported supervisors. The same is true for any of the various levels of management, all of which may be filled with people trained with local Model Cities funds.

C. Improving Housing

In addition to manpower, the other Model Cities element most often related to local economic development is housing. Almost every model city perceives inadequate housing as a major deficiency. It is not a recent phenomenon that the supply of housing in minority communities is inadequate both in terms of amount and quality. The housing squeeze in most major areas of urban concentration has only compounded the difficulties. As the various model cities have moved to alleviate

---

[24] And, according to the Model Cities *gestalt*, these jobs must be filled primarily with residents of the model neighborhoods.
[25] Which are frequently referred to as reflecting lack of knowledge of the "world of work."

the housing burden, many have appreciated the linkage that housing development can have to economic development.

A nonprofit housing sponsor (a frequent Model Cities mechanism) is, in many ways, not unlike a new business. The management problems have many interesting parallels[26] which are no less difficult for the new housing manager than for the new business manager. If the failure rate is lower, it is only because it is more difficult to kill a house in a market with no vacancies—such as the ghetto market for standard, reasonably-priced housing—than it is to kill a business. To guarantee that the Model-Cities-financed nonprofit housing sponsors provide adequate management for units which are very precious to the community, many cities have made the housing management assistance function part of the economic development technical assistance function, thereby purchasing more specialized services in both areas for the same cost—and without setting up two separate staffs.

As mentioned above, there is a need for housing development to meet the demand created by a new group of well-paid, private-sector workers in the community. Even though the Model Cities program is still too young to have reached that glorious day, the normal program does generate jobs in the public sector, the income from which is already creating a modest housing demand. Presently, the most advanced cities are moving into position to establish their own profitmaking real estate development corporations to build moderate amounts of non-assisted housing in the model neighborhoods. From that experience, those firms should be able to move into the larger housing market at a time when the demand for housing is about to explode.

There is, of course, one additional, obvious advantage that Model Cities programs have in setting out to develop assisted or non-assisted housing, whether or not the linkage to economic development is made. For whatever it may be worth, local Model Cities programs, by virtue of their HUD connections, have some leverage in getting FHA commitments to provide financial assistance and guarantees for housing that is being built in conjunction with the program.

A frequently-discussed but as yet untried gambit related to solving the model neighborhood's housing problems is the formation of a modular housing corporation. The typical model foresees the economic development corporation providing the venture capital, the banks and SBA putting up the loan funds, neighborhood residents being trained as the company work force, and the pent-up demand for low- and moderate-cost housing in the model neighborhood providing a guaranteed market. The problem, of course, with this synergistic system is that the market cannot be guaranteed unless the Model Cities program finances all the housing and the community is willing to accept a standardized product—not just for one or two clusters, but for all new housing. In any event, the market that could be guaranteed would probably not be of sufficient size to meet the minimum produc-

---

[26] Accounting, purchasing, record-keeping, advertising, and site selection are only a few of the common problems.

tion required for a plant to be financially feasible. The economic constraint that most cities thinking along these lines must face is either the necessity to compete in the open market economy[27] or to expand the size of their guaranteed markets, a question of economics which is explored below.

D. Minority Contractors and Urban Renewal

Related to new housing development is the question of how the Model Cities program goes about enhancing the opportunities for minority contractors. For the most part the techniques being used are not unique to the program and are not very successful. Generally, the training and assistance programs are well financed, but the bonding problem has not been successfully approached. Revolving pools for working capital and bonding have been established by many cities, but the funding has not been very significant when compared to the need. While it will not solve the financial problem, there is a means within the Model Cities program for cities to channel more construction activity to contractors from the model neighborhood. The mechanism utilizes the employment-of-model-neighborhood-residents requirement to prevalidate acceptable bidders on the basis of their demonstrated ability to hire residents for construction projects. Under this system the local minority contractor, whose regular work force already lives in the community, gets the advantage.

The ability to help minority contractors and, at the same time, to realize significant economic gains for the community also occurs when HUD's Urban Renewal program is used in conjunction with economic development efforts of Model Cities. The contractors can always participate in the demolition process, which is under public control. However, they rarely get assigned any of the rebuilding activity; the bulk of that is done by private, multimillion dollar land developers who choose their own contractors, and not necessarily by open, competitive bid. When the community controls the process, minority firms are more likely to participate in the reconstruction work, and that requires very effective community organization in the most political way or community control of the land in the capacity of developer. In point of fact, many Model Cities are proceeding in this manner. Communities are putting themselves squarely in the running to become developers of urban renewal projects, backing up their organizational strength with Model Cities money. As in the housing field, the HUD lineage of both Model Cities and urban renewal is a distinct advantage.

Control of land is an important asset for any development effort. Up to this point, the communities seeking to link urban renewal with economic development have focused on projects started long before Model Cities and economic development were heard of. As the result, the projects are not entirely suited to Model Cities needs. Moreover, the community economic development effort has had to catch up rapidly to avoid missing yet another payday. These handicaps can be overcome, however, and no community with the financial and political strength of the Model

---

[27] This would require a very different image for the product to be produced.

Cities program behind it ought to remain idle because the game started before it was ready.

The far better, if longer term, relationship with urban renewal is the one initiated by the local Model Cities agency as part of its economic development program. In this instance, the community is clearly involved from the very beginning. It participates in all critical decisions, including site selection, timing of the project to proceed in line with the community's capability to respond, and planning the eventual re-use of the project. In addition, and possibly most important, the entire cost of buying the land and preparing it for resale can be funded with readily-available HUD funds. Renewal funds to be used in conjunction with the Model Cities program have been more readily available than normal renewal moneys, since the local matching one-third share may be paid from Model Cities grants. By using the renewal process to its best advantage, local model cities programs can easily assemble parcels of land whose size and location are best suited to the needs of their economic development programs. As with any Model Cities activity, land assembled in this manner need not necessarily be included in the model neighborhood area; however, the benefit to be derived from the re-use of the land must accrue to residents.

Having followed the procedure outlined above for new projects or the more difficult route for ongoing projects, the development corporation should be in a position to receive the first-development option on the land of a no-fee basis. The trick, then, is to take advantage of long-term leases to finance the land and plant, turnkey operations for construction contractors, and employment contracts with the eventual users of the land to ensure employment of local residents.

E. Relations with Other Programs

Local Model Cities programs have a special relationship to the institutions that control city planning activities, zoning, taxation, public improvement programs, and other local services that affect a community's ability to make economic gains. An enlightened city, making strategic use of its powers and resources, can provide very valuable assistance to a community economic development effort. In many instances, nothing more is involved than the everyday courtesy of one city agency clearing the way for another's program. On the other hand, the early provision of such public services as roads, lighting, water, sewers, and trees in an industrial setting can be the key factor in making a community's development effort successful. Model Cities programs needing city support in order to accomplish their economic objectives are given a big assist by HUD, which pays regular and close attention to the level of city commitment and the manner in which regular city functions help or hinder the city's program.

Just as development efforts related to Model Cities enjoy a favored position within the normal functions of the city government, so also do they frequently enjoy a position of greater credibility with the private sector than do most other community-based programs. The reasons for this are many, including the program's presupposed good relations with City Hall, the additional relationship with the private financial institutions in the area of housing, and the broad city involvement that usually accompanies Model Cities. The frequent upshot of this advantage is a heightened ability to bring about institutional change, making the private sector more responsive to the community's economic and financial needs. Whereas many programs (such as OMBE) to date have set out to increase the number of interactions between community and downtown, Model Cities also seeks to change the nature of that interaction. Proposed programs in New York City, Tucson, Fresno, and Baltimore involving Model Cities and bank-sponsored credit arrangements attest to the potential in this area.

We have already explored the unique ability of Model Cities funds to be used as the local matching share for other federal grant programs. It is worth noting that the model neighborhood areas comprise geographical and pathological units which make then ideal candidates for the benefits available under EDA's Special Impact designation and OEO's Speical Impact (I-D) program. Several model neighborhoods are expected to be among the few urban poverty pockets that EDA will designate for special assistance. (HUD, of course, has suggested to no avail that EDA designate all 150 model neighborhood areas on the basis that their inclusion in the Model Cities program is prima facie evidence of satisfying EDA guidelines.) Under OEO's I-D program, the United Inner City Development Foundation in Seattle, which has been receiving Model City funds, has been chosen as the recipient of a six-month grant to plan specific enterprises and activities which OEO will fund. By joining a CDC operating with Model Cities funds, the OEO grant realizes significant savings in start-up time, staff orientation, and community acceptance.

As a program, Model Cities have suffered the advantages and disadvantages of being restricted to serving the populace of a given geographic area. One of the positive aspects of that constraint is the understanding of a particular neighborhood that arises over a period of time. In the economic area, this means that markets are measured, business expansion potential is well-evaluated, strengths get exploited, and weaknesses are corrected. In short, economic programs are beginning to achieve their first blushes of maturity. The Model Cities agencies located in close proximity will then be in position to work together in capturing the potential of their several marketplaces, thereby expanding the size and types of business which might logically be started to serve the community.

One very legitimate example of this could well be a modular housing factory sponsored by a number of model neighborhoods. If the potential market for the factory's product can be increased, its prospects for financial success would seem to be far greater than those of the factory built by a single Model Cities program to serve its neighborhood only. The many Model Cities programs in the San Francisco area have indicated a willingness to explore a joint approach to their financing problems at a reasonable point in the near future. Jointly-funded venture capital, venture management, and technical assistance operations are also logical extensions of the economic development programs beginning to function in the many model neighborhoods. In time, of course, the natural alliance that will grow among the Model-Cities-sponsored development efforts in 150 cities will be expanded to include CDC's and all other types of community-sponsored groups.

CONCLUSION

The upshot of these many unique economic and political advantages accruing to Model-Cities-related development programs should be a higher degree of success than the average community development program experiences. In some cities, success will be spectacular; in others, failure will be equally spectacular. Although they will be the exception, a few moderately-sized cities with aggressive programs, can be expected to ameliorate much of their unemployment problem and to establish the kind of viable community-based enterprises and institutions necessary to continue the development pattern. For most, however, success will be achieved in terms relative only to lesser efforts in the past. Success, absolute success, will be too difficult to achieve within the time frame allotted, with the financial resources provided, and with the backdrop of a nation not very willing to accept its responsibility to its poor.

APPENDIX A

POLICY STATEMENT ON ECONOMIC DEVELOPMENT
(CDA Letter 10-C)

1. *General Considerations*

In undertaking economic development projects, each City Demonstration Agency must carefully weigh the full range of approaches to development problems. This examination should enable the CDA to choose the approach or combination of approaches most appropriate to its problem analysis. The various development approaches to be considered may include, but are not limited to:

   a. Economic planning in order to utilize the area's physical and human resource base more efficiently.
   b. Furnishing technical assistance to businesses and development organizations.
   c. Financing development activity and individual business ventures.
   d. Creating and improving the public facilities and services necessary for economic growth, such as development of industrial sites, transportation systems, water, sewerage and other utilities intended to benefit industrial and commercial users.
   e. Impacting municipal policies and practices on land use, taxes and other matters which affect the city's ability to attract investment, particularly in the Model Neighborhood.

2. *Use of Existing Organizations*

Existing organizations, institutions, programs and services shall be used to the optimum extent possible in implementing economic development projects. CDAs are required to demonstrate the ways in which such existing resources will be involved in performing economic development tasks at the time action plans to be supported from supplemented funds are submitted to HUD-Model Cities for approval. Such submission material will be supplied in accordance with the Issuances or Instructions that are contained in Category 3140 entitled Submission Requirements of the Model Cities Operating Manual.

3. *Relationship to Other Components*

CDAs shall extend all appropriate services from other components to support economic development projects. Specifically, manpower training and development services shall be provided to help qualify Model Neighborhood residents for jobs generated by economic development activity and to help residents retain and become upgraded in such employment. Supporting services, such as child care and transportation, shall be arranged where appropriate.

4. *Technical Assistance Functions*

CDA action plans should clearly identify the technical assistance elements of economic development projects and distinguish them from the investment elements listed in Section 5 below. Such a distinction is intended to facilitate application of this policy with respect to those costs chargeable against supplemental funds on a grant, loan or equity investment basis. Technical assistance elements which can be provided from Model Cities supplemental funds on a grant basis may include, but are not limited to, the following:

   a. Performing feasibility studies, marketing surveys and labor market analyses concerning proposed expansions of existing businesses, the initiation of new business ventures and creation of new opportunities for investment.
   b. Providing assistance in the packaging of loan funds or other financial assistance for individual business enterprises.
   c. Furnishing management assistance to business enterprises, including but not limited to counseling in production, finance, marketing, procurement, personnel management and similar aspects of business operations.
   d. Identifying prospective owners, investors and managers of business enterprises and training both potential and actual owners and managers in the techniques of business management.
   e. Performing common services which increase the capacity of a businessmen's association to provide management training and assist in solving mutual problems for its members on a continuing basis.
   f. Performing industrial solicitation and promotion functions.

5. *Investment Functions*

The types of investment in individual business enterprises permitted with Model Cities supplemental funds shall be limited by the following rules:

    a. Supplemental funds should not be used on a grant basis to finance a business.

    b. Every effort shall be made to obtain the participation of private lenders in financing businesses. Where applicable the programs of the Small Business Administration, Economic Development Administration, State lending agencies and other public programs should also be used. Model Cities supplemental funds may be used in conjunction with such private and public lending activities in a variety of ways: to guarantee loans, to provide reimbursement to lenders of all or a portion of the interest charged on loans, to permit the deferred payment of principal or interest on loans, to facilitate special deposit arrangements encouraging the participation of private banks in business development programs or to provide a portion of the total loan financing required by a business venture.

    c. Model Cities supplemental funds should not normally be used to provide loans to business enterprises in the absence of participation by other lenders or guarantors.

    d. Supplement funds may be used to acquire equity in the ownership of an individual business only when such investments are not prohibited by State or local law and only when the development corporation or agency taking such an equity position is a nonprofit organization, or, if a for-profit organization, it is broadly-based and controlled by residents of the Model Neighborhood.

6. *Investment Guidelines*

In administering investment programs of the types permitted above, operating agencies shall observe the following procedures:

    a. Prior to using supplemental funds for investment purposes, the agency operating the component project must ascertain the potential viability of the proposed business venture. If the owners or managers of the proposed business do not have experience in the successful operation of similar ventures, management assistance must be provided as appropriate to insure the success of the venture.

    b. Any financial assistance furnished to a business shall be conditioned upon a requirement that all employment generated will be available on a preferential basis to Model Neighborhood residents in accordance with HUD-Model Cities policy on resident employment. Such financial assistance will be further conditioned upon a requirement that the business will conform to HUD policy on equal opportunity.

    c. Agencies administering investment programs shall establish criteria under

which proposed ventures shall be eligible for financial assistance.
   d. In addition, agencies administering investment programs shall establish objective criteria under which preference will be given among proposed ventures meeting the eligibility requirements set in accordance with c. above. Such preference criteria may include: ventures which support other aspects of the Model Cities program, investments in labor-intensive businesses, and business ventures which provide subcontracting opportunities to Model Neighborhood enterprises.
   e. The agencies administering investment programs financed with supplemental funds must maintain for public inspection copies of the eligibility and preference criteria required by c. and d. above, together with a list of the businesses assisted by such investments. This list must include the names and addresses of the businesses together with the names of the proprietors, partners or those shareholders who hold more than 20% of the outstanding stock in the corporation. Records should be kept of all applications for assistance received, including those which are not approved. Such records are necessary for internal evaluation and need not be available for general public inspection.

7. *Structure of Development Corporations*
Prior to creating any new economic development corporations, the CDA must demonstrate that there are no experienced, existing institutions performing the same or similar functions or else justify any decision not to utilize the services of such institutions. Any newly created development corporation or other private organization which receives investment capital from Model Cities supplemental funds for reinvestment in individual business enterprises shall be organized in such a manner as to comply with applicable Federal, State and local statutes. In addition, new development corporations shall meet each of the following requirements:
   a. The governing board must be broadly representative of the community within the Model Cities target area. In general, participation should also be sought from the broader city community. Participation by private businesses, individuals and agencies with particular expertise in economic development shall be provided, either on the governing board or in advisory capacity.
   b. No more than one-third of the members of the governing board may be selected, directly or indirectly, by the citizens participation body which serves the city demonstration program.
   c. In designing the structure of the development corporation and composition of its governing board, CDA or other local officials should consider the the requirements of the various public programs which can provide capital

to the development corporation. For example, if the development corporation expects to participate in the development and financing of land, buildings and equipment for small businesses, it should be organized in such a way as to meet the requirements imposed by the Small Business Administration on local development corporations under its Section 502 program.

d. Prior to considering any applications for financing which involve Model Cities supplemental funds, the development corporation shall establish rules prohibiting conflict of interest by development corporation officials responsible for determining the investments the corporation will make.

OPPORTUNITY FUNDING CORPORATION: AN ANALYSIS

SAMUEL I. DOCTORS* AND SHARON LOCKWOOD†

The Opportunity Funding Corporation's primary novelty is that it is the first attempt to determine experimentally how to build a capital base in low-income communities. It attempts, in effect, to transfer the experience and learning of the banker, the securities analyst, and all the other financial specialists who help to create the money markets and the investment opportunities that leverage the use of capital in this country. It is thus an attempt to experiment in the transfer of financial technology from the affluent, capital-rich economy of Wall Street to the poor, capital-starved economy of the urban and rural ghettos and barrios. It may, of course, be inappropriate to suppose that the financial technology common in the non-minority community can or should be transferred to the minority community.

The Opportunity Funding Corporation (OFC) was born in controversy, and it has been initiated in spite of substantial protest by the very groups it seeks to serve. Officially, OFC is an experimental economic development effort designed to test and demonstrate the effectiveness of various incentive, guarantee, and rediscount techniques in attracting private capital to low-income areas. Unofficially, the new program has been labeled by some community leaders as a white-run boondoggle—just a new way of taking money away from the poor and giving it to non-minority capitalists.[1] Reverend Douglas Moore of Washington's Black United Front has called OFC "an example of OEO money wasted on a white-run 'phony outfit.'"[2]

There is a requirement that the local Community Action Program (CAP) agency must approve OEO anti-poverty grants in the Washington area. The Washington anti-poverty agency, the United Planning Organization (UPO), which was the agency responsible for approving the initial OFC grant, refused to do so. The

---

* Associate Professor of Management Environment, Northwestern University Graduate School of Management. Professor Doctors acted as a consultant to Ted Cross during the development phase of OFC, and he is the editor of the Report of the President's Advisory Council on Minority Business Enterprise.

† Economic Advisor to the President's Council on Minority Business Enterprise; Financial Economist, Small Business Administration.

Much of the material presented in this paper was gathered during the course of the authors' work with Ted Cross, officials at OEO, members of the OFC Board of Directors, and staff members of the President's Council. However the views presented are only those of the authors and do not necessarily reflect the views of any other individual or organization.

[1] *See* Rosenthal, *Investment Test is Slated by OEO*, N.Y. Times, Mar. 22, 1970, § 1, at 53, col. 3; OFFICE OF ECONOMIC OPPORTUNITY, FACT SHEET ON THE OPPORTUNITY FUNDING CORPORATION: DESCRIPTION AND PURPOSE (1970); OFFICE OF ECONOMIC OPPORTUNITY, OPPORTUNITY FUNDING: AN ECONOMIC DEVELOPMENT DEMONSTRATION PROGRAM (1970).

[2] Bowman, *Poverty Agencies Quarrel Over Black Capitalism Plan*, Washington Post, Aug. 18, 1970, at C-1 to C-20.

reason given by UPO officials was that the project was "unworkable, would cost too much money, and might compete here in Washington with UPO itself."[3]

Rev. Moore and other community leaders complained of the vagueness of the proposal to OEO.[4] Nationally, a fairly broad spectrum of community leaders have also expressed the feeling that OFC was set up in secrecy and without any real input from the very community groups it was intended to serve. On the other hand, Eli Goldston, a member of the OFC Board of Directors, and former OEO Administrator Donald Rumsfeld felt the proposal for funding had to be worded vaguely in order to give the experimental program the necessary freedom in planning and operation.[5] Mr. Rumsfeld also felt that there was some urgency in launching the OFC project and that inputs from the various community groups would be useful in shaping OFC programs after the project was in operation.

Why so much protest against an organization that on paper sounds like a cross between a Harley Street banking house and a Hartford-based insurance company? Why have community leaders been so vociferous in their opposition to the OFC concept and to OEO's efforts to establish it? Why have many financial and business leaders been so enthusiastic in their response?

The answers to the questions of why the protest and why the enthusiasm are not hard to find. The protest arose from the way the OFC concept was formulated and established as an operating entity. The enthusiasm was the result of the OFC philosophy of minority economic development which is largely a "business" approach to such development. To understand both the protest and the enthusiasm it is necessary to examine the brief history of OFC and its creator's philosophy of minority development.

I

HISTORY

A. The Formative Concepts

OFC officially became an entity in June of 1970 when it was incorporated as a non-profit corporation under the laws of Delaware. For months before the incorporation, the concept had been in the development process at OEO. In the fall of 1969, Donald Rumsfeld, then Administrator of the Office of Economic Opportunity, asked Ted Cross, who was later to become the author of the OFC concept, to come to Washington to develop a program based on his book, *Black Capitalism*.[6] Cross, a New York City attorney and an expert on banking law, decided to under-

---

[3] *Id.*
[4] *See* OFFICE OF ECONOMIC OPPORTUNITY, THE OPPORTUNITY FUNDING CORPORATION STATEMENT OF WORK (1970). This document was initially drafted by Theodore Cross and reworked by OEO officials, and consists of a forty-three page description of the proposed OFC program. It does not state explicitly which projects OFC would undertake; rather it describes a variety of possible projects and generally describes the concepts underlying the OFC program.
[5] Bowman, *supra* note 2.
[6] T. CROSS, BLACK CAPITALISM (1969).

take the project on a half-time basis as a consultant to OEO. He maintained his law practice and other business interests in New York City on a restricted basis for the duration of his work in Washington. He was supplied with three secretaries, an aide who was a White House Fellow and several offices at OEO headquarters. He spent the next six months working with a few Rumsfeld aides in designing a program that would pass bureaucratic inspection. He also talked with scores of business and financial leaders, minority businessmen, government officials, and academicians. The result was OFC.

Cross argued that there will never be enough money available to fund minority economic development programs from government sources alone and that ways and means must be found to substantially leverage the resources from standard money markets. He further argued that only by inducing such substantial private sector investment of resources and expertise can sufficient effort be brought to bear on the problem. The rationale for these arguments had been developed earlier while he was writing his book on black capitalism.

The major thesis of the Cross book is that the ghetto economy does not obey the rules of the larger economy. Cross argues that credit, at a reasonable cost, is unavailable in the ghetto, that savings as a source of equity capital are almost nonexistent, and that the ghetto entrepreneur is a "missing person." Many of the incentives which would promote business and economic development are missing. The full magnitude of the problem must first be understood before any action can be taken to remedy the situation. Cross states that viewing the ghetto as merely a reflection of the larger society has, in the past, only provided palliatives as a solution and that such palliatives have had no long-term impact on getting at the root cause of ghetto poverty.[7]

Cross maintains that fifteen million or more black people live in 163 isolated slums whose economics are fundamentally structured to prevent the accumulation of wealth because they:

(1) are inhospitable to investment or technical assistance;
(2) have little motivation to save or convert even available savings to venture capital;
(3) have little or no entrepreneurial opportunity in legitimate business; and
(4) are isolated from the mainstream economy by a series of tariffs on retail sales, rents, and credit, but are totally dependent on imports from the mainstream economy for most of their basic goods and services.[8]

Cross feels that the economic system of the ghetto economy militates against traditional programs of poverty aid or charity as a vehicle for change. He also concludes that the federal government has been unable to demonstrate competence

---
[7] *Id.* at 21-69.
[8] *Id.* at 204-05; *but see* J. DUESENBERRY, INCOME, SAVING, AND THE THEORY OF CONSUMER BEHAVIOR 50-52 (1949) for a quite different view of the motivation for savings and investment. See also pp. 17-68 for a general theoretical discussion.

in implementing effective anti-poverty programs.[9] Thus he advocates a system of federal incentives, guarantees, equity insurance, rediscount arrangements, and subsidies which will induce a massive infusion of private sector capital and know-how into the ghettos to create viable capital creation and retention institutions. This new system of incentives, guarantees, and subsidies must be structured to provide a compelling reason for private investment, not one based primarily on charity or guilt feelings.

B. Formation of OFC

The early OFC developmental work at OEO was dubbed "Project X." Project X went through a number of written drafts which were carefully circulated to a select group within the agency. Circulation was limited to less than ten copies of the document. The document consisted of a hypothetical press conference by Rumsfeld explaining the nature and purpose of OFC, a functional description of the OFC organization, and a series of possible experimental projects. Many of these experimental projects were added by Mr. Cross after discussions with a number of businessmen, financiers, community leaders, academicians, and governmental officials.

It was decided that OFC would take the form of a non-profit corporation whose funding would come largely from title I-D Special Impact Funds.[10] It was felt that OFC should be relatively independent of the government in order to have more freedom to experiment. To help insure this independence a highly prestigious board of directors was assembled:

Dr. David Hertz, Chairman
(elected October, 1970)
Director, McKinsey & Co.
New York, New York

Rev. Leon Sullivan
President and Founder
Opportunities Industrialization Center
Philadelphia, Pennsylvania

Eli Goldston
Chairman and Chief Executive Officer
Eastern Gas & Fuel Association
Boston, Massachusetts

Dr. Robert Vowels
Dean, School of Business Administration
Atlanta University
Atlanta, Georgia

Alex Mercure
State Project Director, Project HELP
Albuquerque, New Mexico

Robert O. Dehlendorf, II
President, Arcata National Corporation
Menlo Park, California

---

[9] In his *The Age of Discontinuity*, Peter Drucker has generally concluded that federal government programs in such social areas as poverty and education have largely failed because government is not equipped to implement or carry out programs. Thus Drucker, like Cross, advocates a restructuring of federal programs to require the government to provide the overall strategy and financial incentives, while the implementation is left to the private sector. P. DRUCKER, THE AGE OF DISCONTINUITY 212-42 (1968).

[10] See description detailed in note 12 *infra*.

John Mabie
Vice-President and Director
A. G. Becker and Company
Chicago, Illinois

Dan Lufkin
Chairman, Executive Committee
Donaldson, Lufkin, & Jenrette
New York, New York

James M. Hall
Secretary, Business and Transportation
 Agency
State of California
Sacramento, California

The board is divided fairly evenly between Republicans and Democrats. It contains three minority group members and is headed by David Hertz. Names of board members were solicited from a variety of sources, both inside and outside of government. The major criteria, aside from political considerations, were a history of active participation in minority economic development, clout in the corporate world or in minority communities, and a willingness to devote substantial amounts of personal time to OFC. Every candidate was cleared through the White House, and several potential candidates were dropped because they were unacceptable to the White House. However, the White House was liberal in its view of candidates' political orientation and four of the first five appointments were Democrats.

It was decided that most of the programs would be channeled through the OEO-initiated and supported community development corporations (CDC's). This decision was made, in part, to mute pressures exerted by the CDC's against the establishment of OFC. Community development corporations draw their principal support from title I-D funding and were not pleased at the prospect of competing with OFC for limited funds.[11]

Little thought was given to possible alternatives or supplementary sources for OFC funding from other government agencies. It was assumed that most of the funding for the forseeable future would come from OEO title I-D research and demonstration appropriations and from public offerings of OFC securities, "Opportunity Bonds." Cross contemplated that OFC would acquire significant independence and power if it could market Opportunity Bonds in public markets. Initial funding of OFC was pegged at about $20 million, but only $7.4 million actually was made available.[12] Approximately one half came from title I-D funds and half from research

---

[11] Approximately $10.6 million was available in fiscal 1969 and $31.2 million in fiscal 1970 from title I-D. Fifteen existing CDC's and 21 new CDC's received title I-D funds in fiscal 1970. Thus, less than an average of $1 million was available per CDC in fiscal 1970. DEPARTMENT OF COMMERCE, REPORT TO THE PRESIDENT ON MINORITY BUSINESS ENTERPRISE, at III-32 to III-33 (1970).

[12] An OEO news release (June 30, 1970) indicated that the newly created non-profit OFC was incorporated in Delaware and would have its principal offices in Washington, D.C. Its initial funding of $7.4 million would come from title I-D ($3.9 million) and from research and development funds ($3.5 million). "Title I-D" refers to the section in the OEO Act of 1964 which provides development funds for "special impact areas." What the news release did not say is that OFC was originally to have received more than $20 million in first year funds. But internal pressures at OEO and pressures

and demonstration funds.[13]

In addition to the board of directors, the corporation was to have a president and a small professional staff, perhaps three to five in number most of whom were minority group members.[14] Although OFC was incorporated in June, 1969, little was done to find a president until the fall of 1970 when David Hertz engaged a private consulting firm to assemble a list of potential candidates. By October, the list had been reduced to eight candidates, each of whom was to be interviewed by members of the board. In late November, the decision was made to name John Gloster of the Urban Coalition as the first president of the OFC.

Mr. John Gloster presented his initial plan to the board in December, and three of the OFC pilot projects are currently underway: (1) surety bonding for minority contractors in cooperation with black and Chicano contractors in Los Angeles, and with black contractors seeking a substantial part of the Metro transit program in the District of Columbia; (2) consumer credit for low-income citizens, including those on welfare and those unemployed, in cooperation with the National Congress for Community Economic Development and community development corporations and their constituents; and, (3) supplementary funding for low-income area minority lending institutions.[15]

II

OPERATION OF OFC

A. Components of the Opportunity Funding Corporation

OFC has three principal components: Opportunity Guarantee, Community Development Discount, and Incentive Simulation (figure I). The first component, Opportunity Guarantee, is designed to reduce the aversion of private institutions to committing capital and credit to low-income communities by providing a variety of guarantees. It will operate only when comparable guarantees are not available from existing federal, state, or private sources and where the perceived risk is quite high. The second component, Community Development Discount, is designed to demonstrate the feasibility of establishing a secondary market for SBA- and EDA-backed obligations and other commercial paper generated in low-income communities. It will purchase this paper, repackage it, and resell these new securities with a guarantee to such institutions as pension funds, churches, and others seeking a safe, yet socially useful investment opportunity. This guarantee will be similar to that of the Federal National Mortgage Company in the mortgage market. It

---

from the community development corporations led to the cutback of almost two-thirds of the original pledge amount.

[13] Initially, when the funding was to have been more than $20 million, it was thought that the staff might have to be considerably larger than the presently planned four or five professionals. One of the authors had been asked to design an organization structure for this larger organization.

[14] PROFITS, Jan., 1971, at 3 (monthly newsletter of the Institute for Minority Business Enterprise, Howard University).

[15] Id.

is designed to test whether such a facility can provide substantially increased liquidity for lending institutions serving low-income communities.

In briefings Cross always emphasized that the great gamble of OFC was that development in ghettos, barrios, and reservations could ultimately become self-financing. He argued that historically bankers have always been wrong—that the non-bankable goals of today always become the solid collateral of tomorrow. He urged the analogy of the World Bank which is currently making development loans to fund housing and health care for the poor of East Pakistan and other underdeveloped nations.

The third component, Incentive Simulation, is intended to test various incentives, such as simulated tax incentives, to promote private investment in disadvantaged communities. Of course, OFC is not organized with these three distinct elements, and one staff member may be responsible for projects in several component areas.

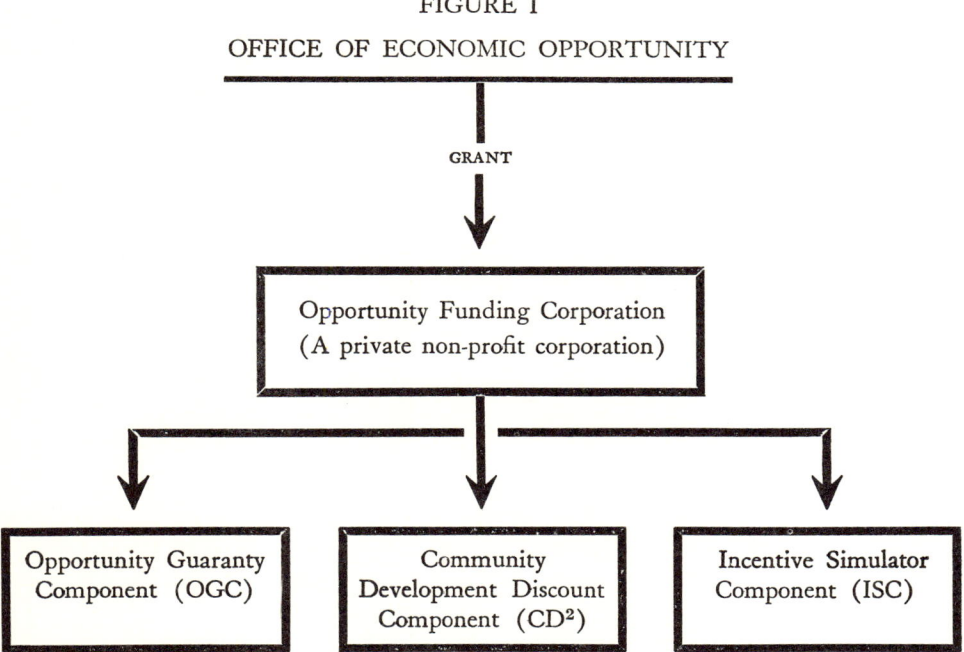

FIGURE I

OFFICE OF ECONOMIC OPPORTUNITY

Source: OEO, Opportunity Funding: An Economic Development Demonstration Program (1970).

B. OFC—A Demonstration Vehicle

It is important to understand OFC as one of the very few minority economic development programs which has the full support of the Nixon Administration. On several occasions Cross presented the OFC program to the White House staff and, in March, 1970, to President Nixon and the full Cabinet. OFC seeks to apply the traditional techniques of financial leveraging to minority economic development. It is not a welfare program; it is not meant to provide outright grants; rather it seeks to use modest sums of government money to attract large sums of private capital into the nation's rural and urban ghettos and barrios.

OFC is not truly an operating arm of the federal government, rather it is a test and demonstration vehicle like its parent organization, OEO. Its stated purpose "is to test the effectiveness of various incentive techniques in attracting private sources of money to rural and urban low-income areas." Each of the pilot projects is designed to establish a specific need for legislative and/or administrative changes. Thus the OFC has chosen four criteria for the selection of projects for funding:

1. The project must be innovative in concept and must provide leverage for OFC's investment.
2. The project must have national impact, as distinguished from meeting a local economic need under specialized circumstances.
3. The project must be capable of being reproduced in other localities.
4. The project must have demonstrable benefits for poverty area residents.[16]

III
POTENTIAL PROBLEMS

Ted Cross is a consummate technician. He knows the art of finance and the related areas of law, but he was unaware of the intricacies of governmental agencies or community development politics. He also was unaware of the need to cultivate various members of the OEO bureaucracy as well as community development leaders who would be most affected by OFC. Donald Rumsfeld, Cross' leading backer, assumed that OFC could be conceived and set into motion with only minimal interface with community leaders or with OEO's own internal departments. Rumsfeld did check out the OFC concept with a number of influential persons such as McGeorge Bundy, President of the Ford Foundation. However, the failure to fully inform those most directly affected by OFC, such as the CDC's and other community development groups, has resulted in substantial criticism both inside and outside OEO, often more because of ignorance of the proposed program rather than genuine criticism of its substance. In private, most community leaders are enthusiastic about the OFC concept and few OEO staff members can be found to argue against the substance of the OFC program.

The original framework for restructuring ghetto economies presented by Cross in *Black Capitalism* assumed a massive simultaneous onslaught on many fronts such as designing programs to reduce the risk on "soft" commercial loans, developing a secondary market for ghetto installment paper, stimulating deposits in slum area banks, establishing special ghetto development banks, increasing the amount of capital available for ghetto ventures, and planning other programs to develop and

---
[16] *Id.*

train ghetto entrepreneurs.[17] Although not explicitly articulated, it is apparent that Cross assumed that the synergy developed by these various complementary programs would provide a critical mass for significant change. While economists are not entirely clear about all the prerequisites for economic development in underdeveloped areas, it is fairly clear that such development requires the interaction of many individual components to achieve significant growth.

OFC, on the other hand, proposes to initiate at most one or two experiments in any one ghetto area. Thus, these experiments are not likely to be more than a pale shadow of the real capital base-building and leveraging techniques commonly used in the larger economy, which depend for their success on the existence and interaction of a whole series of financial and business institutions. OFC has very limited resources, only $7.4 million for the first year of operation, which would not even provide the capital for one medium-sized development bank. OFC will have to concentrate on a limited number of projects in a relatively small number of poverty areas and thus will not be able to really simulate an overall economic development program in any community.

There is the very critical question of measurement of results. What can be measured and over what period of time? Donald Rumsfeld in the hypothetical Project X press conference says, "The guaranty and loan discount arrangements should prove out quite quickly. In six months we'll know if inner city CDC's and others are using our new facilities. It will probably be another year before we will know about our costs, which are overhead plus bad debt experience. The tax simulations will take longer. We should know a lot in a year."[18] Given the complexity of the development process generally, along with the additional problems of operating in a ghetto environment, it would seem that Rumsfeld's optimism is scarcely justified. Mere use by CDC's or other community groups is hardly proof of the relative success of OFC experiments. These groups may use OFC simply because it represents an additional source of funding, not because they foresee any long-term economic benefit to themselves or to the community. Nor is it clear that measurement of usage is any indication of the capital base building potential of any particular item in the OFC repertoire.

Another important problem is the fact that the OFC may be continually in the spotlight, subject to political pressures from a variety of sources. These pressures are likely to require that OFC produce immediate, visible successes. The initial projects must be successful, at least in terms of what can be easily measured, such as the number of users of OFC services or the number of dollars attracted into a particular project. Such measures, however, may not indicate the eventual importance of OFC experiments.[19] Economic development is a long-term process

---

[17] T. Cross, *supra* note 6, at 159-209.
[18] T. Cross, Project X, Mar. 10, 1970, at 9-10 (unpublished OEO memorandum).
[19] For a discussion of the difficulties of measuring the results of CDC programs, see M. Brower, The Criteria for Measuring the Success of a Community Development Corporation in the Ghetto, Mar., 1970 (unpublished paper in Cambridge Institute).

and as such is not likely to yield much in the way of early success stories. In fact, it may be necesary to sacrifice early numerical usage figures for long-term impact.[20]

OFC is at present in direct competition for funds with the various CDC's. This has already created substantial hostility to the concept of OFC. Thus OFC must prove, fairly rapidly, that it does in fact make it possible to leverage CDC funding, or else it will come under increasing attack from the CDC's.

Another substantial problem area is that of transferring the results of "successful experiments" to operating agencies. No one at OEO considered in detail the problems entailed in transferring the results of OFC experiments to the various domestic affairs agencies involved in development, such as the Small Business Administration, the Department of Agriculture, and the Economic Development Administration in the Department of Commerce. Cross did give briefings to a number of agencies and departments, but no real study has been made of the transfer problem. Of course, in those cases requiring legislation, the appropriate congressional committee must be involved early in the experimental process. There is substantial literature available in the information transfer area, most of which indicates the complexity of transferring information across institutional lines.[21]

Continued funding is likely to be a problem, given the general congressional and Administration disposition to cut back on OEO funding. There also will be problems clearing new funding through OEO itself, as OFC fund proposals must compete with numerous other applicants for very scarce economic development funds.

In addition, there is a built-in tension between the desire of OEO to control OFC experiments to maximize their value in terms of OEO goals and objectives and the desire of OFC to operate as an independent entity free to choose experiments from its own agenda. In the initial contract negotiations between OEO and OFC, there was a considerable amount of friction over the degree to which OEO would control experiments. Several board members indicated their unhappiness with what they saw as OEO's attempt to maintain a veto power over OFC operations. This issue was vigorously debated over a period of several weeks before the initial contract was signed, and it is still in doubt. OEO has historically been cited by a number of grantee institutions as unduly officious in the conduct of funded research.[22] On the other hand, OFC does represent the principal vehicle for domestic development experimentation and is therefore of great importance to the success

---

[20] A similar problem was presented for NASA in its spinoff program with its need to produce quickly tangible examples of technology transfer. This emphasis on producing quick success in a very complex problem area may have been the single most important reason for the failure of the NASA transfer program. For a discussion of this similar measurement problem area, see S. Doctors, The Role of the Federal Agencies in Technology Transfer (1969).

[21] See, e.g., E. Rodgers, Diffusion of Innovation (1962); S. Doctors, supra note 20; J. Jewkes, D. Sawers, & R. Stillerman, The Sources of Invention (1958).

[22] The issue of unduly restrictive federal agency contract terms and administration is discussed in Staff of Research and Technical Problems Subcomm. of the House Comm. on Gov't Operations, 90th Cong., 1st Sess., Report on the Use of Social Research in Federal Domestic Programs, pt. 4, at 486-658 (Comm. Print 1967). This report indicates that OEO was the agency most often cited by grantees for its "interference" in their research and development work.

of many present and future OEO programs. Thus, there will be a continuing need to balance the goals of the two organizations to ensure maximum flexibility to experiment for OFC while still maintaining a reasonable amount of direction and control over these experiments, thereby ensuring effective feedback for other OEO programs and for transfer to various operating agencies.

IV
Prerequisites for Successful OFC Operation

For successful OFC operation, the organization must establish its long-term goals and must effectively communicate them to its various constituents. If it is to be a truly experimental agency in economic development, then it must seek to educate the various constituencies to this long-term orientation. These various constituencies include the CDC's, the various congressional committees, OEO, domestic affairs agencies (such as SBA, HUD, and EDA), and the investment community. OFC must avoid becoming just another operating arm of OEO or of any other agency. It must design its projects for long-term impact and work to identify appropriate methods of evaluation which will probably include social as well as economic measures of success. To minimize political pressures, several steps must be taken, such as seeking funds from sources outside OEO, both public and private; selecting a portion of the initial projects for their early, visible impact on the community; seeking to participate in the selection and evaluation criteria; and channeling most of the early projects through the CDC's.

It is likely that the results of the OFC program will be a mixed bag for the immediate future. Nevertheless, it remains the one truly experimental program available to the Administration to test a variety of capital base-building devices. It has a strong board of directors and an able president, and it can operate in a relatively independent manner. To achieve its goals OFC will have to secure sufficient funds from a variety of sources, obtain substantial community support, devise meaningful measures of the various projects undertaken, and find ways and means of transferring its results to operating agencies.

THE EFFECT OF THE PRIVATE FOUNDATION PROVISIONS OF THE TAX REFORM ACT OF 1969 ON COMMUNITY DEVELOPMENT CORPORATIONS

JORDAN D. LUTTRELL*

Ambrose Bierce defined a lawyer as "[o]ne skilled in circumvention of the law,"[1] and it seems likely that it was a similar view of certain exempt organizations which led Congress to enact the "private foundation" provisions of the Tax Reform Act of 1969.[2] The 1965 Treasury Report on Private Foundations had set forth convincingly and at length both the failure of privately controlled foundations to police their own activities, and the law's incapacity to cope with the abuses found to exist.[3]

Private foundations are typically established as nonprofit corporations under state law and, along with other qualifying organizations, may obtain an exemption from federal income taxation under section 501(c)(3) of the Internal Revenue Code of 1954 because they are organized and operated for certain exempt purposes, principally those involving charitable, educational, scientific, or literary pursuits. With a few narrow exceptions organizations so exempt (whether private foundations or not), may accept contributions which are deductible to their donors under section 170. The conclusion of Congress evidenced in the Tax Reform Act was that many private foundations, while affording their financial supporters a tax deduction, were not using those contributions for the stated exempt purposes. Although prior law had provided for sanctions in certain extreme cases, it had not proved capable of dealing effectively with abuses on a lesser scale. The private foundation provisions of the Act attempt to remove that inadequacy by utilizing a series of graduated taxes to discourage private foundations from engaging in any of several kinds of activities viewed as improper. Congress cannot be said to have had community development corporations (CDC's) in mind when it enacted the private foundation provisions. Nevertheless, any CDC exempt under section 501(c)(3), as every other exempt organization, must gauge what impact the private foundation provisions will have on its operations. In addition, a CDC not yet exempt but contemplating the submission of an application for exemption to the Internal Revenue Service will wish

---

* Supervising Attorney, National Housing and Economic Development Law Project, Earl Warren Legal Institute, University of California, Berkeley.

The research reported herein was performed pursuant to a grant with the Office of Economic Opportunity, Washington, D.C. 20506. The opinions expressed herein are those of the author and should not be construed as representing the opinions or policy of any agency of the United States Government. I wish to thank Professor Lawrence M. Stone, Kenneth F. Phillips, Esq., and David M. Madway, Esq., for their criticisms of this article in manuscript. The article itself is a shortened version of a chapter to appear in a manual on economic development in preparation at the Project. Those interested in receiving the longer version may write the author.

[1] A. BIERCE, THE DEVIL'S DICTIONARY 75 (Dover ed. 1958).
[2] INT. REV. CODE OF 1954 §§ 507-09, 4940-48.
[3] U.S. TREASURY DEP'T, REPORT ON PRIVATE FOUNDATIONS (Comm. Print 1965).

to weigh the advantages of exempt status against the potential adverse impact of the provisions.

The term "community development corporation," or CDC, has been used to describe organizations carrying on a great variety of activities, ranging from CDC's concerned solely with educational and social matters on the one hand, to those involved in all types of financing and commercial arrangements and technical and management assistance on the other. All CDC's, however, do share one common characteristic: they are broad-based membership organizations with members (or shareholders) who exclusively or for the most part are poor and live or work in a particular geographic area. The type of CDC to which this article is addressed is one which engages in activities that are more economic in nature, rather than social or service oriented, since in general the greater the commercial and financial activities of a CDC, the more likely it will be that those activities may be adversely affected by the Act. Thus, the type of CDC discussed in this article is one which is or plans to be involved in a full range of the following activities: investing in or making loans to individually or community-owned enterprises, setting up its own businesses as internal divisions or subsidiaries, entering into joint ventures, putting up guaranty money, providing all types of management and technical assistance, and arranging for all of the foregoing from other sources.[4]

In many cases the CDC is incorporated as a nonprofit corporation under applicable state law,[5] and has either obtained an exemption from federal income taxation under section 501(c)(3) of the Internal Revenue Code, or will be considering doing so. Several benefits are gained by taking advantage of the exemption. With an exemption, the CDC is in a much improved fund-raising position. It will be better able to secure charitable contributions from individuals and corporations, since contributions to an organization exempt under section 501(c)(3) are deductible to the donor within the limits specified in section 170 of the Code. The CDC's ability to obtain money from other exempt organizations will also be enhanced.[6] Such other organizations are most obviously acting for exempt purposes and are consequently

---

[4] This article assumes that the CDC will be able to obtain an exemption if it wishes to do so. The CDC may find this to be no easy task for several reasons. First, the Service has not issued any revenue rulings in this area, so that its position is difficult to determine. Second, in those private rulings which have been issued, the Service has imposed restrictions which a CDC may not wish to accept. Third, the Service may be concerned that excessive private benefit will redound to those assisted by a CDC, although this fear should not be substantial where the CDC retains control over the businesses assisted. In such a case, returns from the business will go to the CDC, which will likely be governed by articles which forbid the inurement of any benefit to individuals.

[5] Some CDC's are formed as for-profit corporations, issuing voting shares exclusively or principally to the community it serves. As such, they would not be able to apply for a section 501(c)(3) exemption, since their net earnings could "inure to the benefit of any private shareholder," a consequence prohibited by the section.

[6] Over 90% of foundation grants (in dollars) reportedly go to exempt organizations. *Hearings on H.R. 13270 Before the Senate Comm. on Finance*, 91st Cong., 1st Sess., pt. 6, at 6144 (1969) (H.R. 13270 was the House version of the Tax Reform Act). An Internal Revenue Service Blue Book lists those organizations to which deductible contributions may be made. Eighty-one per cent of all foundations are said to make grants only to these qualified organizations. *Id.* at 6165.

minimizing the risk of jeopardizing their own exemptions by making contributions (usually termed "grants") to exempt organizations.[7] Exempt organizations may also escape a host of state and local taxes and licensing requirements.[8] The advantages of the exemption, however, must be viewed with its attendant disadvantages, one of which is the potentially unfavorable impact of the private foundation provisions of the Tax Reform Act of 1969.

The Tax Reform Act of 1969 is unquestionably the most significant piece of tax legislation since the revision of the Internal Revenue Code in 1954. Approximately one-quarter of the Act is devoted to remedying what Congress viewed as the unacceptable practices of private foundations. In gauging the effect these provisions will have on CDC's, two questions must be answered. Will a CDC be considered a "private foundation"? If so, what provisions restricting the activities of all private foundations will be of practical importance to it?

Generally, every section 501(c)(3) organization, including a CDC, is presumed to be a "private foundation" unless it can demonstrate that it is "publicly-supported" to a substantial extent, and thus classified as a "public charity." There are basically two ways a CDC can establish itself as a "public charity." One is to demonstrate that under either of two similar tests more than one-third of its financial support is derived from "public sources." "Public sources" may generally be defined as any governmental source, other "public charities," and, within certain dollar or percentage limits per contributor, the general public. A CDC may also demonstrate that it is a "public charity" and not a "private foundation" in a second way: by satisfying a "facts and circumstances" test found in the Regulations which stresses factors other than public financial support. These factors include the organization's fund-raising activities and the extent to which it is controlled by the public and makes its facilities and programs available to it.

A genuinely broad-based CDC will most likely be able to meet one of these tests. If the tests are not met, however, what disabilities will a CDC that has been found to be a "private foundation" suffer that a CDC which qualifies as a "public charity" will escape? In general, a private foundation will be potentially subject to six taxes: an excise tax based on investment income and initial and additional taxes on self-dealing, failure to distribute income, excess business holdings, investments which jeopardize charitable purpose, and taxable expenditures.[9] Except for the tax on investment income, all of these taxes are in effect graduated penalties designed to discourage a private foundation from acting in certain ways. Since most of a CDC's activities are not of the types which are intended to be discouraged, the typical CDC will have little to fear even if it finds itself a private foundation.

---

[7] The Tax Reform Act, moreover, requires "private foundations" to make minimum distributions of income for qualified purposes. INT. REV. CODE OF 1954 §4942. Distributions to other exempt organizations probably satisfy these distribution requirements most easily. *See* part III *infra*.

[8] *See, e.g.*, CAL. REV. & TAX. CODE § 23701 (West 1970).

[9] INT. REV. CODE OF 1954, §§ 4940-46.

I

Avoiding Private Foundation Status

Rather than define what a private foundation is, the Code declares what it is not. Section 509, which defines "private foundation," states at the outset that all section 501(c)(3) organizations are private foundations[10] and then proceeds to establish four exceptions to this general rule. Those section 501(c)(3) organizations not fitting into the exceptions are "private foundations" and are subject to the disadvantages to be discussed subsequently. Only two of the four exceptions will be of utility to a CDC attempting to escape private foundation status.[11]

One of the exceptions of which a CDC may take advantage in effect incorporates two tests which have forerunners in post-1966 Regulations: one of the public financial support tests and the facts and circumstances test.[12] As were their predecessors, these new tests, found in the section 170 Regulations are designed to distinguish between "publicly-supported" organizations and all other exempt organizations. The Code since 1964 has allowed a deduction for contributions of up to thirty per cent (now fifty per cent) of an individual's adjusted gross income made to "publicly-supported" organizations, while imposing a twenty per cent limit on contributions to all other exempt organizations.[13] These tests will now take on further importance because any organization meeting them will not only be excluded from the definition of a private foundation, but will also be able to receive contributions of "increased" deductibility by the contributors.

The other exception available to a CDC seeking to avoid private foundation status sets forth a second public financial support test.[14] This test somewhat more broadly defines public financial suppport in order to exclude from private foundation status those organizations which may have had some difficulty fitting within the

---

[10] In a separate section churches and related groups are automatically excluded from even the presumption that they are private foundations and thus do not have to attempt to fit within one of the four exceptions. INT. REV. CODE OF 1954 § 508(c)(1). Authority is delegated to the Treasury, in addition, to exclude in its discretion certain educational institutions and other organizations from the presumption, the latter on the criterion of "efficient administration." INT. REV. CODE OF 1954 § 508(c)(2)(B).

[11] INT. REV. CODE OF 1954 § 509(a)(1) and (2). Of the two exceptions not of importance to a CDC, one is designed for organizations established to support *other* "public charities," and the other for organizations testing for public safety. INT. REV. CODE OF 1954 § 509(a)(3) and (4).

[12] INT. REV. CODE OF 1954 § 509(a)(1) referring to INT. REV. CODE OF 1954 §170(b)(1)(A)(i)-(vi). The tests have only very recently been proposed by the Service and apply to all taxable years beginning after December 31, 1969. Proposed Treas. Reg. § 1.170A-9, 36 Fed. Reg. 9298 (1971). The old tests upon which they are based in large part are applicable to taxable years beginning prior to January 1, 1970, and can be found in Treas. Reg. § 1.170-2(b)(5)(iii)(*b*) & (*c*) (1966).

[13] The 30% limit was raised to 50% by the Act, while the 20% limit was left unchanged. INT. REV. CODE OF 1954 § 170(b)(1). The statement in the text is subject to some refinement and qualification. The standard of adjusted gross income referred to is not quite accurate, as the 50% limit applies to an individual's "contribution base," which is defined as adjusted gross income computed without regard to any net operating loss carry-back to the taxable year. INT. REV. CODE OF 1954 § 170(b)(1)(F). For limitations on contributions of certain capital gain property, see INT. REV. CODE OF 1954 § 170(b)(1)(D). It should also be noted that the 50% limit applies only to individuals; corporations may only deduct up to 5% of their taxable income, with certain modifications. INT. REV. CODE OF 1954 § 170(b)(2).

[14] INT. REV. CODE OF 1954 § 509(a)(2).

forerunners of the other tests, but which were not engaging in the kinds of activities which led Congress to enact the private foundation provisions.[15]

The two public financial support tests follow roughly the same outline, and a CDC which can qualify under one will no doubt be able to qualify under the other, at least while the CDC is primarily dependent upon outside funds rather than those generated from its own operations. If the CDC cannot demonstrate the requisite public financial support to qualify under either of these tests, it still may qualify under the facts and circumstances test, which requires a lesser showing of public financial support, and in rare instances may not require any such showing at all. A CDC should first attempt to qualify under one of the public financial support tests, however, since these standards are more mechanical in nature than those of the facts and circumstances test. As its name rightly implies, the facts and circumstances test involves a greater subjectivity in application, an application made, moreover, by the Service, not by the organization. Before turning to a discussion and comparison of the three tests, it will be of some value to set forth briefly the history of the section 170 tests, because without some explanation their incorporation by reference in section 509(a)(1) is not readily understandable.

A. The History of the Section 170 Tests

After defining a "private foundation" as any section 501(c)(3) organization, section 509 then first excludes those organizations to which individuals can make deductible contributions of up to fifty (formerly thirty) per cent of their adjusted gross income, as opposed to twenty per cent for other organizations. Of all the former "thirty per cent" organizations, only one is of relevance to a CDC.[16] Termed a "publicly-supported" organization in the Regulations, its statutory definition is:

> an organization referred to in [section 501(c)(3)] which normally receives a substantial part of its support . . . from a governmental unit . . . or from direct or indirect contributions from the general public . . . .[17]

This provision was the ultimate result of proposals in President Kennedy's 1963 Tax Message to Congress in which he sought to extend more favorable treatment to those charitable organizations "which are publicly supported *and controlled* . . . ."[18]

---

[15] S. REP. No. 552, 91st Cong., 1st Sess. 56 (1969) [hereinafter referred to as SENATE REPORT]. Organizations escaping private foundation status under this test may also receive contributions which are deductible up to 50% of an individual's "contribution base." INT. REV. CODE OF 1954 § 170(b)(1)(A) (viii).

[16] The others consist of churches and educational organizations, including certain related groups, and hospitals and governmental units, and thus would rarely if ever be of pertinence to a CDC. Even if a CDC carried on some educational activities, it would not be considered an educational organization, and thus a "thirty per cent" organization, since the definition in the Regulations excludes "organizations engaged in both educational and noneducational activities unless the latter are merely incidental to and growing out of the educational activities." Treas. Reg. § 1.170-2(b)(3)(i) (1958).

[17] INT. REV. CODE OF 1954 § 170(b)(1)(A)(vi). Although the reference in the statute is to section 170(c)(2), the language of that section is virtually identical to that of section 501(c)(3), and the few differences which do exist are immaterial to a discussion of CDC's.

[18] Liles, *Qualification of Museums and Similar Institutions as Publicly Supported Organizations*, 45 TAXES 528 (1967).

The provision as ultimately enacted, however, made no reference to public control, but only to "public support." Public support was said in the House Report to be public *financial* support, exclusive of other types of public support or involvement. The significance of this difference in terminology is uncertain. The explanations in the House Report suggested that, although the notion of public financial support was a central consideration, organizations which *served* the public, or a particular portion of the public, or which were *controlled* by it, were also to be considered "publicly-supported."[19] Thus, examples were given of organizations such as museums, libraries, civic centers, and community chests, all of which seem to exemplify service to and control by the public as much as financial support from it.

In the first of what proved to be three steps eventually leading to the issuance of final Regulations designed to implement the provision, the Service provided only for a public financial support test, which basically required that more than one-third of an organization's total financial support be drawn from the public.[20] Substantial pressure to expand the Regulations' scope was then apparently placed on the Service by organizations which served and were controlled by the public, but which foresaw difficulty in demonstrating the requisite public financial support because of their reliance on large gifts and endowments from a limited number of individuals.[21] As a consequence, a facts and circumstances test was added to the final Regulations which, though bowing in the direction of public financial support, allowed much greater emphasis to be placed on other factors in determining whether an organization was "publicly-supported." Incorporation of these factors in the facts and circumstances test swung the emphasis away from the sources of financial support toward public service and control.

The new section 170 Regulations follow the same outline established by the Regulations issued in 1966 in that both a public financial support and a facts and circumstances test are maintained. Some modifications have been made in both tests, however. These were apparently designed to dove-tail the new section 170 tests with the public financial support test added by the Tax Reform Act in section 509(a)(2), which has been further explained and developed in proposed Regulations issued by the Service in late 1970.[22] Since the public financial support tests are basically similar to one another, they will be discussed simultaneously despite their varied history. Subsequently, the facts and circumstances test will be examined.

B. The Public Financial Support Tests

In general the public financial support tests require that to be considered a public charity (rather than a private foundation) an organization must derive at

---

[19] *Id.* at 529.
[20] *See* Rev. Pub. 66-100, 1966-1 CUM. BULL. 51.
[21] Liles, *supra* note 18, at 530.
[22] The passage of the Tax Reform Act has imposed an enormous burden on the Service merely in requiring the issuance of Regulations implementing the Act's provisions. After approximately eighteen months, the Service issued proposed Regulations on all three tests, and set June 28, 1971, as the date on which hearings will be held on them. 36 Fed. Reg. 9298 (1971).

least one-third of its total support from public sources. With one important exception, the definition of public support and total support are roughly the same in both the section 509(a)(2) and the section 170 tests. Both tests establish procedures pursuant to which an organization may ask the Service for a determination of whether it is a private foundation or a public charity at the organization's inception. The new tests, thus, are a substantial improvement over the old public financial support test which required that an organization have been in existence for five years before it could seek a determination under the test.[23] The section 509(a)(2) test provides for the exclusion of unusual grants in certain instances, the counterpart of which is found in the new facts and circumstances test rather than in the section 170 public financial support test. Lastly, the section 509(a)(2) test imposes a one-third limit on the amount of total support which may be accounted for by investment income, and in this respect is more restrictive than the section 170 tests, which set no investment income limits.

Aside from gross receipts, the tests' definitions of support are identical, and include as their more important categories gifts, grants, contributions, membership fees, net income from business activities unrelated to the organizational purposes, and gross investment income.[24] Gross receipts are included in the statutory definition of support in section 509(d), but are excluded under section 170. These receipts are defined as income derived from admissions, sales of merchandise, performance of services, or furnishing of facilities in any activity which is related to the purposes for which the organization was declared exempt. This difference, though insignificant while a CDC remains dependent on outside sources of funds, may gain in importance as the CDC weans itself from those sources and becomes self-supporting.

The tests' definitions of public support are also basically the same (with the same exception for gross receipts), although some differences do exist which may make the section 170 test more attractive in borderline cases where the organization's public support is very close to the minimum one-third floor imposed by both tests.[25] Both tests include in public support only *public* gifts, grants, contributions and membership fees, and, in the section 509(a)(2) test, certain gross receipts. Excluded altogether are investment and unrelated business income, and other income included in total support, as well as that income, such as capital gains, which is specifically excluded from total support.

---

[23] *See* Treas. Reg. § 1.170-2(b)(5)(ii)(*c*)(*1*) (1966).

[24] Both tests refer to the statutory definition of support found in section 509(d). The section 170 test reference expressly excludes gross receipts. Proposed Treas. Reg. § 1.170A-9(e)(7), 36 Fed. Reg. 9303 (1971); Proposed Treas. Reg. § 1.509(a)-3(a)(2), 35 Fed. Reg. 17846 (1970). The definition of support also includes two other categories which should usually be of lesser importance: tax revenues levied for the benefit of the organization and either paid to it or expended on its behalf, and the value of services or facilities especially furnished by any governmental unit without charge. INT. REV. CODE OF 1954 § 509(d)(5) and (6). Specifically excluded from the definition of support, which is otherwise not limited, are capital gains and the value of any tax exemption or similar benefit. *Id.* § 509(d).

[25] Public support is defined in Proposed Treas. Reg. § 1.170A-9(e)(6), 36 Fed. Reg. 9303 (1971) and INT. REV. CODE OF 1954 § 509(a)(2). The latter definition is further explained in Proposed Treas. Reg. § 1.509(a)-3(a) and (b), 35 Fed. Reg. 17845-46 (1970).

Under the section 509(a)(2) test, public sources are governmental units, those public charities which have already satisfied one of the section 170 tests, and those contributors not considered "disqualified." The entire amount of gifts, grants, contributions, and membership fees from such sources are included in public support. Gross receipts are subject to the additional restriction, however, that they may not exceed one per cent or $5,000 (whichever is greater) from any one source, even though that source is public.[26] Gifts, grants, contributions, membership fees, and gross receipts are totally excluded if derived from "disqualified persons," principal among which, for purposes of fund raising, are contributors or grantors who have donated amounts in excess of either $5,000 or two per cent (whichever is greater) of the organization's total support in a taxable year.[27]

The section 170 public financial support test includes in public support all funds obtained from governmental units and other section 170 organizations. Its treatment of donations from individual and corporate contributors, however, is slightly different. The section 170 test includes all such individual and corporate contributions, regardless of source, but only to the extent of two per cent of the organization's total support. Thus, the section 170 test is somewhat more liberal in that it does not entirely exclude those contributions from the equivalent of substantial contributors, but includes them up to a maximum of two per cent of total support. In a borderline case this difference might be sufficient to allow an organization to qualify under the section 170 test even though it would not satisfy the section 509(a)(2) test.

Those CDC's which are largely or totally supported by funds from government programs will obviously have no difficulty qualifying as a public charity under either of the public financial support tests, since funds from a governmental unit are considered to be public in nature.[28] Thus grantees under either the Special Impact program of the Office of Economic Opportunity or the Model Cities program of the Department of Housing and Urban Development would be classified as public charities under either of the two tests. For a CDC not so fortunate as to receive

---

[26] Because of this added limitation on gross receipts, the section 509(a)(2) regulations devote a great deal of space to the proper distinctions between gross receipts on the one hand, and gifts, grants, contributions, and membership fees on the other. Proposed Treas. Reg. § 1.509(a)-3(f) to (h), 35 Fed. Reg. 17849-50 (1970).

[27] For a further discussion of "disqualified person" see notes 76-91 *infra* and accompanying text. In general there are three types of disqualified persons: substantial contributors, foundation managers, and government employees.

[28] In some unusual cases a problem might arise in distinguishing between grants and gross receipts. The distinction maintained by the Regulations is that between the use of funds to benefit the grantor directly and their use to benefit the public in general. Typically, of course, a grant from a government agency to a CDC is for the purposes of benefiting the community which the CDC serves and is not intended to benefit the federal government directly. *See* Proposed Treas. Reg. § 1.509(a)-3(g), particularly example (3), 35 Fed. Reg. 17849-50 (1970).

If the CDC finds that it is in a position to choose between one of the two tests, it should qualify under section 170, since grants which it makes in turn to its grantees will be considered to be from it as a public charity. It can thereby assist its own grantees in attempting to become public charities themselves. *See* INT. REV. CODE OF 1954 § 509(a)(2); Proposed Treas. Reg. § 1.509(a)-3(j), 35 Fed. Reg. 17851 (1970); Proposed Treas. Reg. § 1.170A-9(e)(6)(i), 36 Fed. Reg. 9303 (1971).

government largesse, there are still a number of other sources to which it may turn. Principal among these are its own community, foundations, corporations, and wealthy individuals. If it does so, however, it may encounter problems when attempting to meet either of the public financial support tests. If the CDC is successful in deriving a substantial amount of its funds from the community itself, then it will stand a good chance of meeting the tests. This is because the CDC will be obtaining many contributions of relatively small amounts from numerous contributors, and all of this money will be includable in public support. Similarly, where the CDC is fortunate enough to receive a substantial portion of its funds from other publicly-supported organizations which themselves have qualified under one of the section 170 tests (such as the United Fund or those rare national foundations which depend upon relatively small contributions from large memberships), it will be able to qualify under either of the public financial support tests. Where the CDC is dependent upon foundations, corporations, or wealthy individuals, however, its chances of qualifying will be substantially reduced. With few exceptions all of the national foundations which have been active in making economic development grants to CDC's are themselves private foundations, not public charities. If their contributions exceed the greater of $5,000 or two per cent of the CDC's total support, the foundation, corporation, or individual will be considered a substantial contributor, and the contribution completely excluded from the category of public support under the section 509(a)(2) test. Under the section 170 public financial support test, the CDC will be somewhat better off, in that amounts up to two per cent of total support, even though from such "tainted" sources, can be included in public support. Obviously, however, if the CDC is dependent on one, or even a handful, of such large contributors, the two per cent amounts will not total up to the minimum one-third public financial support.

A CDC which finds itself unable to qualify under either of the public support tests has open to it two other alternatives which it may pursue before resigning itself to private foundation status. First, the CDC may attempt to qualify under the facts and circumstances test recently proposed in the Regulations issued by the Service under section 170. Second, it might attempt to exclude those large contributions from "tainted" sources pursuant to the unusual grant exclusions found both in the section 509(a)(2) test and in the facts and circumstances test.

C. The Facts and Circumstances Test

The facts and circumstances test recently proposed by the Service under section 170 generally follows the pattern established by its predecessor.[29] By continuing to provide for this kind of test, the Service recognizes that the organizations to which Congress addressed itself in the Act were those over which the public at large has little control. Principally, Congress was concerned with those small "family" founda-

---

[29] The new test is set forth in Proposed Treas. Reg. § 1.170A-9(e)(3), 36 Fed. Reg. 9300 (1971). The old test may be found in Treas. Reg. § 1.170-2(b)(5)(iii)(c) (1966).

tions established by an individual for tax, rather than charitable reasons, and over which that individual exercised effective control. It was also concerned with certain of the larger national foundations which were originally formed through endowments provided by enormously wealthy individuals and which now exercise virtually complete control over their own operations as self-perpetuating bodies. The public financial support tests offer a shorthand method for separating truly public charities from such private foundations. The *absence* of public financial support, however, does not necessarily establish the *presence* of private control. Some organizations, even though not publicly supported financially, still are not controlled by the "private" sources from which they derive their funds. It is inappropriate for such organizations to be subject to the private foundation provisions found in the Tax Reform Act, since they do not engage in the type of activities which prompted congressional concern. The facts and circumstances test provides an escape hatch through which such organizations, although unable to demonstrate the requisite public financial support needed to meet the public financial support tests, can still avoid private foundation status by demonstrating that they are controlled by the public and are responsive to it.[30]

An examination of the test itself reveals that some showing of public financial support is still demanded through the requirement that at least ten per cent (rather than one-third) of the organization's support comes from public sources.[31] The inclusion of some mention of public financial support seems necessary, given the statutory language of section 170 that the organization must receive a "substantial part of its support . . . from a governmental unit . . . or from direct or indirect contributions from the general public . . . ."[32] In addition to the ten per cent requirement, the test sets forth one additional requirement and then several factors which, although not mandatory, will, taken together, have a substantial bearing on whether the organization satisfies the test.

---

[30] The Service appears to be recognizing that a community foundation (such as a CDC) may be public in nature regardless of its sources of financial support. The Assistant Secretary in charge of tax policy in the Treasury, John Nolan, has recently stated, "A [public financial] support test is *not* appropriate to determine whether the community foundation is a public charity under § 170(b)(1)(A). The typical community foundation is intended to provide endowment funds for community institutions and future community needs, so that *current* contributions become a progressively smaller part of its total receipts, but at the same time it has received its support from the general public and is as responsive to the public as we need require for public charity status. Accordingly, we are developing a test based on such factors as a continuous program of solicitations of additional endowment funds, receipt of a substantial number of independent gifts over its history from unrelated parties, control by a representative group from the community periodically reappointed, and absence of control by any single individual or family." 9 Non-Profit Organ. Tax Letter, No. 4, at 2 (Mar. 8, 1971).

[31] Proposed Treas. Reg. § 1.170A-9(e)(3)(i), 36 Fed. Reg. 9300 (1971). In the first facts and circumstances test no floor was expressly required in percentage terms, although both the test itself and the examples illustrating it suggested that some public financial support would be required for an organization to qualify.

[32] INT. REV. CODE OF 1954 § 170(b)(1)(A)(vi). The Service's decision to employ a definite percentage figure may be questioned as inserting rigidity into a test which was initially designed to encourage a great deal of flexibility. The Service may have retained the desired flexibility, however, through its provision for the exclusion of unusual grants, while introducing an element of objectivity into the test through the use of the 10% minimum.

The test also requires that the organization must continuously attempt to attract additional support from public sources.[33] These fund-raising efforts can be met either through actual solicitation or merely through the activities which the organization carries on, if those activities are designed to attract support from governmental units or other public charities. Most CDC's would seem to meet this requirement simply through their activities since, regardless of whether their outside sources of financing are foundations, corporations, individuals, or the government, in general their ultimate aims are the same—large scale community involvement in the development, establishment, and maintenance of community-owned enterprises. As added assurance, however, the CDC may wish to engage in formal fund raising.

The most obvious of the several "optional" factors states that the closer the organization comes to the one-third public support figure, the greater will be its chances of meeting the facts and circumstances test. Thus, an organization receiving the bare minimum ten per cent public financial support will be viewed less favorably than the organization receiving thirty per cent.[34] The organization's attempt to meet the test will also be viewed more favorably if it is dependent upon a number of fairly substantial gifts from unrelated persons, rather than grants from members of a single family. In addition, the governing body of the organization will be examined in order to determine whether its representatives are selected by only a few people or, in contrast, reflect the interests of the general public. In the case of a membership organization such as the typical CDC, election of the directors by a broadly-based membership is preferable. Those not directly elected by the membership should represent the public at large—such as elected public officials, civic leaders, or persons representing the views of a broad cross-section of the community—or have gained their place on the board by virtue of their expertise. The organization should also make its facilities or services available to the public and should allow the public to participate in its programs and policies.[35] In the case of a membership organization such as a CDC, there are several other factors which will also be taken into account: whether dues-paying members are solicited, whether the amount of dues required is fixed sufficiently low to encourage a broad-based membership, and whether the organization's activities will likely appeal to those whom the organization intends to serve.

It is certain that a genuinely broad-based CDC will easily meet all of the non-financial factors mentioned in the facts and circumstances test which are concerned with the organization's public control and responsiveness. The only difficulty which may be encountered is the public nature of the funds upon which the CDC depends, a matter which in most cases is outside the control of the CDC.

---

[33] Proposed Treas. Reg. § 1.170A-9(e)(3)(ii), 36 Fed. Reg. 9300 (1971).

[34] These factors are set forth in Proposed Treas. Reg. § 1.170A-9(e)(3)(iii)-(vii), 36 Fed. Reg. 9300-01 (1971).

[35] Of particular importance to CDC's is one of the factors which the Service will consider as evidence of an organization's public support maintenance of a definitive program to accomplish charitable work in the community such as slum clearance or development of employment opportunities. Proposed Treas. Reg. § 1.170A-9(e)(3)(vi)(c)(2), 36 Fed. Reg. 9301 (1971).

It is the Service which will ultimately be responsible for making a determination under the facts and circumstances test, and hopefully it will keep the financial predicament of some CDC's in mind when doing so. Flexibility could be achieved through use of the unusual grant exclusion provided for in both the facts and circumstances test and the section 509(a)(2) test.[36] Before the unusual grant exclusion is considered, however, it seems advisable to treat briefly the procedures proposed by the Service for calculating both the public and total support of an organization.

D. Normality and the Unusual Grant Exclusion

Both statutory provisions, section 170 and section 509, require an organization to demonstrate that it *normally* receives the appropriate amounts of public support. All three tests interpret *normally* to mean *aggregated over a four-year period*. Though differing somewhat in detail, they do not require an organization to demonstrate annually that it has received the requisite amount of public support during that particular year.[37] The tests also make provision for those organizations which have not been in existence for four years and those organizations which have just come into existence and wish to secure rulings on their status in advance of beginning their operations.[38]

The basic consideration of the Service in issuing an advance ruling is whether it appears that the organization will in fact be a publicly-supported organization after it begins operation. In order to make this determination under section 170, the Service requests the organization to submit all the information which the organization would have submitted had it been attempting to meet the facts and circumstances test and, in addition, information on its anticipated sources of funds. The section 509(a)(2) test sets forth factors which the Service will take into account should an organization apply for an advance ruling. Except for the addition of an investment income proviso (designed to determine whether the organization will meet the investment income test of section 509(a)(2)), the factors there listed are similar in substance to those under section 170. There is apparently no definite advantage to an organization's attempting one test rather than the other.

It is definitely advantageous, however, for the organization to attempt to secure a favorable advance ruling. Once the organization has obtained the prior approval of the Service, moreover, it will be regarded as a public charity for a period of two years unless there is a prior public revocation of that status. The organization

---

[36] Although no reason is given for the absence of the unusual grant exclusion in the section 170 public support test, it may be that the Service believed that the availabilty of the exclusion in the facts and circumstances test was sufficient to insure the desired flexibility.

[37] Proposed Treas. Reg. § 1.170A-9(e)(4), 36 Fed. Reg. 9301 (1971); Proposed Treas. Reg. § 1.509(a)-3(c), 35 Fed. Reg. 17846 (1970). The particular four-year period may vary. Under the section 170 tests the four-year period is the four years immediately preceding the organization's current taxable year. In the case of the § 509(a)(2) test the organization may choose between the immediately preceding four years, or its current taxable year and the immediately preceding three years.

[38] These methods are set forth in Proposed Treas. Reg. § 1.170A-9(e)(4)(vii) and (5), 36 Fed. Reg. 9302-03 (1971); Proposed Treas. Reg. § 1.509(a)-3(d) and (e), 35 Fed. Reg. 17848-49 (1970).

which has secured a ruling will more likely be able to secure funds from other private foundations, since the latter will then not have to exercise expenditure responsibility over the grant and will probably be able to claim more easily that the amounts disbursed were made for qualified purposes under section 4942 of the Code.[39] In addition, the organization itself will not be subject to the taxes which may be imposed on a private foundation engaging in certain prohibited activities.

An organization which fails to secure a prior ruling may attempt to qualify as a public charity at the end of its first taxable year. If it is unsuccessful in this attempt, it may again attempt to qualify at the end of its second year and if successful at that time, have any taxes imposed during its first taxable year abated. This procedure is not as satisfactory as attempting to secure an advance ruling. Not only does the organization subject itself to the possibility of taxes being imposed upon it (even though they may later be abated), but it may also find other private foundations reluctant to deal with it. Moreover, should the organizations fail to achieve public charity status at the end of its second year, it will be considered a private foundation for those two years and for all subsequent years until it can establish its public charity status. In comparison, an organization which receives an advance ruling stating that it is a public charity, unless notified earlier by the Service, will be considered a public charity for the first two years, even though it is unable to qualify at the end of that time. In such a case the organization will be considered a private foundation at the begining of the third year, but its status as a public charity will not be revoked retroactively.[40]

The exclusion for unusual grants permits modification of the usual procedures for determining whether an organization *normally* receives sufficient public support to meet either the section 509(a)(2) public support test or the facts and circumstances test.[41] Although the mechanics of the exclusions vary somewhat, the underlying principle is the same. A grant which is unusual in size or is unexpected should not be included in determining whether an organization is publicly supported, since its inclusion would tend to distort the nature of the organization by overemphasizing an amount from only one source.[42] This exception may prove particularly valuable to a CDC dependent upon private sources of support. By excluding one or two contributions, it may be able to achieve public charity status based on the public nature of its other sources of funds. This would be especially true where the CDC has

---

[39] For a discussion of expenditure responsibility and qualified distributions, see text accompanying notes 109-33 *infra*.

[40] There are two exceptions: taxes under § 4940 (the 4% tax on an organization's net investment income) and the determination of substantial contributors under § 507(d) are retroactive.

[41] Proposed Treas. Reg. § 1.170A-9(e)(6)(ii) and (iii), 36 Fed. Reg. 9303 (1971); Proposed Treas. Reg. § 1.509(a)-3(c)(3) to (7), 35 Fed. Reg. 17846-47 (1970).

[42] It should be noted that the exclusion is available for more than one instance of an unusual grant, so that, an organization could exclude several grants over a period of time as long as it was able to convince the Service that all of the grants were unusual. Obviously, the greater the number of grants which the organization attempts to exclude, the more skeptical the Service will become of their alleged unusual nature.

received most of its funds from a foundation, corporation, or individual that was instrumental in getting the CDC started, but which does not wish to exercise significant control over the organization's activities.

Under the section 509(a)(2) test, the year in which the unusual grant is made is simply excluded in calculating the normality of the organization's public support. An organization would normally be required to aggregate its public support and total support either from the four years immediately preceding its present taxable year or the three years immediately preceding its current taxable year plus that year itself. Under the mechanics of the unusual grant exclusion, normality would be based on a three-year rather than a four-year period. In the case of a newly-formed organization which has not applied for an advance ruling, the year in which the unusual grant was made can be excluded when, after two years, the organization attempts to establish that it is a public charity.

The mechanics in the facts and circumstances test are somewhat different. The amount of the unusual grant is simply omitted in the calculation of public support for the applicable period. The remainder of the support of the year in which the unusual grant is made is still included in the amounts aggregated over the appropriate period of time.

The rationale for the unusual grant exclusion is set forth in the Regulations applicable to the facts and circumstances test:

> The exclusion . . . is generally intended to apply to substantial contributions or bequests from disinterested parties, which contributions or bequests:
> (a) Are attracted by reason of the publicly supported nature of the organization;
> (b) Are unusual or unexpected with respect to the amount thereof; and
> (c) Would, by reason of their size, adversely affect the status of the organization as normally being publicly supported . . . .[43]

Both tests expand on this rationale by setting forth several inquiries which are to be made. Was the grant made by a person who created the organization or has stood in a position of authority with respect to it? Has he previously made a substantial grant to the organization? Prior to receipt of the grant, was the organization relatively dormant or was it carrying on an active program? Similarly, prior to the year in which the unsual grant was made, had the organization met the public financial support tests or the facts and circumstances test of section 170? Was the contribution a bequest or an *inter vivos* transfer (the latter being viewed more favorably)? Lastly, was the grant made in the form of cash, liquid assets, or assets which further the organization's purposes, rather than a contribution of property which would tend to benefit the contributor more than the organization?

It can be seen that an unusual grant to a CDC should probably be excludable unless the CDC must rely upon it alone in order to undertake any activities whatsoever. In such a case, if the latter were true, the grant would not be excludable

---

[43] Proposed Treas. Reg. § 1.170A-9(e)(6)(ii), 36 Fed. Reg. 9303 (1971).

since it is likely that the organization was dormant prior to the grant. A similar problem might be raised where the amount of the grant is significantly larger than the amount of funds previously received by the CDC so that the nature of the CDC's operation is likely to change drastically. The Regulations do not indicate whether the mere size of a grant would in itself require the Service to disallow the exclusion of the grant. The Service may take the position that a grant will be excluded if it is unusual, but not if it is inordinately unusual. The language of the Regulations seems to imply that a grant could be excluded no matter what its size, so long as the grant does not "derogate from [the organization's] publicly supported nature and constitute a device to avoid the provisions of chapter 42 of subtitle D of this title [containing the provisions which tax certain proscribed activities of private foundations]."[44] The Regulations go on to note that the exclusion of the unusual grant will be permitted "if no fundamental change has taken place in the normal broad, publicly supported nature of the organization or in its operations."

A CDC should be able to present a convincing case to the Service that, although the *scope* of its operations has changed, both its methods and its ultimate purposes have not. Thus, the CDC may argue that the exclusion of an unusual grant should be disallowed only if the grant would cause an organization formerly publicly controlled to fall into private hands. As long as the CDC continues to control its own activities, the unusual grant should be excluded since the CDC's public nature will be maintained. That public nature can be demonstrated by the CDC through the public contributions which it has already obtained from membership dues, public solicitations, public charities, and governmental agencies. The CDC should be able to couple its past fund-raising efforts with those which it will undertake in the future, pointing out to the Service that as a result of the increased power gained from the unusual grant, its chances for government funds and other kinds of public contributions are probably enhanced.[45]

---

[44] Proposed Treas. Reg. § 1.509(a)-3(c)(4), 35 Fed. Reg. 17847 (1970).

[45] Subsequent to the preparation of this article, the Service issued proposed Regulations which provide that an organization which qualifies as a *community trust* will be deemed to be publicly-supported. Proposed Treas. Reg. § 1.170A-9(e)(10) to (19), 36 Fed. Reg. 19598 (1971). The apparent purpose of the Regulations is to exclude from private foundation status those organizations which are publicly-controlled despite their financial dependence on a limited number of sources. CDC's should fit within the general intent of the Regulations. The CDC thus might attempt to qualify as a publicly-supported community trust by satisfying the detailed requirements of the Regulations, which relate to the structure and administration of the organization, the nature of its support, and the character of its distributions. It should do so only as a last resort, however, since a community trust is precluded from undertaking certain activities which would subject it to taxation if it had private foundation status. For example, a community trust may not engage in acts which would amount to self-dealing under section 4941 if it were a private foundation. Similarly, the trust may not possess holdings which would be excessive under section 4943. Among all of the penalty taxes of Chapter 42, the prohibitions of these two sections are those which a CDC would likely find most objectionable. Consequently, for most CDC's, a Service determination that the CDC satisfies one of the other tests (the mechanical test or facts and circumstances test) is more desirable than a finding that it qualifies as a community trust. On the other hand, most CDC's should find qualification as a community trust somewhat preferable to private foundation status.

E. The Impact of Financial Independence

The above discussion of the three tests has presupposed a CDC depending on a few outside sources for its financial support. As has been seen, the nature of these sources alone as either public or private will very probably determine whether the CDC will meet either financial support tests and possibly the facts and circumstances test. Most CDC's rely on a limited number of such outside sources because of the difficulty of securing funds in any other fashion. Ideally, however, the CDC hopes that through a prudent use of those initial funds, it may wean itself and eventually become self-sustaining. If a CDC can successfully accomplish this feat, its eventual sources of financial support will be quite different from what they were initially. A crucial question, therefore, is whether a CDC will be considered a public charity when the bulk of its financial support comes from returns from its own business operations and its investments and loans in other businesses.[46] The answer to this question requires that those returns be classified under the public financial support tests. It seems obvious that they will not be considered gifts, grants, or contributions since they will be receivable by the CDC pursuant to an obligation of some sort. Rather, the returns will be considered investment income.

The returns from the CDC's businesses, whether operated as subsidiaries or as divisions of the CDC itself, might be considered gross receipts, and thus it would meet the section 509(a)(2) test which permits the inclusion of gross receipts (within certain limits) in calculation of public support.[47] This possibility, however, confronts several difficulties. First, and principally, only those gross receipts which are derived from "related" trades and businesses are includable in public support. Relatedness, in turn, is defined by reference to the Code provisions which tax income from unrelated trades or businesses.[48] In order to satisfy the Service that such relatedness exists, the CDC must be able to demonstrate a relationship between the business and the CDC's purpose other than merely the use of the receipts for exempt purposes. In the words of the Regulations, there must be a "substantial" or "causal" relationship between the business operations and the exempt purposes for which the CDC was formed.[49]

Since only income from *un*related trades or businesses is taxable, the CDC's related gross receipts would not be subject to taxation. Hence, the practical

---

[46] This potential redetermination of the CDC's status will probably take place gradually over a number of years, in part simply because of the time it takes to establish successful businesses, and in part because both support tests determine the percentage of public support by taking the aggregate amounts of public and total support over specified preceding time periods.

[47] This statement presupposes that the corporate form in which the operations are carried out (whether as subsidiaries or as divisions) should not be relevant to a classification of returns as investment income or as gross receipts; rather, they should be uniformly treated as gross receipts if they result from activities carried out to further the exempt purposes of the CDC. By this line of reasoning, returns should be considered investment income only if they are derived from investments which are designed solely as portfolio investments for the maintenance and growth of an organization's endowment.

[48] INT. REV. CODE OF 1954 §§ 511-14.

[49] Treas. Reg. § 1.513-1(d) (1967).

obstacle for the CDC to overcome will be the Service's fear that if it agrees that the returns from a CDC's businesses are "related" in determining whether the CDC is a public charity or a private foundation it must also agree that they are "related" in applying the unrelated business income provisions. In seeking to classify its gross receipts as related, therefore, the CDC must keep in mind that the Service may be viewing consequences other than the determination of public charity status.[50]

Even if gross receipts are "related," a second difficulty remains. Gross receipts may be included in public support only in amounts from any one source in a taxable year not in excess of $5,000 or one per cent, whichever is greater. The importance of this restriction will probably vary according to the type of business producing the gross receipts. In a retail operation, such as a grocery store or a service station, it seems unlikely that one person would account for $5,000 or one per cent of the operation's business. A manufacturing concern with only a few customers, however, might be much more adversely affected.

Lastly, it must be remembered that gross receipts, even though "related" and within the proper limits, must also be derived from proper sources, namely other public charities, governmental units, and other than disqualified persons. One type of "disqualified person" is a substantial contributor—one who during the taxable year has contributed an amount to the CDC in excess of the greater of $5,000 or two per cent of the CDC's total contributions.[51] This limitation might cause difficulty if a customer of the CDC were also contributing goods, services, or assistance to it free or at less than cost, as in the situation in which a well-established company assists in the formation and operation of a minority firm and is also a customer of it. At the point at which the customer would become a substantial contributor, gross receipts derived from it could not be included in support, even if otherwise qualified, because the customer would be tainted as a "disqualified person."

Assuming that a CDC formerly able to meet the public financial support tests can no longer do so, it may still continue to qualify as a public charity under the facts and circumstances test. Under that test, the CDC need only become concerned when its public support will likely fall below ten per cent of its total support. The CDC should be forewarned of this possibility well in advance of its occurrence since a four-year period is used to determine whether it *normally* meets the test and since the profitability of its businesses will probably build up slowly over an extended length of time.

If the CDC has so developed that it is no longer able to meet even the facts and circumstances test because of the amount of its own investment returns, it is unlikely that a section 501(c)(3) exemption would be of any particular value to it.

---

[50] Similar problems may arise in a CDC's attempt to classify an investment as "program-related." See n.87 *infra*.

[51] INT. REV. CODE OF 1954 §§ 4946(a)(1)(A), 507(d)(2). For CDC's in existence prior to October 9, 1969, substantial contributors are those who before that date contributed the appropriate amounts. INT. REV. CODE OF 1954 § 507(d)(2)(B)(ii) and (iv).

Presently, the exemption is worth seeking primarily because a CDC may more easily attract outside funds. Once a CDC becomes self-sustaining, the exemption's attractiveness diminishes considerably. Its principal value then may only be the possibility that the CDC could pull out its "profits" tax-free by successfully classifying them as related gross receipts. Rather than risk subjecting itself to private foundation status, the CDC might be well advised to relinquish its exemption, and merely become a nonprofit corporation under state law subject to taxation at normal corporate rates. If the CDC decides to do so, however, it should act before it is classified as a private foundation, since it will almost certainly be unable to terminate its private foundation status in a manner satisfactory to it.[52]

II

Private Foundation Taxes Affecting CDC's

A CDC which cannot qualify as a public charity under any of the three tests already discussed will be considered a private foundation. The purpose of this part of the article is to set forth those consequences emanating from private foundation designation. These consequences are, briefly, more detailed reporting requirements and the possible imposition of six operating taxes:[53] (1) an excise tax on investment income; and taxes on (2) self-dealing, (3) failure to distribute income, (4) excess business holdings, (5) investments which jeopardize charitable purpose, and (6) taxable expenditures. With the exception of the excise tax on investment income,[54] a general pattern can thus be seen in these levies: certain foundation activities which had led to abuse of the section 501(c)(3) exemption in the past are discouraged through the sanction of graduated taxation. First, initial taxes are imposed on the discouraged activities, followed by much larger additional taxes if the consequences of these activities are not corrected after a specified period of time. Secondly, in the case of three of the taxes[55] both initial and additional taxes are also imposed on individuals, referred to as "foundation managers" by the Act, who either make up the management of the foundation or who are responsible for the particular actions which have led to the imposition of the taxes. Initial taxes are only imposed on a foundation manager, however, if his participation is "knowing"; even then he is excused if his participation is "not willful and is due to reasonable cause."[56] Thirdly, self-dealers and foundation managers are subject to joint and

---

[52] See note 138 infra.
[53] The taxes are set forth in Int. Rev. Code of 1954 §§ 4940-46. The reporting requirements and related provisions are found in Int. Rev. Code of 1954 §§ 6033-34, 6056, 6104(d), 6652(d), 6685 and 7207. See generally Eliasburg, 501(c)(3)—The Private Foundation: New Procedural Requirements and Noncompliance Penalties, 45 J. State B. Calif. 860, 870-71 (1970); Lehrfeld, Private Foundations and Tax Reform: Accounting and Administrative Problems, 1 Tax Adviser 418 (1970).
[54] The tax on investment income was viewed by Congress as a user or audit fee in order to pay for the costs of supervising the activities of private foundations, not as a means of discouraging certain foundation activities. Senate Report, supra note 15, at 27.
[55] The three are those levied on self-dealing, jeopardizing charitable purpose, and taxable expenditures.
[56] This language is found in all three sections. The purpose of the knowledge requirement is pur-

several liability for all taxes imposed upon them, although the latter's liability is limited to either $5,000 or $10,000 depending on the tax involved. Lastly, only after specified correction periods have ended can additional taxes be imposed.

Following is a treatment of each of these taxes, grouped for convenience into those taxes which may affect CDC's directly (the remainder of part II), and those which may do so only indirectly through policies and practices which may be adopted by other private foundations (part III). The two taxes of greatest potential importance to CDC's—those on excess business holdings and self-dealing—are immediately discussed.

A. The Tax on Excess Business Holdings

One congressional concern transformed into law involves the substantial extent to which some exempt organizations had been engaging in conventional commercial activities. Prior law had proven ineffective because it was difficult to establish a definite point at which the business operations of the exempt organization had become so substantial that its exemption should be revoked, a step rarely taken, moreover, because of its severity.[57] Section 4943 attempts to remedy these defects by providing for graduated taxation of business holdings over specified percentage limits. The section's practical effect is to force divestiture of the excess holdings.[58]

A private foundation is permitted to hold up to twenty per cent of the voting stock of a corporation, less the percentage of the voting stock owned by all "disqualified persons."[59] Where all disqualified persons together do not own more than twenty per cent of the voting stock, then the private foundation may hold as much *nonvoting* stock as it wishes. Where a third party exercises effective control of the corporation, the twenty per cent figure is increased to thirty-five per cent.[60] It is crucial to determine whether a CDC would be restricted to the percentage holding of this section since a CDC may in many situations wish to take equity positions larger than those permitted by the section.[61]

---

portedly to establish the proof standard of clear and convincing evidence. CONF. REP. No. 782, 91st Cong., 1st Sess. 280 (1969) [hereinafter cited as CONFERENCE REPORT]; SENATE REPORT 32. Additional taxes are imposed only where a manager refuses to agree to the correction of the action which led to the initial tax. Imposition of this tax should be rare. SENATE REPORT 33.

[57] SENATE REPORT 38.

[58] INT. REV. CODE OF 1954 § 4943. The initial tax is 5% on the value of the private foundation's excess business holdings in a business enterprise. INT. REV. CODE OF 1954 § 4943(a). The additional tax is 200%. INT. REV. CODE OF 1954 § 4943(b).

[59] INT. REV. CODE OF 1954 § 4943(c)(2)(A). The term *disqualified person* is defined in INT. REV. CODE OF 1954 § 4946 and is with two exceptions identical to the term as used in the provisions taxing self-dealings discussed in text accompanying notes 76-91 *infra*.

[60] INT. REV. CODE OF 1954 § 4943(c)(2)(B). Similar treatment is provided for business enterprises which are not corporations, except in the case of proprietorships, in which no holdings are permitted. *Id.* § 4943(c)(3). A major portion of this section sets forth complex methods governing the divestiture of present excess business holdings of private foundations. *Id.* § 4943(c)(4). Since most of the CDC's did not possess such holdings on the cut-off date, May 26, 1969, these provisions will not be discussed.

[61] An example would be a joint venture with a non-minority firm in which the CDC wished voting control of the venture either initially or through buy-out provisions over a period of years. Another example, perhaps even more typical, involves a CDC wishing to run a retail or service operation, such

It seems highly likely that most, and perhaps all, of a CDC's commercial activities should be unaffected by section 4943's taxes since they will be classified as "program-related investments," investments which were expressly excluded from the section's coverage in the Senate Report. In addition to the favorable language contained in the Senate Report, the Service has recently issued proposed Regulations further elucidating program-related investments; these Regulations appear to include as program-related virtually any investment contemplated by a CDC so long as the CDC is able to demonstrate a connection between the investment and the economic well-being or improvement of the area which it serves.[62]

The language used in the discussion of section 4943 in the Senate Report seems clearly designed to exclude some typical CDC business activities from the application of the excess business holdings taxes:

> Business holdings do not include "program-related investments" (such as investments in small businesses in central cities or in corporations to assist in neighborhood renovation) which are part of the foundation's charitable program, where the making of a profit for the foundation is not one of the significant purposes for holding these investments.[63]

The term *program-related investments* is discussed further in the Senate Report's explanation of section 4944 which also excludes program-related investments from the imposition of taxes on investments which jeopardize the charitable purpose of a private foundation.[64] That explanation sets forth further examples of program-related investments:

> [A] program-related investment—such as low-interest or interest-free loans to needy students, high risk investments in low-income housing, and loans to small businesses where commercial sources are unavailable—is not to be considered as an investment which might jeopardize the foundation's carrying out of its exempt purposes (since such an investment is classified as a charitable expenditure). To qualify as a program-related investment, the investment must be primarily for charitable purposes and not have as one of its significant purposes that of deriving a profit for the foundation.[65]

---

as a grocery store or a day care center or planning to control the enterprise initially, divesting its ownership only after the enterprise had become established.

[62] Proposed Treas. Reg. § 53.4944-3, 36 Fed. Reg. 12027 (1971). Program-related investments are also referred to in section 4944 as an exception to that section's prohibition against investments which jeopardize a foundation's exempt purposes. The proposed Regulations which are referred to in the text and which are immediately discussed in some detail are those issued under section 4944, not section 4943. It is thus possible that when Regulations are proposed under section 4943 the treatment of program-related investments there will be different from their treatment in the proposed section 4944 Regulations. Although this eventuality should be kept in mind, the likelihood of its occurrence seems remote in that the Senate Report gives no indication that program-related investments should be treated differently under the two sections. The more likely possibility is, as in a few other instances, that the section 4943 Regulations will merely incorporate the section 4944 Regulations by reference. *See, e.g.,* Proposed Treas. Reg. § 53.4942(a)-2(c)(1)(ii)(g), 36 Fed. Reg. 11037 (1971).

[63] SENATE REPORT 41. Only excess business holdings are taxed under section 4943. The exclusion of program-related investments from such holdings thus excludes them from the section's taxes.

[64] INT. REV. CODE OF 1954 § 4944(c).

[65] SENATE REPORT 46.

Program-related investments thus appear to be those made primarily for charitable purposes and not, at least significantly, for making a profit as illustrated by the examples set forth. One question immediately posed is the meaning of "charitable purposes" in the context of program-related investments. In attempting to answer it, it is instructive to examine the meaning of *charitable* as it is used generally in section 501(c)(3), and then to apply that meaning to the examples of program-related investments found in the Senate Report.

The definition of *charitable* found in the Regulations is extremely (and intentionally) broad, partly as a result of judicial usage of the term incorporated by reference and partly as a result of sweeping language found in the Regulations themselves:

> The term "charitable" is used in section 501(c)(3) in its generally accepted legal sense and is, therefore, not to be construed as limited by the separate enumeration in section 501(c)(3) of other tax-exempt purposes which may fall within the broad outlines of "charity" as developed by judicial decisions. Such term includes: Relief of the poor and distressed or of the underprivileged; . . . lessening of the burdens of Government; and promotion of social welfare by organizations designed to accomplish any of the above purposes, or (i) to lessen neighborhood tensions; (ii) to eliminate prejudice and discrimination . . . or (iv) to combat community deterioration . . . .[66]

Given the typical membership and purposes of an urban or rural CDC, it is not difficult to put their operations within one, or even all, of these general statements of charitable purpose.

Program-related investments, then, appear to be those which serve the broadly-drawn statements of charitable purpose in ways similar to those set forth in the Senate Report examples. Those examples, in turn, are (1) investments in small businesses in central cities, (2) investments in corporations to assist neighborhood renovation, (3) low-interest or interest-free loans to needy students, (4) high-risk investments in low-income housing, and (5) loans to small businesses where commercial sources of funds are unavailable.

These examples imply that a proper charitable purpose can be evidenced in either of two ways: by the nature or location of the recipient itself, or by the terms on which the funds are provided to the recipient. In other words, the recipient must in some way be deserving, and the funds must be provided on favorable terms. The justification for the first requirement seems clear—the benefit of charitable activities must redound to those in need, as in example (4) (potential residents in low-income housing) or example (3) (impoverished students). The benefit, however, apparently need not be direct. It could be to a business located in, and perhaps serving, an area where the recipients live, as in example (1) (small businesses in central cities). If it is thus correct to say that a benefit, directly or indirectly, must result to recipients who are proper objects of charitable largesse, then the purposes and operations of

---
[66] Treas. Reg. § 1.501(c)(3)-1(d)(2) (1959).

a typical CDC will face little difficulty in meeting this requirement. CDC's are located in poor areas, either urban or rural. In most cases their members are black, Mexican-American, or another minority which is and has been subject to discrimination, and with few exceptions whose members have not had equal opportunity to engage in business and professional activities.

The other requirement—that the terms on which the funds are provided must be favorable—appears to restate the Senate's concern that "the making of a profit . . . is not one of the significant purposes for holding these investments."[67] The consequence of this requirement will be that some evidence should be available to distinguish the "charitable" business activities of a private foundation from its other commercial operations that make profits which, as the result of operations unrelated to the foundation's charitable activities, are taxable at regular corporate rates.[68] Terms favorable to proper recipients also provide evidence that it is indeed their interests that lie at the center of the foundation's actions. This evidence reinforces the conclusion drawn from the nature or location of the recipient that the actions were charitably inspired.

The favorability of the terms may be demonstrated in a number of ways. Interest rates may be lower than market, or no interest at all may be charged [example (3)]; funds may be provided where, otherwise, no funds whatsoever would be available [example (5)]; and the investment may involve a high risk [example (4)]. In some cases it appears that the recipient itself (or its location) is sufficient evidence of either the terms' favorability or the propriety of the investment—funds may be invested in a small business location in a central city area on "commercial" terms [example (1)]. Also, investments may be made in corporations to assist in neighborhood renovation [example (2)]. These examples, by not expressly requiring the extension of terms more favorable than those commercially available, support the conclusion that in some cases the recipients themselves will demonstrate the charitable nature of the transaction and that the terms and purposes of the particular transaction may be the same as those which could be found in the business world between two arm's-length parties.

The proposed Regulations recently issued by the Service appear to support fully this analysis of the Senate's intent in creating an exception for program-related investments. In a series of eight examples the Regulations attempt to illustrate the kinds of investments which will be considered program-related in that their primary purpose will be to accomplish the charitable or other exempt purposes of the organization.[69] These examples demonstrate their program-related nature principally

---

[67] SENATE REPORT 41.
[68] INT. REV. CODE OF 1954 § 511 (unrelated business income tax).
[69] Proposed Treas. Reg. § 53.4944-3(a)(1), 36 Fed. Reg. 12027 (1971). In addition to the eight examples, the proposed Regulations also include as program-related investments the five kinds of program-related investments set forth in the discussions of sections 4943 and 4944 in the Senate Report. The fact that the Regulations do refer to investments mentioned by the Senate under both sections appears to indicate that the Service recognizes the identity of program-related investments under both sections,

through the benefit which they will directly or ultimately confer on members of an economically-disadvantaged minority group, and tend to downplay the requirement (as was implicit in the Senate Report) that investments be made on favorable terms in order to demonstrate the absence of a profit motive. Thus, in those examples in which favorable terms are found it is apparent that without such terms it might be difficult to determine whether the investment was commercial or charitable.[70]

It cannot be ascertained in some of the examples whether all of the factors are essential since several are mentioned. It is clear, however, that a CDC may either assist a business controlled by others or one which it owns itself.[71] Moreover, if the business assisted is small, minority-owned, located in a poor area, and unable to obtain funds from conventional sources, then the CDC may make assistance available to it on commercial terms, so long as the CDC disclaims any intent to make a profit and can point to a colorable justification for the assistance being extended.[72]

In addition to investments which encourage minority ownership, those investments which increase employment opportunities to minority people from a poor area are classified as program-related in the proposed Regulations. Moreover, even though the business is not owned by low-income or minority people and not located in the low-income area itself, the foundation may apparently charge commercial interest rates if it appears that the business will be sufficiently profitable to meet the payments.[73] In fact, in only one example is the foundation prevented from charging the commercial rate—when it induces a "financially secure" business enterprise, "the stock of which is listed and traded on a national exchange," to establish a plant in a deteriorated urban area.[74] Even in this instance, moreover, it may very well be that a commercial interest rate would have been permissible because the below-market rate was demanded by the business enterprise itself in order to compensate for the other high risks involved. Since the loan was made by the foundation "to enhance the economic development of the area by providing employment oppor-

and, that when it issues Regulations under section 4943, it will pattern its discussion of program-related investments there on its exposition of them under section 4944.

[70] Proposed Treas. Reg. § 53.4944-3(c), *examples* (4) and (5), 36 Fed. Reg. 12028 (1971).
[71] Proposed Treas. Reg. § 53.4944-3(c), *examples* (6) and (8), 36 Fed. Reg. 12028 (1971).
[72] Proposed Treas. Reg. § 53.4944-3(c), *examples* (1), (3), and (6), 36 Fed. Reg. 12028 (1971). In example (1), a loan is provided "at or below the market rate for commercial loans of comparable risk," because the "terms of the loans are primarily intended to demonstrate to the financial community the economic viability of such [minority] enterprises." Moreover, the foundation's "primary purpose for making such loans is to encourage the economic development of such minority groups." In example (3), the ultimate financial benefit which might redound to the foundation is even greater since there the foundation purchases shares of the common stock of the business in order to convince conventional lending sources to participate, those sources being unwilling to provide funds "unless [the business] increases the amount of its equity capital." By purchasing the stock, the foundation is making a program-related investment "even though [it] may realize a profit if [the business] is successful and the common stock appreciates in value." In example (6), the foundation makes a loan to a business owned by it on the same terms as those demanded by conventional sources ("whose primary purpose for making the loan is financial"). The loan is nevertheless considered to be a program-related investment because it triggered the loan from the other sources.
[73] Proposed Treas. Reg. § 53.4944-3(c), *example* (4), 36 Fed. Reg. 12028 (1971).
[74] Proposed Treas. Reg. § 53.4944-3(c), *example* (5), 36 Fed. Reg. 12028 (1971).

tunities for low-income employees at the new plant," presumably the same would hold true if the foundation were to make funds available to a business enterprise which, for whatever reasons, was itself willing to assume the higher risks involved. Thus, perhaps the mere provision of capital by a foundation would alone be sufficient inducement to a business enterprise, and, so long as the foundation could demonstrate a charitable purpose, would qualify the investment as program-related.[75]

Under the proposed regulations, a CDC should be able to demonstrate that its investments are program-related in all but the most exceptional instances. Even investments in businesses located outside the CDC's usual area of operations might be justified as program-related if the enterprises were within commuting distance, since they could be said to provide employment opportunities. In general, it appears that only those investments of an entirely passive nature will be indefensible as program-related. Since it is difficult to imagine CDC's holding more than the twenty per cent or thirty-five per cent investment permitted by section 4943 in such enterprises, it is likely that the impact of section 4943 on them will be negligible if the proposed Regulations are adopted as final in substantially their present form.

B. The Taxes on Self-Dealing

Prior to the Act, section 503 permitted dealings between some types of exempt organizations and persons related to them if the transactions appeared to be the result of arm's-length negotiations.[76] Difficulties were encountered, however, in determining whether particular dealings met this standard. Moreover, even some that clearly did meet the standard were felt by Congress to be objectionable.[77] Also, the only sanction for engaging in prohibited dealings was removal of the exemption, an extreme step rarely and reluctantly taken. The Act attempts to remedy these deficiencies of prior law by imposing a series of graduated taxes on most dealings between private foundations and *disqualified persons*, whether at arm's-length or not.[78]

There are, in general, three categories of *disqualified persons*: (1) substantial contributors to the foundation, (2) *foundation managers*, and (3) certain government

---

[75] This statement also seems to be supported by more general language found elsewhere in the Regulations which states that "the fact that an investment produces significant income or capital appreciation shall not, in the absence of other factors, be conclusive evidence of a significant purpose involving the production of income or the appreciation of property [which would disqualify the investment as program-related]." Proposed Treas. Reg. § 53.4944-3(a)(2)(iii), 36 Fed. Reg. 12027 (1971).

[76] Section 503 applied only to those organizations could not meet the publicly-supported tests in the Regulations. Section 503 no longer applies to "private foundations," as sections 4941 and 4946 were designated to supplant it. SENATE REPORT, *supra* note 15, at 29.

[77] An example of the latter concern is a loan made by the foundation to a donor on commercial terms but in a tight market where the donor might otherwise have had greater difficulty in obtaining any funds at all. This and other examples are cited in SENATE REPORT 28-29.

[78] INT. REV. CODE OF 1954 § 4941. The taxes imposed are to be paid by the *disqualified persons* and, in some cases, by those responsible for the foundation's part in the dealing, but not by the foundation itself. INT. REV. CODE OF 1954 § 4941(a) and (b). *See also* Proposed Treas. Reg. § 53.4941(a)-1(a)(1), 36 Fed. Reg. 10968 (1971). The Service has recently issued proposed Regulations on disqualified persons. Proposed Treas. Reg. 53.4946-1, 36 Fed. Reg. 6430 (1971).

officials.[79] A substantial contributor is defined as any person (including a corporation or other entity) which gives the foundation more than $5,000 or two per cent of the foundation's total contributions during any taxable year, whichever is greater.[80] The term *foundation manager* includes any director, officer, or trustee of a foundation (or one performing similar functions, regardless of his title), and any employee having authority or responsibility for the act which led to the imposition of the tax. The broad sweep of this definition is curtailed under other sections setting forth specific taxes which require that the foundation manager must know that his act is one of self-dealing. Even where this knowledge exists, the provisions excuse him if his participation is "not willful and is due to reasonable cause."[81] Thus, the treatment of foundation managers and other disqualified persons is substantially different, as the latter are taxed regardless of their state of mind and the responsibility for the transaction at issue.

In addition, persons or organizations may be considered disqualified persons because of their relationship to a foundation manager or a substantial contributor. Entities in which a disqualified person has specified interests will also be considered disqualified as will owners of more than specified percentage interests in a disqualified entity. In addition, particular family relationships also expand the coverage of those considered disqualified. All of these measures are designed to prevent one person or entity from accomplishing indirectly what it cannot do directly.[82] The last general category of disqualified persons, government officials, includes those in public office who are likely to be politically powerful themselves, who are in relatively high-level policy-making positions, or who are potentially influential because of their close relationship to either of the former.[83]

The Code specifies in section 4941 the types of dealings between disqualified persons (as discussed above) and private foundations which are either precluded

---

[79] INT. REV. CODE OF 1954 § 4946(a)(1)(A), (B), and (I); Proposal Treas. Reg. § 53.4946-1(a)(1)(i) and (ii), and (c), 36 Fed. Reg. 6430-31 (1971).

[80] INT. REV. CODE OF 1954 § 507(d)(2)(A). If the foundation was in existence before October 9, 1969, those who are to be considered substantial contributors are determined by first assuming that all contributions or bequests received on or before October 9 were received on that day and then computing whether the particular contributor gave in excess of the applicable limit ($5000 or 2%). Once one qualifies as a substantial contributor, moreover, he remains a substantial contributor. INT. REV. CODE OF 1954 § 507(d)(2)(B)(ii) and (iv); Proposed Treas. Reg. § 1.507-6(b), 36 Fed. Reg. 6429 (1971).

[81] INT. REV. CODE OF 1954 § 4941(a)(2) (self-dealing), § 4944(a)(2) (jeopardizing charitable purpose), and § 4945(a)(2) (taxable expenditures). It should be noted, however, that the limitations on the liability apply only when the individual is acting in his capacity as a foundation manager. When, in contrast, he is dealing on his own behalf with the foundation (as, for example, where a foundation director is selling a piece of land owned by him to the foundation), he would be liable for the tax as a disqualified person. See INT. REV. CODE OF 1954 § 4941(a)(1). *Compare* Proposed Treas. Reg. § 53.4941(a)-1(a)(1) *with* Proposed Treas. Reg. § 53.4941(a)-1(b), 36 Fed. Reg. 10968-69 (1971).

[82] *See* INT. REV. CODE OF 1954 § 4946(a)(1)(C)-(G); Proposed Treas. Reg. § 53.4946-1(a)(1)(iii) to (vii), and (d), and (e), 36 Fed. Reg. 6430-32 (1971).

[83] INT. REV. CODE OF 1954 § 4946(a)(1)(I) and (c); Proposed Treas. Reg. § 53.4946-1(c) and (g), 36 Fed. Reg. 6432 (1971). In its definition of a government official, the Service distinguishes "public office" from public employment. Proposed Treas. Reg. § 53.4946-1(g)(2), 36 Fed. Reg. 6432 (1971).

altogether or substantially restricted. In general, it can be stated that a disqualified person may not enter into any transaction with a private foundation if he will benefit from it in any way. There are two exceptions: he may be a beneficiary of the foundation's programs on the same footing with any member of the general public, and he may be paid reasonable compensation for personal services which are reasonable and necessary to carry out the foundation's exempt purposes.[84] Thus, all real or personal property transactions with a foundation are taxable, including any leasing arrangements, and even gifts of the property if it has been mortgaged in a proscribed manner. Similarly, all monetary transactions are subject to taxation except for no-interest loans which are made by the disqualified person to the foundation and which are to be used for exempt purposes.[85] In addition, no goods, services, or facilities may be furnished by a disqualified person to the foundation, except that he may do so at no cost if what he furnishes is used for exempt purposes, or if certain pre-established business relationships are involved.[86]

These prohibitions may be of importance to a CDC in several ways. Perhaps the most obvious is business dealings between the CDC and other corporations (or individuals). In some cases, one or a number of corporations may assist a particular business operation of a CDC by providing equity capital, loan funds, technical and business advice, or guaranteed markets for the products of the operation. If a corporation has contributed an amount sufficient to render it a substantial contributor, it would arguably be foreclosed from any further dealings with the CDC, except by gift. Thus, contracts for any goods or services might be barred under the prohibition upon the furnishing of these by or to a private foundation.[87]

---

[84] INT. REV. CODE OF 1954 § 4941(d); Proposed Treas. Reg. § 53.4941(d)-1, 36 Fed. Reg. 10970-71 (1971). The exceptions are stated in § 4941(d)(2)(D) and (E), and in recently proposed Regulations. Proposed Treas. Reg. § 53.4941(d)-3(b) and (c), 36 Fed. Reg. 10973 (1971).

[85] INT. REV. CODE OF 1954 § 4941(d)(1)(B) and (2)(B); Proposed Treas. Reg. § 53.4941(d)-2(c), 36 Fed. Reg. 10971 (1971). The Regulations appear to omit the requirement that the loan proceeds be used for exempt purposes.

No loan, regardless of its terms, is permitted from the foundation to the disqualified person. INT. REV. CODE OF 1954 § 4941(d)(1)(B).

[86] INT. REV. CODE OF 1954 § 4941(d)(1)(C) and (2)(C); Proposed Treas. Reg. § 53.4941(d)-1(b) and 2(d)(3), 36 Fed. Reg. 10970, 10972 (1971).

[87] There is one possible exception to this statement. Since a foundation is permitted to furnish goods or services to a disqualified person on the same basis as it does to the "general public" the CDC might argue that its furnishing of goods or services to the disqualified corporation is permissible by defining general public as the class of buyers for the goods or services. The definition of general public in the proposed Regulations is basically conclusory, and thus not of much assistance: "the term 'general public' shall include those persons who, because of the particular nature of the activities of the private foundation, would be reasonably expected to utilize such goods, services, or facilities." Proposed Treas. Reg. § 53.4941 (d)-3(b)(2), 36 Fed. Reg. 10973 (1971). Although this definition certainly leaves room for a general public which is a narrow class of people or organizations, the two textual examples provided as illustrations suggest a broader interpretation. Id.

A second difficulty confronting a CDC in attempting to use the general public exception is that the proposed Regulations require that the goods or services be "functionally related," as that term is defined in section 4942(j)(5). In order to satisfy this requirement, the CDC would have to demonstrate that the goods or services furnished were "related" to its exempt purposes. Unfortunately the concept of "relatedness" set forth in section 4942(j)(5) and found elsewhere in other sections of the Code (particularly those dealing with "related" and "unrelated" business income) have not been dovetailed as yet

The tax on self-dealing would seemingly also operate in the situation in which the corporation provides goods, equipment, land, money, or services to the CDC, not as a gift, but on terms more favorable than those offered to others. Examples include a sale of land to the CDC at less than its original cost or a sale of equipment at a price equal to its adjusted basis. Both seem precluded by the taxation of any "sale . . . of property between a private foundation and a disqualified person."[88] Similar problems might arise if a foundation had made a grant to a CDC and later considered making a loan or providing technical assistance at a reduced cost.[89]

Although it appears that in some instances the corporation or foundation could not deal with the CDC directly, it must be asked whether a transaction with an organization related to the CDC would be permitted. For example, a foundation which had made a grant to the CDC (which caused it to become a substantial contributor) might subsequently enter into a loan agreement with a subsidiary of the CDC. It is unlikely that this would be permitted, as self-dealing is defined to preclude the specified activities whether they are "direct or indirect."

It is of no consequence that an action is undertaken to further exempt purposes. The exceptions to the prohibitions against making loans and furnishing goods, services, or facilities are based both on their being provided cost-free *and* on their being used for exempt purposes. Thus, a loan at a lower-than-market rate of interest, even for exempt purposes, would fail to meet the former standard. In addition, no exception at all is provided for exchanges of property.

The consequence is that a CDC must be constantly aware of the possibility that a benefactor will become a substantial contributor and that the CDC may thus be unable to deal with it, even in transactions which seemingly complement those objectives which led to the initial contribution. It cannot be said that Congress was unaware of problems such as these. The Senate Report notes:

> It has been suggested that many of those with whom a foundation [the CDC] "naturally" deals are, or may be disqualified persons. However, the difficulties that prompted this legislation in many cases arise because foundations "naturally" deal with their donors' businesses.
>
> If a substantial donor owns an office building, the foundation should look elsewhere for its office space.[90]

---

with the program-related investments exceptions of sections 4943 and 4944. It is thus presently uncertain whether a CDC may demonstrate an investment to be "functionally related" merely by showing that it is program-related, or whether additional, or even completely separate, considerations are involved.

[88] INT. REV. CODE OF 1954 § 4945(d)(1)(A).

[89] The Regulations do provide an exception to the prohibitions on self-dealing for certain business transactions, which may in a few instances alleviate the rigor of the self-dealing provisions on CDC's. The exception's standards are fairly stringent, however, requiring that the business relationship exist before the transaction takes place, that the terms of the transaction be as favorable to the CDC as those secured in arm's-length negotiations, and that "severe economic hardship" would be caused the CDC if it were forced to engage in the transaction with another party. Proposed Treas. Reg. § 53.4941(d)-1(b)(1), 36 Fed. Reg. 10970 (1971).

[90] SENATE REPORT 30.

The possibility that a CDC might be unable to obtain assistance which would have been provided but for the taxes on self-dealing demonstrates that a CDC should not be considered a private foundation in the first place. The evils against which Congress was directing these provisions were those arising from situations involving a much closer relationship between the donor and the private foundation, as where the donor, in fact, was able to control or manipulate the foundation to his advantage.[91] This is not the case with the typical CDC. It seems, rather, that the CDC is unintentionally being caught up in the consequences of a literal reading of provisions enacted for other, albeit laudable, aims.

C. The Taxes on Investments which Jeopardize Charitable Purpose

It is virtually certain that the usual activities of CDC's will not be subject to taxation under section 4944 which proscribes "investments which jeopardize charitable purpose." Although the statutory language itself does not define the content of such investments, the Senate Report suggests that the section is intended to affect high-risk, high-yield investments which reveal that the private foundation is engaged in highly speculative financial dealings. For example, the Report disapproves the past practices of some foundations of investing their assets in "warrants, commodity futures, and options, or . . . purchases on margin of [investments which] otherwise risk the corpus of the foundation."[92] Section 4944 thus appears designed to prevent such investments, which are clearly unrelated to the exempt purposes of the foundation.[93]

It is true that investments of the type typically made by a CDC involve extreme risks. The Senate appears to have anticipated the contention that they would be taxed under section 4944, for it excluded "program-related investments" from the section's proscriptions.[94] The Senate Report offers three examples of such investments: low-interest or interest-free loans to needy students, high-risk investments in low-income housing, and loans to small businesses where commercial sources of funds are unavailable.[95] It is apparent that the factor of high risk, while perhaps necessary to trigger the application of section 4944, is itself not sufficient. A finding is also necessary that the investment is unrelated to the exempt purposes of the CDC.

---

[91] Goray, *Private Foundations under the Tax Reform Act of 1969*, 16 Wayne L. Rev. 1277, 1277-81 (1970).

[92] Senate Report 45.

[93] Prior to the Act *income* of a foundation could not be invested if the purpose of the foundation would consequently be jeopardized. Int. Rev. Code of 1954 § 504(a)(3). Section 4944 extends this prohibition to both assets and income. *See* Int. Rev. Code of 1954 § 4944(a)(1) ("If a private foundation invests *any amount* . . . .") (emphasis supplied).

[94] Int. Rev. Code of 1954 § 4944(c). "Program-related investments" are discussed at length in the text accompanying notes 62-75 *supra*.

[95] Senate Report 46. The Senate examples have been adopted and expanded upon in recently proposed Regulations. Proposed Treas. Reg. § 53.4944-3, 36 Fed. Reg. 12027 (1971).

D. The Taxes on Taxable Expenditures

Section 4945 taxes a miscellany of activities, termed "taxable expenditures," which Congress viewed as outside the scope of a private foundation's proper purposes.[96] Most of the proscribed activities would not normally be carried on by a CDC, but a few might be, and the "expenditure responsibility" provisions of the section will prove important if the CDC is receiving funds from another private foundation.

Taxable expenditures are defined as amounts spent on any of the following activities: (1) lobbying and attempting to influence public opinion for the purpose of affecting legislation; (2) attempting to influence the outcome of any specific public election or to carry on voter registration drives unless the organization is a section 501(c)(3) organization specifically formed to carry out voter registration activities; (3) making individual travel and study grants unless such grants are awarded on an approved objective and on a nondiscriminatory basis; and (4) making grants to any organization (except section 501(c)(3) organizations which are not private foundations) unless the grantor private foundation insures that the grant is spent solely for the purpose for which it is made, obtains complete reports from the grantee, and makes detailed reports to the Service (the "expenditure responsibility" provisions). There is, in addition, a general catch-all which taxes all expenditures "for any purpose other than [an exempt] one."[97]

The first three categories reflect congressional concern with activities which should rarely be a part of the operations of a CDC, and need only be briefly discussed. The first two categories discourage those activities which are of a partisan political nature, such as grass roots lobbying, supporting particular candidates for public office, and contacting members of a legislature in an attempt to affect particular legislation. Excepted is nonpartisan analysis, study, or research, and the furnishing of technical information requested in writing by legislators.[98]

The prohibitions on some types of grants to individuals should seldom trouble a CDC.[99] These restrictions do not extend to contracts for services, the arrangement

---

[96] The initial taxes on taxable expenditures are 10% and 2½% for the foundation and the foundation managers respectively. INT. REV. CODE OF 1954 § 4945(a). The additional taxes are 100% and 50%. INT. REV. CODE OF 1954 § 4945(b). The Service has recently issued proposed Regulations for this section. Proposed Treas. Reg. § 53.4945, 36 Fed. Reg. 5357 (1971).

[97] Taxable expenditures are defined in broad terms in § 4945(d), and then treated further in § 4945(e)-(h). The impact of the catch-all provision is difficult to gauge. It could be used by the Service to deter attempted circumventions of the other provisions, especially grants to individuals. Both committee reports mention the provision only in passing; its importance will await the Service's decision on its utility. The proposed Regulations specifically exclude unreasonable administrative expenses. Proposed Treas. Reg. § 53.4945-6, 36 Fed. Reg. 5367 (1971).

[98] SENATE REPORT 48-49. Proposed Treas. Reg. § 53.4945-2(d), 36 Fed. Reg. 5360-61 (1971).

[99] In the recently issued proposed Regulations, however, "grant" is surprisingly defined to include loans and program-related investments. Proposed Treas. Reg. § 53.4945-4(a)(2), 36 Fed. Reg. 5362 (1971). Since there is no mention in either committee report of such an unusual definition, it is difficult to understand the Service's reasoning in adopting it. A CDC must be aware that its investment program may have to meet the criteria established in the Regulations, at least so far as its investments or loans are extended to individuals rather than to legal entities such as corporations or partnerships.

which would usually be found in a CDC's operations.[100] Problems of self-dealing rather than individual grants seem more likely to trouble a typical CDC in this respect. The provisions of section 4945 are not intended to limit those on self-dealing.[101] A grant to an individual who was a disqualified person within the meaning of the self-dealing provisions would probably be precluded as "a transfer to ... a disqualified person of the income or assets of a foundation ...."[102] In any event, should a CDC institute any sort of scholarship or award program, it must be certain that proper objective standards are established and maintained.

The portion of section 4945 most likely to affect CDC's is the fourth category, the "expenditure responsibility" provisions intended to ensure that grants are made and expended for exempt purposes. These provisions apply, however, only where both the grantor and the grantee are not public charities. In the case of a typical CDC, these provisions will be of most importance where the CDC as a private foundation is seeking funds from another private foundation. The grantor foundation will thus have to assume the burden of "expenditure responsibility" if it wishes to make the grant to the CDC. Since the effect of the provisions is thus indirect in the sense that the principal burden is on an organization other than the CDC, it is discussed below with those other provisions similarly affecting CDC operations indirectly.

E. The Excise Tax Based on Investment Income

Every private foundation is subject to a four per cent tax on its net investment income.[103] In contrast with the other excise taxes potentially applicable to a private foundation's operations, this tax is designed as a source of revenue in order to cover the increased costs which the Service will incur in administering the private foundation provisions.[104] Net investment income consists of net capital gain and gross investment income less the expenses incurred in obtaining the latter. The net capital gain is determined by taking the net gain from sale or distribution of property used to generate gross investment income, plus the gain from the sale or disposition of property the use of which results in unrelated business income under section 511, less any net capital gain used in computing the tax under that section.

Gross investment income is defined as income from interest, dividends, rents, and royalties, excluding any such income which has already been used in computing the unrelated business income tax under section 511. Before passage of the Act, investment

---

[100] SENATE REPORT 50; H.R. REP. No. 91-413, 91st Cong., 1st Sess. 35 (1969). That a foundation might attempt to label a questionable grant a "contract for services" was recognized in the House Report, but the problem of distinguishing the two was minimized as no more difficult of solution than questions of excessive compensation. *Id.*

[101] SENATE REPORT 50, n.19. Proposed Treas. Reg. § 53.4945-4(a)(1), 36 Fed. Reg. 5362 (1971).

[102] INT. REV. CODE OF 1954 § 4941(d)(1)(E). This interpretation is suggested by the negative implication of the special exception in § 4941 allowing government officials (who are one type of disqualified person) to receive prizes, awards, and scholarships if made on an objective basis. INT. REV. CODE OF 1954 § 4941(d)(2)(G)(i) and (ii). *See* SENATE REPORT 32.

[103] INT. REV. CODE OF 1954 § 4940; Proposed Treas. Reg. § 53.4940, 36 Fed. Reg. 5355 (1971).

[104] SENATE REPORT 27.

income was not included in unrelated business income. The Act, however, in addition to enacting section 4940, expanded the definition of the unrelated business income to include a certain proportion of income from interest, annuities, royalties, and rents (but not dividends) if that income is derived from a "controlled" organization.[105] The language of section 4940, in excluding investment income already included under section 511, appears intended to avoid the occurrence of double taxation.

A practical consequence of the investment income tax is that tax treatment of dividends may become less favorable to nonprofit corporations. Dividends received by exempt organizations are excluded from unrelated business income. Although still excluded as such, they are now subject to the four per cent investment income tax. For-profit corporations, in contrast, may exclude eighty-five per cent of dividends received.[106] The effective result is that for-profit corporations are subject to at least a 3.3 per cent and at most a 7.5 per cent tax on dividends.[107]

III

Taxes Indirectly Affecting CDC's

Those penalty taxes already discussed may affect a CDC's operations directly. The effect of some of the other taxes, in contrast, will be felt indirectly, if at all, because they may discourage *other* private foundations from dealing with CDC's by imposing taxes on dealings between one private foundation and another. The impact of these taxes will be examined on the assumption that a private foundation is considering a grant to a CDC.[108] As the ensuing discussion will attempt to demonstrate, the effect of these taxes should be minimal. The possibility of their affecting CDC's in any substantial manner in the short run will be due to the cautious advice of the grantor private foundation's counsel, reflecting his uncertainty as to what the Service's position will ultimately be. Over the long run, it should become clear that the additional burden will be insignificant.

---

[105] Int. Rev. Code of 1954 § 512(b)(15). This amendment to the unrelated business income provisions may have important consequences to a CDC which controls its commercial operations through subsidiaries, as it will no longer be able to extract profits in the form of interest on loans. Prior to the Act it was desirable from a tax standpoint to capitalize the subsidiary as thinly as possible, since interest payments were deductible to the subsidiary, and not includable in the parent's income. Dividends, in comparison, enjoyed only the latter advantage. Section 512(b)(15) defines "control" by reference to § 368(c), which establishes, very roughly, a standard of 80% stock ownership. Section 512(b)(15) may thus encourage a CDC to divest its holdings in its subsidiaries below the 80% mark so that the subsidiaries may take advantage of deductions for interest on loans from the parent CDC to them.

[106] Int. Rev. Code of 1954 § 243(a)(1).

[107] The 7½% figure is based on the maximum corporate tax rate of approximately 50%. An 85% exclusion leaves 15% subject to tax, half of which is 7½%. The difference is even less, of course, where the corporate profits are not sufficiently large so as to be taxed at the maximum rate.

[108] It is possible, of course, that the CDC might be the grantor and another organization the grantee, in which case the CDC would be directly affected by the taxes to be discussed. Given the early stages of development of the business operations of most CDC's, however, the emphasis at this time seems better placed on the CDC as grantee.

A. The Taxes on Failure to Distribute Income

Before the Act an exempt organization which made an unreasonable accumulation of income faced possible loss of its exemption.[109] Problems were encountered both in attempting to gauge when unreasonable accumulations should be found to exist and in justifying a sanction as harsh as removal of the exemption. Section 4942 attempts to remove the subjective element previously inherent in a standard of unreasonable accumulation by requiring a private foundation to make qualified distributions of either its adjusted net income,[110] or an amount equal to a certain percentage (termed the "minimum investment return") of the foundation's "net" assets, whichever is greater.[111] The all-or-nothing approach militated by the sole sanction of removal of the exemption has also been replaced by taxes graduated in severity.[112] As a consequence of these changes, exempt organizations should cease to be a haven for tax deductions from their donors while never, or rarely, expending funds for exempt purposes.

The typical CDC itself will not likely be subject to the taxes imposed by this section, as it will undoubtedly be making qualified distributions in an amount easily in excess of the amounts which it must disburse in order to meet the section's

---

[109] INT. REV. CODE OF 1954 § 504(a)(1). Section 4942 (taxing failure to distribute income) is intended to replace the repealed section. SENATE REPORT, *supra* note 15, at 35, n.6.

[110] Adjusted net income under this section is similar to adjusted gross income as defined in section 62 except for certain added income and deduction modifications. INT. REV. CODE OF 1954 § 4942(f).

[111] Quite detailed proposed Regulations have recently been issued by the Service under Section 4942. Proposed Treas. Reg. § 53.4942(a), 36 Fed. Reg. 11034 (1971). Net asset value is determined by establishing the fair market value of the foundation's assets *not* used for exempt purposes less certain kinds of debt (termed acquisition indebtedness) to which the assets are subject. INT. REV. CODE OF 1954 § 4942(e)(1)(A); Proposed Treas. Reg. § 53.4942(c)-2(c), 36 Fed. Reg. 11037-38 (1971). The minimum investment return percentage applicable to organizations organized on or after May 27, 1969 is 6%. Those organized before that date are subject to lesser, but increasing, minimum investment return percentages through 1974 in order to allow them sufficient time to alter their present investment policies. INT. REV. CODE OF 1954 § 4942(e)(3) and (4); Tax Reform Act of 1969 § 101(l)(3)(A), 83 Stat. 534; Proposed Treas. Reg. § 53.4942(a)-2(c)(3), 36 Fed. Reg. 11038 (1971).

The alternate requirements of the higher of adjusted gross income or the minimum investment return are designed to force a private foundation to distribute at least a certain minimum amount (the minimum investment return), and possibly more (all adjusted gross income), if its investment policies prove successful. Without congressional imposition of the floor of the minimum investment return, private foundations could have modified their investment policies so that no income was generated. The floor encourages a private foundation to attain a return on its investment at least equal to the minimum investment return, since it will otherwise be forced to deplete its corpus in order to make the distributions. To illustrate, assume that the foundation's net assets are found to be $100,000, and that the applicable minimum investment return is 6%. If in fiscal 1970 the foundation had an adjusted net income of $9,000, it would be required to distribute all of the $9,000 for qualified purposes. If its adjusted net income was only $4,000, then it would have to distribute that income for qualified purposes, and $2,000 in addition, since the minimum investment return at 6% of $100,000, would be $6,000. In order to obtain the $2,000, the foundation would presumably have to draw from its corpus, thus reducing its net assets to $98,000. See Proposed Treasury Regulations sections 53.4942(a)-1(a)(1) and 53.4942(a)-3(d) and (e), 36 Fed. Reg. 11035, 11042-43 (1971) for the timing, carry-forward, and carry-back provisions for undistributed amounts.

[112] The initial tax imposed under this section is equal to 15% of the undistributed income of the private foundation, with an additional tax equal to 100% of the amount remaining undistributed at the end of the correction period. INT. REV. CODE OF 1954 § 4942(a) and (b); Proposed Treas. Reg. § 53.4942(a)-1, 36 Fed. Reg. 11035-37 (1971).

requirements. Qualified distributions are defiend (1) as program-related investments, and (2) by reference to section 170(c)(2)(B) as those for "religious, charitable, scientific, literary, or educational purposes, or for the prevention of cruelty to animals . . . ." Qualified distributions may take a variety of forms other than a grant. Assets purchased for qualified purposes, for example, will be considered qualifying distributions.[113] Loans will almost certainly qualify as well, if made for proper purposes, on the condition that repayments of principal and interest be again considered distributable income.[114] Lastly, a private foundation may make a qualifying distribution by setting aside funds to be used for future exempt purposes if the foundation can satisfy the Service that the amounts will be used for a specific project and that the project will be better accomplished through the postponement of a present qualifying distribution.[115] Assuming that the typical CDC has been granted a section 501(c)(3) exemption initially to carry on activities such as making loans to appropriate businesses, guarantees of bank or other institutional financing, or equity investments in appropriate businesses or in its own concerns, there should be little doubt that it has made qualified distributions well in excess of the relatively small amounts required by section 4942.

The only likely instance when this section will have an impact on a typical CDC is the limited case where the CDC, as a private foundation, seeks funds from another private foundation which is attempting to qualify its grants as a proper distribution under section 4942. Assuming that the distribution is for qualified purposes,[116] then it can be made by the private foundation to any grantee without further concern under section 4942, unless the grantee is also a private foundation. In that case, unless the grantee is a special type of private foundation (termed an *operating foundation*), the grant must be either redistributed by or pass through the grantee within one year, and the grantor must obtain sufficient evidence that this

---

[113] INT. REV. CODE OF 1954 § 4942(g)(1)(B); Proposed Treas. Reg. § 53.4942(a)-3(a)(1)(ii), 36 Fed. Reg. 11040 (1971).

[114] *See* INT. REV. CODE OF 1954 § 4942(f)(2)(C)(i); Proposed Treas. Reg. § 53.4942(a)-2(d)(2)(iii), 36 Fed. Reg. 11038 (1971). The obscurity of the statutory language and the Regulations is illuminated by language in the Senate and Conference Reports, both of which state clearly that loans made by a private foundation should be treated as qualifying distributions at the time when they are made. SENATE REPORT 36; CONFERENCE REPORT 282. The same principle will apply in any case where an amount once treated as a qualifying distribution is later returned or made available to the foundation. SENATE REPORT 36, n.8.

[115] INT. REV. CODE OF 1954 § 4942(g)(2); Proposed Treas. Reg. § 53.4942(a)-3(b), 36 Fed. Reg. 11040-41 (1971). The statute expressly includes as part of a qualified distribution administrative expenses incurred in making it, except where assets are purchased and amounts set aside. *Compare* INT. REV. CODE OF 1954 § 4942(g)(1)(A) *with Id.* § 4942(g)(1)(B) and (2). This distinction appears to be maintained in the proposed Regulations. *Compare* Proposed Treas. Reg. § 53.4942(a)-3(a)(i) *with Id.* § 53.4942(a)-3(a)(ii) and (iii), 36 Fed. Reg. 11040 (1971).

[116] Regardless of the status of the grantee (whether individual, exempt organization, for-profit corporation, etc.), the distribution must be a qualified one, that is, one which is a program-related investment, or one made for section 170(c)(2)(B) purposes. The language of that section is virtually identical to the language of section 501(c)(3). *See* text accompanying note 113 *supra*. Neither the statute nor the regulations further explains these distributions, with the apparent result that a private foundation will be confronted with the difficult task of determining whether each grant (or other distribution) made by it satisfies the generally-phrased standards of section 4942 and its Regulations.

in fact has occurred. The practical consequence for a CDC which is a private foundation is that a donor private foundation may be hesitant to make a grant to it because by doing so the donor may feel that it will be increasing its own difficulties under section 4942. The following discussion attempts to determine whether the typical CDC will be able to avail itself of the operating foundation exception.

Private foundations which are also operating foundations are accorded more favorable treatment than other private foundations, despite their lack of public financial support, because in various ways their assets and income are directly devoted to their exempt purposes rather than to grant-making.[117] Examples offered by the Senate Report include museums, libraries, and research organizations.[118] In order to qualify as an operating foundation under section 4942, an organization must make qualifying distributions which are equal to substantially all (eighty-five per cent) of its adjusted net income and which are to be used directly for the exempt purposes of the organization (the income test).[119] In addition, the organization must meet one of the following three criteria: (a) substantially more than half of its assets (sixty-five per cent) must be devoted directly to the activities for which it was organized or to "functionally related" businesses, or both, or be stock in a comparable controlled corporation (the assets test); or (b) it must make qualifying distributions in an amount not less than two-thirds of the "minimum investment return" to be used directly for the exempt purposes for which it was formed (the endowment test); or (c) substantially all (eighty-five per cent) of its support, excluding investment income, must come from the general public and five or more unrelated exempt organizations with no one organization contributing more than twenty-five per cent of the support (the support test). In other words the would-be operating foundation must meet both the income test and either the assets, endowment, or support test. In attempting to meet any of the tests other than the support test, the principal task is to demonstrate that funds are distributed or assets are held *directly* for activities which further the exempt purpose of the aspiring operating foundation.[120]

Recently proposed Regulations set forth the manner in which each of the four tests may be met. To satisfy the income test, the organization must demonstrate

---

[117] SENATE REPORT 60. The definition of an operating foundation is set forth in INT. REV. CODE OF 1954 § 4942(j)(3).

[118] SENATE REPORT 61.

[119] INT. REV. CODE OF 1954 § 4942(j)(3)(A). *Substantially all* was set at a minimum of 85% in the committee reports, SENATE REPORT 60; H.R. REP. No. 91-413, *supra* note 100, at 42, and the same figure was adopted in the proposed Regulations recently issued by the Service. Proposed Treas. Reg. § 53.4942(b)-2(e), 36 Fed. Reg. 107 (1971). The percentages in the other tests discussed in the text below were similarly incorporated by the Service from the Senate Report.

[120] If an organization could become an operating foundation by meeting, directly *or* indirectly, the income test and any one of the other three tests, then it would be easier to achieve that status than to meet the requirements of § 4942. Absent the requirement of directness, to become an operating foundation an organization would only have to distribute substantially all (85%) of its income (the income test) and not less than two-thirds of its minimum investment return (the assets test). But section 4942 requires an organization to distribute *all* of its income, or a sum equal to 100% of its minimum investment return, whichever is higher.

that it is making qualifying distributions "directly for the active conduct of the activities constituting the purpose or function for which it is organized and operated [in an amount] equal to substantially all [eighty-five per cent] of its adjusted net income."[121] Qualifying distributions are elsewhere defined in section 4942 as program-related investments and as those made to accomplish, among others, charitable, scientific, literary, or educational purposes.[122] A distribution will be considered to have been made directly if the organization uses the distribution itself or if it makes a distribution to individuals or other organizations and continues to maintain a "significant involvement" in the recipient.[123]

It has already been noted that the typical CDC will usually distribute, directly or indirectly, all of its adjusted gross income. There is even less likelihood, of course, that the CDC will not distribute the smaller percentage (eighty-five per cent) of its adjusted gross income required by the income test. Rather, the question will be whether it distributes that percentage "directly." If the CDC is putting enough money into businesses which it is operating itself, then it will meet the requirement of "directness." In some instances, however, a CDC may avoid generating businesses within its own corporate shell by choosing instead to utilize subsidiaries or other organizations.[124] In such cases the "significant involvement" test will have to be met. In most instances a CDC should be able to meet the criteria for significant involvement set forth in the Regulations; it will have (1) developed expertise, (2) maintained a staff which offers support for the uses to which the distributions are put, and (3) encouraged others to become involved in the organization's area of interest. The numerous examples set forth in the Regulations suggest that an organization will be deemed significantly involved if it performs functions other than that of merely screening distributions.

A CDC which can satisfy the income test will likely be able to meet the endowment test as well, since the same considerations are involved. An exception is that the CDC must expend an amount equal to two-thirds of its minimum investment return, rather than substantially all of its adjusted net income.[125] In the rare instance where this proves not to be the case,[126] the CDC might be able to meet the assets test, which requires that at least sixty per cent of the CDC's assets

---

[121] Proposed Treas. Reg. § 53.4942(b)-2(a), 36 Fed. Reg. 107 (1971).
[122] INT. REV. CODE OF 1954 § 4942(g). The definition of a qualifying distribution for an operating foundation, however, is slightly more restrictive in that the twelve month "pass-through" device cannot be used by operating foundations to make a qualifying distribution. See INT. REV. CODE OF 1954 § 4942 (j)(3)(A) and (B)(ii). "Pass-throughs" are discussed in text accompanying notes 128-31 *infra*.
[123] Proposed Treas. Reg. § 53.4942(b)-2(b) and (c), 35 Fed. Reg. 107-08 (1971).
[124] It might be possible for a CDC to argue that funds distributed to controlled subsidiaries were in effect used by it. The proposed Regulations, however, do not discuss this possibility. See Proposed Treas. Reg. § 53.4942(b)-2(b)(1)(i), 36 Fed. Reg. 107 (1971).
[125] Proposed Treas. Reg. § 53.4942(b)-4, 36 Fed. Reg. 110-11 (1971).
[126] This would be so only where the adjusted net income of the CDC was extremely small, since two-thirds of the minimum investment return (assuming the return is at 6%) is only 4%, and that percentage is calculated only on those *net* assets not directly used for exempt purposes. INT. REV. CODE OF 1954 § 4942(e).

are being used by it or its controlled subsidiaries for exempt purposes. The only test which should create difficulty for the average CDC is the support test, which requires that at least five organizations and the general public support the CDC, with no one organization accounting for more than twenty-five per cent of all support. It is not enough, of course, for the organization to believe that it is an operating foundation; other organizations will demand evidence that the Service has made this determination. The Regulations recently proposed set forth four ways by which an organization may attempt to secure this determination from the Service.[127]

If a CDC were found to be a private foundation and not an operating foundation, what additional burdens would be placed on the CDC and a grantor private foundation in making a qualifying distribution to the CDC? The CDC would itself have to redistribute or "pass through" the grant for qualified purposes in the taxable year after receiving it. In addition, it could not redistribute the income to another private foundation. The grantor private foundation would be required to verify that the CDC had in fact done so through "adequate records or other sufficient evidence."[128]

The principal disadvantage to a CDC in obtaining a grant would simply be that it would have to redistribute it; the option to utilize the funds directly for its own activities would be foreclosed. Other than utilizing the funds itself or in any operations controlled by it,[129] however, the CDC would be free to dispose of the funds—for qualified purposes and not to another private foundation—as it liked. From the grantor's viewpoint it may even be an advantage for it to make a grant to another private foundation, since it allows the grantor to make the grant without ascertaining that it is for qualified purposes until the donee redistributes it. The grantor consequently will have a twelve-month grace period during which it can decide on a proper qualified purpose.[130] Noting that this twelve-month "pass-through" provision was a "significant exception" to the purposes of section 4942, the Senate Report explained, somewhat unconvincingly, that it "believed that this was necessary to provide adequate flexibility in operations for private foundations."[131]

B. The Expenditure Responsibility Provisions

The "expenditure responsibility" provisions may also indirectly affect CDC's because of their impact on the policies and procedures of grantor private founda-

---

[127] Proposed Treas. Reg. § 53.4942(b)-6, 36 Fed. Reg. 111 (1971).

[128] If notions of adequacy of record-keeping found elsewhere in the Act can be taken as guideposts, a grantor private foundation should easily be able to satisfy its responsibilities. INT. REV. CODE OF 1954 § 4942(g)(3)(B). See text accompanying notes 132-33 *infra*, and particularly the language from the Senate Report quoted there.

[129] Although the term "controlled" is used in section 4942, it is not defined. If the definition of section 368(c) is applicable, then the standard of control would be 80% of all classes of voting stock.

[130] The grantor would have to ensure, of course, that it conditioned the grant so that it could reserve some power over the "pass-through." The most inoffensive manner of doing so would probably be a "sign-off" or veto power. The power to direct the grant in the absence of a veto would give the grantee a reason to serve as the pass-through when it could not use the grant itself.

[131] SENATE REPORT 37.

tions. The provisions, designed to ensure that grants are expended for exempt purposes, should create few problems, however, because their requirements are set forth with considerable clarity in both the Senate Report and the recently issued proposed Regulations.[132]

Where both the grantor and the grantee are private foundations, section 4945(h) requires that the grantor must "exert all *reasonable* efforts and . . . establish *adequate* procedures (1) to see that the grant is spent solely for the purpose for which made, (2) to obtain full and complete reports from the grantee on how the funds are spent, and (3) to make full and detailed reports with respect to such expenditures to the Secretary or his delegate." The emphasized language implies, and the Senate Report and the proposed Regulations confirm, that no absolute liability is to be imposed on the grantor, but rather that a "prudent man" standard is to be employed. The contents of this standard are set forth at length in the Senate Report:

> It is contemplated that a [private] foundation will be required to specify the purposes of any grant clearly in the terms of the grant itself. The terms of the grant should, also, state plainly the limitations upon the recipient's use of the grant. After the grant is made, the granting foundation must take reasonable steps (a) to secure reports from the grantee on its use of the funds, and (b) to report to the Internal Revenue Service the amount and purposes of the grant, the identity of the grantee and the data which the grantor obtains on the grantee's use of the funds. The Internal Revenue Service is expected to provide an appropriate schedule or attachment for the annual information return, so that all reports which a grant-making foundation must make to the Internal Revenue Service for 1 year can be consolidated in the foundation's information return for that year. If the grantor discovers a misapplication of the funds by the grantee, it would normally be required to withhold any further payments to the grantee (to the extent that it is legally able to do so) until the misapplication has been corrected, or adequate assurance provided that it will not occur again. Where a grantor foundation adheres to these rules, and a misuse occurs which it has no reasonable means of correcting, it will be deemed to have discharged all responsibilities under this section by reporting the default to the Internal Revenue Service.[133]

"Expenditure responsibility," in sum, should entail no more work than that formerly assumed voluntarily by some foundations.

Summary

The impact of the private foundation provisions of the Tax Reform Act on community development corporations may be summarized as follows. If one-third or more of a CDC's financial support comes from public sources (the government, the general public, or other public charities), it will be considered a public charity under

---

[132] INT. REV. CODE OF 1954 § 4945(d)(4) and (h). *See also* SENATE REPORT 50-51; Proposed Treas. Reg. § 53.4945-5, 36 Fed. Reg. 5365 (1971).

[133] SENATE REPORT 51. This language has been followed and elaborated in the proposed Regulations and confirms that a grantor acting in the prescribed manner will be able to avoid taxation. Proposed Treas. Reg. § 53.4945-5, 36 Fed. Reg. 5365 (1971).

either of two public financial support tests. Even without such public financial support, a CDC responsive to a genuinely broad-based membership should also be considered a public charity under the facts and circumstances test. Under proposed Regulations, this test requires only that ten per cent of a CDC's support be public support if the CDC's public nature can be otherwise demonstrated. Lastly, under both the facts and circumstances test and one of the public financial support tests, provision is made for the exclusion of unusual grants. By making use of this exclusion, a CDC may be able to reduce substantially the amount of private contributions includable in total support, and thus increase the possibility that the amount of its public support will equal or exceed the percentages required to meet either of the two tests.

If a CDC is considered a private foundation, it will have to guard against the imposition of taxes on self-dealing, and may confront problems in attempting to maintain sizeable business holdings. Most holdings, however, should come within the exceptions to the section setting forth the taxes on excess holdings for program-related investments. In light of the proposed Regulations recently issued by the Service, this exception should cover the investments of CDC's which are not purely commercial.

Other provisions may also offer some difficulties, though hopefully they will be little more than nuisances. The CDC will be forced to avoid certain activities which might be classified as taxable expenditures. As a potential grantee, it may also indirectly feel the impact of the provisions taxing the failure to distribute income and to exercise expenditure responsibility. In the long run, these should only be significant where the grantor-private foundation is overly cautious in establishing its own operating policies. The CDC will also probably find its paperwork increased by the Act's expansion of the reporting requirements imposed both on all exempt organizations and on private foundations.

If a CDC does not yet have an exemption, it should carefully consider the potential adverse impact of the private foundation provisions before submitting its exemption application. A CDC already possessing the exemption, in contrast, has little choice but to live with the provisions, if it is in fact a private foundation, since the methods of terminating private foundation status are of little practical value to it.[134]

---

[134] The Tax Reform Act of 1969 permits a private foundation to terminate its private foundation status by either of two basic methods. It may transfer its assets to a public charity, or it may begin and continue to operate as a public charity itself. These methods have since been spelled out by the Service in recently issued temporary Regulations. T.D. 7063, 1970 INT. REV. BULL. No. 44, at 8, *as amended by* T.D. 7085, 1971 INT. REV. BULL. No. 5, at 14. The possibility of terminating by either method will probably be of little practical importance to a CDC. By pursuing the first method (transferring its assets to a public charity), the CDC, of course, would be putting itself out of business. Since the CDC can probably live with private foundation status, it is obviously much worse off in terminating its status in this way especially if there was a substantial likelihood, in the opinion of the CDC prior to its attempt to obtain a section 501(c)(3) exemption, that it would be designated a private foundation. Were the CDC to wish to terminate such private foundation status, the initial decision should therefore be not to seek such exemption but to remain a nonprofit corporation. The second method available to

the CDC to end private foundation status would be to begin operating as a public charity. In doing so, however, it would find itself confronting roughly the same problems obtaining designation as a public charity as would a recently formed CDC which had just applied for an exemption and was seeking to avoid private foundation status. A CDC that finds itself a private foundation is likely to have recently obtained that status, so attempting to terminate it would in effect be an attempt to reopen a determination just made, and the result is likely to be the same.

POLITICS AND BUREAUCRACY IN COMMUNITY-CONTROLLED ECONOMIC DEVELOPMENT

GEOFFREY FAUX*

INTRODUCTION

A white businessman recently concluded a speech at a conference on ghetto development with the words, "Stay away from the government." He then described his experience in trying to start a minority-owned business with financing from the Small Business Administration. It was a story of delay, incompetence, and bureaucratic interference. The result was not a new business, but an increase in frustration and bitterness on the part of everyone concerned. At the end of the presentation, a black man rose from the audience and said that he had gone through similar experiences. "But," he asked, "where else do you get the money?" He then described his own efforts to get *private* financing for a ghetto business. There was not nearly the same red tape and infuriating bureaucracy as in the public sector, but in the end the answer was "No." The risks were simply too large and the private companies and banks would not ask their stockholders to invest in an enterprise whose major pay-off would be in social benefits.

The dialogue reflects a basic dilemma for those who have been struggling with community-controlled economic development programs. Government support is essential, but the bureaucracy that accompanies such support often dooms a program to failure.

There are three essential ingredients to effective economic development in poverty areas:

1. Social investment, which requires government—usually federal—resources;
2. Community control, which requires local organization;
3. Business organization, which requires freedom from bureaucratic constraints.

The ghettos, barrios, and poverty-stricken rural areas of this country are not attractive places in which to invest. Their labor forces are not competitive and the management talent is thin. In urban ghettos, physical safety is threatened and the population is likely to be black or Mexican-American, which is itself a major disincentive for outside investment. Effective economic development of these areas therefore requires that someone cover the costs of developing the labor force and management, of providing for the organization of community support and ownership, and for making long-term investments to improve the economy of the impoverished area. Only when these largely social investments make the area and its institutions attrac-

---

*(Mr. Faux is the former Director of the Economic Development Division of the United States Office of Economic Opportunity. He is now a Fellow of the Institute for Politics, John F. Kennedy School of Government, Harvard University.—Ed.)

tive places in which to invest, will private sector funds flow. Since these investments are recoverable in the form of benefits to society as a whole (higher tax revenues, lower welfare costs, and so on), society as a whole should pay for them.

Public investment alone, however, is not a sufficient condition for the economic development of poverty areas. The experience of the last decade with urban renewal, anti-poverty, manpower training, Model Cities, and similar programs is ample evidence that the direction in which the benefits of any government program flows is in part a function of who controls the program. Thus far, the major domestic programs have been put in the hands of local politicians and social scientists. If the social investment necessary to stimulate poverty area economies is to be effective in helping the poor residents, the poor residents must control it. Only they have the incentive to assure that benefits flow in their direction. To be of lasting value for the poor, economic development must be self-development.

To public investment and community control must be added a third item: the set of techniques and organizational forms that have proven effective in producing economic development in the private sector of the economy. One condition for organizational effectiveness is freedom from entangling bureaucratic red tape and interference. The great advantage private businesses have over government institutions is that they have the freedom to act decisively in their own interests. Economic development requires that the developer be able to take immediate advantage of sudden opportunities that cannot wait for approval through layers of bureaucracy. A piece of land becomes available and has to be purchased now or it is lost. A chance to invest in a good business having cash flow problems appears and disappears often in the space of days. A talented potential manager must be offered a job when he becomes available or he will go somewhere else.

I

FREEDOM VS. ACCOUNTABILITY IN ANTI-POVERTY PROGRAMS

To some extent, there is a natural tension between public investment and business organization. It is the proper concern of any financier, public or private, that funds are used as intended, and it is the proper concern of a business development organization that it have as much freedom as possible.

Where financing is done from the public sector, the tension is made greater by the natural tendencies of bureaucracies toward caution and delay. These tendencies are not due so much to the type of individual who becomes a bureaucrat as they are results of the incentive system in most government organizations; the rewards for accomplishment are much less than the penalties for failure. Furthermore, failure often is not identified in any objective way. For the bureaucrat, avoiding political embarrassment rather than accomplishing program goals is the first priority.

In order to protect himself from being held responsible for such embarrassment, the bureaucrat and the bureaucratic organization spread the risk through systems of coordination and multiple review of decisions. Where everyone is responsible for a decision, no one is responsible for it. Thus, the recipient of government aid has to contend with not just one set of bureaucratic forces, but as many as are needed by the bureaucracy to spread the risk. The familiar result is delay, obstruction, and interference in the internal workings of the program, all of which are accurately recorded by the businessman mentioned above who feels that dealing with the government is too difficult.

The power to delay and to obstruct is directly related to the power of the program's beneficiaries, or constituency. Thus the private contractors that deal with the Defense Department, the large farmers that deal with the Agriculture Department, the banks that deal with the Federal Reserve Board, and the airlines that deal with the Federal Aviation Agency or the Civil Aeronautics Board experience a level of bureaucratic frustration that is minimal compared with that experienced by poor people who deal with the local welfare department, or the community organizations that deal with the Office of Economic Opportunity (OEO) or the Model Cities program.

The power of the constituencies of the former set of agencies is not necessarily coercive. It may be primarily permissive in that it permits the individual bureaucrat wider latitude in serving the needs of the constituency. People who form the permanent labor force of a government agency generally identify with its constituency. As the constituency becomes more important, as the public treasury provides more resources to support it, the promotions and rewards come to the bureaucracy through which the support flows. The function of an organized constituency, therefore, is to protect its own interests by protecting the bureaucracy that is fighting for its interests and by seeing to it that the bureacracy continues to do so. Where the constituency does not play this role, the bureaucracy will try to protect itself, sometimes at the expense of its own constituency.

The history of the war on poverty reveals a weak constituency that could neither protect its bureaucracy nor prevent its bureaucracy from exercising the self-protective devices of delay and interference. In 1967, the power of the constituency to defend itself against local governments was tested and found deficient with the passage of the Green Amendment to the Economic Opportunity Act which gave local governments the power to control the Community Action Program.[1] Soon after this defeat, there occurred a "tightening up" of OEO management procedures which meant a dramatic expansion in federal rules and regulations and a marked increase in the exercise of government power over recipients of anti-poverty money.

The crumbling of the anti-poverty constituency's power over the bureaucracy caused many people to look for new means of financing independent programs. One such means, the possibility of generating independent funds for anti-poverty programs, provided a partial reason for the attractiveness of community-based

[1] Economic Opportunity Act (1967 Green Amendment), 42 U.S.C. §§ 2790, 2791, 2795, 2796 (Supp. V, 1969).

economic development. Frustrated anti-poverty workers grasped at the notion that profits from economic development programs could generate funds for social programs. From the same frustrated sources the idea appeared that the private sector could finance such development with a little bit of prodding from the government. The idea was encouraged by both the Johnson and Nixon administrations whose budgets were being drained by the Viet Nam war.

The political failure of the anti-poverty constituency also led to the search for ways around the legislative process. Backdoor financing and a heavy dose of business philosophy were the twin features of the Community Self-Determination Act introduced into the Congress in 1968.[2] Although the bill had a number of legitimate defects, many liberals who opposed it completely lost the point that it was an attempt to continue financing anti-poverty efforts in an increasingly conservative environment.

Political weakness could not, however, be wished away. OEO-funded community economic development programs quickly became vulnerable to political pressures and the increasing dominance of the bureaucracy over the community organizations which it served. The earliest of these, Crawfordville Enterprises in Georgia, the Southwest Alabama Farmers Cooperative Association, and the Harlem Commonwealth Council were subject to political pressures and bureaucratic abuse. The first two, located in the South, where the political power of the minority anti-poverty interests was weakest, were particularly battered. Demands that the projects become self-sustaining in unreasonable periods of time, changes in directives from Washington, and visits by consultants and OEO staff members with conflicting authority and advice were added to the burdens which predictably affect black-controlled projects in hostile southern surroundings.

Another reaction to the weakness of the anti-poverty constituency was the placing of control of the Model Cities program in local governments. The resultant layering of bureaucracy has thus far prevented the Model Cities from making a meaningful impact upon poor neighborhoods despite the fact that the legislation has been in force since 1966. Of the more than one billion dollars appropriated to the Model Cities program, only about fifty percent had been committed and only about ten percent had been spent by June 30, 1970.[3] The inability or unwillingness of local city governments to spend Model Cities money despite the obvious need is another piece of evidence of how bureaucratic pipelines quickly clog when the constituency is too weak to demand that the flow of resources be maintained.

Although the anti-poverty constituency is too weak to take control of the Model Cities program, it is strong enough to press its claim. In city after city, conflict between city hall and neighborhood organizations over the issue of community con-

---

[2] S. 3875, 90th Cong., 2d Sess. (1968).

[3] As of July 31, 1970, the exact figures were: appropriations, $1.073 billion; obligations, $534 million; expenditures, $97 million. The source of this information is Mr. Harry Nolan, Division of Financial Management, Office of the Assistant Secretary for Model Cities, Department of Housing and Urban Development.

trol has stalled both planning and project implementation. In part, the Model Cities program is failing because the Department of Housing and Urban Development (HUD) refuses to recognize the reality of organization in urban neighborhoods. The 1960's saw a political awakening of minorities in ghettos and barrios all over the country; they will not be put back to sleep. By demanding that the mayor be responsible for programs even when he has agreed to turn programs over to the neighborhoods, HUD is creating unnecessary bureaucracy at city hall and unnecessary tension between that bureaucracy and the neighborhoods.

The community control issue has been particularly visible in the establishment of economic development programs, to which HUD has already committed over $30 million, more than half to support community development corporations (CDC) and their investments.

II

THE SPECIAL IMPACT PROGRAM

The Special Impact Program authorized by title I-D of the Economic Opportunity Act,[4] used for the most part to support community development corporations, illustrates the manner in which the absence of a strong constituency contributes to a distortion of program objectives and a hardening of the bureaucracy's demands for accountability at the expense of the CDC's freedom of operation. It also illustrates the degree of power which a constituency can develop when it is properly organized.

The Special Impact Program was written into the Economic Opportunity Act in 1966 in order to support a specific economic development project in the Bedford-Stuyvesant section of Brooklyn. The late Senator Robert F. Kennedy was the principal force behind the project. The Program was based upon the following assumptions:

—the war on poverty, particularly its major component, the Community Action Program, was insufficiently concerned with jobs and economic development;

—the conflicts and political influence which inevitably accompany a program run through city hall prevent accomplishment;

—the approach of the war on poverty was piecemeal while what was required was a comprehensive strategy.

—the business community must play a major role in solving poverty problems.

The last notion came from several sources. First, Kennedy saw, as Lyndon Johnson was to see shortly afterwards, that the Viet Nam war was draining away funds that had been promised for major domestic programs, and he postulated that the private sector might be persuaded to pick up the slack. Secondly, Kennedy saw that championing the role of business in the poverty program would moderate the hostility toward him among businessmen. Finally, the presence of influential businessmen in a ghetto development program would free the community organizations from

---

[4] Economic Opportunity Act, tit. I-D, 42 U.S.C. §§ 2763-68 (Supp. V, 1969).

dependence on the local politicians. Thus, the program embodied an alliance of businessmen and ghetto residents and specifically minimized the influence of the city and anti-poverty bureaucracies.

This alliance was reflected in the structure of the project that emerged from Kennedy's efforts. Two separate corporations were set up to run the Bedford-Stuyvesant program: the Restoration Corporation, composed of twenty-six leaders chosen from the community, and the Development and Services Corporation, composed of twelve white establishment figures. In addition to Kennedy and his fellow Senator Jacob Javits, the Development and Services board included Thomas Watson of IBM, Douglas Dillon, William Paley of CBS, George Moore of the First National City Bank, and Benno Schmidt of the J. A. Witney Company.

To finance the program, Kennedy and Javits introduced an amendment to title I of the Economic Opportunity Act which authorized Special Impact Programs for urban areas with high concentrations of low-income people. Projects were to be designed "to arrest tendencies toward dependency, chronic unemployment, and rising community tensions."[5] They were to be carried out in the poor neighborhoods themselves and they were to be of "sufficient size and scope to have an appreciable impact."[6]

The language of title I-D is imprecise. The details of the program had not been thought out, but they did not need to be. It was the intent of the program that decisions should be made at the local level and that the business-community alliance should be as free as possible to respond to needs and opportunities.

Reflecting, in part, the desire of Kennedy and his staff to keep the Bedford-Stuyvesant project out of the hands of the local Community Action Program and the New York City bureaucracy, the Senate committee specified that the Department of Labor should initially administer the program. Twenty-five million dollars were appropriated for the program in fiscal year 1967, and of this sum, $6.9 million went to the Bedford-Stuyvesant project. The remainder was scattered in various projects throughout the country to supplement the Labor Department's concentrated employment program.

Such a scattering of the funds was not what the Senate committee had intended. The committee criticized the Labor Department in its Report on the 1967 amendments to the Economic Opportunity Act[7] and strengthened the language of the legislation to eliminate a special focus on youth employment, to concentrate on economic development programs, and to include rural areas in the program. In addition, because of the difficulty Kennedy had encountered in putting together the Bedford-Stuyvesant project, and also apparently because of an evolution in the Senator's thinking, the report of the Senate committee drew attention to the importance of community participation. The report commented:

---

[5] Economic Opportunity Act, tit. I-D (1967 Kennedy-Javits Amendment), 42 U.S.C. § 2763 (Supp. V, 1969).
[6] *Id.* § 2764.
[7] S. REP. 563, 90th Cong., 1st Sess. (1967).

Experience of the first year's operation demonstrates that successful program operation, including the participation by business, requires and depends on the utmost cooperation of community residents. That cooperation, in the view of the committee, will best be achieved through effective and substantial participation of the residents in program decisions, responsibility and benefits. Community and community-based corporations, which have demonstrated their potential utility as vehicles for such participation should be encouraged by the Secretary of Labor to undertake sponsorship of programs under this part.[8]

There was great resistance to implementing title I-D in the Johnson administration. Part of the resistance was programmatic; officials in the Office of Economic Opportunity and the Labor Department wanted to concentrate on education and manpower training programs which would encourage the poor to disperse from impoverished areas. It was felt that the development of inner-city ghettos and poor rural areas would defeat that purpose. Part of the resistance was political; the White House under Lyndon Johnson was not anxious to build up a program identified with Robert Kennedy.

At the same time, some middle-level administrators in the Office of Economic Opportunity had developed an analysis of the weaknesses of the anti-poverty program which in part paralleled Kennedy's. The parallel was strongest in the perceptions that diffuse responsibility and a large bureaucracy were hobbling efforts to help the poor and that the growing interest in building up community controlled economic institutions could be a constructive movement. These bureaucrats felt that ghetto development could be a more certain stepping stone to social and economic integration than an approach emphasizing instant dispersal. They argued that dispersal as a short term solution was neither politically realistic nor economically sound and that concentration on dispersal was becoming a political excuse for not financing the immediate, practical needs of the poor. Despite the importance of the dispersal-development issue to urban strategy, the only national political dialogue on the subject occurred briefly during the Kennedy-McCarthy television debate preceding the 1968 California primary. Kennedy argued for the development strategy.

After a great deal of bureaucratic maneuvering, the Special Impact appropriation for fiscal year 1968 was finally split up among four federal agencies: the Departments of Labor, Commerce, and Agriculture, and OEO. OEO received the smallest part of the pie—$1.6 million of the $20 million total—to implement the ideas of some of its staff. The goal of the OEO program was the economic development of the poverty area under the control of indigenous institutions. It was built on the assumption that in order for institutions to evolve, they had to have control over resources—that is, they had to have real power. Without such power the institutions could not attract the talented, but cynical and alienated, males who held the key to strengthening ghetto economic life.

The emphasis on alienated males led to one other assumption. It was that the

---
[8] *Id.* at 34.

election process was not necessarily the best means of establishing leadership. Elections under the Community Action Program had produced one disappointing turnout after another. People were elected to CAP and neighborhood boards with two, three, five percent of the eligible voters participating. Moreover, many boards seemed to be dominated by women and clergy who tended to have a strong social welfare orientation. The young alienated male did not participate.

The economic assumptions of the program were also based on the experience of the past. OEO staff members felt that attempts to induce outside established businesses to move into poverty areas had failed, and would continue to fail, because of the unattractive economic environment and racial fear. They had also concluded that economic development could not be built on the small marginal ghetto entrepreneur because of the need for both planning and large scale interrelated projects that could make an impact on the poor population.

The economic and political role of the business community was also recognized. However, the OEO staff did not attempt to replicate the Bedford-Stuyvesant model. They felt that in most places such a formal partnership would result in the "community" partner being the junior one, which would restrain its growth and development into a strong institution. They also felt that a sharing of power between the business establishment and the ghetto community would lead to the same tension that had characterized the sharing of power between the local political establishment and the ghetto community. Finally, the unusual circumstance of having a powerful Senator put the time and energy into a program in order to get the right balance between forces most likely could not be duplicated in other places.

Rather than have the federal or local government attempt to effect the business/community alliance, the OEO program left that task to the community organization itself. The community organization had to negotiate its own arrangement with the local business community as a requirement of the grant. A premise of the program was that it would build on *existing* neighborhood institutions, rather than establish new ones. Thus, the degree to which the community organization had the respect of the local business community was another measure of its ability to run an effective economic development program.

The grants were to be made directly from Washington to avoid the multiple levels of bureaucracy in OEO regional offices as well as in the local Community Action Agencies (CAA) that Kennedy's staff had also feared would hobble the program. The grants themselves called for maximum flexibility. In particular, they could be used for seed (equity) money in the establishment of businesses and housing projects. The question of political acceptability was left to the political abilities of the community organization. No formal approval rights were given either to the local government or to the local CAA. It was understood, however, that the local agency would be informed in advance of the program and that it would be up to the community development corporation to draw up sufficient political strength to overcome any objections. The selection of the organizations was entirely in the hands of the OEO staff.

In June of 1968 the OEO program began with a grant of $1.6 million (the total OEO allocation) to the Hough Area Development Corporation in Cleveland. In the winter of 1968-69, Bureau of the Budget officials under the outgoing Johnson administration determined that the OEO project had met the intentions of title I-D but that the projects in the Departments of Agriculture, Commerce, and Labor had not. The Bureau recommended that the entire program be run by OEO. The incoming administration concurred and the Special Impact Program became the first and only program to be "spun-in" to OEO. The agency spent $11.4 million in title I-D funds on community development corporations in 1969, and almost $36 million in fiscal year 1970. The estimated appropriation for fiscal year 1971 is approximately $31 million.

III

Pressures for Government Controls

The restrictions on the flexibility of community development corporations financed by the Special Impact Program sprang from three separate, but interrelated sources: (1) political pressures arising from local opposition to projects in specific localities, (2) bureaucratic pressures arising from the natural tendency for the bureaucracy to protect itself with delay and obstruction, and (3) ideological pressures arising from the basic philosophy of the representatives of the administration who controlled the program.

A. Political Pressures

In April 1969, three months after the Nixon administration had taken over the Office of Economic Opportunity, a Special Impact grant was made to the Foundation for Community Development, a non-profit corporation in Durham, North Carolina. The grant was intended for the use of United Durham, Inc., a profit-making CDC which the Foundation for Community Development had helped establish. The grant raised a political storm among Republicans in North Carolina because of the presence on the staff of the nonprofit corporation of a controversial "black militant."

The bureaucrat who was in charge of the Special Impact Program, was called to the White House to explain. After listening to the rationale for the grant, White House aide Harry Dent said, in effect: "Oh, I understand all right. But now you have to understand that the South is very important to this administration. I know that OEO money has been used to start riots and elect Democrats and it is going to stop. The President wants that grant killed."

The CDC had the involvement of a number of highly respected businessmen, black and white. It was, however, in the South, and it was aimed at putting almost a million dollars of investment capital under the control of poor black people who were not part of the Republican constituency. And where there is no constituency there is no power. For example, Robert Brown, the only black White House assistant, who is from North Carolina, had personally intervened with the OEO staff to support the grant while it was being considered. But Brown was not at the meeting with Dent and could not be reached for weeks by those who were trying to save the program.

Ultimately, the grant was not killed, primarily because of the determination of some of the OEO staff to save it. It was held up for approximately a year, however. Legally, the grant could be terminated only "for cause."[9] Practically, however, the Republican administration would not release funds to a project that was so clearly in conflict with its southern strategy. Finally, as a result of the intervention of a white Durham businessman, OEO permitted the release of funds for a specific business project on the condition that it not go through the controversial nonprofit organization.

The delay was costly. A site for the location of a modular housing business which was available at a reasonable cost had to be given up. Committed orders for two hundred units of housing were lost and a potential manager had to be kept on the payroll. It cost the organization about $20,000 of scarce foundation money just to negotiate with OEO.

At the other extreme were projects that had too much local political support. One example was an urban CDC in the Midwest which was offered federal assistance for a ghetto transportation program. It was a sorely needed venture which would have had a great economic impact upon the neighborhood and would have established the credibility of the CDC. But the project would have caused conflict with the city-owned bus company. Since the mayor had supported the CDC, the corporation felt it did not want a confrontation with city hall so soon after it was funded. Such a confrontation might have strengthened the community support for the CDC and permitted it to be more independent of the mayor, but the CDC was not willing to take the attendant risk.

Political pressure took another twist in Cleveland, where the Hough Area Development Corporation (HADC) was attacked by the *Cleveland Plain Dealer* for what the newspaper strongly implied was a mishandling of public funds. While the focus of the attack was the CDC, the obvious target was the black mayor of Cleveland whom the newspaper tried to link with HADC. The *Plain Dealer's* case turned out to be weak, and a number of prominent citizens and businessmen came to HADC's defense. The result, however, was a freezing of HADC's funds by the Office of Economic Opportunity and a halt to negotiations between the Small Business Administration and HADC over the financing of a shopping center. After an exhaustive investigation and "evaluation" by the OEO and the General Accounting Office—which duplicated previous investigations by the FBI and the McClelland Committee—funds were released, but with a significant tightening in the power of the government to control program decisions.

In eastern Kentucky, a CDC was funded over the strong objections of the

---

[9] Economic Opportunity Act, tit. I-D, 42 U.S.C. § 2765 (Supp. V, 1969).

governor of the state. The governor's representative had approached OEO staff people and agreed that in return for adding seats to the board for some hostile local officials, he would get the governor to withdraw opposition. Since the governor was a Republican presumably in favor at the White House, the deal was assumed by OEO staff to be the price for the grant. The governor opposed the grant anyway. Despite his opposition, the grant eventually was made, but the enlarged board remained, even though there was no longer a political rationale for it. It is worth noting that the OEO staff, and not the CDC, made the decision that the grant was worth the governor's price.

CDC's survive political pressures when they have strong establishment allies. One program in the South was funded by the Republican administration because of the involvement of a major corporation and the personal interest of the corporation's president in the program. Before the corporate involvement the program was considered too controversial *by Democratic appointees.* The program had not changed—the political support had.

The experience of two other black-controlled programs in the rural South presents an interesting contrast in ability and willingness to react to political pressures. Both CDC's were bitterly attacked by local white officials and conservative congressmen. The leadership of one CDC entrenched itself and waited for its white liberal allies in the North to rescue it. The rescue never came. The leadership of the other program confronted the white establishment politicians with the implicit threat that the growing black voting majority in the county could cost the congressman his next election and the explicit argument that the federal funds being spent in the poor county would bolster the local, white-controlled economy. It is uncertain which consideration was the decisive one, but the opposition to the grant was withdrawn with no damage to the CDC's independence.

B. Bureaucratic Pressures

The bureaucracy-generated pressures on CDC freedom are in many ways more damaging than the political pressures. Bureaucratic pressures tend to push against the entire program rather than against specific projects. They tend to affect the day-to-day workings of the community development corporations and in the long run have a greater effect upon the CDC's performance. The first issue to arise in the OEO bureaucracy concerned the degree to which CDC's would be able to make independent investment decisions. The designers of the program proposed that CDC's have the freedom to make any investment decision without approval from OEO as long as the decision met some general criteria as to benefits going to the poor and as long as the CDC could give reasonable evidence that the feasibility of the business or housing venture had been established. Accountability was to be determined by a periodic review of the program. This proposal was rejected by the Acting Director of the agency as not fulfilling OEO's responsibility toward the public funds. As a result, OEO insisted upon approval rights on all investment decisions.

The history of the first OEO Special Impact grantee, the Hough Area Development Corporation, exemplifies the gradual loss of freedom from bureaucracy-generated pressures. Initially, only accounting and auditing procedures were to be established, evaluation visits were to be made, and reports on the progress of the program were to be filed. In addition, a number of legislative prohibitions, such as those pertaining to the use of federal funds for political activity, had to be observed. There were no other serious restrictions on the freedom of the Hough Area Development Corporation in the first grant. By the winter of the following fiscal year (1968-69), however, the program had gained some prominence in OEO and the noose of bureaucracy began to tighten.

There were many hands on the rope: lawyers who lacked precedents, administrators who saw a need for massive reporting and who wanted the right to approve every action which fell within their jurisdiction, and researchers and planners who were concerned that CDC's produce simple programs which could be readily evaluated.

1. *Lawyers*

Some of the lawyers' problems were understandable. OEO had been set up to provide the poor with services, not to give them independent economic power. Conventional service programs, such as recreation or manpower training, did not generate permanent income-producing assets. The legal problem was that both the income and the assets would be free from federal control after the twenty-four month grant period. How could OEO be sure that the poor community would always benefit from the successful investments made with the federal funds?

The question was an important one. Assuming that a community development corporation was responsive to the needs and interests of the poor area to begin with, what was to insure that it would always be so? The argument centered on projects with self-selected boards. Despite the history of meaningless elections, the lawyers were satisfied that elected boards were always "representative."

Out of the arguments over this point, there emerged the notion that a CDC had a choice as to how it would be accountable for its assets after the federal grant expired. On the one hand, the CDC could establish a structure whereby the board would be chosen in a neighborhood election or by future low income shareholders. On the other hand, OEO could retain the right in the future to step in and take over the CDC if OEO felt that the CDC was no longer responsive. All but one of the CDC's with self-selected boards chose the former arrangement.

In the negotiations between OEO and the CDC's over the question of corporate structures, the OEO lawyers revealed a creative flair for postulating every conceivable contingency. Charter provisions were included to accommodate each of these. The result in many cases was a legal monstrosity which most poor people could not comprehend, much less utilize. The negotiations over the structure of one grant continued for more than six months after the grant was made.

Precedent existed for the making of federal investment grants to be without such complexity. The subsidization of private business is well rooted in the nation's economic history. Railroad, shipbuilding, and airline subsidies; land grants to farmers; and tax subsidies for the oil and real estate industries are but a few examples of the use of public funds to achieve social goals through private institutions. Certainly the plight of the nation's poor is at least as important as the problems these other subsidies are intended to solve. For the OEO legal staff, however, there was a practical difference. There were no influential interest groups to argue the cause of the poor and no congressional committees eager to please a rich and powerful constituency.

Traditionally, government agency lawyers take for themselves the task of standing guard against agency decisions that may be politically controversial. The Durham episode, therefore, gave the Office of the General Counsel the opportunity to expand its influence over the Special Impact Program. Several lawyers began to exercise rights of review of programs, as well as of legal problems.

One such instance occurred in connection with a CDC project in Chicago. The proposal called for the renovation of a four block area in North Lawndale for a commercial and housing program. It had been developed by a community organization with the assistance of a number of established banks and businesses in Chicago. It was one of the most competently written proposals that OEO had received. During the last two weeks of the fiscal year, however, the project almost collapsed when an OEO lawyer demanded that the calculations involved in projecting the million dollar program be explained in detail. A half-dozen experts traveled from Chicago to explain such matters as the projected cost for maintaining white lines in a parking lot over a twenty year period! Such absurdities and indignities would have never been suffered by a business applicant. In fact, only when the nature and depth of the business involvement in the Chicago project became apparent did the politically sensitive General Counsel's office back down.

2. *Administrators*

The increase in the number of forms that accompanied the growth of the Special Impact Program was illustrative of a familiar bureauratic phenomenon. Each week the program staff was notified of another obscure governmental regulation which required another form. At first, the program staff consciously resisted. As the program came under political criticism, however, the bureaucrats in charge of the program had to spend their time in other battles, and the complicated procedures grew relentlessly. When complaints were made, those responsible for the increase in paperwork would reiterate their devotion to principals of efficiency. While each form seemed to have a reason, together they were an irrational burden.

This paper snowstorm had two effects. First, it added to the number of things a CDC had to do in order to get and keep a grant. Failure to fill out each form or otherwise fulfill the new requirements put the CDC in violation of its agreement with OEO. The CDC therefore had to spend more staff time filling out the forms and less time doing economic development. The second result was delay. Failure to fill out all the forms properly and in the right order meant that funds could not be released. These delays were in addition to those caused by an overworked staff having to approve every CDC investment decision.

The delays in approving projects lengthened from weeks to months. CDC's made business deals on which they had to renege because OEO could not process the papers in time. The credibility of the CDC's with their neighborhoods and local business communities was seriously eroded.

Along with the delays came increasing insensitivity to the CDC's problems. For example, in June 1969, a grant was made to a CDC in Hancock County, Georgia. In late October, money still had not been released because the clerk with the authority to release the funds had not completed a review of all the forms. The director of the Georgia CDC had to track down the clerk himself. He told her that the people in Hancock County had concluded that he had taken the money himself and that if she didn't release the funds, they would kill him when he got back to Georgia. He was quite serious. The clerk released the money but only after making it clear that in the future such a situation would not be a sufficient excuse to go out of channels.

Jurisdictional disputes were perhaps inevitable. Regional offices wanted the right to approve and monitor all programs in their regions. This added another layer of bureaucracy. The Community Action Agencies wanted the same right to approve programs as did the state Offices of Economic Opportunity. Topping it off was a thick sauce of interagency committees, administrative offices, advisors to the director, and "liaison" offices which was beginning to make the Special Impact Program indigestible to the poor.

The first grant to the Hough Area Development Corporation required the approval of three separate offices within OEO. Two years later, the number was ten and rising. The saving grace was that some of these offices were interested only in being consulted and made little or no effort to contribute to the grant-making process. In these cases the major result was delay. In other instances, however, attempts were made to change the program and, at times, to thwart it. In the rural South, for example, one project was stopped, and several seriously hampered, by the opposition of local Community Action Agencies which preferred that resources *not* go to the poor of their counties if the money was to be controlled by an independent organization.

3. *Social Scientists*

The program was also subject to pressures from that part of the bureaucracy interested in research and planning. The people involved were primarily social scientists who were spending a few years at OEO away from the university or the RAND Corporation. Their complaint was that the objectives of the program did not fit into neat categories. Employment was not, for example, the chief goal. It was one of several goals which included developing the economic base of the poverty area, spreading ownership and control of enterprises, providing managerial and entrepreneurial opportunities, and developing community institutions. Quantitative analysis, which the planners felt should be the major determinant of a program's value, could not handle such multiple objectives and interrelated goals. Although such goals reflected the needs of the community as seen by the community, they could not easily fit the academic frame of reference of the planners. The Program Planning and Budget System required simple "inputs" and simple "outputs." There is nothing simple about organizing people for economic development in a place like Hough or Bedford-Stuyvesant.

At OEO, the planners had great influence on the budget, and the result was a pressure upon the CDC's to concentrate on projects that maximized one goal. Thus, a project like the combination shopping center-public housing project in Cleveland, which was the single most important project in the Hough community, became much harder to justify than a project to create a few unskilled jobs with no future and no impact upon the community. The multiple benefits of a shopping center-public housing project on employment, ownership, community services, and the economic base were hard to quantify; employment of the poor was easier.

Another result was a narrowing of the concept of economic development. Rather than a broad comprehensive program such as that originally envisaged by Robert Kennedy for Bedford-Stuyvesant, and by those who put together the Hough Area Development Corporation, the Special Impact Program gravitated toward the small business-oriented "minority capitalism" program of the Nixon administration. The concept of using public funds for basic investment in the ghetto to some extent gave way to an objective of creating individual businesses, *which had been rejected originally by the designers of the program as doomed to failure.* But individual businesses were easier to count.

The final and politically most tragic limitation imposed by the social scientists was the insistence that all Special Impact Programs be judged on their direct impact upon the poor as defined by OEO. The agency's definitions were kept deliberately low for political and program reasons. Politically, it was and is important to the Johnson and Nixon administrations to show a relatively small amount of resources being devoted to poverty programs. Given the low level of resources, the OEO budget planners insisted upon keeping the poverty definition low so that the funds could be concentrated on the lowest portion of the poverty population. Although this limitation made some sense as a device for maximizing the delivery of services to those most in need, it was a destructive notion in an economic development program which required the involvement of many skilled individuals. Moreover, a large portion of the key target population—adult males—could not be drawn into a program with arbitrarily low income standards.[10] The demand that the benefits be limited to such a small segment of the population also defeated the notion of developing community institutions, and had the effect of limiting the constituency for the program. The insistence of the social scientist planners that OEO funds be used only for the poor in the interests of program efficiency, combined with the decision to keep the income definition unreasonably low, cost the poor and their programs the chance to broaden their base of support.

C. Ideological Pressures

The ideological pressures on the Special Impact Program reflected the way in which OEO's leadership looked at the problem of poverty. While these pressures had political implications, their source was not so much specific political problems as a desire to operate programs according to a general political philosophy. In the last year of the Johnson administration the ideological opposition to the Special Impact Program centered upon two points: (1) that development programs, particularly in the cities, would lead to racial separatism, and (2) that the development of businesses would necessarily mean concentration on the nonpoor.

As indicated previously, the designers of the program had argued that development would lead to integration and not separatism. The second point was answered by the argument that the benefits of an economic development program in large part was a function of who controlled the program. If the poor controlled it, they would benefit. The differences between those who designed the program and the OEO leadership were not completely resolved, but the ideological concerns of the latter were recognized by the designers as reasonable concerns. When these were approached with sufficient seriousness, a limited number of projects was approved.

Donald Rumsfeld, the Republican OEO director, and his staff brought an entirely new set of objections to the program. Shortly after he assumed the directorship, a report to Rumsfeld written by one of his assistants recommended that the program be terminated immediately and all of the oustanding funds returned to the treasury. Another report to Rumsfeld stated that the primary question was whether the program was consistent with the *Protestant ethic*. Rumsfeld declared that making grants without very tight controls was irresponsible. "What happens," he asked, "if ten years from now the Black Panthers are chosen by the stockholders to run one of these CDC's? How are you going to prevent that?" The program staff replied that businesses could not be run effectively under government controls, but that argument was brushed aside. "They" were using "our" money and "we" had to control its use. Thus, it was the Republicans—the party of business and advocates of local control and freedom from government regulation—which gave the final shove that pushed the Special Impact Program into the bureaucratic quicksand.

---

[10] Some notion of the adequacy of OEO poverty definition ($3800 for an urban family of four) can be gained by a comparison with the Bureau of Labor Standards minimum level of $6960. *See generally*, Bureau of Labor Standards Press Release, Dec. 21, 1970.

The lawyers were set to work creating still more restrictions upon the program. Ironically, it was a point on which the lawyers previously had insisted—the CDC's electoral responsiveness to the neighborhood—that most concerned the Republicans. But there was no attempt by the Geenral Counsel office to defend the program. The theme was *control*, control over staff, control over investment decisions, control over strategies.

The concern for controls, however, was selective. Those projects such as the original Kennedy program in Bedford-Stuyvesant, which had strong establishment support, were not questioned. In fact, so that Rumsfeld might have something to deliver on a trip to New York City, he announced the $10 million refunding of the Bedford-Stuyvesant program before the basic documents had been prepared. Neither Rumsfeld nor anyone else on his staff knew what they were announcing. But with important business leaders involved in the project it did not seem to matter.

Another example of the selective concern for accountability for federal monies was the creation of the Opportunity Funding Corporation (OFC). The OFC was the creation of Theodore Cross, author of a book on black capitalism who was hired by Rumsfeld to come up with innovative business-oriented programs.[11] Cross proposed that the OFC be formed by a small group of financiers and businessmen and be supported by OEO for the purpose of experimenting with new ways to encourage investment in poverty areas. While no one could quarrel with the general goals of the program, none of the ideas to be pursued were defined. Nonetheless, Rumsfeld agreed to terminate the entire CDC program and use the funds for the OFC, sight unseen, programs undefined, and relationship to the poor unclear. The important thing to Rumsfeld was that the OFC would be run by reliable white businessmen. So anxious was Rumsfeld to shift resources from control by the poor to control by the rich, that he announced the OFC program to the press before it had been reviewed for legality. Only after the community development corporations themselves organized to fight the plan, and several members of Congress joined in their protest, was the Opportunity Funding Corporation modified. The monies for the support of OFC that were to come out of title I-D were decreased considerably, and two CDC leaders, one of whom was a Special Impact grantee, were added to the board.

Despite the Republican Party's rhetoric against federal controls, particularly economic controls, those who ran OEO favored central state control when it came to programs in which the poor were participating. Freedom and independence were reserved for the higher social orders.

IV

THE NEED FOR AN EFFECTIVE CONSTITUENCY

The history of the Special Impact Program illustrates that the tension between

---
[11] T. CROSS, BLACK CAPITALISM (1968).

a community development organization's need for freedom and the bureaucracy's need for accountability are directly related to the political support that the former can muster. Individual community development corporations successfully defended themselves against political and bureaucratic pressures only because they had been able to secure influential allies. The Bedford-Stuyvesant program with its built-in alliances with the business community has been most successful. The Hough Area Development Corporation's program was saved by supporters in Cleveland's business and political community. The key individual in saving the Durham project was the local manager of an IBM plant. In Chicago, the prestigious group of businessmen which agreed to help the North Lawndale Economic Development Corporation was instrumental in overcoming its problems with the bureaucracy. Where such allies have been absent, projects have experienced more difficulty, particularly in the rural South and in Appalachia.

Most of the support has come from the business community. Thus the original hypothesis of the Kennedy-Javits Amendment that established businessmen could act as effective guards against political and bureaucratic interference has proven correct. Usually some price must be paid for local business support. In some cases the price is tangible; deposits are expected to be made with a particular bank, or real estate transactions must be handled by a particular downtown firm. In some cases, the price may be less tangible but higher—a reliance on the protection of a dominating institution which prevents the community development corporation from solving its own problems and growing into an independent institution.

Business support is also of uncertain stability. As the memory of urban riots fades and business conditions deteriorate, the enthusiasm of businessmen in assisting community organizations diminishes. The assumption of many that the business community would provide the massive resources to develop rural slums and urban ghettos has not proven correct.

That community-controlled economic development programs were forced to rely upon outsiders for protection was inevitable. Just as a degree of economic protection in the form of subsidies and guaranteed markets is needed at the beginning stages of economic development, a degree of political protection is also needed. Those who support anti-poverty programs are still small in number and the hostility in Washington to community control has never been stronger. But if the public investment necessary to develop urban and rural poverty areas under community control is ever going to be made, CDC's, cooperatives, and similar organizations will have to develop their own constituency on a national, as well as a local level.

Businessmen cannot be expected to give the kind of political attention to the needs of poor people that they give to their own needs. An example of the political priorities in the private business sector is the Administration's recent success in persuading Congress to approve a loan to the Lockheed Aircraft Corporation to enable that firm to survive its own mismanagement of the C5A program. The estimated cost of this loan—to help one firm recover from its own mistakes—is ten times what the same Administration is seeking from Congress so as to support CDC's throughout the entire nation under the Special Impact Program in 1971.[12]

Moreover, the private business sector has been of help primarily in the large urban areas, where local self-help organizations pose no immediate threat to the establishment. On the other hand, the histories of both the Community Action Program and the Special Impact Program have demonstrated how thin the support is for social and economic change on the part of those who control the destinies of small cities and rural areas. When the relationship between the economic facts of poverty and the structure of political influence becomes clear, the mere existence of a semi-independent organization with the responsibility to "eliminate poverty" is enough to cause uneasiness at city hall and the county courthouse.

The rhetoric of community economic development often tends to emphasize the conservative aspects of self-help. Indeed, the notion of people organizing for their own economic improvement is in the best traditions of American business. But it would be a fatal mistake for those interested in strengthening the movement for community economic development to forget that on the national level their cause is linked to the cause of anti-poverty efforts in general. The notion that political conservatives who opposed social welfare programs would support local control and economic independence for the poor and disadvantaged has been tested in the first years of the Nixon administration, and it has failed. Only as part of a reconstituted and revitalized anti-poverty constituency which crosses racial as well as programmatic lines will community economic development organizations gain the scale of resources and degree of freedom they need.

To begin playing this role, community economic development organizations will first have to organize themselves. Even now, most of these organizations define themselves nationally in terms of their financiers—as OEO programs, Model Cities programs, Ford Foundation programs—rather than in terms of what they themselves do. A network that cuts across such lines is needed to share experiences and for mutual protection and reinforcement. Efforts also should be made by those concerned to encourage the expansion of the community development corporation idea to groups that thus far have not been much involved, such as the white urban poor and near-poor. To the extent that these groups are more concerned with *community* development than with *economic* development, it may require a broadening of the concept of "community economic development." As the history of the Special Impact Program shows, a social scientist's concern for definitional purity can be detrimental to the building of a political constituency. If efforts at community control of an area's economic development are to be taken seriously, they must be seen as applicable to disadvantaged people generally and not simply as a program just for ghetto residents or minority businessmen.

Outside alliances, of course, should be maintained and strengthened. At present,

---

[12] N.Y. Times, June 30, 1970, at 82, col. 4.

businessmen will play an important role in any economic development program. But other players must also be drawn into the game, including the more progressive elements in the labor movement who in areas such as Los Angeles have given financial support to community economic development organizations.

A Washington consultant with long experience in the economic development field recently noted that when people come to Washington to lobby for urban programs, they concentrate on programs such as education, welfare, and housing. The issue of economic development programs rarely comes up. Therefore, senators and congressmen assume that it is not very important. If community economic development is to be a claimant for public funds, community organizations will have to talk to those congressmen and senators and talk to those who influence them. If community organizations are to use economic development funds to respond to the needs of their people rather than the political needs of Washington or city hall, the process of building political strength cannot begin too soon.

NATIONAL POLICY AND THE COMMUNITY DEVELOPMENT CORPORATION

Stewart E. Perry*

As the community development corporation (CDC) becomes more familiar to those concerned with public law and policy relating to inner city problems, there is a tendency to consider CDC's merely as part of some federal program and therefore relevant to federal or national policy primarily on that ground. An OEO program does in fact support about forty CDC's, and other CDC's are organized under HUD's Model Cities programs. Yet the CDC is much more than a federal program vehicle. It is in fact the expression of a socio-political movement and process that is much broader than the urban renewal and poverty programs.

Although the main goal of the CDC is inner-city or rural economic development, it is actually a multi-purpose social institution and can take different forms.[1] This results from the fact that CDC's originally emerged spontaneously in widely separated cities and rural areas and were not the product of a governmentally prescribed pattern. In fact, federal officials and others have specifically turned to CDC's because as a pre-existing organizational form, they are presumably more effective and credible in low-income areas.[2] The form itself, however, is not as significant as the nascent social developments that it represents. From these social developments come its significance for national policy.

This article will describe briefly the more recent historical background of the CDC movement, try to suggest the similarity of the CDC movement to a similar middle-class concern, link these to general policy problems of decentralization and rural development, and, finally, discuss some specific, though minor, restrictions in federal policy that prevent full utilization of the energy that the CDC expresses.

The immediate historical background of the CDC both as an idea and as an institution offers a clue to social trends in our country. The problems associated with these trends have been conceptualized in the bureaucracies and agencies of

---

* Director, Center for Community Economic Development, Cambridge, Massachusetts. I owe a debt to Jeff Faux and Helen Perry for their colleagueship on this article.

[1] For descriptions of a wide variety of CDC's, see a joint publication of the Center for Community Economic Development and the Cambridge Institute, Profiles in Community-Based Economic Development (1971). Only urban CDC's are included in this pamphlet, which describes 27 groups.

[2] This history appears in a paper by the author prepared for the Society for Applied Anthropology in 1968, to be published under the title *Black Separatism, Black Institutions, and Economic Development* in Human Organization. Essential reading is a book just published by the Twentieth Century Fund Task Force on Community Development Corporations: CDC's: New Hope for the Inner City (1971). The conceptual framework for the CDC was a collaborative effort at Harvard's Kennedy Institute by Gar Alperovitz, John McClaughry, and Roy Innis. One of the earliest published treatments of the CDC concept is in Social Innovation in the City (R. Rosenbloom & R. Marris, eds. 1969). I have drawn from my own earlier paper, *A Note on the Genesis of the Community Development Corporation*, in Case for Participatory Democracy (G. Benello & D. Roussopoulos, eds. 1971).

Washington for federal programs. Yet the connection between what is happening in city neighborhoods and rural communities in the evolution of the CDC and what must be dealt with on a national level has not yet been clearly made. If we are ever to make those connections, we must go back at least a few years, though an even longer view must eventually be taken.

First, *as an idea*, the CDC arose in reaction to the successes and failures of the civil rights movement. The significance of this movement as part of broad social trends in America has not yet been adequately described in the near-revolutionary terms it deserves.[3] The successes of the movement in bringing about improvements in the legal status and privileges of blacks only put into high relief the basic economic deprivation that this group suffered. The main beneficiaries of the successes were and are in many respects the middle-class blacks who can take advantage of newly opened opportunities. The vast majority of the black people, despite all the civil rights victories, still face an economic future that raises basic questions about the means and processes of an economic system that has cost the blacks so much. Thus, various civil rights activists of the last decade began again to raise the idea of a different economic system, using the principle of a group rising in economic status as a group, as contrasted with the conventional conception of individual improvement by individual effort. In the early 1960's, this idea was espoused in the political demands that finally brought forth President Johnson's poverty program.[4] Later, a more sophisticated and precise expression arose in the form of the CDC as the instrument of what government officials began to call "community capitalism," but which was, in fact, a movement for neighborhood-controlled and neighborhood-owned economic enterprise.

Second, *as an institution*, the CDC evolved as a reaction to the promise, the accomplishments, and the disappointments of the central institution of the antipoverty program, the community action agency (CAA). The promise of the CAA was that it would be an instrument that would represent the poor (especially the black poor) and be their advocate in eliciting resources for them from the more affluent environment. The reality was a disappointment. It was clear that the CAA did not swiftly or surely elicit enough resources for the poor. But that might have been tolerated as part of a long-term struggle if the CAA had really offered the poor a social instrument of their own. The worst disappointment was that the CAA *did not* represent the poor; it really represented the whole local community, the rich and middle class as well as the poor. This was in part a result of the composition of the CAA boards. One-third of the board members were appointed by local government; one-third came from social and welfare agencies; and only the remaining third were selected by the poor themselves.

Insofar as a majority of CAA board members did not come from the ranks of the

---

[3] Preliminary insights are presented in the examination of the relationships between the blacks, the civil rights movement, and the youth culture in H. PERRY, THE HUMAN BE-IN (1970).

[4] *See* S. LEVITAN, THE DESIGN OF A FEDERAL ANTIPOVERTY STRATEGY (1967).

poor themselves, the CAA certainly was not an instrument controlled by poverty area residents even though its aims were geared to those areas and those residents. Therefore, the CAA became a forum in which many interests of the whole community were compromised before outside demands were made by the agency in the name of the poor. The representatives of local government, charities, businesses, foundations, and social welfare agencies who sat upon the CAA boards had first to fight out among themselves the different demands that they brought from their varying allegiances before they could do battle in the name of the poor. Naturally, the demands defined by this compromising process often differed from what the poor would have expressed for themselves.

However, among the accomplishments of this institutional instrument was one that offered the springboard for a new approach. The CAA personnel budgets subsidized many poor neighborhood residents in low-level jobs that either left them free or actually enjoined them to organize their neighbors to make more effective demands, within and without the poverty program. A whole new cadre of leaders developed as a result. Included were some people who might never have had a chance otherwise to escape from the daily grind of more meaningless occupations, people who had not previously had the economic freedom to participate as leaders in the civil rights movement. Free to think in basic political terms and to organize neighbors on those terms (usually without respect to conventional partisan groupings), these people became a new resource to their neighborhoods.

In this sense the CAA's were successful; by investing in the development of human leadership capital (however unintentionally), they produced a new resource for the poor neighborhoods—a pool of individuals with the social vocabulary of experiences and skills necessary for moving through the system to secure opportunity for their neighborhood. These people together with others who had already provided civil rights leadership, and who were also occasionally subsidized for a time by the poverty programs, made up a critical mass of articulate and insightful spokesmen on the local level. They were able to support each other when it finally became evident that the old goals and the compromising instruments of the CAA no longer fit the rising expectations of an activated neighborhood.

The conventional CAA did not fulfill enough of what the poor came to see as their needs, and out of the ferment created by the rights movement and the poverty programs, a whole set of new or rediscovered activities arose, including the collective civil disorder or riot. Among the many other social creations of the black poor in this period were organizations that exemplified three principles: (1) the instrument of action must be controlled by the neighborhood and the neighborhood alone; (2) neighborhood political power requires economic power embodied in control of existing economic institutions and the creation of new ones; and (3) the improvement of the political, social, and economic status of the neighborhood requires a coordination of efforts in all three sectors and a coalition of all those active in the neighborhood.

The CDC was only one of a wide variety of models based on these principles, and it too varied in form. In its most powerful form, the CDC is intended to include a broad representation of the spectrum of leadership, ranks, and class in the neighborhood, and thus to act as a unified spokesman. An example of this potential scope is the Hough Area Development Corporation of Cleveland, Ohio, a CDC which included in its membership virtually every influential leader in the Hough neighborhood. Another example is Fighton, an economic development corporation in Rochester, New York, that was organized as a *subsidiary* of a federation of all local civil rights groups and interests.

In black communities, the CDC has sought, by business and other economic development activities, to strengthen black power with economic muscle. It is not designed for the limited purpose of providing services for the neighborhood, as the CAA usually is. It also has sought a coordination of plans for the neighborhood by persons exclusively responsible to the neighborhood and representative of it—unlike Model Cities programs, which are run by the city mayor or his delegate. In these ways a CDC is designed to avoid the political and functional limits of the CAA (and Model Cities units) and thus to broaden the scope of the civil rights movement.

The structure of this new institution has varied considerably, since in each location it was a local response. There was no model to be copied. The original innovations of the Zion Investment Associates in Philadelphia, the Fighton Corporation in Rochester, the Hough Area Development Corporation in Cleveland, and so on, were in 1967 truly indigenous inventions.[5]

The degree to which the CDC's are truly responsive to their constituency also varies from case to case, but not in relation to such structural features as direct election of leaders by residents at large. This is not to say that both questions of structure and of responsiveness will not jeopardize the future of the CDC's in general or in some specific cases. The point is that the source of their initial energy was their credibly representing their constituencies.

Today, in recognition of the fundamental flexibility of the CDC, many groups other than blacks have established their own versions of this institution. The underlying conception is expressed in still other structural forms, some of which had existed before—such as production cooperatives of the rural poor. What underlies them all, however, is adherence to the principle of community-based economic development—economic development activities controlled by the heretofore underrepresented, under-privileged, and under-developed communities or neighborhoods and their residents. That is perhaps the only common characteristic that describes the members of the National Congress for Community Economic Development—an association recently founded for mutual support by leaders of some of the new

---

[5] Actually the Reverend Leon Sullivan's ZIA did not become open to any but Zion Baptist Church members until 1968, but its roots in the so-called "10-36 plan" (ten dollars a month from each member for thirty-six months) date back to 1962.

CDC's. Mexican-Americans, Indians, Puerto Ricans, Appalachian whites, and urban ethnic whites, as well as blacks, are among those now who are working with a CDC tool for economic development. The CDC idea has also been under consideration recently in at least one upper-middle-class suburban attempt to gain local hegemony —in the Isla Vista neighborhood of Santa Barbara, California.

The impetus for new structures comes from a demand in local neighborhoods for a return of a measure of control over their immediate environment. This neighborhood trend in depressed areas coincides with the upsurge of concern in middle-class communities with a different facet of the issue of self-determination—that which is exemplified by increased feelings of personal alienation from social, political, and economic institutions. In middle-class communities the problem is defined in individualistic terms rather than group or neighborhood terms. For example, with the middle-class citizens, especially younger ones, the solution to alienation is through a search for different styles of personal relatedness—greater intimacy in communal living arrangements, encounter groups, and the like. With the low-income minorities, on the other hand, the solution to alienation is to get together for *group advancement* through joint economic endeavors. Thus, the CDC is only one institutional precipitate from only one social stratum responding to increased demands for autonomy, self-determination, or participatory democracy in a mass society. Yet because it is in fact a part of a broader social trend affecting other strata, it is especially important. For one thing, it is possible that the CDC as an institutional form will attract middle-class citizens who seek economic decentralization as a solution to alienation in the economic sphere.

II

Decentralization of Power

The generalized application of both the institution and the idea of the CDC from low-income blacks to other groups has implications for national domestic policy and, hence, for programs based on that policy. Governmental policies favoring decentralization are the most obvious concomitants of the present local trends. Revenue-sharing or other decentralization proposals founder, however, on the problem of finding, creating, and defending institutions which can carry out the activities to be decentralized. For example, decentralizing federal manpower programs to the state employment services surely means miring these programs in distracting politics, institutionalized racism, and inefficient bureaucracy. Or to take another example, a revenue-sharing plan that will leave it up to a city or state to decide whether low-income areas or more influential higher-income areas are to benefit does not inspire confidence in the future of urgently needed urban and rural development.

Whatever decentralization eventually emanates from Washington will involve usually unresponsive state, county, and municipal entities, even when the rhetoric of that decentralization calls for broad citizen control over the new transfers of authority. Yet, depending upon local political alignments, the CDC could become a final repository of that authority for the CDC's neighborhood. It is this potential which gives the CDC relevance for national policies of decentralization, including revenue-sharing. Where the CDC in fact lives up to its ambitious aim, it will be a citizen advocacy center for a neighborhood or region and can coordinate and focus the special demands of that area. And because of its administrative experience in other activities, it will also be a natural candidate for delegation of municipal service functions.

The organizational flexibility of the CDC will enable it to move into different fields through the use of semi-independent sub-organizations. It could, for example, take over activities such as low-income housing construction, refuse removal, street maintenance, and institutional supplies and services for public schools and hospitals on delegation or contract from local entities. Insofar as the CDC represents no single entrepreneur or group of persons who will privately benefit, but rather an entire geographical neighborhood that will publicly benefit, the delegation of such functions is politically defensible. The degree of the CDC's responsiveness to and control by the citizens in its area will be the key to its salience as the incontestable local instrument for local affairs. The presence of local responsiveness and control makes it politically necessary for outsiders to deal with the CDC. Of course, this assumes both that the area is sufficiently organized to have a real identity vis-à-vis the rest of the city or county and that its constituents can be mobilized on election day. An effective CDC will meet these assumptions.

Middle-class areas ordinarily do not have such identities, probably because the individual resident finds its easier, without high levels of local organization, to direct municipal attention to a neighborhood problem. For example, the pot-hole in the street just beyond a middle-class driveway gets fixed more quickly as the result of a telephone call than when the call is about a repair need in a low-income neighborhood. When the central administrations become unresponsive, however, it seems likely that even middle-class neighborhoods will organize an instrument like a CDC to accomplish local goals. That seems the lesson of Isla Vista which experienced a police riot that ordinarily occurs only in a slum. Indeed, it is precisely the fact that a CDC arises to meet local needs that makes the CDC much more likely to fit those needs than some externally induced subdivision of the city, county, or state.

In short, it would seem that a rather natural political and social evolution could occur, mainly out of local needs, to give meaning to decentralization as a national policy. True decentralization cannot occur unless the recognition of what needs to be done happens at the lowest level of citizen organization—the neighborhood. This of course has been argued by many observers, most recently by Milton Kotler.[6] The CDC is the embodiment of much of what Kotler foresaw as the necessary beginning to the return of local affairs to local control.

---

[6] M. KOTLER, NEIGHBORHOOD GOVERNMENT (1969).

III

THE COMMUNITY DEVELOPMENT CORPORATION IN RURAL AREAS

The CDC has evolved in the urban areas, gaining much of its potential from the fact that its members live in close proximity to each other and, therefore, are mutually accessible for communication and mobilization on common problems. Quite a different situation, of course, characterizes any attempt by rural people to join in common action. The dispersal of population and, often, a great heterogeneity of class, status, and perspective pose more significant barriers to community organization. Nevertheless, the economic situation of the rural poor and near-poor offers a strong common bond for one major CDC activity—the creation of new employment and income opportunities in tune with local needs.

The need for employment and other income opportunities in rural areas is very different from that which exists in the urban neighborhood. In the cities, there are unfilled job opportunities even in the midst of recession, albeit to a considerably lesser degree. Housing patterns, inconvenient transportation, and a variety of artificila barriers including discrimination, tend to prevent the filling of those jobs from among the ranks of the unemployed or underemployed. But in the depressed rural areas, often there are no jobs; and often there is no particular likelihood that jobs will open up even if great prosperity covers the rest of the nation.

It is true that federal programs have been devised for these forgotten areas. But efforts such as the Appalachian Regional Commission and the Economic Development Administration have not produced any convincing evidence of major success. These programs apparently continue because more promising alternatives have not appeared.

The recalcitrance of the rural problem has led some to suggest that it be ignored, that "uneconomic" areas be allowed to die or simply remain stagnant. In this unencouraging context, the arousal of hope and the harnessing of joint energies that only a local institution like a CDC can achieve may be a new tool. CDC's could not or would not supplant any of the other rural development activities. The point is that here, too, decentralization to locally evolved institutions may play an important supplemental part in any attempt to devise a broad strategy for rural development.[7] Certainly, the usual policy based upon giving local incentives to outside companies to move their plants to rural locations cannot solve the rural problem. First, what is one area's gain is another's loss. Second, we have witnessed how little effect county booster groups, even with state help, have in such efforts. And finally, there is in-

---

[7] A particularly instructive comparison is the miserable record of a Department of Agriculture project in economic development in southeastern Kentucky, as juxtaposed with the moderate success of a coincidental project in an equally distressed area of North Carolina. In the first case, interference by the federal agency stymied any meaningful activity and encouraged a destructive atmosphere of inter-county competition; in the latter project a more representative group of the counties concerned effectively capitalized on the opportunities for economic development that were open to them. *See* I & II WESTINGHOUSE LEARNING CORPORATION, AN EVALUATION OF FISCAL YEAR 1968, SPECIAL IMPACT PROGRAMS (1969).

creasing evidence that even when an industry is brought in from the outside, the costs to the community may be more than the benefits, under existing incentive programs. For instance, unemployment may be little affected if the plants bring their own employees. Perhaps, on the contrary, new possibilities for local control and change—that is, for self-determination—through a different institutional tool can mobilize a local rural community to a different pattern of combining the local and the necessary outside resources.

Rural cooperatives, and in recent years other CDC-like organizations,[8] are able to arouse new activity because the institutional limitations of conventional county government can be transcended. New human resources can be tapped from constituencies that have been ignored in the past. The most obvious examples are the minorities in the South and Southwest. As illustrated in the case of HELP in Northern New Mexico and ECCO in Hancock County, Georgia, new economic energy can be released with benefit to an entire rural area.

The special advantages of a new institution responsive to a previously underutilized constituency is threefold at least. First, new knowledge is brought to bear on local problems, so that the creation or attraction of new industry or business can be adapted more specifically to local needs for jobs in terms of local skills available. For example, those who know the job needs of the community will not seek an industry which will bring its own employees. Second, the multi-purpose design of the CDC, together with emphasis upon community ownership, brings to light many considerations in local business development that are usually ignored. The CDC can assess trade-offs between community needs and profit level in a way that organizations with more restricted ownership and single-minded profit considerations cannot. Third, the CDC as a new instrument can do things that long-established institutions cannot. It may be argued that the under-utilized constituencies can make their influence felt through extant local government institutions by the simple process of registering and voting. It is true that electoral influence is essential in any case, but it is also well recognized that any major redirection of the whole set of established local government bureaucracies is impossible even with the election of sympathetic executives. It is, then, for this reason also that the CDC or its analog can be especially effective in stagnant rural communities.

The common feature of the energy released by the CDC in the urban areas and by the CDC in a rural area is the new sense of community self-determination. In the urban areas, this has primarily reflected the energy potential of the racial identity movement. The same potential is possible in racially or ethnically distinct rural areas of Chicanos or blacks. Yet, the necessary sense of new community possibilities can occur even in mixed or white rural areas because rural people can

---

[8] As has been made plain, the CDC is significant as a multi-purpose development institution. Insofar as cooperatives serve only to reduce their members' production, marketing, or purchasing costs, they are not capable of the same systematic development of their area. Many co-ops, however, do engage in multiple activities, such as community organization on local issues, initiating credit unions, and so on. In these instances they then perform the same broad community function as a CDC might.

more clearly sense the handicaps of their economic environment. It is easier for them to recognize that whatever is wrong is not an individual matter, but rather a community or area condition of lack of opportunity.

IV

RECOMMENDATIONS FOR SPECIFIC ACTIONS

There are certain specific actions which can be taken on a national level by congressional or executive initiative to insure that new and existing domestic programs benefit from the CDC phenomenon. Basically, the policy position must be one which is permissive rather than prescriptive.

Presently, many federal laws are framed or applied in such a way as to exclude CDC's from participation in benefits available to other business or community groups. At a minimum, we need to insure that federal law does not stand in the way of use of this new social institution. But mere neutral openness to the CDC's will not always be enough; at some later date, there will have to be massive encouragement through federal grant and loan funds.[9] However, at this point, some fairly limited federal actions can create a generative climate for CDC growth, and that alone can be extremely useful at the current stage of CDC development. Administrative interpretations and existing legislation can be modestly changed now so as to permit the utilization of a CDC whenever a CDC is prepared to carry out a project within a current federal program. Similar opportunities, of course, must be provided by state and local law and regulation.

The most important areas of national programming that are relevant here are business and agricultural assistance, urban renewal, housing, and what is being called the "new communities" approach. Other potentially relevant federal programs —for example, in environmental protection and conservation—ought to be scrutinized to make sure that the instrumentalities for carrying them out are so defined as to permit the use of CDC's; but the former programs are so central that I shall concentrate on them in illustrating the constraints placed on community-based development groups.

First, the economic development assistance provided by EDA goes only to depressed areas approved by EDA in accordance with administrative regulations which require a submission by a local governmental unit, or delegated body, of a comprehensive development plan—the Overall Economic Development Plan (OEDP). The

---

[9] The experience of similar development groups abroad (such as the *kibbutzim* in Palestine) established the need for considerable outside assistance, both in the initiation stages and in continuing development. Presumably the same will be true in any American models, with the federal government being the major source of outside assistance. Among the mechanisms that will eventually be necessary is some sort of national development bank. Various congressional proposals have been advanced on this instrument over the last few years. However, a bank is only one part of the necessary system, and an integration of many elements will be necessary. The proposed Community Self-Determination Act (now known as the Community Corporation Act, proposed in a Senate Labor Committee print) is one form of a systematic federal program, and the current Special Impact program of OEO is a microcosm test of what some of that program might look like.

approval process has been administered so as to militate against the channeling of assistance to certain low-income areas (called Special Impact areas) which are now being developed by CDC's. Legislative provision in the Economic Opportunity Act encourages the designation of these areas by EDA as eligible for assistance. Yet, they have not received that assistance, mainly because the CDC's working in them are not given appropriate recognition by EDA.

For example, the author was present during a discussion between EDA officials and a group of OEO CDC directors in which the EDA position was made explicit: the Special Impact areas would not receive assistance despite the legislated mandate. Earlier, EDA designation of the eligibility of these areas for assistance had been denied on the technicality that an approved OEDP must precede EDA designation. The CDC directors were told, however, that EDA would not approve any plans or, if approved, the plans would not lead to assistance. The reasons for this remain unclear.

More recently, EDA has indicated that it will provide that assistance in one or two cases on a "demonstration" basis. A recent legislative proposal by Senators Kennedy and Javits to strengthen the claim of the OEO CDC's to EDA assistance may have been a factor in prompting this change.[10] It was formulated in part as a result of the history of EDA's denial of assistance to the Special Impact areas. Whether the new provision would be effective despite an apparently unsympathetic agency is still problematic. The point here is, however, that the record on EDA assistance is only one illustration of the problems that arise if the use of the CDC movement in national policy is desired.

Second, the creation and expansion by CDC's of businesses in their localities is hampered by regulations which exclude nonprofit corporations and cooperatives from benefits administered by the Small Business Administration (SBA). For example, SBA regulations specifically deny section 8(a) assistance to nonprofit CDC's or their instruments.[11] The 8(a) program is the potentially powerful resource of government contracts which may be allocated to smaller companies, in the so-called "set-aside program" of federal procurement that would otherwise go to major corporations.[12] Since CDC's are in most cases nonprofit, this means that a major economic development resource is denied them. Even in those instances in which they are in a for-profit form, CDC's may be linked to a nonprofit corporation in such a way as to still be excluded from the small business assistance. Yet, the goal of much CDC activity is, of course, the same as that of the SBA, stimulation of business activity. Since the profits of many CDC-sponsored business ventures are used for the benefit of a larger group, SBA funds channeled through a CDC would seemingly have a greater total impact than those directed to small privately-owned concerns.

---

[10] S. 2007, 92d Cong., 1st Sess. (1971). The measure has been incorporated as a part of title VII in the Amendments to the Economic Opportunity Act of 1964, the new (1971) OEO authorization bill that at this writing has gone to the President for action.

[11] 13 C.F.R. § 124.8-1 (Supp. 1971).

[12] Small Business Act, 15 U.S.C. § 637 (1970).

Third, although inner-city revitalization is the special goal of the majority of CDC's, they are not given reasonable access to the resources that HUD is devoting to this goal. For example, Model Cities regulations prevent the designation of citizen participation units as the arm for economic development.[13] This should be changed. The needed change would not mean that HUD should *require* the local mayor to designate citizen-controlled CDC's for administration of development programs. That may be politically impossible for the present. However, HUD should not, as it has in the past, administer the program so as to prevent that designation even when the mayor and the local groups prefer it.

An illustration of the effect of the present limitation is the two-year struggle between HUD and the local Model Cities group in Boston. Although HUD prevailed, its victory was pyrrhic. Economic development now is divided between competing units including the city's community development administration, a CDC created by the model neighborhood board, and citizen groups that have resisted capitulation to programs directed from outside the community.[14] The result of course is duplication and waste of very scarce resources in ideas and people, as well as funds.

Similar federal agency regulations tend to inhibit the energies of local development groups in the field of housing. For example, nonprofit sponsors of low-income housing, such as CDC's, usually have difficulty getting the necessary seed money to start a project. Although FHA construction loans will retroactively cover the preconstruction investment, the loans cannot be awarded until the preliminary work is done. The Housing and Urban Development Act of 1968 provides for preconstruction loans,[15] but the amount authorized is small and would support a total national housing investment of no more than $75 million—a pitifully insignificant amount. A minor modification in the legal structure in favor of CDC's could permit them to secure combined preconstruction and construction loans, rather than rely upon the inadequate preconstruction appropriations of the 1968 Act.

A final example of the limitations of the current assistance structure is the "new communities" program of HUD, which is designed to insure the orderly increase of sites for new towns. As currently framed, the program requires large amounts of private capital, which of course are ventured only on the prospect of high profits. No CDC is likely to have the necessary capital in its own investment fund, and if it wished to undertake a new town project, it would have to enter into the kind of arrangements for private capital that would rule out the community control approach

---

[13] *See* Policy Statement on Economic Development for Model Cities Programs, CDA Letter 10c, MC 3135.1 Supp. 2 (Nov. 1970). This regulation *does* provide that the economic development corporation must be "broadly representative of the community within the Model Cities target area," as well as include people from the "broader city community." However, local city politics being what they are, the governance of this board is securely in the hands of a mayor, if he wants it to be—and of course he usually would.

[14] For details of the HUD restrictions, see M. Dean, Boston Model City and the Community Development Corporation, 1968 (unpublished course paper, Harvard Business School).

[15] 12 U.S.C. § 1701X(a) (1970).

that marks CDC ventures. Thus, probably the most exciting new town project in the country, a 5000-acre tract known as Featherfield Farm developed by a community group in southwest Georgia, has struggled against impending disaster for three years without even the necessary seed money to plan properly because of the inability of community-controlled development projects to attract capital comparable to that available to large private developers. Their tenuous hold on the $1 million property is a major success story in itself; whether they will in the end manage to attract church and foundation money holds the key to that new town to be built by a CDC. Federal funds are virtually denied them.[16]

Conclusion

None of these administrative and legislative restrictions are necessary for proper federal control over the use of federal funds. They tend to frustrate the approach to local development that CDC's exemplify, simply because the task tackled by the CDC is so overwhelming. CDC's appear to be an energetic innovation with high potential for local revitalization programs. They could become the instrument for a renascence of our most depressed areas, and national programs, laws, and policies must be reviewed carefully to remove obstacles to this new democratic development.

---

[16] *Cf.* THE TWENTIETH CENTURY FUND, NEW TOWNS: LABORATORIES FOR DEMOCRACY (1971). For a description of the Featherfield Farm project, see Gottschalk & Swann, *Planning a Rural New Town in Southwest Georgia*, 1 ARETÊ 3 (1970) (journal of the Graduate School of Social Work, University of South Carolina).

139912